Accounting for Capitalism

Accounting for Capitalism

The World the Clerk Made

MICHAEL ZAKIM

The University of Chicago Press
Chicago and London

The University of Chicago Press, Chicago 60637
The University of Chicago Press, Ltd., London
Published 2018
Printed in the United States of America

27 26 25 24 23 22 21 20 19 18   1 2 3 4 5

ISBN-13: 978-0-226-97797-3 (cloth)
ISBN-13: 978-0-226-54589-9 (e-book)
DOI: https://doi.org/10.7208/chicago/9780226545899.001.0001

Library of Congress Cataloging-in-Publication Data

Names: Zakim, Michael, author.
Title: Accounting for capitalism : the world the clerk made /
   Michael Zakim.
Description: Chicago : The University of Chicago Press, 2018. | Includes
   bibliographical references and index.
Identifiers: LCCN 2017035753 | ISBN 9780226977973 (cloth : alk. paper) |
   ISBN 9780226545899 (e-book)
Subjects: LCSH: Clerks—United States—History—19th century. | Capitalism—
   Social aspects—United States—History—19th century.
Classification: LCC HD8039.M4 U59 2018 | DDC 331.7/6165137097309034—dc23
   LC record available at https://lccn.loc.gov/2017035753

♾ This paper meets the requirements of ANSI/NISO z39.48-1992 (Permanence of Paper).

For Netanel, Itai, Aviya, and Shira
and for Zivya

Contents

Acknowledgments

Accounting for Capitalism is an ambitious interdisciplinary history and, as such, a faithful reflection of its subject since capitalism's own greatest conceit is the relevance of truck and barter to the whole of social experience. It was not infrequently the case, then, that in the course of writing this book I found myself lecturing to audiences about constipation rather than capital, or vice versa, and provoking considerable consternation, if not confusion, about what I actually had to say about the economy. If I have ultimately produced a convincing account of the interaction between the moral and material, between "Mammon and Manhood," in nineteenth-century America, much of the reason is to be traced back to those occasions and, more generally, to the critically important practice of universities in bringing guests from near and far and engaging them in conversation.

Additional conversations with two remarkable historians of the modern economy, Roy Kreitner and Jonathan Levy, have been even more essential to my education, and I wish to thank them for the time and talent they devoted in responding to the work in progress. I also want to acknowledge the effort expended by anonymous readers invited by the University of Chicago Press to review the manuscript, and then review it again. Tim Mennel, meanwhile, has guided this study through to completion, becoming its most patient and sensitive reader of all. Katherine Faydash then copyedited the final draft with incisive flair.

The Gilder-Lehrman Institute in American History provided fellowship support in the early stages of research. This was followed by a generous grant from the Israel Science Foundation, which, despite the pressures of international academic boycotts and political reaction at home, remains steadfastly committed to the humanist project. I have sought to honor that commitment in the history that follows.

Introduction: The Clerk Problem

Walt Whitman printed an insolent picture of himself on the frontispiece of the first edition of *Leaves of Grass* in 1855. It was a portrait of déclassé insouciance and cheap clothes that marked the poet, in the words of the *New York Tribune*, as one of that "exemplary class of society . . . irreverently styled 'loafers.'" In fact, Whitman was quite explicit about his identity as a loafer: "I lean and loafe at my ease observing a spear of summer grass," he wrote at the beginning of the poem that later became known as "Song of Myself." It was one of those rhetorical provocations that gave his poetics such startling resonance, as Whitman conspicuously sought to turn the tables on a favorite expression of moral censure employed by the better classes at midcentury.[1]

The age abounded in loafers. There were literary loafers, Yankee loafers, French loafers, genteel loafers, common loafers, and country loafers—the latter observed by Nathaniel Hawthorne at the Brighton Cattle Fair "wait[ing] for some friend to invite them to drink." Nevertheless, loaferism was most essentially a metropolitan phenomenon, strolling the city's avenues, wharves, parks, and museums, and serving as a ready epithet for anyone seeking to hurl an anxious insult. The young New York conservative George Templeton Strong thus ascribed the worst tendencies of democracy, "so called," to the loafer, while the *Southern Literary Messenger* accused him of advocating no less than "the sublime doctrine of social equality." Loafers were known for cursing without shame and for smoking cigars. They cared little for the law and exhibited a studied disregard for public mores in general. They were eccentric, if not impudent, in their personal habits. They had a weakness for billiards and barrooms and were maddeningly self-satisfied, if not philosophically reclusive. And they wore stand-up collars that were, more often than not, covered in stains.[2]

This stream of invective was not without its own logic. The loafer's ubiquity in American conversation—the wide currency, that is, accorded to accusations of idleness and indolence—was testimony to an emerging labor problem: a crisis in the meaning of industriousness that was provoked, aptly enough, by industrial revolution. As someone "whose aim is to get through the world with as little energy as possible," the loafer presented an adamant rebuke to productive effort and labor theories of value that had long informed republican thought and American political practice. "The only real employment intended for man was to eat and sleep," the *Ladies Companion* sardonically observed in an essay on the subject in 1837, "and the Loafer's principle and practice on the matter, were in unison." And yet, as the *New-York Daily Times* noted some years later, the loafer was deeply implicated in the forward march of progress: "In a barbarous state of society loafers were, without doubt, scarce; in fact, their very existence is doubtful." This was in pointed contrast to the present day, when their numbers "increase with hundred-fold rapidity beneath the benignant influence of civilization." Loafing, it consistently followed, was no less than "the consummation of all industry."[3]

And so "the real employment intended for man" became an open question in the age of capital. That was why the talking classes fretted incessantly about Americans becoming "impatient of hard work out of doors." Henry Ward Beecher opened his best-selling *Seven Lectures to Young Men* in 1846 with a sermon on industry and idleness that warned of a "pestilent sediment" forming under society's foundations, an expanding class of sluggards who preferred to sleep late rather than wield a plow. Beecher's rhetoric was characteristic of a nationwide trope—shared by conservatives and radicals alike—protesting the ruinous effects of too much easy money. "The stampede towards the golden temple became general," Joseph Baldwin observed in his *Flush Times of Alabama and Mississippi*, while Jesse Chickering, a Boston minister, physician, statistician, and writer on political economy seemingly far removed from the speculative fever of the southwestern frontier, lamented to local audiences that "we have become emphatically a commercial community." Chickering meant that the once axiomatic relationship between labor and its fruits was coming undone, and that trade seemed to be the basis of industry rather than the opposite.[4]

The logic of accumulation that drove men to buy in order to sell, "and sell to buy the more," as another pundit remarked of the spiraling effects of the commodity form, was poised to assume sovereign control of the economy. The *Treasury of Knowledge* consequently noted that if shopkeepers and manufacturers could not turn a surplus on their goods, there was little point in putting them up for sale in the first place since "it is only the profit that they live upon." The primary purpose of wealth in such a system was to make more wealth, to which end men made things.[5]

But who made the market where all the goods were accordingly trans-formed into so much surplus value? Francis Walker, director of the federal government's Bureau of Statistics after the Civil War, discovered the answer to that question by analyzing the nation's census returns from 1860. They revealed the products of American industry being "conveyed from the pro-ducer to the consumer by a series of exchanges which can hardly average less than three in number, and with a percentage of expenses and profits . . . that must amount to fifty per cent upon their original cost. What a tremendous fact!" Such facts attracted Walker's attention because they showed that men "taking the whole product to themselves . . . asking no favors of capital on the one hand, nor of hirelings and slaves on the other," as Lincoln described an ostensibly ascendant free-soil ideal, were nevertheless beholden to the enter-prise of those who produced nothing of value themselves. Champions of the commercial life could thus contend, as Charles Edwards did in the premier volume of *Hunt's Merchant's Magazine*, that trade enjoyed a distinct advan-tage over all other sectors of the economy because it increased the wealth of a nation "without the labor of producing or fabricating a single article." Digging up rocks on a virgin hillside in preparation for planting might re-main a defining moment of American civilization, in other words, but such heavy lifting was increasingly dependent on the offices of bankers, brokers, factors, and wholesalers who specialized in disposing of the surpluses of others' productive efforts. Indeed, not fewer than three quarters of a million persons, Francis Walker continued in his survey of the census data, directly participated in bringing the products of the nation's industry to market.[6]

All this buying and selling begat a giant class of "merchant clerks," the generic nomenclature for an expanding cadre of young men finding employ-ment in counting rooms, credit agencies, import houses, commission busi-nesses, trust companies, law offices, insurance brokerages, auction firms, savings banks, retail stores, wholesale warehouses, and the era's new "marble palaces," where they devoted long hours to taking stock, keeping accounts, displaying wares, delivering bills, distributing samples, paying import duties, figuring interest charges, and copying out a constant stream of correspon-dence that tied the nation's far-flung merchants and manufacturers together in an opportunistic negotiation over the ever-shifting terms of exchange. Ed-gar A. Poe took note of this phenomenon and called it deskism, "for want of a better word." In fact, there was no better word, both because it perspica-ciously accorded business administration the status of doctrine and because it acknowledged the growing preponderance of a modern tribe of scriveners

who "bend over a desk and scratch from 'morn til dewey eve' without inter-
mission from day to day," as a young general store clerk in Bangor, Maine
named Benjamin Foster testified to the mass production needs of a modern
"paper machine" designed to transpose the material world into commensurable units of exchange.[7]

Clerking had become the third-largest (male) occupation in Manhattan
by 1855, trailing only behind the city's petty laborers and servants, encompassing the "thousands and tens of thousands who get their living in one way or
another by the pen," as Benjamin Franklin Foster, America's "counting-house
oracle" who is not to be confused with the young man from Bangor, identified the vast matriculation pool of candidates for his Commercial Academy,
which opened its doors on Broadway in 1837. Almost every family has sent
one or more representatives, Walter Barrett also observed in his *Old Merchants of New York City* of the mass movement of talent and enterprise out
of rural New England and toward the emporium. "All do not succeed, but
some do, and this is quite sufficient to keep the ambition to get a clerkship in
New York alive." Advertisements for a sales position at the counter, "at a salary less by half than a bricklayer can earn," were answered by fifty applicants
within six hours, according to other reports, "each eager to enter the field and
try his chance in the mercantile world." Twenty-year-old William Hoffman,
recently arrived from an upstate farm and "ready to turn my hand to any thing
that was honest, in the way of selling goods, figuring accounts, or fingering
cash," was tipped off about an opening at a Manhattan dry-goods firm only
to discover that twenty others had preceded him there that same morning.
In fact, the numbers were often much larger. Charles French counted two
hundred responses to an employment notice his father's hardware business
placed in Boston in the winter of 1859, and a hundred more when Charles
opened his own establishment several months later. He eventually hired a
young man from upper New England who soon moved on to a new job in
Providence.[8]

All these sellers of goods and figurers of accounts were hired to administer a system of "fast property," Charles Briggs's pithy characterization of the
new industrial economy that appeared in his *Adventures of Harry Franco: A
Tale of the Great Panic*, which was published in 1839. Briggs was referring to
the growing number of business obligations dissolved upon the completion
of each transaction, allowing the contracting parties to resume their former
autonomy without any further regard to each other. The ensuing freedom
from traditional tenets of commonweal—equity and just price, for instance,
or kin and community, for that matter—proved essential to anyone seeking to
calculate his own best interest. Property, which once served as the foundation

of a thick web of household mutuality, deference, and constraint, was consequently converted into the fungible object of restless relations between anonymous persons associated solely through the equivalencies of floating prices. The revolutionary character of this development was evident in Ralph Waldo Emerson's contention in 1841 that "Reliance on Property . . . is the want of self reliance." There was no more incisive summary of the death of a yeoman ideal that had rested on the opposite reasoning, namely, that property constituted the surest guarantee of personal as well as political integrity.[9]

Too many wish to reap before they have plowed, Henry Ward Beecher protested, adopting the most—and the least—appropriate simile in reprimanding a postagrarian generation of youth "fired with a conviction that shrewdness, cunning, and bold ventures, are a more manly way to wealth." It was a shame, the *New York Tribune* editorialized as well, "that fine, hearty lads, who might clear their 50 acres each of western forest in a short time, and have a house, a farm, a wife, and boys about them in the course of ten years, should be hived up in hot salesrooms, handing down tapes and ribbons, and cramping their genius over chintzes and delaines." Virginia Penny, meanwhile, blamed them for female poverty in her *Employments of Women*. The reason there were so many young men performing the duties of clerks and salesmen, she explained, is that "they are lazy, and do not want to perform hard work." And yet why would anyone undertake "bona fide physical labor," Horace Greeley fretted, when he could more comfortably obtain a living without it? "I am the Counter-jumper, weak and effeminate," the New York satirical monthly *Vanity Fair* thus retorted in an especially malevolent piece of Whitmanesque doggerel. "I love to loaf and lie about dry-goods."[10]

A clerk problem was born, symptomatic of the "restless, nervous, bustling, trivial Nineteenth Century," as Henry David Thoreau remarked in registering his own apprehensions about modernity's preference for relative over absolute value. Even *Hunt's Merchant's Magazine* expressed concern over the wholesale enlistment of the country's youth in the forces of market revolution. "Where lies the charm that turns so many young men to the counting-room," *Hunt's* inquired, "and puts so many tender boys behind the counter?" The charm lay in their emancipation from the inspection, admonition, and restraint of household government in favor of a freedom of contract that offered an alternate livelihood to that once gotten from the land. Because Americans had long considered growing and making things to be more than just a category of material life—seeing in productive labor the means by which culture reliably, and virtuously, reproduces itself—a sales-driven existence dedicated to the ephemera of marginal profits surely heralded the end of business as usual. The spectacle of so many tender boys engaged from morn till night "in the

SHAKSPEARE FOR THE COUNTER-JUMPERS.
You should be women,
And yet your beards forbid me to interpret
That you are so.—MACBETH, *Act* 1, *Scene* 3.

occupation of writing down figures" and "taking down . . . bundles, rolls, and boxes" thus signaled a crisis in the republic's defining notions of industry and economy. "Taxes increase, and rents rise, and the goods are marked up again," as someone sardonically observed of the public's obsessive interest in these servants of yardstick and ledger. "Upon whom shall our indignation be expanded? On the clerk, of course. Who got up the war? Who levied the taxes? Who raised the rents? Who, but the clerks?"[11]

A vision of social life organized around the bargain was only one of several competing programs for American civilization, of course. Hard-money Locofocos, western farmers, New England transcendentalists, and Southern slave owners all advanced their own designs for the nation's future.[12] And yet, as the *United States Democratic Review* concluded in 1855, "human Nature . . . was consummated in the person of a Modern Clerk." Horatio Alger's Ragged Dick, for instance, that paragon of self-made manhood for the industrializing age, discovered that the best avenue out of his hardscrabble life as a bootblack lay in improving his reading, writing, and arithmetic ("as far as Interest") in hopes of landing a situation in a store or "countin' room." *Scribner's Monthly* subsequently observed that "clerk" had emerged by the 1870s as a common rubric for "nearly everybody who lives on a salary," the avatar of a population embedded in market relations. Certainly, there was no more authentic agent of society's transformation from "stability and absoluteness" to "motions and relations," which is how Georg Simmel synopsized the coming of modern capitalism. Negotiable, impermanent, uprooted from the soil, and carried along by commerce's cycles of boom and bust, the clerk did not, in other words, just produce the market. He was himself one of its products. Benjamin Foster, the general-store clerk in Bangor, confirmed as much in noting his own "irresistible impulse for wealth," which led him to spurn the prospect of "settling on some farm to some safe, secure, contented, domestic life." Anyone could become a capitalist, Americans were told, a possibility that acted as "a spur to exertion to the very news-boy in our streets," as did the popular intelligence that the great majority of the country's businessmen had "commenced life behind the desk or the counter." This did not mean that everyone actually became a capitalist. It did mean, however, that everyone became capital—or what we so casually refer to as "human capital" today—rendering their own lives the subject of utility and enterprise.[13]

Trade unionists and New Harmony radicals could only dream of effecting such change in America's social fabric. But what might at first appear to be a rather Whiggish account of capital's rise to dominion in the person of the merchant clerk was anything of the sort. His trajectory off the land and into the store is revealing, in fact, of the enormous effort required to domesticate the profit motive and turn it into the practical foundation of social intercourse. "To make Adam Smith's 'simple and natural liberty' compatible with the needs of human society was a most complicated affair," Karl Polanyi observed in *The Great Transformation*. Indeed, to presume otherwise is to embrace the market's own ideological conceits about the transcendent status of truck and barter. The power and privilege of dead white capitalists, in other words, had to be earned, for there was nothing natural or preordained about the stunning ascendance of this radically new form of economy, one that relentlessly violated the temporal, physical, moral, and political boundaries that had undergirded the social order, turning apples into oranges, upstate butter into French silk shawls, and healthy plowboys into lank and sallow clerks.[14]

For all their disdain of tradition, however, the bourgeoisie were also frantic system builders striving to resolve the central conundrum of market society, namely, how to bring the constant mayhem of commodity exchange under control without sacrificing the earnings derived from that same tumult.

While undermining older sources of authority, in other words, there was no intention of undermining the authority of authority. The exponents of fast property consequently invested enormous moral and material effort in converting a centrifugal system of commercial opportunity based on the perpetual movement of goods and persons into the reliable foundation of civility, and in adapting the continual tug-of-war of interested exchange between anonymous parties into the source of commonality, and of commonwealth. This was the clerk's most important assignment, in fact, and his emergence at the center of popular attention—a poster boy for the profit principle—was a testament to how the flux of trade was recast as the key to stability, how personal ambition ceased to pose a threat to human civilization and became identified as its most natural expression, and how mutual cooperation was founded on the basis of pecuniary gain.[15]

The story that follows is, as such, an account of the winners written from the bottom up. This is a social history of capital that constitutes an alternative kind of subaltern study—not an attempt to redeem the social margins from the amnesia of a ruling ideology but a search for the everyday sources of that amnesia, an exploration of the minutiae of a cultural system that so resolutely, and convincingly, reinvented civic life in the form of a business deal. This was not just a function of rates of capital turnover, secondary multiplier effects, or subsidiary feedback processes, but the stuff of filing systems, aniline inks, bookkeeping techniques, life insurance premiums, salary negotiations, personal diary entries, gastrointestinal complaints, census blanks, and the cost of postage. These might seem to be procedural banalities, and so they were. But they were also the key operations of a new ruling class in the making, one that established social experience on the same axioms of interchangeability, impersonality, and mutability that proved essential to the commodity. "In the total movement of this disorder is its order," Karl Marx thus wrote in 1849, referring to the peripatetic nature of prices in the labor market. In so doing, he provided an embracing maxim for capitalist civilization *in toto*, one by which "industrial anarchy" emerged as the very source of "balance."[16] As a result, the bottom line became synonymous with truth in an age shorn of absolutes, and the market's relentless logic of universal equivalence and mutual estrangement was grafted onto our very sense of the good life.

1

Paperwork

All basic histories of the American economy report that by the third decade of the nineteenth century the nation's aggregate wealth began to register dramatic gains. Wheat, flour, corn, butter, pork, tobacco, hemp, coal, lead, and cotton were shipped in increasing volume—and decreasing cost—from Buffalo, Cincinnati, Pittsburgh, Louisville, Nashville, St. Louis, Galena, and Mobile to points north, south, east, and west. The raw goods were then exchanged for finished ones in a melee of converging prices and marginal profits that turned the United States into "but one extended counter from Maine to Texas," as a contemporary soon quipped. Nor was all this surging business activity the exclusive focus of a narrow class of commercial agents who bought and sold things for a living. Trade was becoming a practical concern of the public at large, a public that earned, and often grew, its bread in an economy increasingly driven by capital, credit, and collateral, not to mention "the efficiency of the markets."[1]

Such industrial revolution was inventoried by the yard, ton, box, piece, bale, bundle, barrel, keg, pack, case, and crate. These quantitative measurements were a function of qualitative processes that transposed the general miscellany of wares into a standard set of commensurable values, reinventing trade as a far more universal, abstract grid of relations than anything previously known in the marketplaces and seasonal fairs of older systems of exchange. *Hunt's Merchant's Magazine* celebrated the dematerializing character of this surfeit of goods by invoking the efficiencies of a modern port warehouse where tens of thousands of dollars worth of merchandise changed hands every day, but "all the bustle perceivable . . . is one quiet clerk calling and taking away a bundle of warrants." Such operations rested on a close management of the files that was evident, as well, in the administrative routines of a commission house specializing in the transfer of western produce to

metropolitan shippers and home buyers. Four partners—the three juniors respectively assigned to the flour, grain, and cotton "departments"—were served
by a cashier who oversaw office operations and a head bookkeeper charged
with assembling an "accounts current" of ongoing sales and purchases. They
were assisted, in turn, by a pair of book clerks responsible for generating
an itemized record of all the firm's transactions and by a third entry clerk
who maintained the senior partner's "private books," which encompassed ad
hoc ventures and supplementary partnership arrangements. Meanwhile, a receiving and delivery clerk kept a transcript of freight and storage costs that
comprised a second running account of the business's activities, the direct
outcome of trades negotiated by a corps of salesmen who attended " 'change"
each day. A collector then took over the ensuing demands for remuneration,
including remittances to grain elevator operators, city weighers, and various
inspectors of goods. He also delivered the company's own bills and receipts,
visiting clients between ten and three o'clock before continuing on to the
bank and reporting back to the cashier on the status of payments.[2]

This recombinant flow of business data underwrote the age's accelerating circulation of money and merchandise, prompting Samuel Wells, a prolific author of popular guidebooks at midcentury, to declare paper "the most
convenient material ever discovered." The ancillary piles of warranty deeds,
bills of sale, powers of attorney, and inventory lists, among an extensive catalog of other "useful forms of writing," thus proved no less critical to material
progress than the thick yards of muted flannels, brilliant tartans, and serge
twills that served as the commonest emblems of industrial prosperity. Capitalism could not function without such a vigilant disposal of the books, in
fact, which is why the attendant documentation constituted far more than the
mere detritus of modern life. Truly, the pen was "mightier than the sword,"
A. Morton pronounced in advertising a new set of steel writing nibs, which
also meant that the clerk's desultory schedule of desk assignments—running
"a day and night line, copying by sun-light and by candle-light . . . silently,
palely, mechanically," as was remarked of Bartleby, Herman Melville's troubled Wall Street scrivener—emerged as a defining act of the age. Trade might
increase the wealth of the nation without fabricating a single article, as Charles
Edwards told his audience at New York's Mercantile Library with such evident
self-satisfaction, but there was still plenty of work to do.[3]

Producing the Market

All that attendant effort was on display when Edward Tailer arrived at New
York's Custom House one morning in December 1849, delegated by his firm,

Little Alden, to arrange the discharge of sixty-five boxes of foreign-made shawls, which constituted the bulk of the company's upcoming spring inventory. Edward encountered a phalanx of desk-bound officials charged with moving the profusion of imported cargoes in and out of the harbor, preparing the goods, that is, for general circulation in the American market. To that end, tariff categories and prices were assigned to all the wares, making it possible to assess and pay duties, either in cash or in bonds posted as security. Permits, clearances, and debentures needed to be processed as well, then countersigned and certified. Merchandise was inspected and checked against manifests, and reexamined if doubts arose regarding the accuracy of the original documentation. All these sundry operations generated revenue for the federal government, of course. They also provided an effective, if controversial, means for regulating the nation's economic development. More fundamentally still, Custom House clerks transcribed this vast assemblage of wholesale stock into a common denominator of money values, thereby facilitating its transfer from one owner to the next. In so doing, they helped establish the very conditions of trade.[4]

So did Benjamin Foster, positioned as he was at the other end—or beginning—of the nation's commercial food chain, the lone clerk employed in a general store in Bangor, Maine, in 1847. "My past season's labor has been . . . almost incredible," Benjamin reported upon reviewing the four hundred or so pages of daybook he had managed to fill up in the course of just a few months. The accounting was far from over, however. All those entries had to be reviewed and independently posted to the ledger, and each posting examined. Only at that point could Benjamin then draw up the store's final balances for the season, producing the tersely enumerated rows and columns that coordinated the ninety-day notes at sight issued by a transcontinental consortium of bankers, importers, wholesalers, and jobbers with the six-, twelve-, and eighteen-month rhythms of cash crops and household needs that circulated between hinterland and entrepôt. In so arranging this flow of values within the grid of accounts, Benjamin effectively flattened out time and space, transforming the economy into strictly calculable dyads of credit and debt, and profit and loss.[5]

Railroads and telegraphs might thus be the favorite expression of a new "information infrastructure" taking shape in these early decades of capitalist revolution, but bills of lading, warehouse receipts, shipping records, weekly trade reports, and regular fee schedules proved no less essential to the exploding volume of industrial-age business. Indeed, how could anyone navigate the "myriad of rivulets" of antebellum finance—the promissory notes, for example, signed over by one merchant to another that, once endorsed by

a third party, became negotiable currency—without the "modern instrumentalities of commerce" ready at hand? These included indexes and digests
providing reliable updates on tariff rates, the liabilities of shipping agents, and
revised procedures for insolvency hearings. The foreclosures, debt judgments,
state chancery proceedings, and private assignments to creditors generated
by a risk economy were likewise dependent on a coherent paper trail of notes,
bills, and drafts. "Market reviews" and "prices current" published in the daily
press, meanwhile, supplied itemized summaries of the ever-shifting prices of
stocks, staples, and a widening assortment of additional merchandise reaching market. Such inventories did not, in fact, contain a new kind of information, but their systematic circulation was an entirely novel event. So was the
fast growth of insurance, which reflected the rising costs of not having enough
information.[6]

The very semantics of all this commercial paper proved no less indispensable to the logistics of exchange. Such penned incantations as "jointly and
severally," "for value received," and "accepted" were routinely inscribed onto
promissory notes, and serial designations of "first," "second," and "third" were
appended to copies of bills drawn to remitter, acceptor, and endorser, respectively, which would then continue to circulate if superscribed with the
supplementary encryption "in case of need with Messrs. . . ." Variations of
personal assent, often inked in red—"as advised," "per advice," and "without
further advice"—were affixed to bills of sale once the drawee was apprised of
their issue, and the exact sum, date, and place of origin of bills of exchange
was compulsory when passed from one trader to another. This compendium
of literary abridgements and abbreviations—"E.E.," or "errors excepted," was
another common entry, inserted into invoices to protect the holder from
errata inadvertently introduced into the text—acquired unprecedented significance as traditional styles of commercial intercourse were replaced by a
new emphasis on formality and legibility. The fact is, business obligations
reduced to writing were accorded greater evidentiary stature by the country's
courts of law, which increasingly insisted on "putting it all down on paper."[7]

"Never, perhaps, was it so true as now, that 'the seller has need of a hundred eyes,'" a Boston dry-goods jobber consequently remarked of the requirements for doing business in an expanding economy filling up with anonymous agents. It was no longer possible to infer the intention of one's trading
partner by studying his countenance, for instance, or by relying on any number of other time-honored practices once considered mandatory for closing
a deal. "I cannot recollect a single instance when 'Co.,' represents nobody,"
a veteran wholesaler complained of the impersonalized quality of modern
commercial relations. Face value acquired a far less intimate meaning, in

other words, as reciprocal exchange was reestablished around a disembodied mass of pertinent facts that each merchant—or each merchant's clerk, to be more precise—labored to "harmonize into a consistent and satisfactory whole." Only then, after the papers were suitably arranged, did it become possible to impose legibility on the market and inscribe a deliberate course of action onto the economy. Only with answers to an elementary set of inquiries— "What has been done? What is the state of the case at present? What can be done next? What ought to be done?"—could self-maximizing agents hope to effect their maximizations. Hierarchal methods of information storage were developed with such goals in mind, coded by color or pigeonhole, or by brass-hinged labels offering enough taxonomic flexibility to be rearranged in response to the fluid conditions of trade. These cross-indexed records of the minutiae of exchange proved both highly stable and highly mobile, capable of achieving "a command of the subject, and a comparative fearlessness of surprise," which is how contemporaries characterized the value-added quality of properly arranged files.[8]

This modern scriptorium was not yet accorded the appellation of "paperwork," which would become a twentieth-century shorthand for the routinized ubiquity of bureaucratic management. But the *New York Star* pointedly, and sardonically, observed in 1870 that more bookkeepers than books were to be found in New York City. And it was certainly no anachronism to speak of an American "knowledge economy" firmly in place by the Civil War, operating through an extensive network of information industries specializing in credit, communications, transportation, and insurance, as well as the training of a professionalized cadre of "subaltern officials and scribes" who, according to Max Weber, underwrote this new regime of command and control. The mercurial growth in the production and dissemination of commercial information constituted no less than a "business revolution," Thomas Cochran once explained, becoming the basis of a "new politico-business system" that lay the practical foundations for the era's other, more spectacular revolutions being wrought by steam and iron. Indeed, without this knowledge-driven infrastructure firmly in place, modern industry would have been a far less serviceable—and far less profitable—undertaking.[9]

"You should endeavor to establish a system of arranging your papers, as may insure their being readily referred to," *Hunt's Merchant's Magazine* therefore advised its readers. These might seem like little things, "and so they are, unless you neglect them." Such practices—prescribing the production of three facsimiles of each piece of correspondence, for instance, in the event that one was lost in the mail, while the third was kept on file to ensure that both parties were working off the same text—removed communications from the idiosyncratic oral flow of interchange between acquaintances in favor of precision, unambiguity, continuity, discretion, and subordination, to borrow another roster of techniques of rational administration from Max Weber. That "competence at method" is what kept records from devolving into "a shapeless heap," *Hunt's* further determined, which is why those traders who most consistently applied these tenets to their office routines were the most successful at business, and why the failure to keep a regular accounting of one's activities, the *Philadelphia Merchant* also averred, was the cause of "nine-tenths of the Insolvents in every Commercial City in the world." Business was a matter of habit, William Ross declared in summarizing prevailing professional opinion in his *Accountant's Own Book and Business Man's Manual* in 1852, the soul of which was system. "Like the fly-wheel upon a steam-engine, regularity keeps the motion of life steady and unbroken—thereby enabling the machine to do its work unobstructively." Ross's technologized metaphors were an apposite invocation of the new conditions of trade, for they recognized business administration to be the very power source driving the central production project of the capitalist economy, production of the market.[10]

And so, while the intensifying paperwork might seem devoted to bringing the commotion of exchange under manageable control, the opposite was actually the case. The market was not a living system that needed to be regulated and regularized by means of artificial information technologies; it was itself an artifice. Business administered the market, that is to say, by inventing it. Before anyone could produce for exchange, it was necessary to produce the actual system of exchange, to create those structures that allow goods to "encounter" each other by suspending all their other attributes, save what makes them mutually replaceable. "The commodities are transformed into bars in the head and in speech before they are exchanged for one another," as Karl Marx remarked at the time. "They are appraised before being exchanged, and in order to appraise them they must be brought into a given numerical relation to one another."[11] The clerk thus only appeared to be producing nothing of value. In fact, he was busily producing the very system of value, arranged into a labile index of prices for coordinating the indeterminable jumble of trades issuing from the inveterate supply and demand of everyone with property rights. Such an economy was a cultural achievement, not a force of nature, which meant that the market was a quintessentially industrial event, a man-made reconstitution of the material world.

Business knowledge also soon emerged as a commodity in its own right, produced, that is, with the intent of being sold. Credit reports are the best-known example of this new exchange value, not least because the practice struck many contemporaries as a cynical, if not illegal, intrusion into the proprietary affairs of others. But proponents of the system argued that the ability to purchase reliable intelligence regarding the financial condition of otherwise unfamiliar trading partners illuminated the opaque, faceless quality of the mass market, turning it into a viable structure of trade. There was nothing cynical about that. If anything, the general interest would be far better served once "what is known to one is known to all," as a sympathetic observer wrote in praise of the activities of the Mercantile Agency, whose subaltern staff of thirty was kept on the job at Exchange Street in Manhattan—and at additional branches that opened in Boston (1843), Philadelphia (1845), Baltimore (1846), Cincinnati (1849), St. Louis (1850), and New Orleans (1851)—copying and cataloging the interminable flow of financial reports arriving every day from the field. Country store owners and proprietors of limited means would, as a result, enjoy "the range of the entire market," able to trade with anyone who kept an active file on their assets and credit histories rather than having to confine their purchases to those few wholesale houses where they were personally known. "He need not even leave home to make his purchases," it was remarked of a market system expanding its reach to every place, and so no longer restricted to any place at all.[12]

Facts on paper accordingly replaced facts on the ground as the operative reality in this increasingly immaterial world filling up with goods. Veteran traders still remembered Michael Boyle making his rounds of Pearl Street and Maiden Lane, "panting under the load of a bag of silver" while collecting on the various notes that had come due that month. Boyle's old-fashioned efforts gave way to a system of discarnate records arranged in standard categories that could be reproduced, transmitted, and disseminated with infinitely greater facility. Those occasions, "as in days of old, to weigh the shekels of silver in cumbrous scales," were supplanted by the digests of a paper apparatus that operated as both archive and action, amplifying the age's "mental labor" no less spectacularly than steam engines augmented humanity's physical exertions. "All the instants of time and all the places in space can be gathered in another time and place," Bruno Latour has observed of modern science's technical success in processing empirical information, a technique that proved equally relevant for doing business. In fact, capitalism was no less infused with this Enlightenment bias toward abstraction, which allowed humanity to distill the flux of events into their constituent parts and then reconfigure them into more useful patterns. Liverpool, New York, and New Orleans consequently sat an inch apart from each other on the written page, making the extraordinary scales of capitalist exchange an increasingly conventional operation.[13]

Desk and ledger thus rivaled the machine as both sign and praxis of the new age. The tractability of the written documents matched the plasticity of the market, revealing a close affinity between paper and profits. Certainly, paperwork proved to be an essential complement to paper money: both systems demonstrated a remarkable ability to transcend distance, reshape relations, and refocus power in the hands of men with access to information. The reign of the document and its extensive infrastructure of knowledge production subsequently effected a redivision of commercial labor that brought an end to the era of the all-purpose merchant. In that earlier system of global trade, capitalists often owned their own ships while operating in wholesale and retail circuits of exchange. They imported, exported, financed, and insured their own cargoes. Many also served as agents for foreign houses and provided funds to local craftsmen and even to farmers. In the industrial economy, shipowning, banking, transporting, insuring, financing, and marketing were reorganized as discrete operations, a function of the general effort to narrow the scope of information necessary to do business and so enhance the capitalist's practical mastery over what had become distinct departments of trade.[14]

Commission houses were a case in point, respectively trading in specific types of commodities, or categories of buyers, or regions of the country. Some represented foreign concerns. Others devoted themselves to domestic products while supplying loans, discounts, advances, and sometimes their own paper to home manufacturers. Those financial activities even prompted numerous firms to abandon merchandising altogether in favor of an exclusive focus on the capital market, which itself became constituted of "informational niches" filling up with assorted brokers of bills, stocks, loans, real estate, bullion, and insurance. There were also exchange brokers who specialized in grading goods before they reached the market, or who subdivided large lots into manageable shipments destined for hinterland stores, confining themselves to a single line of wares—cattle, cotton, drugs, dyestuffs, spices, fruit, hay, hemp, metals, oil, rice, cigars, scrip, tea, tobacco, wine, wood, or "China goods," to name a few—which then became the same conduit for trading in credit. Jobbers emerged as another essential cog in these ramifying networks of exchange. They purchased, or transferred without ever actually purchasing, exiguous assortments of merchandise destined for local retailers who lacked the resources to buy but small quantities. Jobbers also extended credit and accepted notes and checks from inland cities at competitive discount rates, which turned them into bankers of sorts. By so doing, they hastened the decline of a far less specialized auction system that served as the primary channel for moving consumables around the country before the 1820s.

None of this extensive new business structure reduced the risks inherent in trade. In fact, the industrial-age merchant was generally more vulnerable to market commotions than his predecessor had been since he confined himself to a narrower segment of the economy. This effectively limited the scope of his response when encountering the invariable threats and pressures of doing business, whether these issued from changing fashions, rising duties, expensive credit, or failing crops that affected the customer's ability to pay when bills came due. Specialization, in other words, proved essential for rationalizing exchange and standardizing markets, as well as generating opportunities for ambitious men jockeying for a start in business. At the same time, and for the same reason, it exacerbated competition, which would now be decided by ever-smaller comparative advantages. Edwin Freedley, a popular writer on commercial subjects, observed in his *Practical Treatise on Business* that "the percentage of profits will gradually be less, but the aggregate of profits . . . will be unprecedented and astounding" in the new system of trade. The difference between success and ruin, a dry-goods jobber similarly remarked of the domestic market in cloths, was often a matter of "five to seven and a half or ten per cent." The knowledge economy, as such, relentlessly narrowed profit margins, which then redoubled commercial dependence on information.[15]

That is why the "Basis of Prosperity" became founded on "the vast modern increase of facilities for diffusing and obtaining full and correct information on everything pertaining to trade," *Hunt's Merchant's Magazine* pronounced. Such modern facilities—commonly known as counting rooms, or offices—operated as a veritable assembly line for fabricating, aggregating, duplicating, and transmitting the documents which some now began to refer to as the "capital of mind." Most were initially located in residential addresses. The Manhattan branch of the First Bank of the United States opened for business in what had once been someone's private domicile, for example. Twenty years later, in contrast, the Second Bank's offices were built to order, part of a general reconstruction of Wall Street for commercial purposes. The whole neighborhood was being given over to structures whose Renaissance-inspired palazzo designs replaced the Greek Revival temple as the preferred style for doing business. This did not just signal an aesthetic revolt against federalist neoclassicism. The new architecture also proved better suited to an economy that kept expanding its floor space, adding stories, and rearranging interiors in accordance to the shifting requirements of tenants vying for a prime location in what had become identifiable business districts. A single block fronting Wall Street in 1850 was thus home to seventeen separate banking firms, as well as fifty-seven law offices, twenty-one brokerage houses, eleven insurance companies, and an assortment of notaries, agents, importers, commission merchants, and, of course, stationers. A rental market for office

THE COUNTING ROOM.

(Geo. P. Rowell & Co's Advertising Agency, No. 40 Park Row, N. Y.)

"suites" developed apace, "fitted up with gas and every other convenience," which also included newly invented "acoustic tubes" that allowed managing partners to communicate with porters in the basement and clerks in the sales-room without ever having to leave their desks. A variety of safes for protecting documents and banknotes became commonplace as well, as did self-acting locks and separate rooms for controlling access to conversations and records.[16]

All this office activity spurred a flurry of technological spillovers that in-cluded single standing desks and double-counter desks, sitting desks featuring nine or, alternately, fifteen pigeonholes, and drawers that could or could not be locked. "Office chairs" capable of swiveling and tilting became available as well, together with less costly "counting-house stools" that lacked any upholstery. Paperweights, check cutters, pen wipers (the woolen variety being preferable to silk or cotton, which tended to leave fibers on the nib), pencil sharpeners, rulers, copying brushes, dampening bowls, blotting paper (less important for

PRIVATE OFFICE.

(Geo. P. Rowell & Co's Advertising Agency, No. 40 Park Row, N. Y.)

absorbing excess ink than for protecting the page from soiled hands), waste-paper baskets, sealing wax (including small sticks coated with a combustible material ignited by friction and designed to be discarded after a single use), seal presses, paper fasteners, letter clips (for holding checks while entering them into the daybook), writing pads, billhead and envelope cases, business cards, receiving boxes for papers and letters, various trays (for storing pins, wafers, pencils, and pens), and "counting room calendars" spanning twelve- or sixteen-month cycles—all became standard business tools.[17] So did the expanding inventory of "square inkstands," "library inkstands," and "banker inkstands" designed with narrow necks which prevented evaporation and shallow bodies that kept the upper part of the pen from becoming covered in ink, thus avoiding blackened fingers and smudged documents. Inkstands for office use were almost always corked so that the soot and dust of the city would not end up thickening the mixture. The interiors of the better brands were further lined with rubber to safeguard the point of the pen during the constant, hurried dipping.[18]

And then there was the paper, of course, whether of bond, linen, or led-ger quality, whose porousness and flexibility were the keys to its utility. The best blue laid paper for account books came from England. Its layer of gelatin allowed for the easy erasure of mistakes by scratching at the surface. Con-tinental brands, however, were preferred for correspondence. Glazed with farina and rosin soap, the pages were less greasy under the pen, facilitating a freer hand and reducing the abrasion invariably caused by the sharp edge of one's nib. In either case, the product should never smell bad or display too much sensitivity to changes in the weather. Paper intended for the office also required finer and whiter rags than that used for newspapers and books, which entailed a significantly more complex production process. That pro-duction itself was mechanized in the 1820s, achieving a startling capacity for converting liquid pulp into a uniform writing surface at the rate of twenty-five to forty feet per minute, resulting in a product that featured a more durable weave which better resisted bleeding. Dryers, sizers, slitters, cutters, and cal-endars were still necessary for finishing the process, as were newly developed ruling technologies that standardized ledgers and copybooks, among a bur-geoning variety of other blank forms. Self-sealing envelopes also appeared for the first time, providing significant savings in time "as unnecessary folding is avoided," an attribute that earned this invention a place at New York's Ex-hibition of the Industry of All Nations in 1853. The quality of machine-made paper, what's more, proved highly suitable to the steel pens increasingly com-ing into use.[19]

Handwork

Those pens replaced the traditional quill. The transition was far from immediate, however. "Quills Superseded," an agent for Hayden's metal nibs might
announce in an advertisement taken out in the *New York Tribune* in 1841, but
William Dunlap, a well-known playwright, testified to his ongoing frustrations in adjusting to such instruments. His experience was representative of
what many others continued to claim as well, namely, that a hard quill with a
clear barrel, of sufficient age "to extract the water and oil which [it] naturally
contains when immediately from the wing," remained the best tool for writing. "It is difficult to impart to metal the elasticity of the quill," S. H. Browne
pronounced in the *Manual of Commerce*, while B. F. Foster, whose Commercial Academy offered a dedicated course in modern penmanship, noted the
chronically cramped hands of those who had recently taken up the new steel
devices.[20]

The quill was not only more pliant. It could also be parsed for executing
the variably finer or broader strokes required by the writing itself, shaped
into whatever angle better matched the production needs of the document
at hand. Metal was more impervious to heavy use, it is true, but a quill was
easily refreshed by slicing two or three thin shavings off the sides, an operation that could be repeated several times with one's penknife without having
to extend the slit, which would alter the ratio between the barrel's length and
weight and so upset the system's balance. It also became possible after 1820 to
purchase ready-made quills in a variety of grades. These were simply replaced
once they wore out, an increasingly useful feature as pen-making skills began
to disappear among the giant reserve army of clerical labor flocking to the
nation's countinghouses. Steel nib manufacturers, for their part, strove to duplicate the "soft feeling" and "freedom of action" characteristic of a well-made
quill while emphasizing the distinct advantages of technological innovation,
namely, metal's mobility and durability, which became more pronounced
once the problem of corrosion was solved by the invention of aniline inks in
the 1850s.[21]

By then metal pens were established as the dominant tool for commercial writing, their freedom of action significantly enhanced by the addition
of slits cut along the nib. They were also designed to match the specifications
of the paperwork. Foley's gold nibs, for instance, which even "outwear the
steel pen," became available in a range of sizes and styles adapted to the particular needs of bankers, merchants, bookkeepers, editorialists, and insurance
agents. Similarly, the large No. 1 pens manufactured by Thomas Groom & Co.

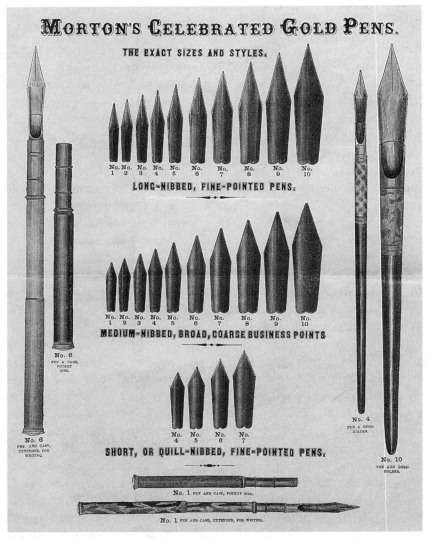

Metal nibs were the new tool of a giant class of scribbling men who administered capitalism's most important production project, production of the market.

best served the requirements of "bold and rapid writing," whereas the medium No. 2 and No. 3 sizes were designated for correspondence, and the No. 4 was recommended for fine work, or "ladies' use." Students at Comer's Commercial College in Boston were instructed to purchase the complete selection of Comer's steel pens, together with copies of *Comer's Penmanship Made Easy*, while P. R. Spencer, who became the dominant authority in the field by the end of the 1850s, typically began marketing his own assortment of signature nibs as best suited to his popular writing method.[22]

The most far-reaching mechanical innovation in writing technologies combined nib, shaft, holder, and inkstand into a single instrument called a "fountain pen," which could be carried about on one's person, ever ready for use. The fountain pen's origins dated back nearly two hundred years, but earlier versions required an external funnel to load the ink. Only now was a reliable reservoir successfully built into the mechanism. Certainly, a pen capable of refilling itself satisfied the through-flow dynamics of mass production, as well as industry's general emphasis on "economies of speed." The fountain pen was also promoted for the relative neatness of its operations since the ink no longer came into contact with one's fingers, which had been unavoidable when having to constantly dip the pen. The problem of splattering was similarly reduced. Once loaded with quality mixtures that effectively reduced blotting and only infrequently thickened into globules—which slowed down the pace of the writing—the fountain pen proved genuinely worthy of the accolades of advertisers. At the same time, complaints could also be heard regarding its high price, as well as the tendency to unexpectedly dry up or fail to throw out the requisite quantity of ink in the course of writing.[23]

All this new hardware was put into the service of capitalism's expansive "writing operations." "Office, great many letters to copy," as George Cayley reported in his diary of the intensifying paperwork, his truncated syntax testifying to business's ascendant demands on his scrivening hand. Albert Norris made a similar note: "Have much writing to do for store etc and shall find less time for my journal I fear." Robert Graham, meanwhile, devoted whole mornings at William Aspinwall's Manhattan countinghouse writing up duplicates of the correspondence until the mail went out at eleven thirty. Afternoons were then given over to transcribing invoices or the accounts current, or to copying additional letters into the firm's correspondence book. Incoming mail also needed to be indexed and filed with a supplementary note detailing "what was done upon any letter, and . . . where it was sent to." Edward Tailer, "engaged at the desk" three blocks away, transcribed thirty-seven pages of invoice into the stock book and returned after supper to write up twenty-seven out-of-town accounts that needed to be sent the next day. "I finished copying the acc[ount] of stock, posted up all the sales which had been made since the eighth of the month, and carried out all the yards upon the Invoice Book," Edward reported in summing up another busy day at the office. "I had but few moments in which to think about myself or other beings."[24]

The industrial century was thus overrun with scribbling men. Their ability to "put a talk on paper, and send it to any distance" became no less than a feature of civilized progress. It had flabbergasted Sequoyah, according to contemporary reports, who went on to invent an alphabet for the Cherokee in their bid to join the ranks of modern nations. William Alcott told a similar tale in his *Structure, Uses and Abuses of the Human Hand*, noting that Powhatan was originally bereft of the practical means for ransoming his prize prisoner, John Smith, in seventeenth-century Virginia. It was pointless to send Smith to Jamestown to announce the conditions for his own release, for obvious reasons. Nor could Powhatan dispatch an envoy, who would certainly be forced to reveal the tribe's whereabouts. It was Smith himself who ultimately proposed that he compose a letter detailing the terms for an exchange. "The half-incredulous but wondering savage accepts of the proposition," Alcott recounted, and "at the appointed spot, on the appointed day, every thing is found. Smith, then, is set free." How truly miraculous such communications must have appeared to the primitive denizens of a preliterate New World wilderness, readers no doubt concluded. In fact, modern sensibilities were no less dazzled. B. F. Foster, for one, celebrated the pen's unique ability "to transmit to others, in places no matter how remote, every species of intelligence, with a secrecy that savors of miracle." The synchronic quality of such writing—allowing speech to inhabit a limitless number of surfaces all at once, to substitute one context for another, and to travel coeval trajectories in endowing an otherwise linear reality with a widening array of temporalities and valences—was an especially compelling demonstration of humanity's growing command over the natural world.[25]

Such command was based on the proper composition of a letter, "to know just what to say, and how to say it," which made that an accomplishment "second to none" for the man of business. This explains Edward Tailer's great excitement upon devoting "an hour or two in the morning to the writing of the first letter which I have ever dispatched." Edward's missive was soon sent off to a correspondent in New Orleans: "[I] will anxiously expect an answer from him in return." Reigning protocol determined that the return mail open with direct reference to the date, subject, and place of origin of the preceding communication, as well as to any other prior exchanges bearing on the matter. That same reflexivity was to inform the entire correspondence, in fact, which was suitably organized into a cadastral sequence of discrete paragraphs addressing one another's concerns in parallel order, and so serving as "the record of the past [and] the regulator of the future," Boyd and Tubb's Commercial Institute in Boston declared in a circular advertising its own course offerings in the field of mercantile correspondence. Such conventions rendered the business letter into a preprinted form, albeit one arranged on a blank page, that was designed to achieve a seamless exchange of commensurate information, the condition for a seamless exchange of commensurate values.[26]

To that same end, B. F. Foster published an extensive selection of archetypes in his *Clerk's Guide*, which modeled the correct "arrangement and phraseology of a Commercial Letter" for a wide array of business situations that included the dissolution of a copartnership and the establishment of a new one, collecting on debts, suspending payments, protesting bills, presenting drafts, making remittances, purchasing insurance, inquiring after goods detained at port, reporting on the state of the market, announcing the failure of a shipment to arrive, and distributing an accounts current to one's agents and representatives. Such standardized epistolary templates would help to rid commerce of superfluous rhetoric—"a waste of words is a waste of time," as Foster exhorted his readers—by allowing the facts to speak for themselves "in plain, bold Saxon," the *American Merchant* further expounded of a business interface shorn of gesture and founded on the self-evident values of "the present utilitarian age." There was no better example of the discursive foundations of the market economy posing as their opposite. Indeed, the cultural authority of commercial exchange came to rest on such performances of "*unequivocalness*," an ethic that Adam Smith had already identified as the source of a new experience of "precision" in language capable of reestablishing human relations on a transparent and therefore more ethical foundation. "Fine writing is ridiculous, and verbose writing is tedious," Edwin Freedley similarly announced in *How to Make Money* while urging business firms to also purge their offices of expensive fixtures and ornamental pediments.[27]

All this utilitarian discourse heralded a new chapter in the history of the republic of letters. The fact is, the price of private correspondence had long been kept high in America by a republican commitment to subsidizing the circulation of public matter, and particularly that of newspapers, "those cheap, useful and agreeable companions of the citizen and farmer." This creed was inverted in a series of postal reforms legislated in the 1840s and 1850s which greatly reduced the price of mailing a letter. "Cheap postage" remained a central tenet of public life, in other words, but its political logic was reversed. Cut-rate personal communications would now secure the "general benefits" of all. Any associated loss of revenue was to be recovered by an increase in the use of the mails, principally by business, for whom the high cost of the telegraph continued to restrict its role to price quotes and urgent orders and updates. Geography, what's more, was eliminated entirely in the system's price structure as the federal government blanketed the continent with uniform postal rates that encouraged an unbounded sense of connectivity. This meant that any piece of correspondence weighing up to half an ounce needed only to be affixed with the same three-cent postage stamp, whether mailed from Maine or Texas, or from California for that matter. Those new adhesive-backed stamps, printed in the millions, functioned as the technical infrastructure for a nationwide grid of prepaid delivery that became another expression of the age's "annihilation of space" while improving the quality of mass communications by no longer requiring addressees to pay in order to receive their mail. Such innovations reflected the growing status of privacy in the bourgeois republic, David Henkin has argued. The fact that the vast bulk of this private communication was devoted to business subjects—contemporary estimates reached as high as 90 percent of all pieces of personal correspondence—reveals just how much that same bourgeois republic was becoming a commercial venture, or, more to the point, how the intercourse between its citizens was increasingly devoted to the exigencies of buying and selling.[28]

"*Business writing* may be said to sway the world!" P. R. Spencer thus declared without a trace of hyperbole. Since its contents had a shelf life, handwork was dedicated not only to producing a continuous stream of correspondence but to realizing its optimal value in real time. "As soon as a young man enters the counting-house," B. F. Foster observed, "he is told that it will never answer to write so slow." Rapid penmen could produce thirty words in sixty seconds, according to one estimation, which required the quill to travel sixteen-and-a-half feet per minute. You say you never saw such a thing, Foster further remarked in his *Prize Essay on the Best Method of Teaching Penmanship*: "That may be: thirty years ago nobody had ever seen a ship impelled by steam." It was a suitably industrial analogy, as was S. A. Potter's warning in another popular penmanship manual of the day about applying too much ink to the pen, for just as "the more dirt a contractor uses in constructing a railroad the longer it takes to make it," the same was true of putting words to paper.[29]

That précis spurred attempts at utilizing "easy combinations of chemical and mechanical skill" to create facsimiles in "scarcely more time and apparatus than is now required to write a single copy." The search for such automated methods of duplication engaged the inventive talents of James Watt, Christopher Wren, and Benjamin Franklin, among others, who were inspired as much by an Enlightenment ethos of mechanical improvement as by commercial utility, although the two motives were increasingly coming to share a common ontology. A version of carbon paper thus became available by the early years of the nineteenth century. This "manifold writer" offered a remarkably facile means of reproducing handwritten inscriptions that required no ink in generating even two copies, "if required," of the same document. Nor were the results easily altered or erased, as judges at the American Institute's

Annual Fair of 1841 noted in praise of this "very ingenious and useful con-
trivance." But because the manifold writer also exuded such a baneful odor,
a result of the oxidation of the oils with which the "carbonic ink paper" was
prepared, its adoption never became widespread. The quality of the copies,
moreover, which for technical reasons could be made only with a pencil or
stylus, thereby leaving no ink-penned "original," proved less than reliable,
often fading into illegibility upon exposure to the air.[30]

Continued interest in the culture of mechanical reproduction spawned
the "polygraph" as well, a device that required neither "considerable labour
or restraint on the fingers," Charles Willson Peale excitedly reported in 1804.
Nor did the new technology utilize special inks or specially treated paper. Instead, it operated by transferring the motion of one's pen to a prosthetic arm
that was attached to a second pen, which then produced an identical version
of the same text, or "two originals . . . at the same instant of time," as Peale
further effused about the wondrous effects of this invention. The *Philadelphia Gazette* similarly pronounced the polygraph to be "one of those things
which when discovered, excite astonishment over how it was ever possible to
do without them." Peale himself soon secured American rights to the original
English patent and commenced manufacture in a workshop he established
alongside his renowned museum of natural history in Philadelphia, shipping
off early models to Thomas Jefferson, a meticulous archivist of his own volu-
minous correspondence, who responded with suggestions for improvements
and then adopted the polygraph for personal use.[31]

Here, too, however, stubborn design flaws restricted the device's wider
adoption. The production of legible copies required a parallel alignment of
the pens, for example, which proved to be an elusive goal because of irregu-
larities in the wooden writing surface. Even when properly adjusted, however, the artificial arm was less than reliable. The beginnings of its lines were
often indistinct, and so too the text appearing at the bottom of the page. And
because no one could effectively watch the progress of his own writing while
simultaneously attending to the condition of the copy, it often went unno-
ticed when the prosthesis had run out of ink. Attempts to solve this problem
by adopting a fountain pen were unsuccessful.[32]

Another means of duplicating written documents became available in the
1830s, executed by a "counting house machine" which constituted the first
such apparatus specifically designed to meet the heavy production needs of
the office. This "press copier" was far more costly and cumbersome than either the manifold writer or the polygraph, requiring both special inks and
preconditioned paper. A newly penned text would be inserted into the machine alongside a blank sheet or bound copybook, the pages of which were

composed of cotton fibers and clay fillers that better adhered to the surface of the original, and that were also treated with tannic acid for darkening the ink upon its transfer to the blank page. The copier was then screwed shut, resulting in the execution of a print. A wide variety of presses, including portable versions weighing less than five pounds, offered a range of power and rapidity of action. All promised relief from the constant scrivening, thus prompting the *Scientific American* to recognize the "great savings for clerks" augured by such a system, which was bound to be embraced by merchant houses everywhere. Sure enough, William Mann Co. of Philadelphia reported on its success in selling a thousand of these copiers within a few years after the company's founding in 1849, together with twenty thousand copying books and three thousand dampeners for prewetting the special copy paper. Charles French, for one, was regularly assigned with impressing letters into the correspondence book at George H. Gray and Company using the new device, which attracted the attention of Charles Babbage, who described its principles in his seminal study *Economy of Machinery and Manufactures*.[33]

The marginal savings in time realized when a clerk pressed a random batch of recently composed texts all at once—presuming the firm had purchased a powerful-enough copier—rather than duplicate each one on its own within a dedicated memorandum book organized by the identity of the corresponding firm, or type of transaction, or particular branch of trade, required new methods of storage and retrieval. The press copier demonstrated a strong predilection toward a compression of the files, in other words, since it was far more efficient to combine documents into a copybook according to the simple order of their production. New systems for administering the flow of information through the office were accordingly developed, ensuring a "competence at method" that allowed convenient access to papers now stored with hundreds of other serially processed records. Nor could this machine-driven taxonomy be based on the production date, since that would still encompass dozens of miscellaneous documents without any other relationship to each other. Instead, each text was to be indexed by a special folio number and individually paginated.[34]

And yet the press copier had only a limited impact on office work. The original document was often rendered illegible, for instance, if too much ink was used up in transferring the text to the copy. The process of dampening the copying paper also proved to be unduly complicated, resulting in sodden or creased and puckered pages when either too much or too little moisture was applied. The paper itself tended to shift position as the mechanism was shut, causing any number of blurred or smeared copies. Neither the press copier nor the polygraph, in other words, and certainly not the manifold writer, could satisfy the escalating demands of the writing operations. Even the country's new Interior Department, which purchased a number of copiers in the 1850s, continued to employ extra copyists at ten cents per hundred words for processing the federal government's own growing volume of paperwork.[35]

As such, ongoing efforts to relieve the office's production bottleneck focused less on the tools and far more on the techniques of writing, driven as they were by the twin desiderata of speed and volume. A "bold, free, expeditious hand" became the primary means for doing so. It was the male equivalent of sewing, a traditional skill, that is to say, accelerated beyond recognition by the "fast property" of the commodity form. Graceful in its proportions, P. R. Spencer remarked of a properly realized commercial script, "it is as attractive as it is useful." In fact, business writing was attractive because it was useful, the outcome of a manufacturing system whose utility was manifest both in the standard nature of its production—all the era's new penmanship systems claimed to rest on a universal model of human physiology—and its product. "The style is so simple that it can be acquired with great ease and rapidity," a coalition of Providence bankers, businessmen, and bookkeepers typically emphasized in endorsing Potter & Hammond's *Revised System of Business Penmanship* for use in the city's public schools. The ensuing "plain, neat letter," consciously expunged of ornament and flourish in favor of "exactness and perspicacity," thus matching the instrumental grammar of business itself, was to be compared to other forms of industrial engineering—to the standardized patterns of the ready-made suit, for example, or the interchangeable jigs of machine parts—as befitted a technology developed to satisfy the mass production demands of the paperwork.[36]

James Guild was consequently entreated by his pupils in Vermont in the late 1820s to teach them "a business hand," for which purpose Guild created a style of his own design that quickened the pace of the writing. In fact, Benjamin Howard Rand had already brought a "running hand" to America several years earlier in his *New and Complete System of Mercantile Penmanship*, characterized by loops and an inclined script that were previously considered effeminate. But since velocity was becoming a priority, and the pen could not be lifted from the page without sacrificing valuable production time, loops were now unavoidable. By the mid-1830s, B. F. Foster was promoting an "American system" of writing adopted from the British innovator Joseph Carstairs, another great champion of speed, which further obviated the need to remove pen from paper while at once reducing the number of strokes required in fabricating each letter. P. R. Spencer, recognizing how "swiftly must the pen glide in these days of steam and electricity," introduced a similarly condensed style in which *y*s and *g*s appearing at the end of the word could be terminated without any loop at all. A straight downward stroke or easy curve to the left would suffice. Spencer also recommended the adoption of simplified forms of capital letters in order to quicken their execution. And while protests against those systems "which would sacrifice everything to rapidity" were to be heard from educators by the 1850s, when Foster himself retreated from his earlier Carstairian zealotry and the Boston Mercantile Academy endorsed a "medium" style that strove to strike a happy balance between an older round hand and the modern running hand—"having the legibility of the former with the rapidity of the latter"—attempts to rationalize, or industrialize, the writing continued apace.[37]

"To run over a page of fair handwriting is like riding over a smooth solid high way," the *Common School Journal* accordingly announced in promoting an early version of the information highway. Spencer, meanwhile, incorporated a metronome into his stroke exercises and called the system "chirythmography," a neologism constructed from the Greek roots for "time," "hand," and "writing" which was said to have first been developed at Albany's Commercial College. The method's incipient Taylorism was unmistakable. The mechanized uniformity of pen strokes effectively broke the alphabet down into an interchangeable collection of basic hand movements divorced from the meaning of the words themselves. "It will be seen that all the letters, long and short, requiring the same number of motions, are executed in precisely the same time," Spencer explained. Heavy, sprawling, blurred, and uncertain marks were eliminated while the text produced by one person would increasingly come to resemble that which was written by another. *Foster's Elementary Copy-Books* were inspired by the same regulatory ideal, measuring the slope of one's lines "with mathematical exactness" and applying those metrics to the thickness of each downward motion of the writing hand, the uniformity of top and bottom turns, and the optimal spacing between each letter, modeled by the width of the letter *o*. Foster then rearranged the alphabet in accordance to such formal production needs, the "short letters" (*a, c, e, i, m, n, o, s, u, v, w,* and *x*) preceding the "long letters" (*b, d, f, g, h, k,* and so on) in a sequence that imbued language with the utility of the age and so satisfied an earlier call by the *North American Review* to introduce science and system to the country's penmanship pedagogies.[38]

All this word-processing rested on a typographic norm that clearly anticipated the typewriter. Friedrich Kittler has forcibly advanced the opposite claim in his well-known study *Gramophone, Film, Typewriter*, arguing that the latter effected the destruction of the word by ushering in a "modern loop of endless replication" that turned the keyboard into a site of industrial alienation and robbed language of its immanent content. Such narratives assign far too much agency to mechanical invention, however. The fact is, machines did not create capitalism. Capitalism created machines. And like so many other mechanical innovations of the age devoted to accelerating the rate of production, the typewriter, which was eventually integrated into office work in the 1870s, together with its female operators, reinforced a process already well under way, one informed by commercial logic rather than any autonomous techno-logic, and patently manifest in the intensifying use of the hand-driven pen. "Write! Write!" as Benjamin Foster declared from his desk in Bangor in 1847. "Be it truth or fable. Words! Words! Clerks never think."[39]

Herman Melville provided additional details regarding the technicalities of this speedup:

> If, for the sake of easing his back, he brought the table lid at a sharp angle well up towards his chin, and wrote there like a man using the steep roof of a Dutch house for his desk, then he declared that it stopped the circulation in his arms. If now he lowered the table to his waistbands and steeped over it in writing, then there was a sore aching in his back.[40]

B. F. Foster explained that such aches and pains were the result of traditional systems of chirography that allowed writers to rest their arm on the paper. This old practice fatigued the fingers and ruined the parallelism of the letters while at once slowing down their execution. Efficient writing required a far more rigorous division of manual labor for which Foster designed a series of exercises that closely coordinated the movement of arm, hand, and fingers. The latter were thus assigned direct control of fine line operations while the forearm supplied the requisite power to the hand and the extended appendage directed all broader movements originating in the shoulder. These mechanics drove the bold, free style to which all now aspired, based as it was on an active physique that annulled the "cramping and effeminate habits" that otherwise narrowed the pen's radius and forced the writer to shift his gravitational center every time he lifted his wrist. "The great fault of turning the hand over to the right, and jerking it from point to point, to keep pace with the progress of the writing . . . is entirely eradicated," Foster happily declared of the resulting liberation of the arm, now free to move "insensibly and without effort" in forming its letters. With a similar goal in mind, P. R. Spencer recommended that the initial curves of words be initiated well below the bottom of each row and terminate above the midline of the shorter letters. This best accorded with the "natural motions" of the writing hand, a natural motion that could only be realized, significantly enough, by means of conscious training.[41]

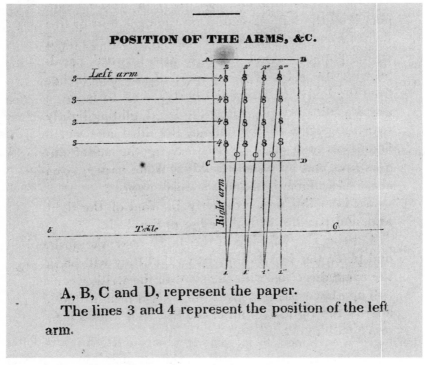

POSITION OF THE ARMS, &C.

A, B, C and D, represent the paper.
The lines 3 and 4 represent the position of the left
arm.

From Benjamin Franklin Foster's *Practical Penmanship*, 1830.

"All penmen know the incalculable advantage arising from the perfect command of the arm," Adam Rapp pronounced as well in his *Complete System of Scientific Penmanship*. In fact, the whole body was mobilized in attaining such command. Keep the mouth open, Spencer urged, since that allowed the tongue and jaw to keep time with the movement of the pen. S. A. Potter, meanwhile, claimed in *Penmanship Explained* that the legs and chest were no less integral to good mechanics than arm and fingers. Downward strokes would be more precise if the feet were firmly planted on the floor, for instance, which is why some experts recommended the use of standing desks, prompting Benjamin Foster to expend a "very dear" dollar and a quarter in 1849 in purchasing a stand that raised his own writing table, "much to my convenience." There were analogous calculations regarding the relative advantages of working on a flat or sloping surface, or for determining the correct height of one's chair, or estimating the optimal distance between the penman's head and the page. The paper itself, meanwhile, was to be strictly parallel to the elbow in order to ensure the regularity of one's rows. This also helped push the body forward, preventing the writer from bending too far over, which would round the shoulders and cramp the chest, obstructing the respiratory tract and making it practically impossible to maintain a single position over time—half an hour, at least—while also interfering with any attempt to shift one's weight during the course of the writing. "Position gives power," Spencer thus concluded, though he did not think it necessary to keep both feet on the floor.[42]

Taking up a pen in the countinghouse constituted an ambitious ergonometric project, it turns outs. All of the era's penmanship systems were consequently based on "philosophical and anatomical principles," as B. F. Foster claimed for his own, an integrated approach for achieving a "free, easy, unconstrained style" that made the "rapid movement of the writing-muscles" a possibility in the first place, as S. A. Potter duly asserted of his own pedagogy for achieving the most proficient use of the writing body. This marriage of freedom and control was as germane to personality as to efficient paperwork, which is why a correct writing style generally served to make us "better men," William Alcott affirmed. George Winchester's "muscular disciplinarian," a set of warm-up exercises incorporated into his *Theoretical and Practical Penmanship*, underscored that relationship by directing pupils to trace a sequence of nonfigurative line patterns fifty times from left to right, and fifty more times from right to left. The goal of the drill, Winchester explained to his method's subscribers, was to effect prompt and rapid communication between one's thoughts and actions. "Not for their own sakes merely" did B. F. Foster similarly recommend "large-hand" exercises to students, for these, too, became "a means to train and discipline the mind or body in order to enable it to effect other things." Proper penmanship therefore emerged as "an aid in the work of self-culture," Samuel Wells contended in his manual *How to Do Business*. The bourgeoisie formed their letters, in other words, as they formed themselves.[43]

Twenty-year-old William Cobbett, ensconced on a stool in copying out deeds and contracts at an antebellum law office, personified this chirographic process of class formation. His awkward, untutored hand was far more accustomed to farmwork, as graphically manifest in the copious blots and erasures he left strewn across the page. These called for conscious, and conscientious, correction, which would depend on William's success in anchoring such efforts in a fine capillary regulation of the fingers, which relied, in turn, on the willful application of his whole corporeal self to the business at hand. Did this make William into an appendage of the machine, or turn his appendage into something of a machine itself, moving "insensibly and without effort" in penning the documentation required by an economy dependent on an ever-growing volume of written records? The muscular discipline that George Winchester identified as essential to such modern mass production—and to modern character as well—together with B. F. Foster's sublime "*command of hand*," as explicated in Foster's *Prize Essay* on the subject, suggested just how much capitalism's divisions of labor dismembered individual bodies even in the ostensibly polite, unmechanized setting of the countinghouse. "Went down with uncle to his office offering him the assistance of my arm," a young clerk wrote in 1838, providing confirmation of Ralph Waldo Emerson's plaint from the year before that "a man in the view of political economy is a pair of hands."[44]

Those same hands were what distinguished men from the beasts, of course, "being the instruments most suitable for an intelligent animal," as Galen had long ago observed in his seminal survey of human anatomy. Handwork constituted mankind's signature achievement, as such, a sign of the civilizing process and a foundation of republican culture. And yet, this triumph was no longer borne by that

> strong arm, in its stalwart pride sweeping,
> True as a sunbeam the swift sickle guides.[45]

The clerk's hard-earned *command of hand* represented a distinctly modern form of man-made mastery, no longer measured by its productive encounter with the material world but by its very ability to turn that world—including itself—into a tool of abstraction.

The Bottom Line

Bookkeeping was the other foundation of paperwork. It was, in fact, an old technology that long antedated business writing, a cultural achievement of the Renaissance developed to enhance the ability of early joint-stock companies and mercantile partnerships to oversee the volume and scope of their trading activities. That same system proved powerfully adept at supervising the proliferating detail and unprecedentedly large numbers generated by industrial-era enterprise as well, measuring assets, mapping liquidity, and regulating temporality in a standard denominator of dollars and cents. "The true state of . . . the merchant's situation may at any time be easily, speedily, and distinctly comprehended and known," as Frederick Beck declared in the *Young Accountant's Guide* of the practical contribution of the accounts to the ramifying dimensions of trade in the nineteenth century. New partnership and corporate forms of business practice, pivotal for channeling investment and limiting liability for financial obligations—thus making risk more tolerable—were increasingly dependent on these procedures. Merchandising houses, for example, mobilized a wide assortment of stock and partnership books, daybooks and journals—or, alternately, a daybook in journal form— together with sales books, invoice books, bill books, cashbooks, and ledgers in seeking to "speedily . . . comprehend" their own situations. Commission businesses principally relied on their accounts current in calculating pay- ment schedules and drawing up notes, drafts, orders, and bills of exchange. Forwarding operations regularly turned to receiving and shipping records while brokerages, exchange houses, banks, steamboat companies (including lake steamboat firms), jobbers, and retailers—for whom the daybook, jour- nal, and invoices could usually be combined into a single register—were all similarly dependent on a proper disposal of the accounts. The ensuing tran- scripts constituted a fundamental tool for acting in the market, "just as tools for apprentices in the mechanical arts," Frederick Beck further explained. Indeed, the sequences of accounts functioned like so many closely calibrated gears driving the "engines of change," which is also why the books were equipped with special bindings capable of enduring the physical wear and tear of constant referral by a variety of office hands.[46]

The "true state of each and all accounts" would only become known, how- ever, if the mass of their constituent figures—the archipelago of liabilities, revenues, costs, and assets—was consistently and continuously engaged. Such diligence served as something of a bourgeois conceit, juxtaposed to aristo- cratic insouciance and to the passive reliance on Providence characteristic of more primitive trading cultures. James Blake consequently devoted a whole day at the office in search of "the precise point of a discrepancy which appears quite perceptible by my balance sheet for the past three years." That strict ty- pology of inputs and outputs, resting on propositions "as demonstrable and universal as those of Euclid," B. F. Foster declared in the *Origin and Progress of Book-keeping*, is what allowed Blake, and everyone else for that matter, to chart the entwined channels of exchange by which capital circulated through the economy before returning to its owner with, or often without, supplemen- tary value. This is why historians have long identified the "science of accounts" as a fundamental condition for the development of capitalism itself.[47]

In that celebrated metric known as double entry, each business transac- tion is recorded twice. Each transaction, that is, consists of two exchanges. In one, something is debited. This means that something else needs to be credited. When a firm sells a hundred linsey-woolsey boys' jackets for $1,000, a credit is thus recorded in the books for the outgoing jackets and a debit is re- corded for the incoming cash. This correspondence between the two entries is what generated an "equilibrium of results" embracing the entire enterprise, the books methodically recording what goes out with the same equanimity as what comes in, obstinately refusing to add up if anyone tried to make the numbers tell anything but the whole story. If one was to then compile all of the resulting accounts, a complete picture of the money economy would emerge since one firm's debits always overlapped with another firm's credits, tying all together in a great chain of exchange. The accounts were uniquely capable of displaying "the mazes of a complicated business with a beautiful regularity," Christopher Columbus Marsh therefore proclaimed in his *Science of Double-Entry Book-Keeping* of this structural commitment to a balanced ledger, which proved particularly adept at transposing discrete qualities into universal quantities and then reducing those quantifications into a singular scheme of commensurable values for sale, five hundred pages of journal postings distilled into several lines of financial summaries that then became the most reliable version of material reality available. The ever-fluctuating signs of value—whether Mr. Holmes's broadcloth, Mr. Brown's hardware, Mr. Lloyd's miscellaneous merchandise, or Mr. Jones's bill payable at thirty days' sight— consequently emerged as the very source of order, and even certainty.[48]

Such conceits marked a dramatic departure from the ad hoc book barter that prevailed in older cultures of exchange. The manner of listing trades and their attendant credits and debts in colonial America, for instance, was principally dedicated to generating a consecutive digest of events. The resulting catalog had little in common with the quadratics vetted by later capitalists seeking to gauge the flux of flux and achieve a synoptic command of the whole. The costs and returns generated by transatlantic voyages required systematic records, to be sure, but little effort was made in the eighteenth century to then utilize those figures in establishing a continuous report of activity at the level of the firm. Indeed, businesses were themselves an amorphous entity since merchant assets comprised a miscellany of separate forms of wealth that included, in addition to gross earnings derived from sundry trading ventures, interest on personal loans, income from legacies, and even the value of family dowries. It was impossible in such circumstances to establish provisional balances, not least because the ledgers consistently failed to distinguish revenue from capital. It was equally impractical to measure appreciation in the value of merchandise, or appraise losses from uncompleted projects, or match receipts to expenditures. Fixed assets—buildings and ships, for instance— were left on the books for years, if not forever. Bad debts were similarly carried at full cost. And changes in the worth of one's holdings were written up or down against income and expenditures, making a calculation of what would later be called net profit a futile endeavor. At the same time, these were all acceptable constraints on commercial knowledge since trade was based

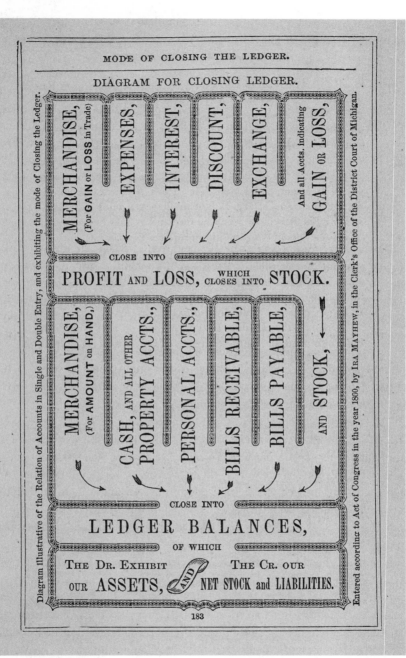

From Ira Mayhew's *Practical Book-keeping*, 1860 (sixtieth edition).

on the flow of wealth rather than its accumulation, on the trader's liquidity, in other words, rather than on any regular summary of the value or equity of the business.[49]

Sometime around 1820 all this began to change. The delineation between debtors and creditors, who were also less often the same person, became far more common, and far more commonly associated through cash payments. Distinctions between income and capital investment were increasingly brought into account as well, while the books, less devoted to maintaining a serial chronicle of goods for sale, were regularly closed in order to generate periodic summaries of assets and debts. Running balances, essential for gauging liquidity and meeting outstanding bills, now entered general use. So did balance sheets. Manufacturing enterprises that produced "solely with an eye to circulation" required a new level of documentary rigor and epistemological invention too. Fixed capital was accordingly separated out from capital currently "employed." Rents, inventories, raw materials, and even the labor of hired hands became the object of systematic measurement dedicated to uncovering the otherwise imperceptible interchange between a gamut of economic variables, both at the level of the enterprise and broken down by article, correlations that subsequently revealed new relationships between the whole and its parts. These then allowed capitalists to observe "at one view the entire result of business, the exact situation of affairs, or, in the brief and pertinent phrase, 'how we stand,'" which is how Christopher Columbus Marsh synopsized the practical effects of such an ambitious system of knowledge production.[50]

Not too many years beforehand, Marsh went on to explain in his *Study of Book-Keeping, with a Balance Sheet* in 1835, "the subject of this pamphlet was thought to be . . . a dark mystery." Since then, however, business accounts had become "so extensively required" that it was no longer possible to say "who may not stand in need of the knowledge embraced under its name." Marsh's own published oeuvre of instructional texts, including a *Course of Practice in Single-Entry Book-Keeping* (soon reissued in an expanded edition featuring a new section on partnerships), *Theory and Practice of Bank Book-Keeping, and Joint Stock Accounts*, as well as the *Science of Double-Entry Book-Keeping* ("respectfully DEDICATED to the CLERKS"), was a direct testament to the growing interest of the public in learning how to balance the books. Henry Patterson, recently hired to clerk at W. N. Seymour & Co. in Manhattan, thus attended a double-entry study group every Tuesday evening that counted among its regular participants "Mr. and Mrs. Crane, Ann Maria, Turner, and Edgar." S. W. Crittenden responded to this popular demand for instruction by publishing an *Elementary Treatise on Book-Keeping* that guided users through the procedures for posting up in the cashbook. Once those elementary skills were acquired, it became possible to advance to the ledger and balance sheet, which then qualified one, in turn, for the high school and countinghouse editions of Crittenden's *Inductive and Practical Treatise on Book-Keeping by Single and Double-Entry*. Irvine Hitchcock was another active pedagogue in the field, proud of his success in integrating "the language of business-men, rather than a childish dialect" into a *New Method of Teaching Book-Keeping* that also featured summary reviews at the end of each unit of study. How should the cash purchase of $1,000 worth of merchandise be listed in the books, pupils were duly quizzed at the conclusion to the *Method's* chapter on journalizing. How should the same purchase be posted if a note were issued in lieu of cash?

> But if, when you buy the Goods, you give in payment for them Cash, $500, and your Note for $500? If you give, besides the Cash, instead of your own Note that of Samuel Archer, due you for $500? If you buy said Good on Book Account? If you afterwards call and pay the Account in Cash? If you give him your Note instead of money?[51]

None of these various *Courses*, *Treatises*, and *Methods* offered a distinct technology for keeping the accounts, only a purportedly better scheme for learning the standard one, "an improved and more efficacious way of teaching the theory and practice of the art," as B. F. Foster advertised his own particular plan. Foster was dismissive, for instance, of those systems which assigned undue importance to subordinate books at the expense of "the LEDGER," that fractal table which contained the fullest, most intricate expression of all of a business's exchange relationships. Samuel Crittenden was equally forceful, however, in defending the organizing principle of his *Elementary Treatise*, based as it was on the cashbook, where each business transaction is initially listed. This method would necessarily "compel the pupil to depend upon his own mental resources," compel him, that is, to grasp the internal logic of each actual exchange and its ramifications for the company's assets, liabilities, and capital in order to then determine whether the reported sale should be transferred to the journal, the sales book, or the accounts current. "To make a correct Journal entry," James Bennett confirmed of this emphasis on the why as well as the how of the accounts in his *American System of Practical Bookkeeping*, "it is first necessary perfectly to comprehend the business transaction on which it is founded."[52]

Comprehending the underlying structure of each exchange rather than simply learning the rules by rote for listing debits on one side of the ledger and credits on the other was a purpose which matched the era's gestalt of social reform, that which strove to nurture each person's own faculties of deduction and generalization. These were the building blocks of rational thought, essential for advancing from "simple elements . . . by gradations, to combined results," as Horace Mann explained in an essay on the "means and objects of common school education." Mann could just as well have been summarizing the theory of accounts, which rested on the same tenets of natural reason and was why bookkeeping was included in the landmark curriculum innovations advanced by Mann in these same years. Lesson plans were accordingly developed in which the raw numbers of a business transaction were dictated to pupils, who were then directed, "as your clerks," to properly journalize the jumble of detail. Once these daybook techniques were mastered, the *Massachusetts Teacher* continued, "let them make a ledger and 'post' into that." B. F. Foster embraced the same pedagogy in his *Concise Treatise on Commercial Book-keeping*, proposing that each student be ascribed a nominal sum of personal capital—distributed in notes "so as to have the appearance of money," since these would clearly attain "a better effect"—which they were to manage as a business asset, requiring, of course, a full accounting. Older habits of "drilling the learner into a calculating machine" were summarily denounced in favor of such more enlightened methods which encouraged the student "to reason upon and comprehend what he is doing, or about to do," as was explained in praise of Foster's plan. Crittenden's *Treatise on Book-Keeping* was similarly lauded for its adherence to the "plain and Philosophical principles" that were inherent to the accounts and which so naturally "guide the reasoning facilities."[53]

Bookkeeping would thus raise up free and responsible agents, as C. C. Marsh declared of double-entry's role in socializing a new generation of Americans. Marsh himself became a persistent critic of commercial orthodoxies that had long considered bookkeeping to best be learned on the job. "A person may keep correctly the accounts of the house in which he was brought up," Marsh contended in rejecting such parochialisms, "but as the business may be quite different in any other house, change his situation, and he who was capable will be incapable." This was not the case for someone trained in the whole theory: "He is at home in the accounts of any business." Bookkeeping was thus consciously industrialized, established, that is to say, on principles of standardization and interchangeability, "as demonstrable and universal as those of Euclid," which effected uniform outcomes no longer dependent on the personal identity of whomever was assigned to keep the books. Such transparency turned the accounts into a science while at once making a mass market in clerical labor a practical possibility.[54]

Cautionary tales consequently abounded which warned of the bitter fate awaiting old-school mercantilists who refused to discipline their numbers:

the idiosyncratic "books of hieroglyphics" kept by such firms would prove utterly useless when the time came to settle up. Similar parables told of the woes of deserving traders who nevertheless faced commercial ruin after miscalculating their discounts, "a subject requiring, at all times and in every branch of commerce, the close and intimate knowledge of an experienced accountant." James Alden, a dry-goods wholesaler forced into bankruptcy, recognized the growing need for such fiscal expertise. "I understand . . . business," Alden pronounced in an affidavit filed with the court in 1842, but "am not a very good accountant, was not educated to accounts, and have no knowledge of accounts but what I have acquired myself." Such lacunae were common enough to warrant the introduction of a new course of study at Foster's Commercial Academy in 1852 intended for those veterans "familiar with the details of business" who nevertheless lacked "a competent knowledge of the principles of double entry." That same situation prompted J. B. Crane to acquire a copy of James Bennett's *American System of Practical Book-keeping* in seeking to improve his own grasp of the procedures for charging interest on receivables and so enhance control over the costs of credit sales at his paper mill.[55]

All this calculus, Thomas Jones explained in his own method for learning double entry, which had garnered a prize from the American Institute, was fundamentally a "problem of arrangement." The accounts constituted an exercise in logic, as such, for listing the trade in its pertinent category. "Each class of items has therefore its proper place assigned, and to know these places, and the object of each collection, is to know the plan." That plan's deep structure was revealed in a controversy which surfaced at the merchant banking firm of Brown Brothers in the 1850s over the best method for recording bad debts in the company's books. As a rule, debts were listed as assets since they were money owed to the firm. In that respect, they principally benefited the bank's senior partners, whose income was calculated on the basis of the value of those assets. But because some debts were bad debts that would probably never be collected, the partners were, in effect, receiving payments that had "not been fully earned," nor would they be. This meant that they were pocketing money that did not exist, a practice that discriminated against those not included in the firm's profit-sharing arrangement while also threatening the firm's very solvency. The practice provoked protest within the bank and eventually led to the creation of a separate "suspense account" for listing the questionable debts. That suspense account was to be written off against the senior partners' personal capital accounts, reducing their income in accordance to the amount of bad debt. However, the amount written off did not cover the entire sum. Part of the debt was left on the books as a real asset, thus showing up in the firm's balance sheet as income and consequently lining the partners' pockets.[56]

This compromise between rival personal interests at Brown Brothers became the company's effective financial situation. It had nothing to do with any kind of "material" reality—not with the legal status of the debt as outstanding, or practical recognition of the debt as worthless. But such materiality was itself a non sequitur, since no one could actually sell off all his holdings on a specific date in determining their "true" market value at any given point in time. What, then, would serve as the basis of value? On what did the balancing act of creditors, debtors, goods, receipts, and cash rest? Actually, it rested on none other than the firm's own particular version of what constituted balance, as arranged in its books. For, regardless of how interested, or even arbitrary, those categories may be, they satisfied accounting criteria as long as they strictly and systematically adhered to the plan's taxonomy, or "arrangement" of the facts, as Thomas Jones explained. The coherence of the books was ensured if all of the parts proved equally consistent with a common governing logic, bringing the concatenation of dollar signs into a stable equilibrium. The invention of a new entity called a suspense account for certain debts thus proved to be a most practical solution, even though it revealed the science of accounts to be an entirely artificial phenomenon.

Of course, this was no contradiction either. Such artifice matched the man-made nature of the market economy in general. Brown Brothers, in other words, functioned on the basis of a balance sheet of discounts, cash flows, costs, incomes, collections, and claims, which rested, in turn, on categories the firm had made up that then accorded it the ability to calculate, devise, adjudicate, and justify—that is, to act in the economy. "Knowledge is power," Warren Spencer declared in rehearsing a favorite slogan of the times in a lecture at Buffalo's Mercantile College in 1857. It was no metaphor. Businesses could only function on the basis of what was known, which made the ledger's production of value the very means for producing the market economy. The process itself was eminently practical, because those categories that effectively informed the firm's actions were invented by the firm in the first place. Tautology turned out to be the system's strength, proof that accounting, which displayed a harmony "more perfect than musical notes," required no further referent.[57]

Not everyone was satisfied with this emerging order of things. "The transactions of business are little better than fictions," Joseph Hopkinson remonstrated against such metaphysics in a "Lecture upon the Principles of Commercial Integrity," which he published in 1832. Hopkinson, a federal circuit court judge, was perturbed by the growing volume of goods circulating in the market that "the seller has not paid for," and which were then sold to customers who gave a note that "will never be paid." Such abuse of the credit relationship by all parties made a mockery of the tenets of mutual exchange, if not the very notion of intrinsic value. A similar protest was registered in response to a "question for accountants" posed in the pages of *Hunt's Merchant's Magazine* in 1844. Should merchandise drawn from a company be priced at cost or on the basis of its current book value? readers were asked. Modern professional opinion endorsed the latter practice, which B. F. Foster, for one, had been promoting since the 1830s as far better suited to the operative exigencies of a dynamic economy in which decisions about spending, crediting, and borrowing could not wait for a complete cycle of commercial events to establish real value, and in which such relatively tangible measurements as cash on hand or the sum total of assets at cost served as a partial indication, at best, of the resources available to merchants and manufacturers seeking the best return on their capital.[58]

And yet, in basing the worth of goods on current book value, the possibility arose in which their nominal worth would be lower than their original cost, resulting in accounts that "exhibit an *apparent loss* on merchandise *not yet sold!*" as was noted with considerable alarm. Conversely, if current value rose above original cost, then the books would show a gain "on what was '*never sold.*'" In either case, the situation proved wholly specious, divorced as it was from what was actually paid for the wares and providing further testimony to the subversive effects of the commodity system on the principles of trade. "He sells a world of goods—he employs a store full of clerks—he piles the boxes mountain high before his door—he takes a prodigious heap of paper—he has oceans of business in the bank—he is continually handling cash"—and he is bankrupt. That increasingly common sequence of commercial events seemed to defy common sense. More to the point, it heralded a new version of common sense, calibrated to a world in which "the old is going down with a crash, and the new is appearing amidst revolutions, as by magic," the *American Phrenological Journal* observed the same year that the "Communist Manifesto" more famously declared that "all that is solid, melts into air." The "questions for accountants" posted in the columns of *Hunt's Merchant's Magazine* were not, as such, a mere technical distraction for professionals in pondering the best method for determining how to properly list the value of assets in the books. They were, rather, a fundamental set of challenges about how to determine value in the first place, and to what purpose. Like the labor on which it once rested, and the republican identification of property with a fixed social order that rested on it, the possibility of intrinsic worth was being rendered obsolete by the "constant and almost ever-varying fluctuations" of the market itself.[59]

"Paper is made from the *rags* of things that did once exist," Thomas Carlyle ruefully remarked in his 1837 history of the French Revolution, that definitive event in the creation of a world shorn of absolutism. Loyalists to a commercial regime of absolute value experienced a similar sense of ennui, if not dread, in response to the modern economy's expulsion of truth from an anterior realm of transcendent meaning and its relocation in each person's "imagination," which is how Horace Bushnell reprimanded contemporaries in his 1851 paean to a lost "age of homespun" for having abandoned an agrarian tradition of equivalent exchange in which value was determined by the tangible effort each person undertook to satisfy his or her needs. Society was consequently slipping out of the control of realists and falling into the hands of nominalists, Bushnell protested, by which he meant that the social order was increasingly a function of humanity's own profane propensities rather than a mirror of what God had originally wrought. This recast truth as a vernacular experience, or contingency, embedded in practical antecedents and their identifiable consequences. "We may legitimately ask ourselves where it originates [and] what good it does," as Émile Durkheim eventually remarked of such plasticity in an essay devoted to the "sociology of knowledge" at the end of the century. Georg Simmel addressed the same market-infused ethics in his *Philosophy of Money*. "We dignify with the name of 'truth' those representations that . . . incite us to useful behavior," Simmel wrote of the instrumental provenance of reason in the age of capital. Utility, it followed, would determine which of those representations was to become established as reality.[60]

That practice found additional expression in a report published in *Hunt's* in 1849 regarding the appraisal of goods at the Custom House. "The invoice price, or even the price actually paid for an article of merchandise, is by no means a true criterion of fair market value," it was explained. That discrepancy might be caused by fraudulently marking down prices in order to pay a lower duty. No less problematic for those assigned with implementing the nation's tariff laws—and of far greater significance for historians investigating the phenomenology of the modern exchange economy—was the possibility that the same false price resulted from the varying fluctuations of trade itself.[61]

The authorities responsible for collecting import duties found themselves arguing, in effect, that the price commanded in the market was not the actual market price. Such claims of "under valuation" flew in the face of plain reason, of course. How could the amount paid for an article of merchandise not be the truest criterion for its "fair market value"? The fact is, however, capitalist economy was not a function of this or that transaction. It was not even a system based on market exchange, per se, but on the general need to bring market exchange under control, or into account. As a consequence, the rubric "market value" had less to do with the fluid movement of prices being paid for the goods than with the attempt to manage that fluidity. In this case, a committee of five merchants, chosen for their "integrity and fair dealing," was appointed to review any challenges to the reappraisals that might be made by customs officers. Continuing disagreements would ultimately be decided by the collector of the port himself, who, if opting for the lower valuation—which would generate less revenue for the federal government—"will give the reasons for the same in his statement, to be forwarded to the [Treasury] department for record." A three-tiered regulatory bureaucracy was thus put into place for determining a "fair and disinterested" price for the goods, the actual market transaction proving to be anything but fair and disinterested, let alone dependable. But let there be no mistake: these new arrangements at the port were no throwback to an earlier moral economy operating on the basis of notions of just price and corporate control over the commonwealth. They were instituted, rather, to facilitate the operations of a competitive market system devoted to the unrestricted accumulation of capital, implicitly recognizing that this same system often undermined its own operations. Fair market value, as such, proved to be another nominal category of account, created by government fiat and founded on the need for a consistent, predictable tariff duty, which would then "secure uniformity of action at the different ports." Like Brown Brothers, the federal state found itself inventing market standards to undergird the "ever-varying fluctuations" of exchange.[62]

The obloquy "fiction" with which Joseph Hopkinson denounced the *ex ante* quality of modern commercial exchange was thus the wrong word. The truth is, "political economy reasons from assumed premises—from premises which might be totally without foundation in fact, and which are not pretended to be universally in accordance with it," as Henry Carey, America's most highly regarded writer on economy at midcentury, quoted John Stuart Mill, England's most highly regarded writer on economy in those same years. The "science of accounts" rested on those very premises, functioning like a tool, "just as tools for apprentices in the mechanical arts," for producing material relations rather than just measuring them. The "proper place" for listing a business transaction, it followed, was not that which best reflected commercial exchange, but that which best integrated commercial exchange, and in integrating it, largely created it. Indeed, the utter clarity of the ledger's outcomes was only further indication of their engineered status, for such balance is rarely to be found in nature. It was "an age of systems," B. F. Foster subsequently declared in his *System of Penmanship*. The accounts underscored his observation for they demonstrated how a system of financial record keeping was stronger than reality, or, to be more precise, how such a system—in this case, a knowledge economy turning unique qualitative differences into universal money values—became reality. The ledger might have ushered in a world shorn of natural value, but that world was, by means of the same ledger, the site of discernable truth.[63]

Only by abandoning absolutes in favor of nominal values could universality even be attained. The account books were the means for doing so, counting and calculating an ever-increasing variety of goods (including such intangible ones as bad debts), and thus showing just how truly marketable everything was. They rendered trade into a unified field theory in which all things became accountable—or knowable—by assigning them a price. The market itself, no longer restricted to any particular time or place, therefore found its most tangible existence here, in the dutifully inscribed rows and columns of the accounts. This was where all parties met—and this was where flesh-and-blood values became abstract equivalencies that made the exchange of commodities synonymous with the economy.[64]

Bookkeeping did not just prove capable of inventing and then naturalizing the market, however, essential as this was to capitalist revolution. By organizing the mass of individual acquisitions (and personal acquisitiveness) into a single universe encompassing all of society's agents—by turning short-term, self-interested truck and barter into the stuff of a broadly secular and even "scientific" order—bookkeeping also helped synthesize the potentially destabilizing dualities at the very heart of the market system: equilibrium and movement, freedom and control, individuality and universality. Enterprises might run out of equity, resulting in bankruptcies that traumatize personal lives and disorder business, but at the level of paradigm, double entry could explain them—and often predict them—making such apparent market failings an entirely normal event. If anything, bankruptcies became the result of a failure to keep proper accounts. A form of knowledge invented in the fourteenth century thus achieved unprecedented importance in the nineteenth, capable as it was of uncovering "general and self-evident truths," as Thomas Jones confirmed in his "Analysis of Bookkeeping as a Branch of General Education," otherwise buried deep within a mass of self-interested figures. The bottom line consequently emerged as the value of values for it provided a structural check on what all agreed to be a national free-for-all in pursuit of the main chance, elevating capital itself into the source of both social and material order, elevating it, that is, into capitalism.[65]

Market Society

Clerks themselves were generally uninterested in the epistemological implications of their employment. "The masses have no desire to spend the best
years of their lives in studying abstract theories," Warren Spencer announced
at Buffalo's Mercantile College. They sought, rather, knowledge with a "direct
bearing upon the practical things of life." Nothing was more practical than
T. S. Arthur's *Advice to Young Men*, counseling his readers to retool for the new
economy. Arthur, born on a farm in upstate New York in 1809 and apprenticed to a watchmaker before finding employment as a clerk in Baltimore,
grew up to become one of the country's best-selling publicists of free-market
hermeneutics, tirelessly explaining in magazine stories and full-length sentimental fictions that the profit motive was a force both for nurturing talent
and for guaranteeing its responsible use. In urging America's young men to
acquire those skills that "could be used to advantage," moreover, Arthur consistently abjured artisanal pursuits. Steam engines and railroads, to cite one
of his examples, had relegated an entire class of harness makers trained to
outfit travelers on the turnpikes to a life of toil in an obsolescent craft and its
deepening web of impoverishment. To avoid a similar fate, the new generation must equip itself with more modern aptitudes, by which Arthur meant
"the whole theory of accounts" and "a fair business hand."[1]

Abandoning plane and anvil in favor of pen and paper was not just a matter of vocational retraining, however. The very notion of leveraging one's personal skill set in the labor market—"Let him ask . . . 'What am I best fitted
to do? What can I do best? What pursuit would be most attractive to me?'"
Samuel Wells advised this same audience of young careerists in *How to Do
Business*—subverted an agrarian logic founded on a far less negotiable system
of landed freeholds and patriarchal hierarchy. Benjamin Foster's pronounced

aversion to a safe and secure future on the farm was representative of such an ethos of "goaheadativeness," which tested success against a sliding scale of personal maximization rather than the static conventions of a yeoman competency. Everyone is succumbing to cash, Benjamin further reported after attending a lecture by Ralph Waldo Emerson at the Lyceum in Newburyport, Massachusetts, to where Benjamin removed from Bangor in favor of employment in a carpet store that offered greater sales opportunities. All that cash, moreover, as he continued in perfect transcendentalist pitch, had begotten an "epoch of separation, disintegration, analysis, individualizing." Clerks and philosophers alike, in other words, understood that personal experience was being recast on the same opportunistic terms that drove the market.[2]

And so, it now became practical to talk about the social life of money, for the same fungibility that facilitated the mass exchange of commodities proved equally applicable to intercourse between persons. True, money itself was an old, well-established means of acquiring property and reproducing community. In market society, however, such currencies of exchange served a fundamentally different purpose, loosening corporate bonds rather than perpetuating them. And though the resulting fluidity did not signal an end to hierarchy, per se, it inverted deference into a highly contingent, conditional relationship. The social contract was thus transformed into a continuous negotiation between citizens determined to replace the protection covenants of yore with liberal propositions that promoted each one of them into his own best agent.

The End of Patriarchy

"Tell them not to be so anxious to exchange the sure results of labor for the shifting promise of calculation" came the nervous response to the age's intensifying pursuit of wealth. "Tell them that the hoe is better than the yardstick." Such admonitions had special resonance in America, where the hoe was never simply a means of material subsistence but a tool for building the political order. As the British reformer and philosopher William Petty once explained, "Labour is the Father and active principle of Wealth, as Lands are the Mother." It was a pithy seventeenth-century formulation of the agrarian marriage of land and labor that served as "*the whole basis of national freedom*," as Noah Webster italicized its critical role a hundred years later, "the very *soul of a republic*." The patriotic zeal with which Americans protected "the HARD EARNED FRUITS OF OUR LABOUR" against imperial corruption during the nation's founding struggle was no rhetorical flourish, it followed, but a pillar of civic life.[3]

These paeans to household government and the homegrown fruits of the farmer's own industry drew on a particularly strong patriarchal tradition in British America, historians tell us, the result of widespread land ownership, a weak established church, and the distant metropolis. This is what made far-reaching experiments in republican politics possible in the first place. "The formerly rude soil has been converted by my father into a pleasant farm [which] has established all our rights," J. Hector St. John de Crevecouer proclaimed of the new republic's foundation of self-government in his *Letters from an American Farmer* in 1782. "On it is founded our rank, our freedom, our power as citizens." Sons accordingly found themselves "toing and froing" in filial service to the estate of their father, whose lands, livestock, tools, and "dwelling houses" would some day become the source of their own freedom and power. Carole Shammas has even suggested that the celebrated absence of entail in the New World—those common-law rules of inheritance that strictly delimited the sale of dynastic property in England to family members, and principally to firstborn sons—actually enhanced the authority of colonial patriarchs. Once land was severed from any preordained path of transmission, discretion over its dispensation only increased, therefore strengthening the incentive of household dependents to obey their masters.[4]

Even when patriarchal prerogative itself was curtailed by legalizing divorce, for instance, or by requiring that children and servants be taught to read, the purpose of legislators was not to grant greater autonomy to members of the household but to transfer certain police powers to the community, and that in order to better check the behavior of the patriarch himself, who was no less bound than others to the common will. This is why "use rights" that recognized a coterie of claims by persons to the same material resources, whether or not they owned them, were also so prevalent in America. Such structural impositions on access to wealth undergirded the mutual reliance and regulation essential for maintaining order on the imperial frontier. Private property was not, then, a wholly personal possession to be disposed of as each individual exclusively saw fit. The pleasant farm that established "all our rights" functioned, instead, as a little commonwealth which bounded polity, economy, and family together into a thick, multigenerational web of duties and collaborations, leaving household members with little choice but to cooperate with one another, even after the death of their parents.[5]

That is also why persons living and working outside the household system provoked so much suspicion, and even trepidation. Social isolation had not yet turned strangers into a source of cheap labor, or into advantageous trading partners. Competency rather than profit anchored the agrarian economy,

which was devoted, first and foremost, to securing each family's own subsistence. Surpluses would come later, if at all, to be disposed of through local networks of trade founded on principles of direct exchange rather than
accumulation, and on use values rather than cash prices. Promises between
neighbors therefore enjoyed far more currency than discrete contracts with
distant agents seeking short-term gains in singular transactions. Farmers also
had little reason, as Treasury Department officials discovered upon seeking to
inventory the nation's domestic manufacturing in 1790, to measure the output
ratios of wives, children, servants, and slaves, or calculate return on capital
investments, or estimate the productivity of the land itself. They also rarely
demanded interest on loans extended to one another, for using money to make
more money rather than acquire goods and services in reciprocal exchange
threatened to undermine the rough equality that underpinned the political
and social fabric. Certainly, such profiteering had little moral or material jus-
tification in an economy that relied as much on credibility as on credit, an
economy in which markets did not so much mediate the relations between
citizens but were mediated by them. Trade was dedicated, in these circumstances, to attenuating risk and enhancing security in an uncertain world that
rested, as everyone intuitively understood, on a fixed fund of wealth.[6]

   This collective regulation over the terms of exchange became the object
of escalating criticism by forward-thinking ideologues who hoped to liberate the economy from a system of controls they saw as hampering talent and
impeding development. The opposition of these free marketeers to household tradition was inspired by a vision of property's dynamic role in society,
reconceived as a vehicle of progress rather than guarantor of the status quo.
Inspection codes, price controls, special incorporation charters, manufacturing bounties, eminent domain rulings favoring landed elites, and long-
standing property restrictions on the franchise all came under withering attack as forms of collusion that protected the prerogatives of the powerful.
And so, for instance, new legislation enacted in the Hudson Valley by the
early years of the nineteenth century required everyone trading in the marketplace to buy and sell to everyone else, "any pretence of prior engagement
or sale notwithstanding." Until that happened, however, the economy had no
separate institutional expression, or even material existence of its own. Like
social life in general, proprietorship was explicitly situated within a family
order embodied in the householder, whose highly personalized rule was itself
embedded in communal structures that allocated both work and its rewards.[7]

   All this explains why the wage system replaced "the very earth as the
ground on which society stands," as Karl Marx summarized the end of land's
long reign over human affairs. The labor market proved far more flexible, and

powerful, than the household in organizing production. At the same time, it provided a direct avenue off the farm to dependent young men determined to liberate themselves from all their toing and froing. Sons did not necessarily inherit the homestead, Frederick Marryat thus reported after a visit to the United States in the 1830s, since they could more advantageously teach school, study the law, move out west, or go into a store. Those very opportunities were what made one "an independent man," Chester Harding wrote in generalizing from his own experience in a privately circulated memoir titled *My Egotistography*. No other period in the life of a youth "awakens so many of the finer feelings of his nature as when he leaves home," Harding declaimed from the vantage point of his own later success, offering a series of like-minded homilies which he distilled into an embracing adage—"Where there's a will, there's a way"—that was arguably the most concise expression of liberal social theory to date. In fact, such slogans abounded. "He can do anything" was another apposite epigram for an "egotistographic" age, this one emblazoned across a banner adorning a Boston banquet hall where the Sons of New Hampshire convened their annual dinner in 1849.[8]

"What Shall I Do for a Living!" thus emerged as a most "momentous . . . inquiry," the *American Phrenological Journal*, the most widely subscribed magazine in the country at midcentury, observed in a multipart series of reports surveying the era's expanding employment opportunities. This meant that only someone who lacked the "ambition to shine" stayed at home, James Guild confirmed upon forsaking his own New England village. William Hoffman, "long . . . abstracted from the desire of making farming my business," was another paragon of such personal ambition in departing the family homestead in upstate New York in the spring of 1848 in order to "install myself in business." "I stood in the Threshold of the hall and with my eyes bent or turned to the east, looked now and then with steady fixedness for the stage to make its appearance." The stage itself was several hours late—a last frustrating encounter with preindustrial time—and William got only so far as the town of Hudson that evening. But he was in Poughkeepsie early the next morning, inquiring after employment prospects in the first dry-goods store he encountered and at the next several establishments as well. It soon became apparent, however, that job opportunities in Poughkeepsie were limited, so William boarded the "through-by-daylight" steamboat service—archetype of the jet age's "red-eye special"—which took him down the Hudson River to New York City, where he arrived just before dawn the following day.[9]

Washing and combing himself in anticipation of another busy day of self-promotion in the anonymous labor market, William began his search for a

New York City clerkship on Greenwich Street. He was soon advised to remove to Stewart's "great store" on Broadway, which was reported to be hiring.
On the way he stopped to borrow an umbrella at a shop where two upstate
acquaintances, Benton Badgley and Lay Bushnell, were employed. At Stewart's William again discovered, as he had in Poughkeepsie the day before,
that his lack of experience was a serious obstacle in landing a position in a
commercial house. Selling choice potatoes in town after a day of hoeing, or
even purchasing a promissory note from a local merchant for a "slick" dollar profit, did not qualify William for a place in the metropolitan world of
business. Rebuffed but not dispirited, he ventured east to Pearl, Nassau, and
William Streets, the heart of the country's dry-goods trade in fabrics. He was
no luckier there. By late afternoon William was back on Broadway. This time
he turned up the avenue, stopping at every establishment along the way until
he reached the northern outskirts of the city. Still no success. He returned to
Greenwich Street, where he began his day, and where William had an unsym-
pathetic encounter with a "Loafer" who played him for a country fool by pre-
tending to be the firm's proprietor and raising false hopes of a job.[10]

At this point William lost track of time. He planned to resume his job
search first thing the next day, until someone told him that it was already
Saturday night. So he spent Sunday waiting for Monday, upon which William
took his efforts to Brooklyn. He ran into Jacob Dewith, who had once worked
for William's uncle in upstate Hudson and who told William to proceed
forthwith to his former employer's store in Manhattan, which was seeking
to hire a new clerk. Reaching the address, William discovered that another
old schoolmate, Bushnell Lumis, was clerking at the same firm. Lumis informed William that the new position had already been filled. Instead of returning to Brooklyn, however, William crossed the Hudson, determined to
try "every store" in Jersey City. There, too, he encountered an acquaintance
from home, but there, too, he "met with but little encouragement" in finding
a job. Clearly, Gotham offered few prospects to a mercantile novice from the
provinces. William concluded that it would be best to remove back upstate
and continue his quest for a start in business in Albany. If unsuccessful there,
he would proceed to Troy. He boarded the *Rip Van Winkle* after dark, sleeping with his head propped up on a table to save the extra fifty cents—which
would have doubled the cost of his fare—charged for a berth. By morning he
was in Albany. Fixing himself "as slick as possible," he struck out for the city
streets. In Albany, William's luck changed, or perhaps his systematic efforts
bore their inevitable fruit, for after meeting with a lukewarm response to his
supplications at a carpet store, William landed a job at a firm specializing in

piece goods. He returned to Hoffman's Gate to pack up his things—and begin planning the sale of the family farm—and was back at S. V. Boyd & Co. the following Tuesday, at once initiated into the art of folding up calicoes.[11]

William Hoffman, like Benton Badgley, Lay Bushnell, Jacob Dewith, and Bushnell Lumis, and together with a "countless throng" of other young men being carried along "by an increasing centripetal force . . . towards the great emporium," as James Alexander observed of the gravitational pull of market forces in his 1857 essay "Merchants' Clerk Cheered and Counselled," were all determined to become "architects of [their] own fortunes." That is how an early biographer of Andrew Jackson described his subject's own self-made success, generally attributed to the fact that Jackson had grown up without a father. So had George Peabody, a celebrated transatlantic financier and pioneering philanthropist, whose "energy and perseverance" were attributed by the *Cyclopaedia of Commercial and Business Anecdotes* to having been orphaned at an early age, leaving young George acutely aware that "in the battle of life before him he must depend on himself alone." In fact, the loss of his father proved to be the key to future success, for the absence of a family patriarch encouraged George, just as it did "many others" of his generation, the *Cyclopaedia* noted, to develop their own ambitions. This emerging creed of autonomy was probably best synopsized by John Angell James in a piece of didactic prose called *Young Man from Home*, which Benjamin Foster perused in his evenings after the store closed. "I am capable of judging, discriminating, and determining between right and wrong," James's young hero exclaims in a burst of self-assertion inspired by his liberation from the restraints of household government. "I have the right, and will exercise it, of forming my own standard of morals, selecting my own models of character, and laying down my own plans of action."[12]

Such personal declarations of independence identified filial deference with cultural reaction, with Asiatic caste systems, for instance, where "every son is born to the business of his father" and thus condemned to a condition from which "he cannot rise." Europe was no less enthralled to such primitive practices. "*Let everyone who is below, or under me, stay there*" remained a practical axiom for Old World society as well. Edward Everett, a favorite on the public lecture circuit, contributed to this waning reputation of patriarchal tradition by telling antebellum audiences about how the young Franklin was "worked hard . . . and beaten" at the hands of a "harsh and unreasonable brother" to whom Ben was involuntarily apprenticed as a child. There was no need to take Everett at his word, however. Franklin himself explained in his best-selling *Autobiography* that deliverance from the arbitrary dominion of family rule—personified by his subsequent escape from servitude and

[YOUNG GREELEY'S ARRIVAL IN NEW YORK.]

The frontispiece of James Parton's 1855 biography of Greeley.

consequent arrival to the distant city—was a critical first step along the path
to personal success. Samuel Goodrich, better known as Peter Parley, the country's foremost author of children's literature, accordingly declared Franklin's
memoir to be the most useful work of its kind ever written: "What a debt of
gratitude does the world owe to Franklin!" It was certainly useful to Thomas
Mellon, a banker who recalled his initial encounter with the *Autobiography*
in the 1830s as inspiring him with "new ambitions." I had never imagined, as
Mellon acknowledged, "any other course of life superior to farming, but the
reading of Franklin's life led me to question this view."[13]

"All the promise of life seemed to us to be at the other end of the rain-bow . . . anywhere else but on the farm," someone else similarly testified to the lure of a landless future. A cousin of Abraham Lincoln also recalled the future president's determination "to cut himself adrift from his old world" and create a life in opposition to the mundane farming routines of his illit-erate father. Young Abe's penchant for "reading, scribbling, writing, [and] ci-phering" eventually took him to the Illinois river town of New Salem, where he opened a store, worked as a surveyor for the county, served as postmaster, and then went into the law. It was an authentic expression of Adam Smith's vision of a society where "every man was perfectly free both to chuse what occupation he thought proper, and to change it as often as he thought proper," a market society, in other words, in which individuals scrambled after the same competitive advantage that likewise drove commodities from place to place in search of a better price. And so it was that "whoever stands still will soon be left behind, by a distance equal to the diameter of the whole visi-ble horizon," the *American Phrenological Journal* pointedly observed in ad-dressing the "demands of the age on young men." Such zero-sum geometries were born of the fact that no one was any longer bound to the condition or occupation of his father, Edward Jarvis, a Boston physician and president of the American Statistical Association, announced in remarks delivered at the cornerstone ceremony for a new hospital being built for the insane in North-ampton, Massachusetts, in 1856. "All the walks and employments are open to all men, and at all times, and they may select whatever they wish . . . and they may change as often as it pleases them," Jarvis continued in describing the unfixed nature of the times, albeit with far less laissez-faire ardor than that which animated Adam Smith. Alexis de Tocqueville, too, was noticeably ambivalent about the chronic restlessness of Americans "in the midst of their prosperity." Tocqueville remained enough of an Old World philosopher to think this still constituted something of a contradiction. "He brings a field to tillage and leaves other men to gather the crops," Tocqueville wrote of the un-restrained pursuit of happiness so characteristic of democracy. "He embraces a profession and gives it up." There was little wonder, as he also reported, that insanity was said to be particularly rampant in the New World.[14]

The resulting separation, disintegration, analysis, and individualizing were commonly juxtaposed to the grounded sensibilities of the farmer who "intends to leave his remains to moulder under the sod which he tills," and of his son, "who, born in the land, piously wishes to linger around the grave of his father," as James Fenimore Cooper, a prominent skeptic of the new world disorder, summoned the consolations of a country existence. That same sod never "fraudulently stops payment" to those who "bring forth its fruits," another neo-agrarian ideologue conjured a more virtuous, and less commercial, application of personal talent and tenacity. And yet, such organic pieties, which cast the merchant's clerk as agonist to the plowboy while fanning complaints of sons running off like "loafers" in pursuit of the "peddler's trunk," obscured the very fact that the land itself was being relentlessly integrated into the mutable abstractions of the market economy. Agriculture requires no eulogy, Edwin Freedley thus proclaimed in his *Practical Treatise on Business*, which featured a long chapter on the utilities of soil management, new forms of animal breeding, and methods of crop rotation. Such capital-intensive farming—which included the Hoffman family's inaugural use of a mechanical thresher to harvest its straw in 1847—represented the redoubled efforts of eastern householders to exploit existing resources in competing with the high yields being sent to market from the western frontier. Their success depended on applying science and system to the land, William Hunter explained at the Rhode Island Society for the Encouragement of Domestic Industry, which would result in an "astonishing" increase in the productive capacity of the farm after centuries of little or no change whatsoever. That industrial sense of boundless improvement is what distinguished American yeomen from foreign peasants. It is also what transformed rents into profits, Henry Carey happily observed of the elasticity of the soil, a conclusion endorsed by the president of New York's State Agricultural Society, who declared the farm to be as "remunerating as any investment in any other pursuit."[15]

The plowboy was no antediluvian gesture, in other words, but an agent of material progress celebrated by such modernizers of country life as "Henry Homespun Jr.," editor of the house organ of New York's Board of Agriculture, which regularly published breathless updates on new breeds and patents that promised to boost the fecundity of the family farm. Those entailed dedicated investments in animals, fertilizers, and machines which then drew an increasing number of householders into the money economy and its constituent flows of cash and credit, to be redeemed by a comparably monetized output of marketable crops. And so, by the time the *Catskill Messenger* announced in 1849 that the value of Hudson Valley produce would "be guided altogether by the prices . . . in the City," this was happy news for farmers who not only relied on steam and rail but a structure of fixed-term credit, price schedules, and redeemable notes that synchronized the variable cycles of crops and capital.[16]

"Counting the costs" thus proved critical for optimizing the value of one's hundred acres. These included expenditures on horses, milch cows, pigs, and a hundred sheep that exceeded $1,000 for converting the farm from grains to livestock, a capitalization that required careful management of factor proportions, output levels, and product prices. It comes as no surprise to therefore find James Bennett, the well-known purveyor of double entry, offering a course of twenty lectures in Hudson, New York, as early as 1816, or to read the *Cultivator* a generation later extolling the vital role of "well-kept accounts" in securing the homestead, a task best delegated to grown sons, as it "would tend very much to benefit [them], as well as to improve the profits of the farm." Those profits transformed agriculture into a full-fledged vocation for the first time, allowing farmers to support a family without the supplementary craftwork and neighborhood barter that had been so central to the household economy. The new income streams also allowed others to leave, for the mass migration of wealth and population off the land in antebellum America was no sign of farming's obsolescence but of the opposite, namely, its integration into the new economy's expanding divisions of labor. A New Englander with four sons could send one to be trained as a lawyer, for instance, another as a physician, and a third as a minister. The fourth stayed home. "Thus, out of the proceeds of a farm, perhaps not containing fifty acres, all these young men shall be properly educated."[17]

The shared rights and lifetime transfers that once made buying and selling a far more cumbersome process were becoming a distant memory. They were certainly absent from William Hoffman's own calculations upon leaving home, at which time his mother transferred ownership of the farm to her three grown sons, all of whom were employed in commercial trades. She was cognizant, William noted, of the insufficient means available to her children and "the absolute necessity of such an addition or increase of our capital." After gaining control of the property, the brothers immediately set about to improve it. This meant renovating the physical plant in hopes of increasing the farm's market value from $7,000 to $8,000, and maybe even $9,000, at which point they planned to sell. In the meantime, they hired a man to manage the place in exchange for a third of everything he grew. The remaining two-thirds of the proceeds from the crops and stock—sheep, pigs, corn, pumpkins, and orchards—would be divided among the three brothers. The land was thus transformed into a capital fund for generating an income based on estimates of its productivity. Problems soon arose, however, for the farm's earnings fell far below expectations, "leaving a small dividend," at best, and leading William to anxiously declare his willingness to sell the property even below its "actual value." "We realize merely nothing from the farm," he bemoaned. "On the other hand the interest of the money is too much to lose year after year—scandalous." He estimated that annual loss—or what his portion of the sales price would have yielded him as an investment—at 7 percent. Sale of the property would also allow William to dissolve his common ownership, or what he called "partnership," with his brother George, with whom he frequently quarreled over money. William was determined to "never again be involved with him or have any interest of our own invested with his." George apparently felt the same way, for he soon proposed to buy his brothers out on the basis of a $7,500 valuation.[18]

In fact, everyone was currently advised to avoid doing business with family and live "*totally independent*, in money matters, of all your kindred." Soliciting financial favors was always an onerous undertaking, as Hubbard Winslow acknowledged in *Young Man's Aid to Knowledge, Virtue, and Happiness*. But it was a particularly thankless task when brothers or cousins were involved, for their "very great" jealousies invariably undermined what should have otherwise been a straightforward set of monetary calculations. B. F. Foster warned readers of his *Clerk's Guide* of the same entanglements. Applications for a loan from friends or relatives, no matter how trifling, were consistently met by condescending disquisitions regarding one's own imputed imprudence. "Doubtless you look forward to the time when you will be able to take a responsible position in the active pursuits of life," James Nixon thus observed in *Rudiments of Book-Keeping*. For that to happen, however, you will need "to depend upon yourself." Such increasingly common sense inverted patriarchal logic, of course, which had insistently wed property and family, and one's personal future to patrimony. But the family's new role as a sanctum of sentiment, born of the widening ideological schism between home and work, sundered that relationship, banishing economy from the household and leading Frederick Marryat to report in his *Diary in America* that when a son went to work for "some merchant, or in some store, his father's home is abandoned, except when it may suit his convenience, his salary being sufficient for most of his wants."[19]

These were the same years when Americans stopped referring to their fathers as Governor, Edward Jarvis later recalled in his memoirs. But the end of patriarchy and its replacement by a fraternity of ambitious sons practicing universal manhood rights that were thoroughly detached from ownership in the land, or any other form of property besides oneself, was no Oedipal catharsis. Family support remained the rule in preparing children for adulthood. "Where lies the charm that brings so many young men into the counting-room and so many tender boys behind the counter?" as *Hunt's Merchant's Magazine* had equivocally asked. "It lies in the urgings of their parents." Charles French accordingly went into a store only after his father decided that Charles was best suited to a career in business, at which point he also assumed the cost of Charles's membership in Boston's Mercantile Library. Eight years later and in business for himself, Charles hired a clerk fresh from the provinces only after receiving explicit promises from the young man's family regarding his character. Henry Patterson's father, too, made arrangements with an acquaintance in New York City to find clerical employment for his son upon the latter's arrival from Suckasunny, New Jersey. William Hoffman eventually landed a job in Manhattan by soliciting a position at Freeland, Stearns & Co., where his father and uncle were both personally known. Edward Thomas secured a job at a Boston hardware firm with family help, and Edwin Morgan received his first clerical opportunity in an uncle's wholesale grocery business in Hartford, Connecticut.[20]

The "empire" of the father which John Locke had promoted in the seventeenth century as a counteragent to the autocratic excesses of the prince was now dismantled by the same tradition of intergenerational cooperation that once secured it. "This day I leave my Father after having got him to consent to my being Free," an eighteen-year-old testified to the paternal countenance he still considered rudimentary in order to "commence my career." That same collaborative spirit encouraged Mrs. Hoffman to abet her sons' decision to turn the family's five hundred acres into a "dividend." Families that were no longer bound together by the legal, material, and moral exigencies of household economy navigated the ensuing market revolution by actively assisting their sons gain a foothold in the new capitalist order, as Mary Ryan showed in her nonpareil account of the making of an American bourgeoisie in Utica, New York. According to Ryan's history of this way station on the Erie Canal, the practical result was a 7,500 percent rise over the following three decades in the number of young men finding employment in town as merchant clerks.[21]

A Cash Fraternity

They faced a "boundless and exulting future," George Hillard, Charles Sumner's law partner, declared of this new breed of strivers in a lecture at the Mercantile Library in Boston, where Charles French was to soon become a dues-paying member. Hillard's remarks were no simple panegyric to commercial ambition, however, but part of a general survey of the "dangers and duties of the mercantile profession," in which he expressed considerable alarm about a social system that would no longer "check your progress," "clog your steps," or "block your path." Such opportunity might now be a natural right, and even central to human progress, but that only exacerbated the unnatural perils of a public order founded on the ever-shifting conditions of personal ambition.[22]

Some responded to this development by urging business firms to assume personal responsibility for the welfare of their waged charges. "So much of a man's character depends on what kind of an employer he had when young," a contributor to *Hunt's* explained in implicitly assigning the role of in loco parentis to senior partners. Clerks should be treated like sons, another observer of the business scene similarly advised, which made it incumbent on merchants to arrange suitable living arrangements, "as much like a home as possible," and that in order to protect their staff from the menacing acquaintanceships so often struck up amid chance encounters in the anonymous conditions of the metropolis. It would be highly advantageous to employers, the *United States Economist* opined too, "if they were a little more interested in the means, and how their clerks passed their evenings." Such supervision should extend beyond business hours and profit margins and include an *"expression of a personal interest in his welfare,"* as well as "such friendly suggestions as may rouse him to resist temptation." A. T. Stewart, whose "Marble Palace," arguably America's first department store, opened on Broadway in 1846, put such counsel into practice by establishing a boardinghouse for his employees and personally stocking its library. Arthur Tappan, a New York City silk importer who established the country's first nationwide credit-rating agency in 1841 in the wake of the country's first nationwide economic panic, also followed suit by disallowing visits to the theater by his clerks while quizzing each of them on Monday morning regarding the texts cited in church the day before.[23]

But there was another kind of response to the congenital dangers of an unsupervised life pursued far from home. It was elaborated in a parable that appeared in the *Cyclopedia of Commercial and Business Anecdotes* and told of a police constable called to investigate the disappearance of a large quantity of stock from a city store. The stolen merchandise is soon traced to one of the firm's own staff, a clerk assigned sole responsibility for overseeing an inventory worth tens of thousands of dollars. Upon interrogation, it becomes apparent that this same young man earned a weekly wage of $3.50. Was that no greater than the sum he expended on room, board, and washing? the constable inquires of one of the firm's partners. Apparently so, the latter acknowledges, not without a little embarrassment. The moral was self-evident. And so, instead of being placed under arrest, the guilty clerk was kept on the job and his salary doubled. Needless to say, he soon proved to be a model employee.[24]

Fair remuneration was a practical substitute for moral stewardship, it followed. Anyone with "a little acquaintance with the abuses practiced upon clerks by employers" understood that loyalty was best secured by coordinating between the respective interests of both sides of the labor relationship. That cooperation, or contractual consent, rested on a modern ethic of "enlightened selfishness," Daniel Haskell, a New York commercial lawyer, explained in another lecture to a roomful of city clerks at the Mercantile Library, seeking to put the best face on a creed of infinite appropriation. It was entirely unreasonable, if not "even laughable," Haskell added, to expect anyone to undertake heroic sacrifices in a world where "pecuniary interest is the lever which moves; money the talisman which inspires and supports." And yet, he continued on a more hopeful note, perhaps heroism was not altogether moribund. Perhaps it had simply been reincarnated as an updated version of the golden rule: "Pay one's debts!"[25]

Of course, debts themselves were an increasingly nominal matter, often melting into air under the aegis of new bankruptcy laws which recognized that such old-fashioned obligations as paying back what one had borrowed could be disastrous for business. Robert Hone, a former mayor of New York, predicted that the city would prosperously fill up with out-of-town buyers once imprisonment for debt was abolished: "As formerly any one who owed anything here was afraid to show themselves even with what little money they might have to pay on a/c and preferred leaving the whole of their debt unpaid and buying their goods elsewhere for cash thus injuring us in a double view." Proponents of the more lenient bankruptcy regime being installed by legislative fiat and judicial activism convincingly, if counterintuitively, argued that repeal of absolute liability would serve to moderate risk and stabilize trade. Creditors would think twice, for example, before extending a loan once borrowers had regular recourse to bankruptcy proceedings. Debtors, meanwhile, understood that formal recognition of their insolvent status and the associated forgiveness of their debts depended on a personal reputation for integrity, not to mention a well-ordered set of books.[26]

Samuel Wells expanded on this new version of moral economy in a popular advice manual *How to Do Business*, which was one of a series of guidebooks that included *How to Write*, *How to Talk*, and *How to Behave*. All could be purchased as a set at discount and were eventually published in a single bound edition:

PA. (Reading a newspaper, mutters)—No rise in the rivers—never going to rise again, I believe, wife.

LITTLE DAUGHTER. I wish the rivers would rise.

PA. Why, what have you got to do with the river's rising?

LITTLE DAUGHTER. A great deal, papa, for then the boats would run.

PA. And what have you to do with the boats running, my child, hey?

LITTLE DAUGHTER. They would bring the cotton down.

PA. (Looking over his spectacles)—And what have you to do, pet, with cotton bales?

LITTLE DAUGHTER. Why, if the cotton was down, pa, you would be able to sell it, you know, dear papa (smilingly).

PA. And what then?

LITTLE DAUGHTER. You would have plenty of money.

PA. Well?

LITTLE DAUGHTER. (Laying her little hand on his shoulder, and looking into his face)—Then you could pay mother that gold twenty-dollar piece you borrowed of her, you know, papa.

PA. And what then, minx?

LITTLE DAUGHTER. Then mamma could pay Aunt Sarah that ten dollars she owes her.

PA. Ay, indeed! And what then?

LITTLE DAUGHTER. And Aunt Sarah would pay sister Jane that dollar she promised to give her on New Year's, but didn't, 'cos she didn't have no cotton, I mean money, pa.

PA. Well, and what else? (Pa lays down the paper and looks at her curiously, with a half smile.)

LITTLE DAUGHTER. Cousin Jane would pay brother John his fifty cents back, and he said when he got it he would give me the half dime he owes me, and two dimes to buy marbles; and this is what I want the rivers to rise for, and the big boats to run! And I owe nurse the other dime, and must pay my debts.[27]

Wells offered a conception of commonwealth—currently in the throes of a credit crunch, no less—founded on the ephemeral, self-interested terms that had undermined it to begin with. This was a vision of money serving as a universal bond in a boundless chain of obligations reaching across society. "Never has a value which an object possesses only through its convertibility into others of definitive value been so completely transferred into a value itself," as Georg Simmel remarked of the unprecedented status of the cash nexus in market society. That convertibility, together with its utter indifference to personality, is what turned money into such a powerfully objective force, a social adhesive for aggregating a mass of promises—or debts—undertaken by one person to another, whether they knew each other or not. And while the abstract nature of this mass circulating currency dissolved the intimate fabric of household economies, money, by the same token, was able to connect all the atomizing interests back together, and do so without relying on the organic hierarchy and absolute value that had once secured the social order. "Money thereby directly and simultaneously becomes the *real community*," Marx also observed at the time, "since it is the general substance of survival for all, and at the same time the social product of all." It was so obvious that even a child could understand.[28]

T. S. Arthur addressed this growing prelation for cash in an anthology of occasional pieces published in 1856 under the apt title *Mother's Rule*. Parents had a duty to teach their children "the value of money," Arthur insisted, for that would imbue the young with a general sense of personal responsibility. Such a goal was best achieved by according them the opportunity to earn it themselves. " 'I remember the first dime I ever possessed,' " Arthur quoted a young man of his acquaintance in an apocryphal story written to alert readers to the pitfalls accompanying the transition to a waged economy. " 'It was given me by a friend of my father's . . . in return for attentions bestowed upon his horse.' " Such well-earned recompense was the object of justifiable pride on the part of the youngster. This did not, however, keep his father from taking immediate possession of the coin and placing it in his own pocket, proving that patriarchal privilege was slow to die. Children brought up under such arbitrary government, Arthur presently adjudged, would never grow up to become accountable citizens. "Their rights have been outraged, and they have been deliberately taught a lesson of dishonesty." How much more enlightened was the attitude of William Hoffman's mother, who, in no less allegorical a chapter in the demise of the household regime, assented to William's request to sell her husband's old sword and military saddle to raise the cash for his move to Albany.[29]

That same money power is what also allowed William and George Hoffman to sever the involuntary bonds of kinship that fed their mutual recriminations, though only after agreeing on a price for the farm, of course. In so doing, they released themselves from any obligations they had not explicitly undertaken, either to each other or to anyone else. Such interaction was founded on another instrument that proved indispensable to the paper economy, the signed contract, which mediated between the disparate, often conflicting desires born of the ambitions of autonomous individuals. Like the account books, in fact, the contract was designed to balance a plethora of separate interests, replacing any supererogatory will or transcendent version of the common good with the signatories' own determinations of what constituted a fair exchange or equitable compensation for goods and services rendered. The notion of just price consequently came to mean what the market would bear, no longer hampered by doctrines of consideration serving a fixed general need. The contract's underlying ethic of personal volition, what's more, recast the very idea of intrinsic worth into an arbitrary, if not inequitable, rubric which denied the primacy of one's own judgment in determining the value of this or that object to oneself. The market was thus the great ally of personal freedom, Henry Bellows declared in his *Leger and the Lexicon*, which took special aim at conservatives who warned of the dangers of unregulated ambition and the ensuing breakdown of social order, and therefore urged humanity to make do with less.[30]

This commercializing sense of self found incisive expression in a draft document submitted to Congress in 1836 by Francis Lieber, who taught political economy at South Carolina College, proposing a nationwide survey of "the welfare of [the] species." Lieber's unprecedentedly expansive census, representative of the decade's fledging statistical activism and a more general culture of calculation, was designed to establish the age's "standards of comfort." These would be derived by comparing the basic costs of human subsistence, determined by political economy's well-worn trinity of food, clothing, and rent. Lieber's initiative was clearly motivated by the era's growing concern with industrial-age poverty, but his plan gave equal expression to an industrial-age commitment to prosperity. Welfare and even comfort, that is to say, were no longer the exclusive prerogative of the propertied classes but universal values to be applied to the population as a whole. If the returns of Lieber's survey thus revealed a chronic condition of want, reforms in the organization of government and the distribution of society's wealth would be called for.[31]

Concern for the welfare of the species found further expression in another novel and highly percipient formula, a "standard of living," which had been unthinkable, and incalculable, in the household economy. Cash inscriptions of the material conditions for one's existence would become the basis for determining whether the economy was supplying the general welfare. The "value of money" was accordingly translated into an ethical category, as T. S. Arthur envisioned, a proto-Pareto gauge not only of social utility, but of social justice and public happiness. Workingmen's movements were soon calculating the routine expenses incurred by a family residing in the city, for example, subtracting the resulting sum from the weekly wages paid on average to a journeyman in order to then demonstrate just how little was left over for ice cream or a trip up the river "to get some fresh air." *Hunt's Merchant's Magazine*, embracing the same logic, constructed personal budgets based on extant wage information to reach the opposite conclusion and so underline the "improved condition of labor" in the age of capital. In either case, and regardless of whose numbers proved more reliable, competence was annexed to commercial arithmetic, reconceived in terms of relative purchasing power. Membership in the community became a function of cash on hand, apprehended in an accounting vernacular whose dispassionate, and even autonomous, enumerations replaced rhetoric and allegory as the grammar of political economy, and of politics altogether. Henry Carey was even inspired to assert that the price system made it possible to talk about equality in practical terms for the first time, and that because such numerators were an indisputably objective reflection of reality, equally valid for one and all.[32]

Edwin Freedley was among the first to deploy this neologism in his volume *How to Make Money*, which incorporated the "standard of living" in a discussion on the earnings of clerks. By subsisting on their wages—"his salary being sufficient for most of his wants," as Frederick Marryat had testified— clerical lives were an obvious model of monetization. Freedley's standard of living transposed their subjective needs into general values within an agora of dollars and sense, suggesting that the popular use of a commercial lexicon in speaking about one's person—in referring to time "profitably spent," for instance, or to an "investment" in character, or, more generally, in "accounting for" one's self—was no metaphorical gesture but a literal expression of the market's new role in the production of meaning. Society was becoming embedded in the economy, which meant that individual lives were increasingly defined as a function of a continuously updated grid of costs and benefits that turned everyone into the subject of accounts. All now resided in a tenaciously Benthamite universe of calculable pains and pleasures that constituted a significantly more reliable calculus—especially when compared to such traditional sources of behavior as "fame, glory, and principle"—in making rational choices. The "money motive" was certainly far better suited to modern social conditions than the "honary motive," as *Hunt's* asserted on behalf of such claims, since the former comprised a universal value "giving to all persons . . . the same impulse for activity," whereas questions of honor remained the purchase of "a comparatively small portion of any community." Cash, once again, provided an ideal means for recollectivizing a commonwealth constituted on the principles of "enlightened selfishness."[33]

"Man's economy is, as a rule, submerged in his social relations," Karl Polanyi once wrote in describing a political order that traditionally subordinated material life to the requirements of stable government. "The change from this to a society which was, on the contrary, submerged in the economic system was an entirely novel development." That essential cultural work assumed a variety of guises. The New York Association for the Improvement of the Condition of the Poor, for example, devised budgets that established a causal relationship between the drinking habits of fathers and their family's subsequent descent into poverty. *Godey's Lady's Book*, meanwhile, itemized the costs of a winter outfit—omitting certain accessories such as gloves, matching gaiters, and a second best bonnet that were clearly unaffordable on "a clerk's or book-keeper's salary"—in its campaign against female extravagance. And yet the principle aim of standardized cash accounts was the policing of neither women nor the poor. It was the disciplining of each citizen's relationship with himself. "Live within your income," William Alcott subsequently urged readers of his *Young Man's Guide*. "To this end you must *calculate*." The countinghouse oracle B. F. Foster quoted John Locke to similar effect, noting that "he who keeps a record of his income and expenses seldom lets his affairs run to ruin." With that object in mind, William Hoffman initiated a daily record of personal expenditures in anticipation of leaving home, something of a dress rehearsal for life in the market. A loaf of bread ($0.05), a trip to the town of Hudson ($0.12), and a new neckcloth ($0.50) were representative entries in this daybook of cash outlays that William then triangulated into a taxonomy of "personal," "domestic," and "unnecessary" expenses that helped him to audit his behavior over time and circumstance, and in so doing measure his character on a fastidiously objective scale. The arithmetic of exchange would, as such, equip William with a reliable moral compass.[34]

Amos Lawrence embraced the same monetary positivism in presenting his twelve-year-old son with a "blank book" of ruled pages. The point of the gift, Lawrence explained in a personal inscription, was to encourage the youngster to develop regular habits of journalizing, essential as these would be "in forming your early character" and developing "a strict regard to truth in all you do." Persons who uselessly spend large sums in adulthood, the *Duties of Employers and Employed* affirmed, do so because they uselessly spent small sums earlier in life. As such, the budget, originally invented to exercise popular control over taxation and hold public officials to account, was adapted to the bourgeoisie's privatized reinvention of self-government, becoming a means, that is, for holding oneself to account. Growing interest in the disciplinary effect of such a personal ethics, or metrics, persuaded Lemuel Shattuck, a leading figure in American statistical circles, to publish a *Domestic Book Keeper and Practical Economist* in 1842 that contained a set of forms and instructions for documenting one's own standard of living. "Having ascertained the point of expenditure, beyond which you ought not to go," Shattuck explained of the contribution of this paper accessory to responsible selfhood, "an account book should be regularly kept, and the price of every article purchased, with the day affixed be accurately and neatly entered, that current expenses, with their annual amount, may be subject to your own inspection." The resulting economy, Shattuck determined, was a foundation of personal autonomy, a key component for "how to live independently, and how to be independent while we live."[35]

Economists, meanwhile, intensified their search for that "natural wage" which would accord all individuals the freedom to make such rational choices.

An account of expenses in 1847

1847				Unnecessary $ c	Personal $ c	Domestic $ c
April	Purchased		Clover Seed			2 00
" 13	"	1	Satin Vest		1 75	
" 17	"	1	Shote of B. Boswell		3 00	
" "	Pay		Mrs Boswell more for Shote		0 50	
" 24	"		for Boot Tapping		0 37½	
May 3	Purchased	1	Broad Cloth Cap		1 37½	
" "	"	1	Pr Gloves		0 18¾	
" 12			Attend Circus	0 25		
" 19	"	1	Neck Cloth		0 30	
June "			Exchange Vests		0 75	
" 26	"		Cloth for Pants		0 94	
" "	"	1	Palm Leaf Hat		0 50	
" 28			Pants Cut		0 18¾	
" 30	Pay		for Making		0 25	
July 3	expended		Fourth of July		1 25	
" 13	Purchased	2	Lemons & Peanuts	0 10		
August 2	Pay		A Miller for driving Horses		0 12½	
" 4	"		C Fowler Boot Tapping		0 63	
" 10	Purchased	2	lbs Candles a 14d			0 28
" "			Gate fees to & from Hudson			0 10
" 15	"		" "			0 06
" "	"		Cloth for Coat cutting &c		8 22	
" "	"		Studs for Bosom		0 12½	
" "			Expenses	0 06		
" 16			Making of Coat		2 00	
" 17	"	1 Pr	Fine Boots		2 25	
" 26			Boots Tapped		0 43	
Sept 6	"	1	lb Candles			0 15
" 14	"	1	" " a			0 14
" "	"	1	Pr Coarse Boots		1 62½	
" "	"	1	Silk Neck Cloth		0 37½	
" "	"		Gate fees to & from Hudson			0 10
" "	"	½	Doz Buttons for Shirt		0 02	0 05
" 17			Gate fees to Hudson	0		
" "			Expense to Hudson	0 06		

A page from William Hoffman's personal budget.

The results could then be synopsized in a balance sheet such as that published in the *New York Daily-Times* in the fall of 1853, under the caption "Living on $600 a Year," which tallied up the annual cost of subsistence for a family of four. A close reading of the same budget's strict symmetries of income and expenses, however, reveals just how much its objective syntax of money values obscured a deeper structure of market-generated imbalance. The cost of a family's yearly rent ($100), groceries ($273), clothing and bedding ($132), furniture ($20), fuel ($18), and lighting ($10) was paid out of pocket, for instance. But the actual prices of these goods appearing in the budget table were based on credit, not cash. That is to say, the costs for the suppliers of the family's basic needs were not paid out of pocket but figured as part of a business's accounting capital, which had a wholly different cost structure—and value—than the money one used to buy food and shelter. Nor, for that matter, did these nominal sums reflect all of the family's real expenses. That was because retail prices already subsumed the profits derived by business from the production and marketing of those goods for sale, a margin that was taken out of the pockets of consumers in their capacity as wage earners. The hidden costs of the market economy, in other words, were much higher than the ostensibly neutral arithmetic on which the standard of living was figured. The family budget, for all its reflexive objectivity, thus became another expression of capitalism's fetishization of social relations under the guise of money's—or the numbers'—emphatic neutrality.[36]

This developing symbiosis between persons and profits found its most perfect expression in the institution of life insurance, which "has suddenly assumed great extent and importance," as the *North American Review* reported in a 1863 survey of the emergent industry. Elizur Wright, a pioneer of actuarial science, explained the mechanics for pricing this novel commodity:

> Let a be the sum to be used for one's family aside from one's self; b, the rate of insurance, that is, the sum paid at the given age to insure 100; c, the rate of interest, and x, the sum to be insured for, in order to yield an interest at that rate, equal to the sum expended yearly, less the premium of insurance. Then we have, $a - bx/100 = cx/100$, which reduced gives $x = 100a/b + c$, the algebraic statement of the rule in question.[37]

Wright's calculations were driven by the need to sell insurance to those "whose income depended upon their lives," persons who owned little or no real property, in other words, and so worked exclusively in the money economy. In fact, insurance served as a vital means for transforming that most ephemeral form of industrial property—the wage—into an inheritable asset capable of spanning generations, functioning as a contingency fund in the event of death, just as land had once done. Now, in the event of a father, brother, or son passing away, and in the absence of any grounded collateral to their name, the family would be protected by a financial contract drawn up well in advance. The system's champions consequently boasted of its success in protecting widows and orphans, assuming, that is to say, the mantel of the deposed patriarch. The purchaser of a life insurance policy was even commended for satisfying the dictates of virtue, sacrificing on behalf of others in putting aside part of his earnings today and so exemplifying the "economy, forethought, prudence, industry, perseverance, [and] self-sacrifice" that the soil could no longer provide to a growing public of wage earners, which is also why the clerk emerged as an important customer base for this newly purchasable good.[38]

Social reformers embraced life insurance's solution to the individuation and fragmentation of the age no less enthusiastically than did industry spokesmen. "In this trying world it seems so indispensable . . . to have *something* certain," the *New England Family* adamantly declared. To that purpose, policies were marketed on affordable terms. This was an obvious strategy for expanding sales, of course. And while innumerable actuarial schemes were developed for turning the insurance technology into a viable business model, these were all "only a matter of book-keeping." The terms for making a profit were singular, and straightforward: insurance required a mass market. "There is really no element of uncertainty in the case, *provided the company can obtain business enough.*" Only if enough policies are sold, the *North American Review* meant to say, will there be sufficient cash on hand to pay out on claims, and then some. The contingency of insuring lives would thus become a reliable investment rather than an irresponsible gamble only when spread over society. In that respect, insurance took the risk out of risk by turning the market itself into the source of stability. The result was a new form of community, populated by policy owners mutually guaranteeing one another's personal security while lacking any personal ties, or even passing acquaintance. "While all other sorts of communism interfere too much with individual liberty to be widely or long tolerated, here is a form of it, which allows unrestrained individualism," Elizur Wright effused. "In life insurance all pay in, and all draw out," the president of the Mutual Life Insurance Company added, offering his own version of this new social contract, or balance sheet.[39]

Like the monetized standard of living, then, insurance simultaneously socialized and individualized. It recast the civic order into a collective but anonymous burden, fixed by a statistics of costs rather than such old-fashioned notions as natural justice and just price. A properly insured society, what's more, was no longer dependent on the good will of family, friends, or neighbors. That was because everyone was in a position to help themselves, turning the annuities into a means of "self-reliance." Or, as Tocqueville remarked in his famous chapter on the emergence of individualism as a social system: "Aristocracy links everybody, from peasant to king, in one long chain. Democracy breaks the chain and frees each link." A market niche had opened up and a new industry rushed in to ensure that democracy.[40]

There were some, of course, who denounced the hubris of such an invention which acted in defiance of "the ways of . . . providence." " 'Tis God alone who holds the key of Life or death," opponents declared in protesting the ontological conceits of the insurance paradigm. They pointed, predictably enough, to the farmer as representative of the proper order of things, investing as he did in "that best of all banks, a bank of earth." But subscribers to postagrarian values of personal freedom and commercial ambition could point to an alternative source of security, one based on the same commodity system that had turned everything upside down in the first place.[41]

In fact, insurance from the uncertainties of life in a market society emerged as a market itself. "A life policy that has been running some time, may become of very great marketable value," *Hunt's* observed of the growing number of policies being assigned to third parties. These were arguably one's best, and often one's only, form of collateral. An entrepreneur without any other assets could thus approach investors who would once have balked at financing his venture, no matter how worthy it might be. A life insurance policy mollified their qualms, allowing talented but undercapitalized men to raise the financing necessary to start out in business. It was credible to claim, then, that "life is not only property, but always the best property a man has." The individual became an asset worthy of the highest credit rating in a cash fraternity born of the axioms of purchasability and personhood. He became human capital.[42]

Homo economicus

Balancing the books, B. F. Foster wrote in his introduction to *Theory and Practice of Book-Keeping*, teaches the young "those things which they will need to practice when they come to be men." Such glib equations of manhood and mammon had become a common currency, on display in Benjamin Foster's bookshelf, for instance, where treatises devoted to double entry lay alongside etiquette manuals, both having become required reading for any "artificer of his own fortune." In that same spirit, the *American Annals of Education* explained that one's time was most "profitably employed" in transcribing archetypes of business letters rather than "writing scraps of poetry."[43]

Americans had proven able translators of Homer, B. F. Foster caustically observed, as well as competent surveyors of the world's oceans. But they remained woefully inept when having to figure interest on accounts or in composing a bill of credit. Classical learning was well developed in the republic, in other words, but no comparable program existed for young men wishing to pursue a career in business. They were left to "grope [their] way in comparative ignorance," Foster protested in the *Prospectus* for his Commercial Academy, whose battery of course offerings in penmanship, double entry, and mercantile correspondence was designed to rectify that regretful situation. Foster's former partner, Thomas Jones, whom Foster accused of pirating his innovative copying exercises, soon opened his own business school a few blocks up Broadway in 1839, announcing that he "will receive on the 1st September next, a class of young gentlemen to whom, during a daily session of four hours, he will devote his exclusive attention." Jones also published a textbook to meet the needs of those seeking "to qualify thoroughly for the duties of the desk."[44]

Within a decade the neighborhood above Houston Street had filled up with such pedagogical initiatives for brokering between the supply of young men looking for clerical work and the demands of the industrial economy for paper documents. One could attend day or evening classes at the Initiatory Counting Rooms, for example, or enroll in C. C. Marsh's Commercial Institute, which pledged in a style typical of the genre to "watch over your work as you advance step by step, from book to book, entry to entry, and transaction to transaction." Aspiring mercantilists could take advantage of Mr. Dolbear's special half-price offer of $10 for a set of lessons in double entry that might not include writing instruction but did promise preparation for positions as bookkeepers and assistant bookkeepers in any commercial house in the city. Winterton's Writing Academy, puffed by the *Tribune* for the "wonderful appropriateness" of its course of study, or Goldsmith's Academy, which reduced the price of a ten-lesson course in penmanship from $5 to $3 after reopening in more spacious apartments at the corner of Broadway and Reade in 1845, presented additional options for clerical training. So did Renville's plan of instruction that "thoroughly fitted for the counting-room," or the Writing and Book-Keeping Academy managed by Brown & Pond, the former a "master of pedagogy" who had recently garnered the highest prize in business writing at the Crystal Palace and organized regular chirographic demonstrations for the public.[45]

The dramatic growth of opportunities for business training reached its acme with the establishment of Bryant and Stratton's national chain of commercial colleges, the first of which was founded in Cleveland in 1853. Additional campuses soon opened in Philadelphia, Buffalo, Detroit, Chicago, St. Louis, and Providence. At the Albany branch, Samuel Munson, hoping to someday "tak[e] the dry goods department of a country town," began a full course of study after deciding, against his father's advice, that he "could not do better than join this school." In Manhattan, Charles Rogers enrolled in a single pro-rated penmanship class with the aim of improving his writing skills after being hired as a government copyist in 1864. Lessons were held each day from eight in the morning until five o'clock. Evening instruction also became available to those holding regular employment. The curriculum was organized around a standard program of "commercial science" that included such basic skills as calculating simple, annual, and compound interest; making discounts for stock purchases and merchandise sales; figuring insurance premiums and rate per-centages; determining profit and loss ratios (by which the most advantageous selling price, adjusted to either specific or ad valorem duties, and including international remittances in foreign currencies, was to be established); and ar-ranging payment schedules for purchases that were executed on separate dates, some in cash and others by credit, while plotting the maturation of each note and the effect of any early payments on the balance sheet.

Bryant and Stratton featured classroom innovations as well, including "black-board elucidations" and personal supervision by business profession-als that supplemented the more pedestrian reliance on textbooks. Updated sales forms and balance sheets, together with ledgers "taken directly from Business Houses," were incorporated into lesson plans designed to function as full-scale simulations of office work, made all the more effective by fitting up the rooms in a "true counting-house style" of counters, desks, and draw-ers. Groups of ten to twelve students would, for instance, be assigned with founding an ersatz banking firm, which required them to open the books, subscribe the stock, issue certificates, draw up banknotes and checks, and schedule payments. A discount policy also had to be determined, for only then could the enterprise actually begin to make money. These approximations of the "realities of that bustling life towards which they have so long and ardently looked" were an effective marketing strategy for increasing enrollments. They also offered the best method for learning the trade of trade, according to James Bennett, America's well-known "professor of figures."[46]

Anyone who paid his tuition could commence studies at any one of the chain's colleges and complete those studies at any of the other campuses, and at any time, which is why enrollment fees were never refunded. That roll-ing admissions policy accommodated the inveterate situation of young men circulating in the labor market. It also helped to integrate that market. The standard business curriculum, which included P. L. Spencer's program for creating a "uniform national system" of writing that Spencer developed as director of the penmanship department at Bryant and Stratton's Cleveland school, would serve to transform local trading practices into generic commercial conventions that linked "the two great emporiums of East and West," establishing "a continuous chain" of exchange reaching across the country. S. S. Packard, hired to produce instructional materials for all the schools, consequently observed that the common course of instruction offered the most practical avenue for finding employment in a nationwide market being reestablished on "enlightened and thoroughly scientific views . . . universally correct, economical, and uniform," as was exclaimed at the 1858 inauguration ceremonies for Bryant and Stratton's new college in Chicago. Business was reinvented as a discipline that "*can be learned*," an object of expertise, that is, which rested on "laws of trade" promising to systematize all the profit making, a critically important contribution to an age when "all things are in a state of metamorphosis and revolution and . . . the new is crowding aside the old," as the *American Merchant*, the chain's house organ, pronounced. Those revolutionary conditions are what distinguished the new business pedagogy from the previous century's corpus of manuals, methods, courses, and instructors that had also sought to introduce a measure of system and technical competence to the commercial economy but which were equally committed to preserving a traditional trading culture based on personality and patronage which never conceived of trade as a force of revolution. Certainly, the acquisition of business skills had not yet become the preferred means for legions of young men to plot their own personal rise to power and position.[47]

Business schools played another central role in the industrializing economy, that of subcontractors supplying metropolitan houses with a steady source of trained manpower. Comer's Commercial College in Boston, where James Blake "struggled thro Dr's and Cr's" every morning in a bookkeeping class, and which boasted of having graduated twelve thousand students in the twenty-five years since opening its doors in 1840—their diplomas serving as "a letter of introduction to the best mercantile houses from Maine to California"—thus invited merchant firms to save on "time and trouble" by applying directly to the college, which would then organize "at short notice and entirely free of expense" a corps of competent candidates for entry, sales, cashier, copyist, bookkeeping, and telegraph positions. Boyd & Stubb's Commercial Institute, doing business down the street from Comer's, offered the same placement services. Meanwhile, Finn's bookkeeping school on Wall Street publicized its close working relationship with New York City wholesalers, fifty of whom had purportedly made inquiries in anticipation of the upcoming spring trade. When the (rather incredible) aggregate value of salaries

CLEVELAND COLLEGE,

Corner Superior and Seneca Streets.

DIRECTORS.

Hon. REUBEN HITCHCOCK, W. J. GORDON, Esq., Pres. LORIN ANDREWS,
JOSHUA R. GIDDINGS, W. F. OTIS, Esq., " CHAS. G. FINNEY,
HIRAM GRISWOLD, CYRUS PRENTISS, Esq., Prof. SAM'L ST. JOHN,
NORTON S. TOWNSEND, C. M. REED, Esq., HENRY WICK, Esq.,
H. D. CLARK, Esq., E. F. GAYLORD, Esq., GEO. WILLEY, Esq.

E. G. FOLSOM, A. M., Associate Proprietor, and Prin. of Cleve'd College.

FACULTY.

INSTRUCTORS IN THE SCIENCE OF ACCOUNTS, AND LECTURERS ON BUSINESS CUSTOMS.

H. B. BRYANT, E. G. FOLSOM, H. D. STRATTON.
S. S. CALKINS,

INSTRUCTORS IN BUSINESS AND ORNAMENTAL PENMANSHIP, AND LECTURERS ON COMMERCIAL CORRESPONDENCE.

P. R. SPENCER, A. J. PHELPS, E. G. FOLSOM.

LECTURERS ON COMMERCIAL LAW.
Professors of the Ohio State and Union Law College, viz:

Hon. C. HAYDEN, L.L. D. M. A. KING.

SPECIAL LECTURERS.

Hon. HORACE MANN, ELIHU BURRITT, Hon. GEORGE W. CLINTON.

LECTURERS ON POLITICAL ECONOMY.

Rev. FRED'K T. BROWN, Dr. JAS. B. BOLLES, Prof. J. A. THOME.

LECTURERS ON COMMERCIAL ETHICS.

Rev. Dr. AIKEN, Rev. JAMES EELLS, Rev. SEYMOUR W. ADAMS.

LECTURERS ON BANKING, FINANCE, ETC.

T. P. HANDY, H. B. HURLBUT,

LECTURERS ON THE GENERAL PRINCIPLES AND DETAILS OF RAILROADING.

H. C. MARSHALL, JOHN B. WARING, H. C. LUCE.

LECTURERS ON COMMERCIAL COMPUTATION.

J. B. MERRIAM, R. F. HUMISTON, WM. S. PALMER.
Prin. Clev'd Institute.

EXAMINING COMMITTEES.

On Banking.	On Rail Roading.	On Commission.
D. P. EELLS,	GEO. B. ELY,	H. B. TUTTLE,
E. L. JONES,	H. C. MARSHALL,	JAMES HALE,
FAYETTE BROWN,	JNO. J. MANY,	H. L. CHAPIN.

From Bryant & Stratton's *Annual Catalogue*, 1859.

being earned by the previous year's graduating class—"$537,250!"—was published in a paid advertisement in the *Herald*, the impetus to enroll in Finn's course of study must have been great indeed.[48]

This widespread purchase of office skills marked a sharp counterpoint to artisanal practices, whose production techniques were still often passed from father to son, and just as often protected as a trade secret, not only in deference to tradition but also in order to defend oneself from the market's drive to generalize knowledge so as to better control and then sell it. The modern clerk was wholly implicated in this latter scheme, of course. He not only traded his labor power on the open market, in other words, but acquired his profession in the same manner, available to anyone with $10 to spend on an accelerated plan of instruction at Marsh's Commercial Institute. If early modern guilds had been the first to define professional skills as a subject of proprietary rights in order to restrict access to the trades, such intellectual property presently emerged as the object of unregulated truck and barter. This mass commodification of business expertise was not to be confused, however, with a process of "deskilling." If anything, the expanding opportunities for commercial instruction made entry into the new economy a practical possibility for someone like John D. Rockefeller, who acquired his bookkeeping skills at Folsom's Business College in Cleveland in the mid-1850s. The aspiring clerk's cash purchase of a "good hand," together with the ability to figure differential interest on net assets and liabilities in a matter of minutes, did not turn that knowledge into a less exclusive source of class identity, or symbolic capital. Indeed, formal training in double entry was the surest sign of Arthur Tappen's seriousness upon first venturing onto the job market, testimony to an entrepreneurial alacrity and personal determination to realize the highest yield on one's own ambition.[49]

That maximization of personal resources suggests that few would therefore be satisfied in serving as a mere "copying machine." Indeed, the "art of selling" was recognized as a more direct avenue of advancement than a neat ledger, the surest means, that is, "to build a Young Man up," as William Hoffman soon discerned after commencing his business career at Boyd & Co. The owner of a carpet business in Newburyport, where Benjamin Foster found employment after leaving Bangor, similarly advised Benjamin to hone his counter skills if he truly hoped to get ahead, despite the young man's obvious talent with the books. William, meanwhile, reported that the petty transactions he managed to complete in Albany when the store's senior clerks were otherwise engaged brought him "more satisfaction and render the state of my mind more composed and settled." William would, in fact, depart before the year was out, frustrated with his ongoing desk assignments at Boyd & Co.

After pondering a move to California, he leveraged his upstate clerical experience into a sales position with the Manhattan firm of Gilbert, Prentiss, and Tuttle, "a desirable one for any clerk anxious to come up, as every opportunity is offered." The main opportunity William had in mind was traveling for the firm. Metropolitan houses frequently hired clerks from the provinces in hopes that their out-of-town contacts would bring in new clients. William soon began to combine upstate visits to his family with the search for hinterland customers. Arriving in Palmyra "with all the grace of a New York Clerk," he set out to convince local store owners to open accounts with Gilbert, Prentiss, and Tuttle on their next buying trip to the city: "I had seen nearly every merchant in town endeavoring to gain their esteem and also to give with my card a lasting impression of my ability to sell them cheap." There was, of course, no guarantee of success. William was not the only city agent promising cut rates and easy credit. Two months later, with the beginning of the fall season, he waited in vain to reap the fruits of his summertime efforts. "My customer did not come and see me today as he promised, buys his goods elsewhere."[50]

How many enter this race "in which the chances of their ultimate defeat are as ten to one," it was remarked of such dashed hopes. Those long odds were a common trope which Henry David Thoreau characteristically worsened by announcing that "ninety-seven in a hundred, are sure to fail." Such pessimism was a consciously nostalgic gesture, referencing an age when commercial striving was confined to a narrow class of traders and not yet embraced by an entire generation of youth driven by the "foolish ambition to see their names over a store door." And yet what choice did they have? The "undue eagerness" and "loud accost" attributed to young men "anxious to come up" was an entirely reasonable response to a social system organized around the main chance. "There is no such thing as a stationary point in human endeavor," Edward Tailer, for one, concluded in assessing his own future at Little Alden & Co. "He who is not worse today than he was yesterday is better. And he who is not better is worse." Was it not the case, the Mercantile Library's *Annual Report* also observed, that very few of the successful men of the day had "not risen to affluence from the smallest beginnings?" Their success was not a matter of fate either, but testimony to their "unflagging exertion," in William Hoffman's terms, a zero-sum confrontation between indomitable energy and idle loaferism. Having become the sole "possessor and *proprietor*" of their lives, this postpatriarchal generation could not "stand with your two hands in your pockets" waiting for opportunity to present itself. Personal advance, rather, was "the handmaid of Endeavor," which meant that everyone was responsible for developing his own assets and turning his life into an enterprise, or a business plan. "I look about me," a young Philadelphia clerk consequently remarked, "and see other young men gaining in the world and I am almost inclined at times to despond." With nothing blocking their path, in other words, there was no excuse not to rise. Who, then, could blame Benjamin Foster for rifling through his employer's "private drawer" in search of letters written on his behalf, or for ingratiating himself with the same boss by devising a plan to ensnare a fellow clerk suspected of pilfering change to buy candy?[51]

That same spirit fed William Hoffman's jealous complaints about the "jealous disposition" of his fellow clerks who kept all the best sales opportunities for themselves. He therefore applauded a reorganization of in-house responsibilities at Boyd & Co. that promised to undercut the established pecking order by assigning each clerk his own counter. This would effectively prevent "shirking from the imperative duty incumbent upon each," William noted in his diary. It also offered him a prime opportunity for demonstrating his own diligence on the job. That redivision of office labor was part of a general program of standardized costing and budgeting in response to the age's depersonalized shopping practices and growing business volume. A Philadelphia wholesale company was accordingly commended in the pages of *Hunt's Merchant's Magazine* for color-coding its counters, which reduced the clutter and confusion of in-store sales operations. At the same time, the firm's cashier introduced an individuated system of sales records that identified each transaction with its attendant clerk. This then made it possible to calculate every employee's respective value to the firm "as a per-centage on each day, week, and year . . . and the per-centage that it has cost to effect these sales." The business would now know "at all times . . . the relative value of the services of each, in proportion to his salary." Such rational management methods did not always effect rational outcomes, however. C. W. Moore reported that a similar plan for booking sales directly to each clerk's account in his New York City dry-goods house ended in disaster. Employees and customers alike became so "caught up with anxiety" that business actually began to fall off. Meanwhile, back at Boyd & Co., the reapportionment of counter responsibilities aroused the ire of another junior clerk who soon accused William of stealing away a customer. Incensed by this incursion into his own recently demarcated sales territory, John Boyd—the boss's son—picked up a board with which to strike William, who was able to dodge the blow but then collided with the counter, sustaining a painful injury. Could there be a more tangible example of the perils of counter jumping?[52]

How quickly the promise of becoming all you can be turns into a taunt, Thomas Augst has observed of the psychodynamics of ambition in an age of universal manhood freedom. "I must put myself ahead more," Charles French concluded upon surveying his own prospects for promotion. "I do not like Eaton at all," he further noted of his immediate superior in the office hierarchy at the Boston hardware firm where he had recently started. "We shall see if he is going to rule me, or someone else." In fact, Charles soon identified a more serious threat to his plans, another newcomer with whom he often shared assignments. "Tobin shall not go ahead of me in the store," Charles irritably resolved after discovering that the former was getting up a price book, which meant that he would either soon be going out on his own or, worse yet, soon be sent out traveling on behalf of the firm. Tobin proved a worthy rival, though, as Charles discovered one afternoon when Tobin asked for his assistance in taking a stock count. Charles had no inclination to help, of course, claiming to be otherwise engaged with his own tasks. Tobin went forthwith to Mr. Danforth to complain about the lack of cooperation, which prompted the firm's partner to approach Charles and inquire as to what was occupying his efforts. Nothing in particular, Charles responded, ever eager to take on whatever assignment the boss might have for him. Then go help Tobin, Danforth tersely directed.[53]

Edward Tailer was no less anxious about his situation at Little Alden & Co. Opening the safe every morning and removing the books, locking them back up again at night, filing bills, refilling the inkstands, and delivering mail to the post office constituted a routine of petty tasks that became the source of constant complaint on his part. Edward was equally unhappy upon being sent around to city firms to collect on outstanding debts at the end of the season, or in delivering parcels to customers, which he considered the work of a porter. He was most chagrined of all, however, when told to venture out to city hotels with pattern cards, an ignominious assignment for drumming up business among out-of-town dealers. "There is not a day which passes," Edward noted to himself, "during which I do not imagine that I might better my situation as a clerk and receive an ample compensation for services rendered." He had, in fact, already broached the subject of his salary by handing a letter to the managing partner "in which my views were fully, and most copiously detailed." In response, Mr. Alden called Edward into the counting room for a private conversation in which he offered the clerk $50 for the year just ended and $100 for the next one. Edward was unassuaged. His efforts were worth at least $150, he announced, for it was time he began to support himself and relieve his father of those responsibilities. Alden countered by observing that the city was full of young men willing to enter a store without demanding any salary at all, happy at the opportunity to learn the business before reaching maturity. That might be true, but it stunk of Old World apprenticeship. The two argued to a standstill, with Alden promising to reach a decision forthwith, leaving Edward to further grumble about the "mean . . . character" that informed his employer's refusal to make "a faithful and hard working clerk . . . feel happy and independent and inwardly bless the bountiful hand which would thus place him above want."[54]

He waited two and a half months before receiving an answer from Alden, who, in fact, acceded to Edward's request for a $150 salary, and even dangled the possibility of a $50 bonus at year's end, "if I continued to please him." Edward was especially delighted when told to post his first business letter. But he "commenced badly and unpropitiously" with his new responsibilities after mistakenly shipping two cases of goods to New Orleans instead of Charleston. "How I could have made this mischievous blunder is beyond my comprehension and has injured me greatly in the estimation of Mr. Alden." The merchandise was returned after two months and eventually disposed of well below the original asking price. Edward therefore found himself increasingly engaged in "writing operations," copying accounts of stock, posting up the sales since the eighth of the month, and compiling an inventory of newly arrived goods in the invoice book. With the firm having grossed $60,000 in the spring season alone, and Edward reassigned out of sales, he was again voicing discontent with what he considered an inadequate appreciation of his talents.[55]

Such frustrations were representative of his generation's "hard fight in the battle of life," which was shouldered, as adherents of the reformist Young America movement protested, with little or no encouragement from their elders. "If he asked to be taken into the firm, he was met with a volume of unprofitable good advice. But was he taken into the firm? Oh, no! Anything but that." Another partner at Little Alden accordingly upbraided Edward for his overeager sales style that "savored too much of the Chatham St manner of receiving a customer . . . every man in the establishment running out to salute and shake a buyer by the hand." Clerks, instead, were told to be prudent and cautious, "to keep cool" and not dare "walk more rapidly than the rule." Even after announcing his departure for a sales position with another firm two years later, Edward Tailer continued to suffer reproof, being told that "my greatest failing was too strong an anxiety to force myself ahead." William Hoffman became the subject of similar injunctions on the part of a senior partner who applauded his disciplined demeanor, by which "I showed every indication of becoming a Business Man," but then reminded William that his continued quiescence to the office hierarchy was a prerequisite for earning the firm's eventual assistance in installing himself in trade some day.[56]

Clerks were thus urged to pursue strategies of cooperation rather than confrontation. John Todd, writing in his best-selling *Student's Manual*, warned that the anxious drive to get ahead invariably devolves into "high hopes, restless

desires, and bitter disappointments." One needed to rein in such passions. With
that same goal in mind, Edward Tailer's mother handed him a "Good Sugges-
tion" clipped out from one of the daily papers:

> A successful merchant who commenced with a clerkship, at a low salary, re-
> marked in speaking of a young man who intended to pursue the mercantile
> life, as follows: . . . he should enter as a clerk in some successful house, without
> regard in the start to the amount of salary, . . . make himself as far as possible
> indispensable to the concern, stick to one place, and in time it cannot hardly
> be otherwise than that he will become a principal.[57]

Not everyone subscribed to such methods of strategic deference. Some
even considered the endorsement of under-remunerated devotion in exchange for vague promises of future promotion to be a naked device for creating a docile class of hirelings. Employers might commend the clerk who undertook his assignments—"that cargo of cotton must be got out and weighed,
and we must have a regular account of it"—with so much energy and precision that "he very soon came to be one that could not be spared," but this supererogatory approach could just as easily turn into a trap. That was the conclusion reached by Charles Rogers, who spent much of his workday at A. T.
Stewart's Marble Palace running down errant packages at the delivery desk
or inquiring after parcels that failed to arrive on time to a customer's home.
Charles aspired to move downtown, to Stewart's wholesale store, and he expended considerable time and effort in entreating his superiors to authorize
the transfer. When that plan failed, Charles sought a promotion from fine white
goods to the retail silk department, not least because his boarding costs had
recently risen to $5 a week. Instead, he was moved to embroideries, which
entailed a longer workday but did pay better, his salary being advanced to
$500. The raise, however, was conditioned on a promise to stay a full year at
the new position, which Charles refused to do. He was subsequently put back
in his former job at his former wage, the failed negotiations leaving him in
a bitter mood. "If I had less scruples about breaking my engagement with a
man who I know would break his with me at any time I might have been getting $500," he remarked, recognizing that all the exertions on his own behalf
had left him high and dry in the race to get ahead.[58]

The regularity of such scenes prompted Daniel Haskell to remark on the
"strange want of confidence exhibited in the intercourse between merchants
and their clerks." Too often, Haskell concluded, that relationship "resembles
what may be termed *cross*-examination," a structural animus belying facile
ideologizations about the mutualities of the market and contractual relations.
Charles French certainly had few illusions. He even decided to "strike" for

The sales counters of a dry-goods emporium.

higher wages after discovering that Tobin was being paid more than he, despite "loafing around the store most of the day." Confident of his value to the firm, Charles only worried that a lack of self-assertion on his part would undermine his designs. In fact, it was Charles's very indignation that frustrated his hopes. Nursing his hurt feelings, he added insult to injury by falling into a series of petty confrontations with the office's cashier, refusing at one point to carry out the latter's explicit instructions. Only after Danforth personally intervened did Charles agree to undertake the requested errand. Upon returning to the office he was summoned into a private room and reprimanded for his obstinacy, which left young Charles on the verge of tears, not least because he realized that another half a year would pass before he could raise the subject of his salary again.[59]

In fact, Charles's contrition came much sooner than that. "I shall turn over a new leaf tomorrow at the store," he wrote the following day in his diary, "and from morning until evening Danforth shall not see me henceforth idle, and if I am told to do an errand by anyone above me, will do it, even though I do not wish to, and without showing any temper whatever. Neither do I intend in the future to speak disrespectfully to or of anyone in the store. Though at times I may forget myself, yet in the long run I will and must succeed." It was a soliloquy worthy of a T. S. Arthur story celebrating the advantages of self-discipline over self-aggrandizement as the key to personal success in the market and, as such, an important moment in the socialization of a maximizing agent. This was also a sober assessment of the relations of power in the office. It was, after all, Danforth who determined which counter or desk was assigned to whom, and how each clerk would consequently be remunerated. Only Danforth decided who was sent out traveling, who was promoted, and who might even be invited into the firm as a partner. And only Danforth was in a position to extend credit to those wishing to start out in business on their own, or provide a personal reference to clerks looking for new employment, often in a distant city.[60]

Six more months passed and Charles's distress reached new heights. "Now the time approaches that I expect to be spoken to about my salary," he nervously wrote on December 31, and "my doubts begin to arise." He had not seen the partners convene their regular end-of-year conference at which they usually decided on bonuses and wages. Yet another week went by, but still no announcement was in the offing. Charles sought to convince himself that the silence was indicative of imminent raises. Personally, he hoped to increase his salary from $300 to $400, and maybe even $500. At that rate, he calculated, he might be earning $800 by the time he turned twenty-one. "If they suppose that because I have never found fault with my salary and am or rather have been willing to work hard on a small salary . . . they will find that they have (to use a vulgar expression) 'got the wrong pig by the ear.' " Charles knew very well—having access to the books—that the firm grossed $400,000 the previous year. He thought it only fair that he be allowed to partake in such success. The expanding economy was, after all, a positive-sum game, no longer resting on virtuous sacrifice or collective want. And, indeed, with still no announcement in the offing, he began to toy once again with the possibility of "striking," a consummately individual act, hoping only that no one else beat him to it.[61]

Instead, Charles plucked up his courage and approached Danforth directly. He opened the conversation by citing local labor conditions, telling him of other young men "who had been in business no longer than I" but were nevertheless paid more money. Danforth responded by informing Charles that the firm paid him more than they had ever given anyone else at a comparable age, an indication, moreover, of how satisfied they were with his job performance. True, clerks at other firms might be earning $500, and perhaps even more, Danforth conceded. The rumor regarding Tobin's salary was also accurate, he confirmed. But none of those other clerks had much chance for significant advancement. Danforth took French into his confidence by telling him that Tobin, too, though a good worker, lacked the qualities that would move him up the ladder of success. Charles's situation was clearly different. If he pressed for more money, however, he would threaten his future prospects with the firm. A raise in salary needed to be based on a clerk's own earnings: whoever brought in more business was "worth more" to the firm, as based on book worth, of course. If Charles could generate $5,000 in sales over the course of the year, for instance, he would be compensated accordingly. To that end, Danforth told Charles that he would be allowed to go around the hotels and pick up custom, for which he would receive a commission. Meanwhile, he insisted, the store's expenses were enormous and profits consequently smaller than they might seem.[62]

Charles was unappeased. "I fear the firm are growing mean." A friend advised him to get as much as he presently could since there was no guarantee that the partners would do "the right thing" when he came of age. "They talk very well but I fear it may be meant for 'salve.'" Only after two more months of anxious waiting did Danforth announce that Charles would receive $400, which might be increased to $500 the following year, depending on his performance. Danforth then suggested that Charles use his annual two-week vacation to travel to Connecticut and collect relevant information from the region's hardware manufacturers. He also urged Charles to develop acquaintances with city traders, since "the amount of custom" he carried was the best way to make oneself "useful" to his employer. In fact, Charles was delighted with his success in winning such a significant raise, "more than I had reason to hope for." But he also understood that the new salary and any future increases depended on how much money he directly brought in to the firm. "I shall also try to sell goods to every customer who enters the store and even go around town to sell odds and ends to the city traders," he resolved.[63]

And so, "cross-examination" proved a most effective vernacular for the growing numbers of men forcing themselves ahead, despite the odds. "Make your views and wishes known," *Hunt's* advised, for there was no advantage in concealing. Employers might still perform an opportunistic paternalism from time to time, but they, too, preferred to establish working relationships on a formal, contractual basis, which then allowed them to organize office production around a fluid roster of clerical hires. The latter, for their part, showed themselves eminently loyal to the commodity form they were employed to administer, promoting money values into the common denominator of personal intercourse and mutual obligation. Did the resulting wage negotiations also achieve the most efficient allocation of the company's resources? Who knows. They did, however, buttress a new proprietary ethic suited to such revolutionary times. For only someone who "owned up" to his personal desires—underscoring the transparency of his intentions—would earn a reputation for integrity. Older styles of deference and deferment would mostly provoke suspicions of dissimilitude.[64]

The "admiration of wealth unpossessed" which political philosophers had once identified as the source "of envy, or of servility," and, as such, a profound threat to civic order, now emerged as the fountainhead of civility. Reciprocity became a pecuniary principle, in other words, and self-interest was redefined as a force that linked as much as divided men. "If you wish anyone to serve you with diligence you must make it for his interest to do so," contemporaries acknowledged in an unmistakable echo of Adam Smith's famous contention from the opening of the *Wealth of Nations* that one should talk to others not about necessities but about advantages. And while *Hunt's* counseled merchant's clerks to do all in their power to make their employer "feel that he may intrust with you uncounted gold," trust was increasingly besides the point. Cooperation would be founded, rather, on the temporary alignment of distinct and even competing designs. To pretend otherwise—to deny the centrality of personal interest in securing mutual agreement—would call the very ethos of the market into question.[65]

Money had become "the prose of life," Emerson announced in his essay on "nominalist and realist" in 1844, which is why the truest test of personal character was how one handled his finances, and why all were advised, once again, to avoid doing business with either friends or foes. Market society consequently filled up with persons indifferent to each other's fate, communicating in "busy, bustling, disputatious" tones, as Rip Van Winkle observed of the vertiginous quality of relations he found upon returning home to his Hudson Valley village after an extended absence. Such mutual dissociation was an ideal condition for negotiating business transactions, the terms of which would be formalized in written agreements between persons who otherwise owed nothing to one another. This fraternity of strangers did nevertheless require everyone to act with a common purpose, namely, a shared dedication to their own best interest, "searching always, falling, picking himself up again, often disappointed, never discouraged."[66] That is why Bartleby, who consistently failed to negotiate on his own behalf, proved so incomprehensible to his employer, and to us. Refusing to embrace the emerging ethic of self-maximization, he proved utterly antisocial.

Self-Making Men

The ascension of *Homo economicus* to the vanguard of the civilizing process provoked as much apprehension as it did enthusiasm in America. Theodore Parker, Unitarian minister, social theorist, and outspoken abolitionist, decried an ethos, for instance, that assigned all men a natural hankering after gain, to be attained, what's more, by a minimum of effort.[1] In an essay expounding his "Thoughts on Labor," Parker compared this emphatically acquisitive self to the organic foundations of an older work ethic in which "God [gave] each man a mouth to be filled, and a pair of hands to work with." If the hands refused to work under such circumstances, then one went hungry. Advancing divisions of labor had since undermined this anatomical equilibrium, however, severing hands from mouth and allowing certain elements of society to avoid the "general and natural lot of man." The result was a fragmented, artificial order that no longer had the ability to govern itself, having been stripped of its original, or natural, foundations. The most glaring example of this wanton fracturing of the body politic was not to be found on the slave plantation, as one might have expected Parker to argue, but in the strivings of "young men . . . ashamed of their fathers' occupation." They were to be observed rushing to the city in search of a fortune, or at least a partnership, without any intention of producing something of value themselves. In the absence of natural checks on their desires—without the hands able to police the mouth now that they were located on separate bodies—the appetite would invariably "run to excess."[2]

"Be men," a writer for the *Phrenological Journal* implored in response, "and with true courage and manliness dash into the wilderness with your axe and make an opening for the sunlight and for an independent home." Another version of true courage, however, divorced from such traditional

asylums though no less dedicated to containing the perverse effects of capitalist disorder, began to take shape in these years. Instead of the farmer's exertions being brought to bear on his independent freehold, this other form of
manliness was grounded in the individual's exertions being brought to bear on
himself. That ethic was famously canonized in the cherry-tree anecdote Par-
son Weems added to the sixth edition of what he also renamed the "Private
Life" of Washington. It was most systematically elaborated a generation later
in William Ellery Channing's *Self-Culture*, a lecture first delivered before
the Mechanics Society of Boston in 1838 and then published the following
year, after which it was widely excerpted in the country's newspapers and
magazines. "We have the power not only of tracing our powers," Channing
explained to readers of his antebellum primer on the proper exercise of personal
sovereignty, "but of guiding and impelling them, not only of watching our
passions, but of controlling them." In so doing, Channing sought to reinvent
self-government for a postpatriarchal age of men no longer looking back, or
up, but straight ahead at a horizon strictly denoted by their own imaginations.[3]

Such "individualism," as the phenomenon soon came to be called, begat a
distinctly modern cultural hero, a "self-made man," who literally turned himself into the object of his own productive efforts. "THE BOY IS . . . FATHER OF THE
MAN," William Thayer wrote in reference to that solipsistic genealogy in *The
Printer Boy; or, How Ben Franklin Made His Mark*. Thayer was paraphrasing
verse initially composed by William Wordsworth in 1802 which attested to the
growing importance of childhood in the development of personality. By midcentury, that same boy had acquired exclusive dominion over his fate, insisting
on a natural right to form "my own standards of morals," select "my own models of character," and lay down "my own plans of action." Such self-making became another of the great production projects of the age of capital, in fact, this
one resting on an infrastructure of self-study, self-satisfaction, self-observation,
self-esteem, self-respect, self-confidence, and self-acquaintance, as one could
read with dulling frequency in such new vehicles of embourgeoisement as the
Young American's Magazine of Self-Improvement, which, significantly enough,
succeeded its earlier incarnation *Boston Mechanic*.[4]

Casualties of Caprice

Flitting to and fro behind the counter, displaying wares he had no real interest in, to those he had no actual acquaintance with, and all the while affecting pleasure at every witticism, "however dismal," the clerk not only failed to
produce anything of value but he sold his manhood for a wage in doing so.
"There is not a more subservient set of men in this country than are the gen-

teel, dry goods clerks," the *American Whig Review* consequently bemoaned. They might exercise the personal prerogative required of someone needing to negotiate his own living and working conditions, but this was not the stuff of independence in any recognizable American form. Indeed, what was the point in sundering the extrapersonal bonds of patrilineage farming if one's deference could then be so casually purchased on the open market? The attendant spectacle of lusty arms measuring out fine millinery conjured the "casualties and caprice of customers" that Jefferson had once identified as the gravest threat to republican government, currently updated into a fast breed of billiard-playing, catfish-suppering rakes who curled each other's hair on Saturday night with the aim of seducing the pretty daughters of Presbyterian stalwarts on Sunday. "With 'neck or nothing' for my watchward," Benjamin Foster pronounced upon commencing his own clerical career, "I have plunged my head in an erect collar and have sported it this week till now I fancy I wear it 'as to the manner born.' " Such dandified artifice was a most authentic expression of the precipitous fall of this somewhat singular set of young men from the intrepid habits of their plainly clad fathers, that which so exercised Theodore Parker's "thoughts on labor." Stay where you are, Joel Ross therefore advised readers in *What I Saw in New-York*. "Pick greens, weed onions, put faggots under the pot . . . lest when you get down here and open your bundle of luck, you find that you have left the all-important article at home, and you regret exceedingly that it was ever your misfortune to be the smartest man in Podunk!"[5]

But the chaste conventions of a country life proved utterly hapless when confronted with the "steam-forced powers and passions of man's restless and struggling spirit," as Ezekiel Bacon attested in an appearance before the Young Men's Association of Utica in 1843. The industrial-age dynamo of personal and professional advance was pulling a whole generation off the land toward a future fixed solely by their own perseverence. Edward Tailer, for instance, attended a Knickerbocker Literary Association debate dedicated to the question of whether ambition or necessity constituted a greater incentive for human action. By the end of the evening the assembled clerks declared in favor of the former, giving collective voice to a post-Malthusian subject who had concluded "that men were not born to be miserable." The result of such convictions was writ large on a landscape of forsaken homes and half-cultivated acreage bearing witness to the misery so "prevalent all around us," Horace Greeley decried, registering his growing distress at the wholesale abandonment of the parental hearthstone and, with it, the "useful labor of one's hands." "You are tempted to exchange the hard work of the farm," the *Cultivator* also protested, "to become a clerk in a city shop, to put off your heavy boots and frock, and be a gentleman, behind the counter!" Stores and countinghouses thus began filling up at the expense of the countryside in a popular declension narrative driven by the confrontation between making things and selling them.[6]

The greatest threat to propriety in the age of capital was not, then, the work of "levelers," "needy laborers," or "protestors against the rich," William Ellery Channing wrote in the wake of the Supreme Court's landmark ruling in the *Charles River Bridge* case in 1837, which realigned property rights in accordance to the perpetuum mobilé of an economy organized around profit and risk. A far more calamitous source of peril issued "from those who are making haste to be rich." Emerson addressed this same turn of events a few years later in an "Ode, Inscribed to W. H. Channing," William's nephew:

> There are two laws discrete,
> Not reconciled—
> Law for man, and law for thing;
> The last builds town and fleet,
> But it runs wild,
> And doth the man unking.

That "law for thing," capable of dissolving the Quincy granite foundations of banking houses, as Emerson noted elsewhere, and send them spinning "at a rate of thousands of miles the hour," posed a far greater menace to public order than did the mob, which explains how an avowed servant of capital such as the clerk could become one of the era's dangerous classes.[7]

The ensuing sense of alarm was commonly acted out in a moral drama by which, "amidst so many tears your mother parted from you, and, with a voice half choked, your father grasped your hand, and sobbed out, 'Farewell, my boy.'" This was one version of what became the primal scene of capitalism, regularly rehearsed in a vernacular of domestic crisis. "Each of them has left behind a beloved circle, which, alas! He has not yet learned to prize, and has entered into a comparatively homeless state," the Reverend James Alexander likewise lamented in "Merchant's Clerk Cheered and Counselled." That homelessness was then exacerbated by the indifference of city crowds who displayed none of "the sympathy, the tenderness, the mutual confidence and refining fellowship of a mother and sisters," as H. A. Boardman testified in yet another variation on the theme of abandoned hearth. All found themselves to be strangers in a strange land, George Whitehouse remarked too upon alighting at Manhattan's East River wharves in 1844, where he was at once engulfed by the cacophony of petty operators—"'are a cab? 'are a Hack, sir? 'are a coach? I'll take your luggage, Here, this way, No, this way, sir"—vying for his custom. The hero of Charles Briggs's *Adventures of Harry Franco*, arriving in Gotham in search of an office situation, experienced a similarly vexed sensation of rootlessness upon moving into a room on the fifth story of the City Hotel and suddenly realizing that he had never been "so far from the earth before." It was a fitting allegory of urban disaffection, not only from the land but from the intimate topographies of the farmhouse.[8]

"Go West, Young Man," Horace Greeley famously retorted in response to the legions preferring to come east. But as Clarence Danhof has summed up a long history of revision of Frederick Jackson Turner's venerable frontier thesis which located the republic's ethos of individualism in the open vistas of a virgin continent, the quest for personal autonomy sent as many Americans to the nation's bustling, disputatious towns as to its distant farmlands, enthusiastic participants in the highest rates of population movement ever registered in the country's history, before or since. "Not a steam-boat reaches the wharf, nor a rail-road car the depot, without bringing a great number of inexperienced youth," it was observed of the through-flow demographics of the dawning age of capital. These newcomers set themselves up in New York City's Third Ward, for instance, a downtown district being refitted for commercial purposes, that is, with office buildings and boardinghouses, where more than four-fifths of the eight hundred clerks registered in the state census of 1855 as residing in the neighborhood had come from somewhere else, three-quarters of those arriving within the past five years. Even in the more domesticated conditions of Manhattan's Ninth Ward, which ran north from Washington Square to Fourteenth Street, and where a much higher percentage of its twelve hundred resident clerks were native to the city, most had nevertheless come from elsewhere. Having reached their destination, moreover, there was no reason to expect anyone to stay put, for the same logic of circulation that brought a person to one place often took him to another. Half of the population of Northampton, Massachusetts in 1850, for instance, where Edward Jarvis would soon make note of the deranged effects of all employments being open to all men, were gone within a decade. Such impermanence found even more emphatic expression when neither the president nor the secretary of the Association of Clerks of Retail Dry Goods Stores, which organized a well-publicized campaign in New York on behalf of a shorter workday in 1850, were to be found in any of the city's population schedules. Existing technologies of social surveillance—Newburyport's first city directory, published the same year that Benjamin Foster arrived in town, also left him out of its listings—clearly lagged behind "the locomotive habits of our people."[9]

The lure of the city, "brilliant and attractive, but certain ruin," thus became an allegory of the clerk's own personal displacement, of the loss of that parental

hearth increasingly relegated to the realm of nostalgia. Certainly, the era's newly
patented parlor stoves offered no substitute for the "log burn[ing] ruddily in the
wide chimney, and the family . . . gathered around it." Horace Paine, employed in
a Manhattan dry-goods store, thus recalled the "cheerful fire" that lit up the old
homestead. "There sits Pa with his foot on the sheet iron," Horace wistfully recalled of Christmas scenes from his boyhood, and "there is Ma with her knitting
work sitting by the stand." Horace Bushnell then transcribed such memories
into a homespun vernacular of yearning for the "large open fire place" and its
steady supply of fine, round hickory. So did Andrew Jackson Downing, whose
hugely popular designs of country homes in the 1840s and 1850s that featured
a "generous-looking" chimney together with an "ample hearth" were explicitly
inspired by the life of "the genuine farmer" who practiced an "intimate relation
with the soil." The generous hearth was fed by a plenitude of fresh air entering
the home through well-proportioned windows while older sons were further
aerated upon being sent out to chop more wood to build up the boisterous fire.
It was a veritable "seminary" of moral virtue, Samuel Goodrich testified in his
Fireside Education, "where the wisdom of one generation was passed on to the
next," exercising a calming influence over the "feverish unrest" of the age.[10]

Those fevers were not so readily relieved, however.

> He puts the books into the safe [and] locks it. Calling to the porter . . . he tells
> him he can close the office now for he's going home. Home, indeed! A home
> from necessity, not from choice—a boarding house.[11]

The boardinghouse was the definitive community of strangers, which continued to strike many as an alarming contradiction in terms. "Instead of sitting down at a snug family board," boarders found themselves dining at "a
table with two or three hundred guests, and these changing every day." Indeed,
the city itself was becoming one "vast boarding-house," James Dabney Mc-
Cabe observed in *Lights and Shadows of New York Life*, his dire pronouncement corroborated by directories that listed more than a thousand such establishments operating in Manhattan alone by the mid-1850s. They were the
practical means for accommodating the locomotive habits of the age. William
Hoffman, for instance, let a room on Greenwich Street upon his arrival in
New York from Albany in March 1849, left for a "better" situation on Warren
Street two months later, was residing on Fulton Street by the end of June, and
moved again after another month to Booth's Boarding House, where residents
were allowed to supply their own meals to save on expenses. Walt Whitman,
who confessed to having done a lot of "boarding round" himself, played on
the public's growing anxiety regarding such restlessness by invoking scenes of
young men rushing out from anonymous suppers in the direction of saloon

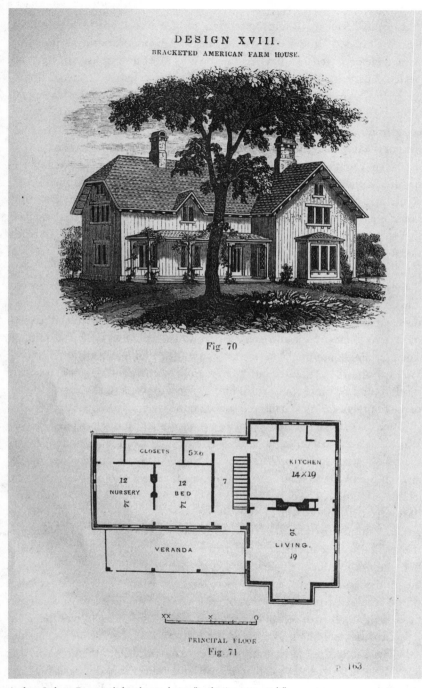

DESIGN XVIII.
BRACKETED AMERICAN FARM HOUSE.

Fig. 70

PRINCIPAL FLOOR
Fig. 71

Andrew Jackson Downing's farmhouse design "in the American style".

and brothel. Richard Robinson, employed at a respectable merchandizing firm on Maiden Lane at the time of his arrest for murdering a prostitute named Helen Jewett in what became the era's most notorious sex crime, appealed directly to these concerns in framing his defense. "I was an unprotected boy," the eighteen-year-old Robinson testified, "without female friends to introduce me to respectable society, sent into a boarding house, where I could enter at what hour I pleased—subservient to no control after the business of the day was over."[12]

"Torn from the parental stock," Horace Mann exclaimed in response to this horrifying repudiation of household government, Robinson and his ilk were abandoned to market society's worst fears of itself. The fact is, the boarding-house not only failed to supervise the comings and goings of its tenants, failed, that is, to offer a reliable substitute for the parental eye, which was "only less sleepless than the eye of God." It operated as an agent of subversion in its own right, peddling a version of home life founded on pecuniary motives that recast domesticity as nothing more than a business initiative. In so mixing family and market, private and public, and love and gold, the boardinghouse became a most egregious example of capital's distressing promiscuity by which the commodity insinuated itself into every aspect of life, including the most intimate. The boardinghouse might have been a quintessential bourgeois invention, as Wendy Gamber has pointed out, an essential niche in a social system based on motions and relations, but that did not make it any less stark a transgression of the bourgeoisie's most hallowed social boundaries.[13]

Such dialectics left contemporaries gasping for air. "It is astonishing," Henry Ward Beecher proclaimed in another jeremiad against the art and artifice of the times, "that God should have . . . provided such wondrous abundance of air, and men take no hint from it of the prime necessity of this substance for health, brightness, and enjoyment." In fact, the suffocating effects of industrial life were a well-known danger. Since every adult required four cubic feet of oxygen each minute in order to breathe, an average-sized room could only support the respiratory needs of six grown men for an hour and a half. The numbers bode ill, not just for the denizens of city tenements and crowded workshops but for those employed "in the damp underground rooms of dry-goods dealers or the cramped dimensions of accounting desks." The threat was actually far more acute than such arithmetic suggested. For while oxygen was being inhaled, rooms were filling back up with the carbonic acid everyone was at once exhaling. Air was not just running out, in other words, but the little that was left was being progressively contaminated, corrupting the body's basic function and undermining "the laws of our government," as Edward Jarvis explained in his *Lecture on the Necessity of the Study of Physiology*. The actuarial tables of insurance companies verified these findings by ranking the life expectancy of clerks as among the lowest in the city, additional testimony to the pernicious effects of indoor work, if not the pathological nature of their "mental labor."[14]

New techniques were required for injecting a continuous stream of oxygen into closed rooms by "excit[ing] an artificial circulation," as *Hunt's* acknowledged in an essay on "air for merchants and business men." The Boylston Medical Committee at Harvard responded to the problem by establishing a prize for the best dissertation on the subject of ventilation, while the American Academy of Arts and Sciences appointed a committee to test various devices meant for removing vitiated air from enclosed spaces. These included perforated glass and "ventilating bricks," iron valves placed in exterior walls or inside chimneys, air pumps, revolving cowls, fans driven by the external air current itself, and tubing that fed the malapropos gases directly into the flue. But working conditions at the office did not so easily lend themselves to such environmental control. When the heating stove at C. W. Moore's countinghouse was removed to the cellar in the early spring of 1847, no doubt to enhance the quality of air in the rest of the rooms, three of the firm's clerks immediately came down with colds.[15]

Faulty ventilation was exacerbated by the era's dramatic advances in illumination. Gas lamps, in particular, which generated an unprecedented quantity of light together with the unprecedented ability to regulate it, used up oxygen at an alarming rate. In addition to the usual carbon dioxide, what's more, they emitted equally unfit quantities of ammonia and sulfur into the air. That same gaslight was, of course, a popular measure of the technological sublime, an astonishingly effective expression of "the conquest of mind over matter," as the *North American Review* celebrated humanity's dramatic success in overcoming the fixed limits of the natural world. "The whole street must be lighted up with harmless bonfires in every shop window!" one passerby effused over the munificent contribution of gas to retail culture—"Well, it's a blessed country!" Others were notably less sanguine. In a well-publicized appearance before the Association of Dry Goods Clerks of New York in 1850, the Reverend E. F. Hatfield delivered an impassioned diatribe against modern industry's destruction of the formerly sacrosanct distinction between night and day. Gas lamps extended business hours beyond any discernible limit, Hatfield complained, undermining the natural rhythms of human labor, "the first great law of our being." No "sweet repose" would ever come to those who toiled in the "almost numberless shops and stores by which our principal streets are illuminated night after night, until nine, ten, eleven, or even twelve o'clock." The clerk had been made into a "Slave of Mammon," Hatfield protested, shackled by the elasticity of industrial time to a marketplace that never slept.[16]

In fact, sleep itself emerged as another subject of the new economy's perverse effects on the human condition. How "very lazy and weary" George
Cayley became, for instance, "whenever I get with in those 4 bare walls" of
the South Street office where he was assigned with copying out the correspondence and checking on the interest of accounts, a decidedly "not interesting"
task, as he feebly punned. "Dull monotonous life is mine!" a Philadelphia
clerk similarly intoned in response to the anomie of his own work routine:
"Yesterday was the type of today, and today is the mold of tomorrow." Edward
Tailer, meanwhile, returned home after spending the whole day sorting and
arranging the thousands of shawls he had released from the Custom House
in December, "and then being greatly fatigued sought soon after my couch
where I forgot the trials of the day." And although Edward Thomas insisted
that he was "becoming a little used to my labors" at the Boston hardware firm
where he had recently been hired, Edward could barely get through Sunday's
sermon. "I succeeded in keeping awake but I was so overcome with fatigue
that all my powers were put into use to keep myself awake."[17]

All were suffering from a peculiar form of "nervous exhaustion," the *Atlantic
Monthly* observed of the chronic fatigue that plagued young men crowded into
subservient occupations which dwarfed their muscles and manhood. We fancy
that we are exhausted, the *Massachusetts Teacher* discerned of such lethargy,
"but we are in fact only *suffering for want of work*." How else could a careless
writing posture leave the penman's "arm, hand, and . . . whole body . . . weary,"
though he had barely even lifted a finger? Benjamin Foster too noted how "the
monotonous, unvaried, dull, tedious life of this store fatigues me." And yet he
could barely fall asleep at night, having failed to earn his rest, as Benjamin himself recognized. "Toil is the price of sleep," the *New England Farmer* explained
of such modern insomnia in an essay extolling the manual foundations of "industry" and its restorative effects on the body and soul, all of which prompted
the *Atlantic Monthly* to refer to the "dishonest" quality of the clerk's postindustrial fatigue. The best that these desk-bound victims of ennui could do was day-
dream of a "mouthful of open air and a cool draught from 'the old oaken bucket
that hangs in the well,'" as *Hunt's* also acknowledged of the endemic languor
of their artificial existence.[18]

The clerk thus acquired the persona of a Daumier caricature, "with ledger-
lines ruled along their brows," as Melville testified, promoting him into an
icon of both the pettiest and the most presumptuous corruptions of this age
of small profits and quick returns. "I am the essence of retail," *Vanity Fair*
seethed in sarcastic mimicry of the clerk's empathy with the commodity and
his subsequent pursuit of little more than affect calibrated to enhance one's
value in the market. The clerk's hands were indeed remarkably white, Asa

Greene noted in *Perils of Pearl Street,* while the ladies declared "that he smelt delightfully." Accoutred in neckcloth and paste brooch, rings adorning each finger in what was surely the most conclusive repudiation of productive industry of all, the clerk found himself enthralled to the whim of every "painted and padded form of humanity," provoking Henry David Thoreau to observe in an essay on "Life without Principle" (which was originally delivered as a lecture titled "Getting a Living"), that while God accorded righteous men a certificate entitling them to food and raiment, the unrighteous had simply "found a facsimile of the same."[19]

Self-Culture

Thoreau soon made the culture of the bottom line the subject of extensive ridicule in *Walden,* which he wrote in general protest against the commodity form's deleterious effects on American civilization. His assault on the ledger was most pointedly on display in the facetiously pedantic record of expenditures with which Thoreau pretended to document the superiority of his alternative economy. We are thus privy to an account of food expenses incurred over an eight-month period:

Rice	$1 73 ½
Molasses	1 73
Rye meal	1 04 ¾
Indian meal	0 99 ¾
Pork	0 22
Flour	0 88
Sugar	0 80
Lard	0 65
Apples	0 25
Dried apple	0 22
Sweet potatoes	0 10
One pumpkin	0 06
One watermelon	0 02
Salt	0 03

"Yes, I did eat $8.74," Thoreau deposed after balancing the books, cash now serving as an equivalent source of human sustenance. Even at Walden, that is to say, household subsistence proved inconceivable without the syllogisms of credit and debit. Thoreau accordingly observed his neighbors plowing and sowing, hoeing and harvesting—practicing what appeared to be a venerable tradition of work on the land—but he was not fooled. They were

no longer growing crops or flowers or fruit but dollars, and thereby "contracting [them]selves into a nutshell of civility." The expanding reach of the cash
nexus had made even the simplest competence into a business opportunity,
turning everyone into a bookkeeper. Penmen and plowboys inhabited two
sides of the same devalued coin, while the countryside became a site of no less
quiet desperation than the recreant city.[20]

Some sought to salvage a sense of absolute value from the industrial wreck-
age. William Leggett, a hard-money radical and well-known Locofoco journal-
ist, found consolation in contrasting the natural dignity of a hundred hardy
plowmen to the derelict posture of an equal number of "lank and sallow accountants worn out with the sordid anxieties of traffic and calculations of gain."
The *Cultivator*, too, strained to reclaim a tradition of proprietary virtue, announcing that "all necessary labor is honorable," whether undertaken on the
land or in the workshop. But was "necessity" a relevant measure of value in a
culture of accumulation? Wasn't Thoreau's whole project at Walden, in fact,
inspired by an understanding that modern civilization had progressed far beyond such Malthusian laws of nature, which meant that human industry was
no longer dedicated to securing a competence but to producing a surplus? The
natural dignity of the plow was an oxymoron, it followed, and men "labor under a mistake," as Thoreau declared in the opening chapter of *Walden*, which
was dedicated to the subject of "economy." Neither the sweat of the farmer's
brow nor the fruits of his manual exertions any longer constituted the basis of
a higher law. If anything, "we are made to exaggerate the importance of what
work we do," as he observed in dismissing labor theories of value as a false
messiah in the age of capital. Americans would have to transcend such clichés
if they were to rescue themselves from a market system that had destroyed the
traditional synthesis of property and propriety.[21]

But if growing and making things no longer served as the reliable foundation of a virtuous social order, what would fill that role? What was the proper
object of man's prodigious powers of production and his breathtaking command over nature? The response to this peculiarly industrial predicament
was that man himself would become that object, "necessarily an end, not a
means," as William Ellery Channing explained in *Self-Culture*. Nor was this
the quixotic illation of a handful of arcane transcendentalists or Unitarian
intellectuals, as was evident in the general embrace of the "self-made man,"
a new kind of hero who literally declared himself to be the ends of his own
productive means. Just as no one "expects golden harvests without digging
in his field or sowing seed," the *American Phrenological Journal* elaborated,
a person's own growth could only be secured by "expending living labor in
cultivating it." Those truths informed the advice Alexander Bryan Johnson,

an upstate New York banker, offered his son—or all sons, for that matter—namely, to "mark out for yourself such a character as you desire to possess and by speaking constantly thereto, you will attain the desired character as certainly as you will a coat, by going to your tailor and ordering it." Personal existence was a matter of "labour and toil," a young clerk in Middletown, Connecticut, affirmed of this distinctly industrial production project that could be said to be of but not in the capitalist economy.[22]

Self-making recommended itself as the only form of labor safe from the abstractions of commercial exchange. The sovereign individual would serve as a bulwark against commodified forms of wealth that were "held by a precarious tenure at best," the agricultural improver Jesse Buel lectured an audience in Albany on the importance of "self-instruction." "I should not talk so much about myself if there were anybody else whom I knew as well," Thoreau announced, too, in explaining the prevailing use he made in *Walden* of the first-person singular. That innate interiority was meant to strike a pointed rebuke to the chimera of the market system, for Thoreau's "*I*" was an organic whole, identical with itself and so seemingly immune to the divisions of labor, the transmutations of form, and the constantly renegotiated value that were coming to define all other forms of property. "Self-possession" was thus divorced from its earlier incarnation as a dominion "over the external things of the world," which is how the British jurist William Blackstone defined the foundations of political economy and its labor theories of value in the eighteenth century, and reconceived as an exclusive domain over oneself. Rather than mixing physical labor with the world's bounty, the new ethic directed citizens to apply mental labor to the production of their own lives. That interior effort, Channing declared, "transcends in importance all our power over outward nature."[23]

This *res privata* was elucidated in a series of biographical sketches devoted to the subject of "self-made men" which appeared in the *Family Lyceum* in 1832 and featured philosophers born into slavery, the sons of untutored fathers who grew up to become eminent scholars, and poets forced to labor as blacksmiths in their youth. Together, they comprised a celebrated gallery of personal virtue overcoming the conventions of patronage and deference by raising themselves up from obscurity through the natural force of their own character, which proved superior to the repressive forces of tradition. A generation later Charles Seymour published an anthology of similarly inspired narratives under the title of *Self-Made Men* that further elaborated on the qualities of such individual assertion. These included a chapter recounting Andrew Jackson's refusal to allow the militia of volunteers under his command to be conscripted into the regular army in 1814. "It was the men he thought of," Seymour explained in comparing Jackson's integrity and independence of thought to "the pusil-lanimity" of a privileged officer caste whom Jackson threatened with arrest if they were to enter his camp in search of recruits. Daniel Webster was another recruit to Seymour's bipartisan pantheon of earnest self-making. Born on a farm and educated in a log schoolhouse, Webster dedicated his life to the pur-suit of knowledge. Even as a youth he carried a volume of Shakespeare along on fishing expeditions while further "economiz[ing] his time" by perusing school texts when assisting at the family's sawmill.[24]

No cash changed hands in any of these accounts of self-made success, for such productive virtue was adamantly divorced from property relations. Personal advance was not to be measured, that is, by how "much money, . . . houses and barns and woodlots" a person owned, as Thoreau explained, but by the superior ambitions of one who seeks "to invent and get a patent for himself." And though Thoreau himself was generally dismissed by contempo-raries as being little more than "a "ranting . . . half-crazed radical," as Benja-min Foster derided the zealous style of the author of *Walden*, Thoreau never-theless gave expression to the popular adulation of those who remain "above the influence of merely external influences," as the more reputable Horace Greeley declared in an essay on "how to make a man," that appeared in the *Young American's Magazine of Self-Improvement* in 1847. It was this ability to keep "nobly independent of others' aid," the *American Phrenological Jour-nal* pronounced as well, which proved that "*self-made* men are heroes in the moral world."[25]

Private devotion to the moral life was not unknown to former generations, John Angell James acknowledged in *Young Man from Home*. The ancients, for instance, considered the proper care of the self to be nothing less than a heavenly injunction. But such divine aegis had long since waned, James also observed, which meant that "we must OURSELVES be the grand Instruments for accomplishing the purposes of our creation." This exclusive responsibil-ity is what spurred an outpouring of "letters" to young men, "lectures" to young men, "thoughts" for young men, "considerations" for young men, and "counselors" to young men that collectively extended practical guidance to their readership for assuming sovereign control over their own fate. This was "a fearful as well as glorious" prospect, the Reverend Channing remarked in one of the more compelling passages of his *Self-Culture*. And while Channing might seem to be recapitulating a well-worn Christian binary between godly damnation and salvation, his dictum rested, in fact, on the opposite premise, namely, that personal fortune had become independent of any deity, or any other supra-authority, save for oneself. *Harper's Monthly* published a graphic version of this condition in a pictorial parable depicting the "two paths in life"

CHILDHOOD.

YOUTH.

YOUTH.

TWO PATHS IN LIFE.

THESE contrasted pictures furnish texts for a whole volume of sermons upon human life and destiny. The CHILD stands at the parting of the ways, and he may run through in succession all the phases depicted in either series of portraits. The essential elements of either course of development lie alike in those smooth features. Which shall be actually realized depends mainly upon the influences brought to bear upon him from without. A few years of training in our schools upon the one hand, or in the streets upon the other, will make all the difference, in the YOUTH, between the characters that stand opposed to each other in these opposite pictures. A youth of study and training in a few years moulds the lineaments of the face into the resemblance of the first picture of MANHOOD; while, by a law equally inevitable, idleness and dissipation bring out all the lower animal faculties, which reveal themselves in the depressed forehead, the hard eyebrow, the coarse mouth, and the thickened neck of the opposite picture. The short-boy, and rowdy, and blackleg, if he escapes the state prison and the gallows, passes, as he reaches the confines of MIDDLE AGE, into the drunken loafer, sneaking around the grogshop in the chance of securing a *treat* from some one who knew him in his flush days; while he who has chosen the other path, as he passes the "mid journey of life," and slowly descends the slope toward AGE, grows daily richer in the love and esteem of those around him; and in the bosom of the family that gather about his hearth, lives over again his happy youth and earnest manhood. What a different picture is presented in the fate of him who has chosen the returnless downward path, another and almost the last stage of which is portrayed in the companion sketch of AGE. The shadows deepen as he descends the hill of life. He has been successively useless, a pest, and a burden to society, and when he dies there is not a soul to wish that his life had been prolonged. Two lives like these lie in possibility enfolded within every infant born into the world.

MANHOOD.

MANHOOD.

MIDDLE LIFE.

MIDDLE LIFE.

AGE.

AGE.

faced by one and all. Parallel columns arrayed along opposing margins of the same page presented diverging visions of the same life as it passed through the respective stations of existence from youth to old age. One column exhibited a benevolent trajectory inspired by love, learning, and earnestness that culminated in a gracious apotheosis of personal fulfillment and benevolence. The other path was strewn with idleness, dissipation, and uselessness, whose unhappy denouement was no less predictable. Since "two lives like these be in possibility enfolded within every infant born into the world," the choice as to whom one was to become rested exclusively on the efforts of none other than ourselves.[26]

Charles French responded to such moral imperatives by pursuing plans to "improve my mind" at the Franklin Library, the Webster Literary Association, and at a special meeting of disgruntled members of Boston's Mercantile Library which was convened to organize an extra series of public lectures once the regular subscription had sold out. The library's lecture schedule was meant to pull young men into the reading room, in fact, "and perhaps to the classes," as Eliza Cope Harrison, president of the Board of Managers of the Mercantile Library in Philadelphia, explained in happily noting a steady rise in the number of members devoting their evenings to seeking out "useful knowledge." That usefulness was measured by its success in countering the baneful influence of theaters and billiard rooms, for "when the mind acquires a taste for literature," Harrison went on to report, "it will have less relish for indulgences of a debasing character." *Hunt's* reached the same conclusion in nothing that no member of the Mercantile Library had ever been known to defraud his employer.[27]

Mercantile libraries were initially established in the country's larger cities in the 1820s for "the especial benefit and intellectual culture of young men, who, in the position of clerks, bookkeepers, salesmen, etc., were engaged in the mercantile profession." Within a generation, these associations could be found in every medium-sized trading hamlet in America, from Sandusky to Peoria, operating at the heart of that "centripetal force" set into motion by industrial opportunity, and so positioning themselves "between the schoolhouse and manhood." By thus socializing a vast public of strivers newly arrived in the emporium and raising them above the commotion of the passions and appetites unleashed by the market, the library associations proved to be a critical "social invention," *Hunt's* further declaimed, giving hope "for the perpetuity of our government." As such, they helped to establish a public of private persons and encouraged them to make active use of their reason, as Jürgen Habermas referred to liberalism's general mobilization of popular enlightenment that also encompassed literary guilds, debating societies, re-

gional lyceums, mechanics' institutes, gymnastic clubs, and an extensive miscellany of other civic organizations that brought upwards of half a million
Americans together every week, according to some estimates, eager consum-
ers of a culture industry offering them the raw materials of good character.[28]

William Hoffman, for instance, joined "a full House" of clerks at an evening lecture in Poughkeepsie on his first day off the farm. Benjamin Foster
attended a talk by Ralph Waldo Emerson on the "spirit of the times" at the
Newburyport Lyceum, where he heard Horace Mann and Horace Greeley
speak as well. Edward Tailer spent an hour and a half "perusing an able article
upon the Importance of the study of Rhetoric" before then borrowing a copy
of Say's *Thoughts on Marriage* from the Mercantile Library. Charles Rogers
enrolled in algebra classes at the Cooper Institute, where he also went to hear
"an interesting lecture" on political economy. Samuel Munson attended public
orations addressing such themes as "the Christian merchant" and "national
prosperity," the latter presented by Henry Ward Beecher. Albert Norris rode
to Springfield, Massachusetts, to hear Beecher speak too. Henry Patterson,
meanwhile, stopped off after work to view an exhibit of Audubon's birds at
the Library Association. And Robert Graham enlightened himself at a series
of lectures respectively devoted to astronomy, anatomy, and Fourierism, the
latter in an especially well-attended event.[29]

Something more was clearly required for self-made success than could be
gotten in the counting room, which is also why city clerks organized regular
campaigns on behalf of "early closing." "Tell me how a clerk spends his evenings," William Thayer wrote in *Poor Boy and Merchant Prince*, "and I will
tell you how he will come out." Popular stereotypes, of course, placed him in
scenes of thoughtless merriment, if not sinful dissipation. But how could it
be otherwise, James Carlile angrily retorted in *Wrongs of the Counter*, since
fourteen hours on the job denied them the opportunity to cultivate their intellect and elevate their morals. "The store detains me late in the evening," a
Philadelphia salesman testified to his own frustrated program of self-culture,
and "makes me undecided about subscribing to a course of French, for fear
of interruptions." The same young man was upbraided for reading on the job.
William Hoffman likewise coveted a "little time left for meditation" and "improvement of the mind," or at least an hour to peruse the papers at the Mercantile Library. But as long as he was assigned with closing up the store every
night at ten o'clock, his best intentions went unrequited. E. F. Hatfield attributed these aborted plans for personal improvement to the shameless race to
accumulate, according to which "not an hour can be spared from the everlast-
ing drudgery." The *New York Tribune* registered a similar protest against the
working conditions at store and office, attributing the clerks' general want of

"mental and moral culture" to the exclusive focus of their employers on the bottom line. The mayor might ask city businesses to close up early in observance of the festive opening of the Metropolitan Fair in the spring of 1864, Charles Rogers exasperatedly reported, but A. T. Stewart simply ordered the shutters lowered and everyone kept on the job.[30]

Long hours "chained to tasks which have very little tendency to expand the mind" were ruinous to one's physical as well as spiritual health, resulting in scenes of destitution that rivaled the suffering of society's most degraded classes. Impassioned calls for the "emancipation of the clerks" followed, referencing reformist crusades against ignorance and unreason, if not, more provocatively, against the dehumanizing effects of chattel exploitation. Such rhetoric was designed to position the clerk on the barricades of civilization, mobilizing the same arguments so often leveled against him in condemning a commodity system that turned men into little more than instruments of profit. Denunciations of the "long hour system" were subsequently couched in a vernacular of righteousness and outrage that consciously targeted the "hearts and conscience" of women. "Wives, mothers, sisters!" were thus beseeched to curtail their evening purchases in a strategy that was less devoted to organizing a consumer boycott than to embarrassing employers by using "the Ladies of New York" to claim the moral high ground. Private sensibilities rather than the public regulation demanded by trades unions also campaigning for a shorter workday were the preferred means of protest for clerks hoping to seize their "only opportunity for rational enjoyment and mental improvement," and so assume a place in those betterment schemes "which tend to promote the best interests of society," as the *Young American's Magazine of Self-Improvement* pronounced in offering its support to the cause as well.[31]

"The ignorance, emptiness and foppery of Clerks have been the theme of popular ridicule long enough," Greeley's *New York Tribune* vowed in endorsing a ten-hour workday that was to award all of the city's wage earners an opportunity to pursue their own "self-education." Ten hours were enough to accomplish the day's business, the Association of Dry Goods Clerks affirmed in its 1850 campaign. Stores should close their doors by six o'clock, marking an escalation over demands from the 1840s which sought an eight o'clock closing, and by three o'clock on Saturdays. The dry-goods clerks insisted, meanwhile, that their object was "not to secure immunities to one class at the expense of another, but to promote the weal of all." They had little interest, in other words, in promulgating wage solidarities with a separate working class. Though engaged in a common struggle over control of the clock instigated by capital's reorganization of labor, young men "clinched to desks" demonstrated little inclination to share their fate with those "nailed to benches." If anything, they strove to distinguish their cause from that of metropolitan journeymen, "inasmuch as it is not money but time they want . . . to improve their mental capacity and enable them to keep pace with the spirit of the age." Agreements on the curtailment of store hours were often reached, as a matter of fact, if only because they also served the interest of the firms in reigning in competition. Those same competitive conditions, however, also meant that any such arrangements soon broke down.[32]

The "abridgment of hours" emerged as the focus of so much polite protest because it promised to redeem the clerk's failure to control his own labor—increasingly subject to color-coded counters and the supervision of junior partners, not to mention the less visible forces of the market—by providing him greater opportunity for controlling himself once the workday was over. That second half of his existence, for which no one else had contracted and so could "properly be regarded as one's own," was known as "*leisure.*" This was the most precious aspect of our existence, the Reverend George W. Bethune exclaimed to an audience at the Mercantile Library, since only leisure made it possible to "devote ourselves mainly and exclusively to the great end of our being." These were the hours that allowed men to nurture the faculties by which they could then "better fit themselves to be good citizens," *Hunt's* pronounced in less redemptive but equally emphatic terms. In either case, such leisure time was clearly no idyll, no supine preserve of the loafer, but a "systematic employment" of oneself, to be expended in tracing our powers and "guiding and impelling them."[33]

The demand for more time of their own, as the dry-goods clerks formally resolved at various protest meetings, was not motivated by "mere sordid or selfish considerations, but by the loftier aspirations of duty," and first and foremost their "duty to themselves." Dr. Franklin was a popular model for such aspirations, often depicted with a book ever ready at hand so "that he might improve every leisure moment," as William Thayer reported in a chapter of *The Printer Boy* aptly devoted to the subject of "industry." This leisure class was not to be identified by its conspicuous consumption, then, but by its conspicuous production, that which secured the "integrity of their own self-isms" and heralded the appearance of a new species of *Homo faber* who separated out industriousness from the workplace and relocated it in the private exertions of each person vis-à-vis himself. One hour of private study a day throughout the year, according to contemporary calculations, resulted in the equivalent of two months in the classroom, a tangible demonstration of just "how much might be saved from sleep, from Broadway, and from the theatre." Such an effective accumulation of leisure hours, another audience of clerks at the Mercantile Library was apprised, would afford them the "intelligence

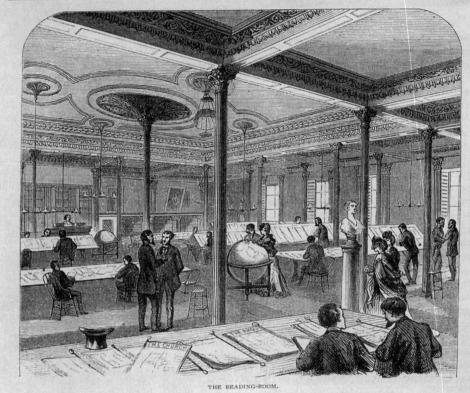

THE READING-ROOM.

and love of order" that were essential for preserving civilization from "the storms of civil revolution."[34]

Most significantly of all, the demands for leisure—for more self-making, in point of fact—were an implicit avowal that plow and plane had lost their pride of place in the republic. The end of the labor theory of value, as the supporters of early closing understood, marked the end of labor as a value. God might have given Adam "a Spade into his hand, to subdue the Earth," as John Locke once declared in promoting productive industry into the corner-stone of the social contract, but a single brain had since become "the concen-trated essence of much land," as *Hunt's* now determined in amending such outmoded axioms of political economy. If that same man then empties his purse into his head, Franklin, too, was quoted as saying, "no one can take it away from him."[35]

Labor on the land was accordingly stripped of its privileged status in favor of an ethos of mental labor that lay claim to sobriety, prudence, resolution, cleanliness, vigor, and duty, among other Franklinesque recipes of civic rectitude. Those who continued to follow the plow, weave the basket, or tend the loom were no longer the "chosen people of God," Jefferson's acclamation from an earlier stage in the moral and material history of the republic. And, indeed, a society filling up with hired labor could no longer subscribe to the proprietary culture of the agrarian freehold. What relevance did such "self-evident" readings of life, liberty, and happiness have once ownership of the means of production became subject to a market-driven system in which hands and mouth were increasingly located on separate bodies? Were the growing numbers of Americans no longer drawing their sustenance from the soil or their own craft tools to be relegated to a subordinate place in the social order? Obviously not. Instead, older notions of self-possession needed to be adapted to a society of landless—and even "homeless"—citizens shorn of any real possessions save for their own selves, which is what informed Orson Fowler's epigraph on the frontispiece of *Self-Culture and Perfection of Character* in 1847 proclaiming that men were "SELF-MADE OR NEVER MADE." In fact, this new mode of self-production constituted a far more universal experience precisely because of its divorce from the economy. With personal existence thus separated from the external things of the world, William Ellery Channing could explain to his audience of Boston mechanics in 1838 that "intellectual and moral culture," rather than their manual toil, was the source of "pleasures worthy of men." His liberalism did not issue from an embrace of the market, as such, but from the opposite, while it at once removed questions about wealth from the realm of moral virtue altogether.[36]

Max Weber would eventually explain that the "spirit of capitalism" has little to do with human greed, which is to be "found in all ages and in all countries of the world." A society organized around the market needed to invent new ways of reigning in covetousness and the unbridled desire for gain. Or, as George Hillard reminded his audience at Boston's Mercantile Library upon addressing "the dangers and duties" of the age, it was not money but the love of money which constituted the root of all evil. "Mere business astuteness," Weber further exclaimed, only resulted in chaotic cycles of profit and loss. Capital's transformation into capitalism, into an embracing system of ethical as well as material relations, required a social praxis, or "occidental rationalism," that obliged individuals operating in the absence of fixed hierarchies and traditional restraints to police the porous boundary between fruitful ambition and baneful aggrandizement on their own. Weber considered Americans to have been particularly effective in doing so. So did Michel Chevalier, who announced after a tour of the republic in 1834 that the reason the United States was able to dispense with Caesar was because its citizens were "ready to act the part of constables." This was the basis of "real self-government," Chevalier concluded, which is also why William Alcott told readers of his well-regarded *Physiology of Marriage* in 1866 that public life rested on each person's private efforts: "Shall he not, at least, take the first step—that which must, forever, be the first step—shall he not reform himself?" Such maxims were to be juxtaposed to Old World practices still mired in the assumption that men are not competent to take care of themselves. Americans act on the opposite principle, John Todd wrote in an *Address* to the nation's rising generation, which explains why the United States had uniquely become "a country of self-made men."[37]

Government required everyone to "turn the mind on itself," Channing elaborated, and embrace a style of introspection that was no longer to be associated with the prerogative of extraordinary men. Nor was such a life of rumination to be dismissed as a foreign or elitist affectation, as was often charged in an earlier age that pitted agrarian against aristocrat. Reason and reflection, rather, lay "within the reach of every individual in this favored nation," John Todd further asserted in extolling a version of the *viva activa* by which sedentary types, able "to think and act" for themselves, became a model of the "*practical man*," exhibiting as they did the "strong, masculine qualities of the mind."[38]

Accounting for Oneself

William Hoffman encountered an acquaintance from home en route to his new job in Albany in the spring of 1848. Apprised of William's exciting prospects to "enter into Business," Henry Coon nevertheless saw fit to caution the young man about the temptations certain to rise up and lure him away from the path of virtue. William remained nonplussed, confident of his ability to ward off any "moral depravity and disregarded looseness, etc.," while establishing effective command over himself once no one else would be around to do so. It was a reasonable assumption on his part. But who would establish effective command over the half dozen "rowdy clerks" Benjamin Foster encountered on the streets of Bangor a year earlier? Neither patriarchal hierarchies or liberal strategies of self-government offered practical means for containing their unruly behavior. A recent review of Ariel Livermore's *Lectures*

to Young Men on Their Moral Dangers and Duties reached the same conclusion. Incessant cries of "'Beware! Beware!'" that suffused the era's countless
etiquette manuals had proven to be little more than empty slogans, it was observed, and that was because "the connection between virtue and happiness is
so much and so constantly insisted on it seems a mere matter of policy to be
good." The problem did not so much issue from this instrumental coupling
of virtue and self-interest, but from the structural contradictions that under-
lay it. For the fact is, those "Young Men" most in need of counsel—whose
"recklessness or stupidity" left them indifferent to the consequences of their
errant ways—were, for that same reason, the least likely to consult the advice
literature, let alone apply it to their own lives. When everyone has the "full
liberty of choice" to do good or evil, in other words, only the good will choose
to be good. Such solipsism threatened to undermine the whole apparatus of
self-making.[39]

The social control of young men was not a new problem, and certainly not
one born of capitalist disorder. Fears of disobedient youth, including the alarming specter of parricide, were a regular feature of Puritan discourse mobilized
in defense of public order. Increase Mather, best remembered for overseeing
the witch trials at Salem, thus invoked the Gospel of Luke in denouncing the
prodigal son's rejection of paternal government. "Do we not fear just so in
many Young men amongst our selves?" he pointedly asked about conditions
in seventeenth-century New England. "Nothing will serve them, but to be going
far from their fathers house, that so they may without control walk in the way
of their heart and after the sight of their own eyes." Similar complaints about
"haughty sons" overly intent on "minding the main chance" were commonly
aired in the next century as well, provoked by concern over the condition of
the little commonwealth and the authority of its titular head. And yet such traditional fulminations against filial challenges to existing hierarchies rested on
the assumption that the lives of the next generation would resemble those of
their parents, and that the past was a practical precedent for the future. All this
changed once the son became father of the man and acquired exclusive control
over his own fate, undermining codes of deference that had shaped the relationship not only between fathers and sons but magistrates and subjects, lords
and servants, and, soon enough, masters and slaves. "I am not under inspection
now," John Angell James reminded his readers in Young Man from Home. "Restraint is over, I can go where I like, associate with whom I please, and fear
neither rebuke nor reproach."[40]

How had the public order ever come to rest on this "right of every one to
do pretty nearly as he pleases?" an incredulous Horace Greeley was still wondering in 1853 about the "age of Individualism." A sarcastic aside directed at

Greeley himself exposed the profane character of the new regime and under-scored the equivocal nature of governing a society in which everyone had be-come his own sovereign. Horace Greeley, it was observed, is a self-made man who worships his creator. It was a most pithy, and precise, characterization of the tautologies of the first-person singular. Benjamin Franklin had, in fact, al-ready grasped the circular nature of that condition. "Even if I could conceive that I had completely overcome it," Franklin wrote in one of his better-known passages about the acquisition of virtues, "I should probably be proud of my Humility." This was not a problem in moral philosophy, however, but in so-cial practice. Nor was Franklin the first to notice it. "Whatsoever is the object of any man's appetite or desire, that is it which he for his part calleth good," Thomas Hobbes remarked on the relativist quagmire that ensued once the general good was entrusted to the particularist sensibilities of individuals.[41]

Hobbes's seventeenth-century solution was to enhance the authority of the prince. But Americans had sundered the links binding society together "from peasant to king," as Tocqueville noted in 1840. The result, which conservatives had been lamenting ever since the storming of the Bastille, left everyone with "a curious strange feeling . . . of fear, suspense, desire, anxiety and numerous other nameless ills," if not a growing sense of terror at the inverted logic of a society founded on the discrete desires of autonomous individuals. This was not the terror of Robespierre, however, but of Bartleby, the Wall Street law clerk in Herman Melville's two-part story published in *Putnam's Monthly* in 1853 who suddenly refuses to perform any more paperwork, and then refuses to explain why. All we definitely know about Bartleby is that he might have once been employed at the Dead Letters Office in Washington, where all the nation's undeliverable mail was sent, its addressees having disappeared with-out a trace into the era's growing public of strangers. Bartleby himself was surely such a stranger: none of the familiar codes of personal behavior seemed to guide his conduct. He was a proud proponent of self-abnegation, an active agent of passivity, and a vagrant who stubbornly refused to budge. Bartleby's subjectivity, in other words, comprised a bundle of contradictions that left his employer feeling altogether "unmanned." Most ominously of all, Bartleby showed how subversive individual prerogative could become in a society that promoted personal preference into a natural right, allowing everyone "to do pretty nearly as he pleases." That was not just because Bartleby preferred not to copy any more deeds and contracts despite being an assiduous and talented penman. A far greater threat to the civic order was contained in Bartleby's pronouncement that "at present I would prefer not to be a little reasonable." How perilously close individualism thus veered to the precipice of chaos, and liberal government to paradox.[42]

"However strange it may seem to the English ear," the first translator of *Democracy in America* remarked of Tocqueville's most famous neologism, "I know of no English word exactly equivalent." In fact, the strangeness of "individualism" was as conceptual as it was phonetic, for promoting the private self into the foundation of public order undermined centuries of political orthodoxy. Sylvester Graham, the country's most influential champion of the proper care of the self, and so an important political theorist in his own right, accordingly described the emergence of the sovereign individual in strikingly discordant terms: "Continually seeking happiness, he is unhappy; inventing new modes of pleasure, he is miserable; desirous of preserving health, he is diseased; a lover of virtue, he is vicious." Such oxymorons were symptomatic of an age in which everyone was a hero—"worshipping his creator"—but in which heroism itself was the relic of a more primitive past based on the "honary motives" of exceptional men. Self-making individuals therefore acquired cultural authority just as authority itself was in danger of collapsing. Such inversions reached their acme in a short notice appearing in the *New York Herald* in 1849 that sought moral solace in the rampant success of cheats. "It is a good thing," the *Herald* announced, "and speaks well for human nature, that, at this late day, in spite of all the hardening of civilization and all the warning of newspapers, men *can be swindled*." Modernity was not, as such, to be measured by either gas or steam, Charles Baudelaire sardonically observed of a problem that continued to agitate Melville until the end of his life as well, but by "the diminution of the traces of original sin."[43]

The demise of original sin, together with other transcendent forms of truth, threatened to touch off an inflationary moral spiral in which success became "its own reward," as contemporaries were prone to exclaim. "It is a great misfortune of the present day," the *Cultivator* protested in an essay on "industry," "that almost everyone is, by his own estimate, *raised above his real state of life*." But what, in fact, constituted a "real" state of life in the elastic conditions of a self-making age? John Todd fell into the same contradiction when he warned readers of his *Student's Manual* about the "vexations of the ambitious man" born of an overeagerness for success, and then acknowledged that anyone reading his admonition was no doubt doing so because of their own ambitions. Self-making, as such, rested on a proposition—"to create and in creating to be created"—whose circularity foreclosed any possibility of testing one's claims on anything but one's own terms, which was especially problematic once everyone was free to be not a little reasonable. Bartleby might have been a schizophrenic, in other words, but his eccentricities were no personality quirk. They were a sign of the general vulnerability of a society composed of persons serving as the source of their own truth. "Ah Bartleby, Ah humanity!" Melville wrote at the conclusion of his tale, just in case the reader had missed its universal moral, namely, that individualism was one long chain of epistemological crises. Humanity—and not just the commodities—threatened to melt into air.[44]

Daniel Haskell responded to this conundrum at Boston's Mercantile Library in a lecture that sought to reground the era's restless signifier and situate self-culture deep within the collective memory. "Our fathers left, three thousand miles behind them, the feudal institutions and corruptions of the old world," Haskell recounted, "in favor of a system that allowed each to attain his own station in life." Ever since that foundational moment, "our people are particularly prone to worship the man who rises from obscurity to eminence by the natural force of his character." Self-made men, Haskell effectively explained, were present at the creation. What's more, their self-making was synonymous with the nation's own mission, which meant that the new generation of "emphatic . . . artificers of their own fortune," as the New York Mercantile Library's *Annual Report* characterized the association's membership, had nothing to apologize about. Personal ambition was a venerable American practice, which meant that when Warren Spencer lectured another roomful of young clerks on the right of each to pursue his own happiness—for "neither wealth nor the prestige of name and ancestry avail anything" in the United States— no one suspected that he was inventing a revolutionary tradition.[45]

The most popular model of self-invention—inspiring contemporaries to view their lives as a full-fledged product of their own imaginations while at once tying those efforts to the nation's founding impulse—was not, of course, Bartleby but Benjamin Franklin. More specifically, it was Franklin's own version of himself as presented in his *Autobiography*, of which more than a hundred editions had appeared by 1860, including sundry abridgments and adaptations for schoolroom use, in addition to an incalculable number of excerpts circulating as biographical sketches in collected volumes and the popular magazines. "The life of Benjamin Franklin is one of deep interest to every young man who feels ambitious," the *Cultivator* acknowledged. "His life is remarkable for two things," Charles Seymour further observed in his anthology of *Self-Made Men*, "great ambition and great virtue." In fact, Franklin's signal contribution to capitalist civilization was in making these into one and the same thing.[46]

The relevance of Franklin's life to the new regime can be gleaned from two separate reviews of his autobiography that appeared in the *North American Review*, the first in 1818, and the second in 1856. The earlier essay, devoted to previously unpublished sections of *History of My Life* and to newly available private correspondence, described a personage making his way in the world by force of great talent and industry, and, as such, lacking a moral compass.

"The groundwork of his character," the *Review* declaimed in an attack exuding neo-Calvinist smugness, "was bad; and the moral qualities, which contributed to his rise, were of a worldly and very profitable kind." Franklin's ambitious rise, the *Review* protested, was grounded in his ethical failures. He abandoned his childhood home early on and remained indifferent throughout his life to the consequent suffering this caused his parents. His views on the nature of vice and virtue, furthermore, were underdeveloped, and that because "no such things exist[ed]" as far as Franklin was concerned. This is what allowed him to practice a "libertinism" in his daily life that prompted no expression of shame or repentance in his memoirs. Franklin's well-known inventory of acquirable virtues—temperance, silence, order, resolution, frugality, industry, sincerity, justice, moderation, cleanliness, tranquility, chastity, and humility—which were published for the first time in 1818, revealed a notion of duty that extended no farther than himself. This suited his habit of keeping an exclusive eye on what was "*most profitable*" for him, turning virtuous self-improvement into a miserly matter of utility and calculation, nothing more than a vehicle by which to "crane" the main chance, weighed and measured as inert data arranged in a table.[47]

With personal interest serving as his sole guide, there was little wonder that Franklin "was not a man to distinguish himself by bold efforts or thankless sacrifices." That became wholly evident in his behavior during the Revolution, characterized as it was by indecision and wavering and by "too great a readiness" to compromise with, and even embrace, the British position. Franklin's failure to rise to the occasion of national crisis was indicative of his lack of "severe integrity" and "disinterested patriotism." It was simply wrong, then, the *Review* concluded, to rank Franklin as a father of the nation or a visionary of the American future. Rather, as someone who "regards man principally as being of this life, with certain natural wants and desires," Franklin represented the banal pursuit of profane success.[48]

A review of the ten-volume collection of Franklin's works recently edited by Jared Sparks that appeared in the *North American Review* almost forty years later offered little disagreement on the facts. "The pervading trait of Franklin's character was allegiance to the Practical," it observed, an allegiance that found expression in a consistent neglect of idealistic and intellectual subjects. But rather than the source of moral failure, such pragmatism was identified as the commendable portent of modern utility. Franklin had imbibed the New England values of "self-dependence" and "self-control" while wisely dispensing with the inflexible habits and narrow vision of Puritan culture. The result was uniquely cosmopolitan: "Commerce one moment and a *jeu d'esprit* the next, advice to a Yankee tradesman and a bagatelle for a Parisian lady, seem equally congenial themes; a state paper and a proverb, allegory and statistics, the way to save money and the way to form a government." Ambition and moral integrity no longer constituted an opposition in Franklin's gestalt, which is what recommended him as an archetype of industrial-age consensus. Of course, there were still blemishes, particularly of a sexual nature. But these were insignificant when compared to "the silent dignity with which he was content, amid the inevitable attacks, and even insults, misrepresentations, and sneers." Such modesty, in fact, was one of Franklin's most admirable character traits. It allowed him to recognize that "happiness was the aggregate of small satisfactions," just as fortune was "the reward of assiduity." This is what then turned him into a true "American philosopher." As such, Franklin's documentation of his own rise "from poor mechanic to statesman and philosopher" was no less than "a triumph of self-culture."[49]

Boston's sesquicentennial celebration of Franklin's birth consequently featured a banner saluting the "Dry Goods clerk, 1727" in reference to the *Autobiography*'s account of copying letters, keeping the books, attending the store, and even demanding a commission on sales. Franklin, the archetype of self-making, became the seminal merchant clerk as well, an occupation that proved a propitious stepping-stone to future success, including a career as founding father. In fact, Franklin's industrial-era standing rested no less on his role as a founding son, for the autobiographical drama actually begins with young Ben's escape from the "Harsh and tyrannical Treatment" of his brother James, to whom he was apprenticed by his parents. "I took upon me to assert my Freedom," Franklin wrote of his subsequent arrival to New York in a precocious version of what became the nineteenth century's ubiquitous trope of forging one's own path in life, "near 300 Miles from home, a Boy of but 17, without the least Recommendation to or Knowledge of any Person in the Place, and with very little Money in my Pocket."[50]

"I wish I was like him," George Cayley wrote in his diary in 1844, by which time Franklin's self-made narrative of self-making had become a favorite gift book in the United States. The text's immense popularity was revealing, in fact, of biography's general emergence as a vehicle of self-instruction in which the private experiences of others, organized into a conventional drama of linear coherence and causality, functioned as a worthy object of study, and emulation, another of the era's oeuvre of behavior manuals. There is no history, Emerson was even led to declare, "only biography," while T. S. Arthur underlined the importance of spreading "the histories of our self-made men . . . before us that we may know the way they came up from the ranks of the people." Those histories translated self-knowledge into "useful knowledge," casting the individual into a mass phenomenon, or "individualism." James Brewster, a carriage manufacturer from Connecticut, consequently advised the "Young Men of New Haven" to "always keep in your rooms some standard works, the first of which was Franklin," readily available for "frequent reference." Brewster himself read Franklin in the most apposite manner, namely, an hour each day after work.[51]

Autobiography proved even more relevant to such cultural work. It was, in fact, a novel literary form, and even a new word—Franklin had referred to his own memoir as a "Recollection"—which replaced such older styles of self-reflection as the confession or the conversion narrative. Those earlier genres of personal experience were dedicated to discovering a consonance between the author's life and the eternal laws of being originating outside of that life. Autobiography, in contrast, presented a subject who had no recourse to any reality preceding his own. The form belonged, as such, to modernity's divorce of truth from a saintly realm and its relocation in the here and now, where it became a function of vernacular experience instead of divine revelation and accessible to anyone willing to interrogate the antecedents and consequences of his own actions. This necessarily made personal life into a highly fluid event since the autobiographical narrative invariably rested on the disparity between what one once had been and had since become. In facing the inherent uncertainties of the future, in other words, the autobiographer effectively tamed them—the drama was explicit proof of that—and so established himself as the sovereign author of his own life. This turned him into a Cartesian hero, not because he aspired to lead an exemplary life—there was nothing new about that—but because the exemplum was no longer the work of God but of one's own imagination, an "exercise of myself," as Benjamin Foster referred to his own diary writing, which was something of an autobiographical working draft.[52]

Such exercises constituted a "bold and arduous Project," Franklin himself testified. Horace Greeley echoed that claim in an essay on "Self-Made Men" appended to James Parton's *Life and Times of Benjamin Franklin* in 1865. Franklin's "service to mankind," Greeley asserted, was most perfectly realized in the systematic record he kept of his youthful mistakes. "I was surpriz'd to find myself so much fuller of Faults than I had imagined," Franklin had acknowledged in his *Autobiography*, for instance. That very interrogation was a fundamental condition for then guiding subsequent efforts at self-improvement. It was indeed a bold act requiring far greater personal courage than anything to be witnessed on the field of battle, Greeley added, which was no empty cliché in 1865.[53]

Franklin transcribed his self-making into ledger form by means of a method of his own invention, elucidated in that passage from the *Autobiography* which provoked so much indignation on the part of the *North American Review* in 1818. I compiled "a little Book," Franklin explained, "in which I allotted a Page for each of the Virtues":

> I rul'd each Page with red Ink, so as to have seven Columns, one for each Day of the Week, marking each Column with a Letter for the Day. I cross'd these Columns with thirteen red lines, marking the Beginning of each Line with the first Letter of one of the Virtues.

In filling out the corresponding cell with "a little black Spot," Franklin was able to create a running account of his respective success or failure in performing any given virtue on any given day. He could then evaluate his character by a glance at the page, or sequence of pages, which revealed "at any given time the true state of each and all the accounts [that] may at any time be easily, speedily, and distinctly comprehended and known," as Frederick Beck had described the practical goal of bookkeeping in the *Young Accountant's Guide*, and which proved equally relevant to Franklin's accumulation of personal capital. No wonder Max Weber identified Franklin as a prophet of capitalism, and Charles Baudelaire less flatteringly referred to "the inventor of the ethics of the shop-counter."[54]

Lemuel Shattuck, a leading educator from Concord, Massachusetts, and "a good specimen of a self-made man" in his own right, adapted Franklin's taxonomy to his *Scholar's Daily Journal*, patented in 1842, for exhibiting "at one view attendance, character, and intellectual progress during each month." Shattuck's field of rows and columns was arranged on a typographed folio that resembled the manuscript blanks of the state census, obviating the need for anyone to rule his own sheets. Nevertheless, the *Daily Journal* closely recapitulated Franklin's original method. Each page was subdivided into a standard grid for tracking personal performance. Supplementary columns were included that kept the running totals. All the pertinent data would be recorded, what's more, by the pupil himself, who thus assumed direct responsibility for plotting his own successes and failures. "The very consciousness that a person has to make entries in his book of every thing that he does," Shattuck wrote in explaining the logic that informed his system—and self-making more generally—"keeps his attention alive to what he ought to do; and the act of making these entries is the best possible training to produce active and painstaking habits."[55]

"Journal" was, in fact, an old word that originally referred to a day's labor or to a measure of land and, by implication, to a close connection between the two. That relationship was severed by capitalist revolution, of course. But Franklin and Shattuck both suggested that journalizing and laboring remained highly relevant to each other if it was the individual's own life that

FORM OF THE PAGES.

TEMPERANCE.

Eat not to dulness : drink not to elevation.

	Sunday.	Monday.	Tuesday.	Wed'ay.	Thur'ay.	Friday.	Sat'ay.
Temp'ce.							
Silence.	*	*		*		*	
Order.	*	*	*		*	*	*
Resol'n.		*				*	
Frug'ty.		*				*	
Indus'y.			*				
Sincerity							
Justice.							
Moder'n.							
Clean'ss.							
Tran'ity.							
Chastity.							
Hum'y.							

* This little book is dated *Sunday, July 1st*, 1733.
*16

Franklin's table of virtues.

was now being produced. For that purpose, William Alcott recommended to readers of his *Young Man's Guide* that they each "carry a small blank book and pencil in their pockets" for the purpose of recording "any interesting fact" as it occurs, or, alternatively, for writing it up in one's "first spare moment." Such documentary habits were essential since "an event of perhaps no present importance may through the mist of years be magnified into something worthy of a moment's notice," as Benjamin Shillaber acknowledged in a New Year's Day entry he posted into his diary. These "copy-book maxims," in fact, rendered the personal journal into a model of empirical rigor for developing "a strict regard to truth in all you do." William Hoffman embraced that same spirit in his own diary's inaugural entry, in which he outlined a plan to keep "a strict account of the transactions and occurrences of each day—Good—Bad—or otherwise—believing that such a source if rigidly adhered to will be highly beneficial in the end."[56]

The Daily Journal of																								in the					

The table is a blank "Scholars Daily Journal" form with columns for Date, Character (Attendance M./A., Industry, Behavior), The highest Credits given or required (Reading, Spelling, Writing, Arithmetic, Grammar, Geography, History, Algebra, Geometry, Music, Astronomy, Philosophy, French, Latin, Greek, Composition, Declamation, Extra Lessons), Daily Totals (Recitations, Highest Credits given, Highest Credits received, Hours' Study at Home), and Age (yrs., mo., dys., Remarks). Rows numbered 1–31.

At bottom:
No. Recitations in . . . . .
Highest Credits given for .
No. Credits received . . . .
Rank number in the Class .

School has kept, half days.
Tardy, times, (excused .)
Absent, times, (excused .)

Total monthly Credits. For Exercises, . For Character, . For both, . Deduct for Errors, . Balance, . Rank No.
The School contains Classes or Divisions. I am No. in the Class, or Division, which contains members.
The school hours are from to A. M.; and from to P. M.

I have examined and this record.   I have reëxamined and it.
                                    Teacher.   *Parent.*

Lemuel Shattuck's *Scholars Daily Journal.*

"We need more and better knowledge of ourselves, and of our powers, their nature and their limit, their uses and their relations to the outer world," Edward Jarvis declared at the ground-breaking ceremony for the new hospital for the insane in Northampton. Diaries were especially effective in generating that kind of knowledge. They helped to determine whether one's life was advancing in a proper direction or had been diverted, and whether such diversions were the result of false steps or of external forces, the fruits of private consciousness, that is, or public constraints. In thus bringing one's behavior into a "regular course of account," the diary functioned as something of a management tool, or a "book of memorandums" in which one posted regular notations to oneself on matters of ongoing significance, establishing an archive for future reference and action. "Use the pen," *Hunt's* advised in a separate but analogous context, for "it forces you to methodize your thoughts." The diary rested on these same principles of paperwork, which cast the diarist as his own clerk, administrating a system of record keeping and review that aided him in achieving a "command of the subject." Nothing is likelier to keep a man within compass, as T. S. Arthur paraphrased the British reformer Samuel Smiles paraphrasing John Locke, "than having constantly before his eyes the state of his affairs in a regular course of account."[57]

If the diary served as a personalized accounts current, then the diarist could be said to be carrying on a debt relationship with himself. "One month of the new year gone and in what have I improved?" Samuel Munson wrote in taking stock soon after beginning a new job at a Boston dry-goods store. "This is the first day of the coming six months," Edward Thomas similarly noted on July 1, 1853, dissatisfied with "the little intellectual progress" he had made over the previous half year. "If my health is spared I promise that the next six months will be more creditable." Such entries functioned like so many promissory notes in which one undertook an obligation to build up and improve upon one's holdings, namely, one's self. As in any system of credit, moreover, the present was acted on in the name of the future in hopes of reducing the radical uncertainty of a life in which nothing any longer blocked your path, checked your progress, or clogged your steps. Glib pronouncements regarding the pedagogical value of a balanced ledger in teaching the young what they needed to learn to become responsible adults therefore acquired a deep resonance.[58]

Thomas Tyler, who clerked for a druggist in Connecticut, affirmed such parallels between personal diaries and account books that refused to add up if anyone tried to make them tell anything but the whole story. "It is often the case that we hesitate about recording some action or thought because it will apt to offend the wiser ears of our future selves," Tyler observed. That was a bad plan, "for when the future comes, if we recollect nothing else of the days when the journal was written we are sure to remember the fact that we practiced deception in writing it." This logic spurred a young Cincinnati lawyer named Rutherford Hayes to purchase a blank book in 1851 with the intention of filling it with expansive posts about "persons, thoughts . . .

and events, great and small." These would be of far greater value to him
than the "mere logbook" that had served his previous attempt at journalizing and which such experts on self-making as William Alcott criticized as
morally indifferent. "Pages, instead of a few lines" were required for one to
effectively become an object of self-knowledge and, as such, the subject of
one's own life. And, indeed, Rutherford's more comprehensive entries soon
proved their worth, revealing just "how aimless are many of my efforts . . .
and how weakly the firmest resolves are pushed towards their results." With
his personal shortfalls thus exposed, he was in a position to undertake remedial steps. Upon reviewing his very first post, for instance, Rutherford
already appended a critical assessment of its slovenly grammar: "Must try
to mend that, too." Benjamin Foster likewise discovered indications in his
diary of being on a "false track." An avid reader of himself, Benjamin's journal "plainly" revealed that something in his everyday practice had deviated
from his original plan. The first matter requiring correction, he soon concluded in an admirably recursive moment of self-study, was none other than
the manner in which he kept his diary, which he adjudged to be overly affected and even "garish," and so incapable of generating a reliable account of
his life.[59]

"It is worthy of observation, that we are able to discern not only what we
already are, but what we may become, to see in ourselves germs and promises of a growth to which no bounds can be set," William Ellery Channing
exclaimed of this knowledge economy of the self. Bradley Cumings honed
such techniques of observation by creating a running subject index that facilitated his access to past posts. How appropriate it was, too, that Charles
French commenced his personal journal in the same composition book that
had previously served him for penmanship lessons, or that Benjamin Shillaber kept his diary in a former business ledger, personal entries filling up the
columns originally established for recording the day's financial transactions,
all of which led Thoreau to complain that "I cannot easily buy a blank-book
to write thoughts in; they are commonly ruled for dollars and cents." Like
those ledgers, in fact, some diaries were designed to exert typographic control over their author. James Blake devoted twice as much space to summarizing each Sunday's sermon because the formal divisions of the printed week
assigned the Sabbath a double field, which he dutifully filled. Others pedanti-
cally stayed within the lines, completing each day's entry just as the page ran
out. But most diarists preferred to author their lives on an ostensibly "blank
page," unhampered by any form of predestination, so to speak. The resulting
spontaneity seemed to offer the best opportunity for autonomous reflection.[60]

The diary thus served as a singular method for processing the raw materials of existence into the building blocks of consciousness, the writing hand and ruminating mind transposing experience into a coherent narrative of personal development. Upon closer examination, however, that turns out to not be the case. The diary—again, not unlike the ledger—actually operates as an insistently proleptic device for constructing and reconstructing oneself in a process that resembled art more than nature. If business accounts were a tool for documenting reality which, in fact, produce that reality, the diary did the same. Written in the present, reporting on the past, and addressing the future, the journal conflated all three tenses. Each discrete entry consequently functioned as a synchronic event, or autonomous variable, arranged within a balance sheet that suspended the relentless movement of daily life in order to assess its value, those assessments then directing the diarist in shaping that life to begin with.

William Hoffman, for example, often wrote in his diary on Sunday afternoons while "the boys are dozing on their beds, etc." It was a commendable expression of self-culture and William was justifiably proud, comparing his conscientious journalizing to the patently unproductive leisure of his fellow clerks. The fact of the matter is, William wrote on Sundays because he had far less opportunity to do so during the week. His journal entries were not, as such, unmediated transliterations of direct experience. They were processed data, often based on notes made in real time that could be reviewed and organized before being inscribed at a later date, not unlike the process William followed in copying sales figures from daybook to stock book. There was, in other words, far less epistemological innocence at play than the diary's strict linear pagination suggested. Instead of constituting a "straight-forward" recapitulation of objective reality imprinting itself, *a posteriori*, on the tabula rasa of individual consciousness, the diary operated on the basis of the opposite teleology, one in which no event preceded its recounting. The journalizing of one's life, that is to say, informed that life. "Each is at the same time means and end," Marx observed of the circuits of market exchange, "and attains his end only in so far as he becomes a means, and becomes a means only in so far as he posits himself as end." He could just as well have been describing the phenomenology of the diary. The present, which ostensibly matched chronometric movement itself, appeared to be mediating a "dialogue" between past and future. But because the present is what writes the past, which then informs our actions in the future, it is no less true to say that the past and the future became mediators of the present. The diarist, as such, established a sense of mastery over his fate by continually resetting the relationship between past, present, and future—and vice versa—and so turning his life into a sequence of calculations in a production economy devoted to making the self. The individual was not a natural event needing to be brought under control, in other words. Like the market, he had to be invented in the first place. It is not preposterous to even ask if one's experience produced the diary or whether the diary produced experience, although it should be rather obvious at this point that both conclusions are equally pertinent.[61]

Robinson Crusoe—whose "rash and immoderate Desire of rising faster than the Nature of the thing admitted" prompted him to defy parental authority, and eventually emerge as a hero of classical economics, his stranded existence bracketed off from all exogenous social obligations—helps illustrate this dynamic. Crusoe scrupulously kept a journal throughout his years on the island. It was especially important for him to maintain a careful record of the Sabbath during his forced absence from civilization. At one point in the story, a bout of fever suggests to the reader that Crusoe might, in fact, be marking the wrong day. Upon further reflection, it becomes equally clear that the question of when Sunday actually falls is entirely immaterial. As sovereign of his own universe, Robinson Crusoe was in a position to rehearse the creation all over again, which meant that any seventh day so designated could serve as Sunday, as long as the measure was consistent. Such a man-made chronology did not make his observation of the Sabbath any less real, or effective, in guiding his actions. That same ontology informed the modern diary. Its strict recounting of daily experience, resting on the natural passage of time, constituted a wholly artificial palimpsest shaped by the needs of the diarist to draft and redraft, erase and revise himself. That artifice was neither quixotic or arbitrary. The ability to arrange and rearrange one's experience—in a manner reminiscent of the Brown Brothers' creation of a suspense account for bad debts—was an authentic expression of subjectivity. There was no truer account of personal sovereignty.[62]

Man is a changeful being, as Benjamin Foster testified in his own diary after he finished reading Emerson's "Self-Reliance." "Change in an individual," what's more, Benjamin then continued, "never ceases till he ceases, and that is never." Such maxims explain why "plastic" became a common expression in the literature written for American youth at midcentury. The fact is, "I" had shown itself to be a thoroughly plastic event, resting on the same operative values that governed the market, namely, the ability to remove knowledge from its immediate context and rearrange it in order to enhance performance. Paperwork thus proved as relevant to making persons as to making profits, which is also why the two great production projects of the day—the making of the self and the making of the market—became so closely intertwined, formalized in the two most significant neologisms of the age, individualism and capitalism. "Economic production and the production of subjectivity . . . are indissociable," Maurizio Lazaratto has since observed of the human condition in our own neoliberal moment.[63] Nineteenth-century liberals already recognized that dynamic, which is why the self-made man, despite his best efforts to inhabit a space outside the commodity system, became synonymous with *Homo economicus.*

4

Desk Diseases

In his *Recollections of a Lifetime*, S. G. Goodrich cataloged the "demagogism and democracy, dyspepsia and transcendentalism, vegetarianism and spiritualism" that had been serially embraced by the American public ever "since old federalism went down." Dyspepsia is the least familiar of Goodrich's litany of systems for reconstituting order in an age of industrial upheaval. It was, in fact, a common diagnosis for a range of digestive ailments. These were symptomatic, in turn, of a general outbreak of nervous disease principally affecting sedentary men furthest removed from the agrarian tenets of household mutuality and hard work out of doors. "Their digestion is bad, their respiration imperfect, and their brain languid," Edward Jarvis typically noted in a lecture on "the necessity of the study of physiology" of those merchants and their clerks, together with lawyers, industrialists, and students, who chronically employed their minds at the expense of their bodies.[1]

The outstanding trait of such modern nervousness, the cultural historian Peter Logan has observed, is its tendency to talk, "especially to talk about itself." That chatter was to be compared to public conversation fifty years earlier, which had been entirely mute regarding the "particulars which might not be discussed to ears polite," as a Boston physician now observed in the 1850s. In contemporary society, in contrast, everyone openly acknowledged that "men have bowels, loose, or costive," and that the diagnostic history of their consumptions was a matter of common concern. Indeed, the status of one's constipations, or, alternatively, one's incontinence, together with a thick nosology of additional headaches, dizziness, deteriorating eyesight, liver dysfunction, deafness, piles, and failing bladders collectively listed under the rubric of "desk diseases" in a volume bearing the same name that first appeared

in London in 1826, emerged as a somatic bildungsroman of the price humanity was forced to pay for abandoning the productive arts.[2]

The bilious physiologies of the desk bound which were "unknown to our
forefathers" did not just signal a world turned upside down, however. Desk
diseases also helped to put things right, doing so, what's more, on the same
volatile terms that so upset the social order to begin with. "Every human being
is responsible for the care of his own health, and the preservation of his own
life," the prolific Edward Jarvis explained in *Primary Physiology for Schools*,
which was representative of a growing corpus of medical primers introduced
into the common school curriculum after 1830. These instructed young and
old alike that illness was no longer to be considered a heavenly punishment
visited upon mankind in retribution for its sins but rather, a condition "of our
own begetting" whose cure would issue from the same source, that is, would
be no less of our own begetting. "Knowledge is what we want," John Gunn
accordingly announced in his *Domestic Medicine*, an antimonopolist tract
dedicated to Andrew Jackson and reprinted in a hundred editions by 1870
that aspired to turn every citizen into "his own physician." Apprised of the
methods for treating an extensive roster of common and less common ills,
as well as the proper manner of eating, sleeping, bathing, and exercising, individuals would learn to minister their own bodies and, in so doing, secure the
welfare of the body politic. Nervous disorder, as such, brought a welcome dose
of organic certainty to a solipsistic age of self-making men in which success
had become its own reward.[3]

I Make Myself Sick

William Hoffman succumbed to dyspepsia "in its worst forms" after moving
to Manhattan. Edward Tailer was increasingly preoccupied with a sharp pain
he traced to an optic nerve "being strained and tasked too much by the miserable blinding light which finds its way into our counting room." Robert Graham complained of enfeebling headaches that came on after long days spent
copying out the correspondence, comparable to the "torturing headache and
wretched nausea" Allen Richmond attributed to the same labor-intensive office routine. Charles French's eyes, meanwhile, swelled up so grievously when
he finished posting his store's back journals, "that I was unable to leave the
house for a week, and . . . obliged to wear a covering over them, and keep
them constantly closed."[4]

Hoffman, Tailer, Graham, Richmond, and French were all suffering from
a bad case of capitalism, their infirmities a direct outcome of the "fast walking,

fast driving, fast eating and drinking, fast bargains, [and] fast business" endemic to an age of fast property, as the *Boston Medical and Surgical Journal* determined. Modern man, Catharine Beecher further explained of the era's epidemic of nervous ailments in her *Physiology and Calisthenics*, his "brain throbbing with excitement and circulation all disarranged," inhabited a world of overstimulation that invariably drove him in search of more stimulation. It was a vicious cycle that turned his person into something resembling a speculative inflation that must, sooner or later, lead to a disastrous run on his depleted resources and then to general collapse. This was why "our fathers and grandfathers" enjoyed far better health than we, Beecher admonished her readers. And that was also why William Hoffman eventually announced that he had cured his recurrent bouts of constipation with a visit to the country, for only there could one's "natural vigor" be repaired and restored.[5]

Hardy men could still be found in the western states, the *Atlantic Monthly* confirmed, and in upper New England as well. They were constitutionally and philosophically immune to the pandemic of disorder overtaking all those for whom "that which was once esteemed manly is forgotten in the rivalry for [the] whitest, softest hands," as the *New-York Daily Times* invoked the spreading incapacities of the sedentary classes. "The sorrowful companionship with disease and anticipations of an early grave" soon followed. The oblique angle of the head as it bent over the paperwork, the *Medical and Surgical Journal* added in greater clinical detail lifted verbatim from *Desk Diseases*, obstructed the flow of blood to the brain, resulting in recurrent headaches that were further aggravated by the fastidiously arranged cravats prescribed by office etiquette. Apoplexy, palsy, and delirium then signaled the next stage of decline.[6]

Was it any wonder that at the end of a workday spent in a closed room filling out the accounts, breathing "an atmosphere . . . contaminated by being again and again taken into the lungs"—in effect, poisoning themselves—those young men forced to "vegetate behind the salesman's counter in a dry-goods establishment" or "tied to the pen in a counting-room" became so irritable, their tongues turning white and furred, and their stomachs distended as dinner lay there "like a lump of lead"? "Performed little or nothing bodily," William Hoffman testily confessed in reference to his own desk-bound habitus. The resulting languor and dizziness, weariness and confusion, flushed cheeks, aching heads, unnatural thirst, "and the thousand excuses to get out of doors" were all indicative of the enervating grip of a money economy and the softened manner of an indoor way of life devoted to mental calculations. "Look at our young men of fortune," *Harper's* importuned in a discussion of effeminacy and ill health. "Were there ever such . . . a pale pasty-faced, narrow chested, spindle-shanked, dwarfed race?" Even such innovations as

Dr. Oliver Halsted's "anti-dyspeptic chair," patented in 1844 to ease the afflic-
tion of persons "compelled to be sedentary" by approximating the motion of
equestrian exercise, were a stopgap solution, at best.[7]

Nature therefore continues to leave her mark, the *Massachusetts Teacher*
noted with discernible relief, manifest "in every pain we bear; in every hacking
cough; in every halting footstep; by every apprehension of approaching death."
No one could escape the facticity of their own body, which meant that the
medically indifferent individual was fated to suffer the consequences that "his
multiplied aberrations from the laws of [health] are sure to bring upon him,"
Andrew Combe declared in *Principles of Physiology*. According to those same
principles, disease was not an autonomous entity following a discrete path of
development and reenacting the same array of symptoms in each host while
spreading through the population. This only became the dominant model of
pathology after the discovery of germs later in the century, at which point it
also provoked the protest of social critics worried about the resulting erosion
of personal responsibility for one's health. Before that happened, "the realm of
causation in medicine was not distinguishable from the realm of meaning in
society generally," as Charles Rosenberg observed of a therapeutic ethos deeply
embedded in social experience. Andrew Combe accordingly urged readers of
his *Principles of Physiology* to "trace the connexion between conduct in life and
broken health" by identifying the causes of whatever was making them sick. In
the anatomical lexicon of the day which had replaced older notions of bodily
humors, that connection was located in the spine "and its innumerable ramifications, called nerves." The nerves, the *Massachusetts Teacher* further professed,
were what linked "physical and moral law," tethering corporeal atrophy to mental corruption in a causal symbiosis that was to be recognized in the Greek ety-
mology for disease—*pathos*—which encompassed psychic experience as well.
Circulation of the blood, the vitality of the limbs, and the specific operations
of the internal organs were all incorporated into a holistic model of the body
that was inseparable from the circumstances and habits—or "constitution"—of
the same person's way of life, which is why Edward Jarvis could so seamlessly
tie bad digestion, imperfect respiration, and a languid brain to the deadening
routinization of indoor employments. "The ancients were right in the supposi-
tion that an unsound body is incompatible with a sound mind," the *Annals of
American Education* affirmed. That reciprocity between body and soul—which
informed such other popular diagnostic models of the day as mesmerism, spiritualism, physiognomy, and phrenology—effectively cast the individual rather
than any particular ailment as the primary subject of medical attention.[8]

And so, alongside public health crusades organized by a state administration increasingly concerned with mass pauperization and the deteriorating

conditions of crowded tenements and stultifying factories, a second medical project for the masses was undertaken in these years. This latter effort required the self-making class to attend to its own ills with no less urgency than it devoted to society's less disciplined hordes, albeit in a distinctly different manner. William Hoffman gave expression to that difference when recording the daily toll of New York City's cholera victims in his diary during the summer of 1849, and immediately following up those figures with a far more alarmed account of his own digestive travails and the associated efforts "to rid myself" of such loathsome costiveness. In fact, cholera was no less symptomatic of the age than were William's desk diseases, traveling the same circuit of canals, railroads, and metropolitan entrepôts along which the era's growing inventories of merchandise were reaching market. Cholera, what's more, attacked bodies made especially vulnerable by "the customs and circumstances of artificial life," Sylvester Graham noted in reference to the growing number of urban denizens caught in the enfeebling grip of industrial poverty. But cholera also constituted a highly focused event, confined to foreigners and the poor, as the new "vital statistics" persistently showed. Such plebeian crises were medical emergencies affecting specific swathes of population and geography, and doing so within bounded spans of time, all in marked contrast to the intimate, enduring spaces occupied by nervous disease. Henry Ward Beecher bravely documented the terrifying results: "Clutching his rags with spasmodic grasp, his swoln tongue lolling from a blackened mouth, his bloodshot eyes glaring and rolling, he shrieks oaths; now blaspheming God, and now imploring him." There was little point in assigning such victims sovereign responsibility for their physiologies. Instead, public sanitation measures were mobilized to rescue them, turning these epidemics into a paternalistic quarantine of marginalized drunks, gamblers, and whores who lacked any semblance of control over their own selves and were perishing by the thousands, or into essentialist campaigns for bolstering the physical stamina of the nation's laboring classes. This was to be contrasted to the establishment of a durable, neurotic regime based on personal hygiene and self-diagnosis. Plagues came and went, in other words, but frayed nerves were a permanent, even normal, presence in a market society that obliged individuals to exert their own private efforts at recovery. While cholera required the centralized administration of social welfare, desk diseases were left, by their nature, to the private administration of each person.[9]

In a discussion of indigestion and the body politic, *Harper's New Monthly Magazine* thus made note of the propertied class's growing habit of "continually feeling its pulse or looking at its tongue, and asking the doctors what can be the matter." Such behavior provoked the scorn of medical circles who dismissed their anxieties as a rampant form of hypochondria. "The attention of all, sick or well, is turned to their health," one physician remonstrated in a series of essays attacking William Alcott, who, together with Sylvester Graham, founded the American Physiological Association in 1837, the first organization of its kind in the world dedicated to disseminating medical knowledge to the public at large. Motivated by an ethos of professionalization seeking to carve out greater authority for formal expertise, these critics accused Alcott and his allies of having "caused and aggravated, beyond calculation, the class of complaints which they were intended to prevent and remove." The result was an obsessive attention on the part of all persons to their internal organs, their diet, and to "whatever concerns their bodies." But such criticism failed to recognize how important the spread of disease was to the very health of the social body in an age of revolutionary upheaval, and how its aggravation was a reliable sign that the public was becoming an obedient subject of diagnosis and an enthusiastic subscriber to the regimens of recovery.[10]

Nor did anyone have to be actively diagnosed in order to become the subject of disease, for whoever ignored the rules of health would "do well to recollect that they are constantly in danger." The whole of the population, in other words, inhabited a universe of chronic illness, which is why "obedience brings its sure reward, and disobedience is followed by its inevitable punishment," as Edward Jarvis declared in endorsing Sylvester Graham's equation of health with self-government and disease with its opposite. The body emerged as a metonym of market volatility, "continually wasting away, and at the same time constantly being renewed by the nourishment which they are receiving, so that, after a time, we come to possess bodies which do not contain a particle of their original matter," the *Young American's Magazine of Self-Improvement* editorialized. This cycle of degeneration and recovery offered everyone the opportunity to personally address the pathologies of the age. Thomas Wren Ward reminded himself each day in his diary, for instance, that "my great object now should be to live right and watch and control myself—and improve—avoiding temptation—know thyself." That self-knowledge was dedicated, first and foremost, to his health, which, as Thomas well understood, was ever subject to crisis and collapse if neglected. This is what detached disease from the metaphysics of damnation, reinventing it as an organic sanction against immoderate and irresponsible behavior, an antidote to the "ambition, avarice, anger, and other passions" that Thomas Hobbes identified as the greatest threat to a society organized around self-interest. "GOD sends *acute* diseases," Benjamin Waterhouse, a professor of medicine at Harvard University, consequently observed, "but *chronic* disorders we create ourselves." That insight turned illness into an ethical as much as a somatic event, privileging each person's

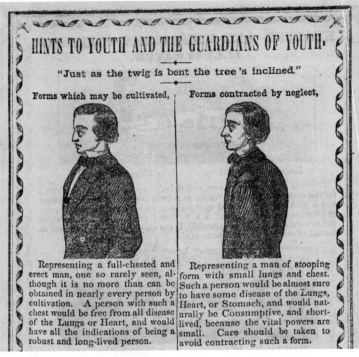

From Jane Taylor's *Wouldst Know Thyself*, 1858.

ability to know himself and, in so doing, obligating each to then act upon such knowledge. The morbid appetite for money that bred so many "self-made victims," Whitman maliciously quipped, would thus be contained by turning the tables on personal ambition. Individuals would resolve the crises of their own making by practicing the same personal prerogative that made their individualism a source of concern to begin with. In this respect, illness provided essential training for the proper exercise of one's sovereignty, an ideal occasion for rehabilitating authority in a liberal age.[11]

Debilitated, degenerate bodies were not, it followed, the exclusive possession of the age's subaltern classes, a means of marking and excluding black, female, or proletarian "Others" from public life.[12] Alongside that well-studied medicalization of deviance, the opposite dynamic proved no less prevalent in capitalist life, namely, the medicalization of normality. The "midnight horrors" of dyspepsia emerged as a near-universal experience for model citizens of the commercial republic, those striving, confident subjects who were nevertheless consumed with their own corporeal selves and the attendant risks to their health. The discourse of America's propertied classes was inundated with melodramatic displays of personal debilitation, suggesting that their social prerogative did not rest on an abstracted persona purportedly immune from the rampant agitations of the times, as numerous historians and theorists have argued over the years in seeking to identify the source of male, white, and moneyed privilege in what was otherwise supposed to be an age of democracy.[13]

Indeed, the massive outbreak of pallid countenances and wasting bodies—when the "sweat of thy brow" no longer attested to a well-turned field readied for planting but to money drafts coming due while buyers continued to hang off—was the setting for an adamant performance of recovery by sedentary types intent on overcoming the very threat they posed to themselves, and to society at large. Personal ambition would prove capable of treating the disorders of its own making, which, of course, perfectly matched its conceits. "What is the best government but that which teaches us to govern ourselves," Daniel Child, a treasurer for a locomotive works, wrote in his commonplace book. Chronic illness served as such a learning experience, prompting individuals to recognize the dangers inherent in their individuality while guiding their own efforts at recovery. The bourgeoisie did not, as such, renounce their bodies but most insistently lived in them, and through them, and so proved far less immaculate—and far more hysterical—than has heretofore been recognized. In an inversion of terms suited to these revolutionary times, one had to be sick in order to become healthy.[14]

Stomach

Paperwork prevented one from purging with regularity since long hours at the desk weakened those muscles in the stomach wall necessary for expelling the contents of the bowels. The ensuing constipation became a subject of widespread conversation, and consternation, because daily evacuations were indispensable to good health. When the equilibrium between the body's input and outflow was disrupted, in other words, disorder invariably set in.[15]

Emetics, cathartics, diuretics, and bleeding were the traditional methods for unclogging obstructions and restoring liquidity and balance. To that end, even leeches were to be found in the battery of nostrums prescribed in the pages of Desk Diseases. But such "heroic medicine," as the dominant therapeutic doctrine in the early days of the republic came to be called, gave way by midcentury to a far less intrusive regime based on perspiration, ventilation,

and diet. These were all self-administered practices and so better suited to
the individual's assumption of political and medical jurisdiction over himself. Walt Whitman celebrated the appearance of this new "art of health," for
instance, which replaced the "old drugging up and bleeding system" and assigned everyone exclusive command over their corporeality. "Frequent lavations of the whole body in pure water," and not just those parts exposed
to public view, thus became essential for effecting a reliable flow of excretions out of the body. By cleansing the skin and opening up the pores—with
a shower bath at home, or at one of the city's washhouses, or by swimming
in the Hudson River, where William Hoffman saved the twenty-five cents
charged at the public baths—twenty-two ounces of waste could be discharged
on the average every day. "There is a whole chest of medicine in a pail of cold
water," contemporaries accordingly proclaimed, whose effect was enhanced
by then drying oneself off with a coarse towel that further stimulated the
skin. No wonder bathing classes at the Mercantile Library were so heavily
enrolled.[16]

And yet the age's recurrent bouts of incontinence could not be resolved
by such superficial attention to one's apertures and orifices. "Due management of the stomach" presented a far more effective treatment plan for gastrointestinal crisis, capable as it was of reestablishing equilibrium in both
individual bodies and in the body politic. This was because the stomach was
"more immediately under the control of the will" than any other organ, which
transformed the digestive process into a matrix of diet, desire, and discipline,
making it the Archimedean hub of personal volition. There was no better measure of an individual's willingness to govern himself, or of the painful price
for failing to do so.[17]

"Over-eating" was thus recognized as "one of the greatest sins and causes
of suffering of the age," the American Health Convention determined. This
was not a particularly modern sin, of course. Humanity's long history of as-
cetic renunciation organized around food makes that clear. Nevertheless, appetite acquired a novel significance in an age of "cheap bread, and plenty of it,"
for once surpluses became a regular outcome of man's productive efforts and
accumulation replaced scarcity as the driving logic of labor, economy was no
longer devoted to staving off privation. Industrial civilization gave birth to
a distinctly different material dilemma, one based on too much rather than
too little. Those who once ate in order to live now lived in order to eat, as was
observed of such revolutionary developments, leading Sylvester Graham to
sarcastically refer to modernity's "abundance of wretchedness and misery." It
was a pithy, and piqued, description of humanity's inverted relationship with
necessity now that the limits on men's appetites had been removed, resulting

in a "frightful and inexhaustible source of calamity," as John Gunn warned in *Domestic Medicine*. Thoreau typically raised the stakes by lamenting the loss of that "unelastic plank of famine" which had undergirded an older, transparent world of absolute value. Hunger, in such traditional terms, served as the main course on a fixed menu of restraint, exemplified by the virtue of necessity, the alimentary foundation of a natural justice in which the hands labored so that the mouth could eat.[18]

But that ethics of subsistence lost its salutary role once men decided that they were "not born to be miserable." The ensuing calamity proved especially frightful because abundance was more easily procured in America, "in the proportion of *five to one*," as Charles Caldwell estimated in his *Thoughts on Physical Education*. "Perhaps no people were ever so blessed in an ample supply of the means indispensable for human comfort," which is why pundits regularly fretted over a population gorging itself on midday dinners comprising two varieties of meat, bread, potatoes, gravies, pickles, and assortments of condiments, often followed by pudding, cheese, butter, pie, and more bread, and all consumed with a "steam engine rapidity." Even the poor could treat themselves to second and third dishes in America, it was observed. Tocqueville, who complained about the absence of wine from the dinner tables of the world's only democracy, was equally flabbergasted by the "sheer quantity of food that people somehow stuff down their gullets." Others dolefully kept watch over the popular taste for half-baked hotcakes saturated in butter, or those pastries that constituted the age's preeminent "instrument of self-destruction," corrupting the miller's snow-white bolts of purity. What purpose could it thus possibly serve, the *Massachusetts Teacher* rebuked the public, "to be able to cover our table with dishes of gold if the stomach is in a nausea at the thought of receiving food"? Americans, who should have been the healthiest people in Christendom as a result of the natural bounty of their vestal continent, were, for that very reason, the sickest.[19]

The modern "bread-nexus" obliged everyone to personally address the consequences of industrial progress by exercising willful control over their intake and, in so doing, curb the boundless stimulations of a market economy that was busily removing all other social and material constraints over the self. "As artificial wants multiply, the temptations increase," Horace Mann, William Ellery Channing's most eminent disciple, remarked of the general outcome of so much freedom and abundance. "Guards and securities must increase," Mann exhorted his audience, "or society will deteriorate." That is why five hundred works devoted to the human digestive system were already in print, the *Atlantic Monthly* reported in inventorying the public's growing interest in eating disorders, appetite having become a favorite parable for the perils of prosperity in such an "ease-loving age" sustained by turtle soups and lobster salads. As such, the stomach continued to play a central role in political economy, but instead of serving as the objective whip of necessity, it emerged as the subjective means of self-government.[20]

Wariness of excess drew on a tradition of country polemics directed against the corruptions of luxury, contrasted to the embracing influence of the "simple life of home." But capitalism had destroyed that home, together with its moral infrastructure of pecuniary frugality, thus democratizing—and Americanizing—the spicy foods and sensual indulgences long associated with aristocratic dissipation. Horace Bushnell might continue to celebrate the coarse virtue of the homespun palate, paying due homage to doughnuts from the pantry, hickory nuts from the chamber, and the smoothest apples from the cellar as essential ingredients of good digestion, "itself no small part of a character." But modern "abuses of cookery" were best contained by the disciplinary force of science. Thyme, cloves, cinnamon, nutmeg, pepper, ginger, mustard, horseradish, garlic, and onions were condemned not just for exciting culinary hankerings, in other words, but for retarding the digestive processes altogether, injuring the stomach "and through it the whole system," as the American Physiology Society explained. In contrast, the *gluten* offered by wheat, together with the *albumen* of eggs, the *casein* in one's milk, and the *fibrin* of animal flesh were identified as essential antidotes to such dangers, critical elements of a properly balanced diet that offered holistic protection to the body's internal systems. "What shall we eat?" and "How much shall we eat?" were matters no longer "beneath anyone's dignity," Edward Jarvis accordingly declared. A "natural diet" of "wholesome food," plainly prepared, certainly never fried, and systematically purged of all seasonings save for a pinch of salt and an occasional dash of vinegar would provide an effective anodyne not just for the turpitude of the intestinal canal but for industrial-age profligacy more generally, aiding citizens to rein in their penchant for more. The modern science of wealth was thus transmuted into "a science of renunciation," Marx wrote in belittling the bourgeoisie's nervous response to its own economic success. Ralph Waldo Emerson epitomized that anxious parsimony upon logging the net weight of his daily intake at meals and happily reporting on a "per diem" reduction from 14¼ to 12½ ounces within just a week.[21]

"*Eating*" is a fearful thing, *Putnam's Monthly* acknowledged, "and is becoming fearfully difficult." The onus fell, predictably enough, on those who devour "as much, or at least as substantial, food, as the farmer or day laborer" without having to. Anyone engaged in mental exertions, the *Boston Medical and Surgical Journal* explained, "must feed himself very differently from what he would if about to exert his muscles to their utmost capacity." George

57. Mean Time required for the Digestion of various Articles of Food in the Stomach.

Articles.	Preparation.	Hrs.	Min.	Articles.	Preparation.	Hrs.	Min.
Apples, sour, hard, .	Raw,	2	50	Corn, green, and beans, ... }	Boiled,	3	45
——— mellow,	Raw,	2		——— bread, ...	Baked,	3	15
———, sweet, do., .	Raw,	1	30	——— cake, ...	Baked,	3	
Aponeurosis,* . . .	Boiled,	3		Custard, ...	Baked,	2	45
Bass, striped, fresh,	Broiled,	3		Dumpling, apple, .	Boiled,	3	
Barley, ...	Boiled,	2		Ducks, domesticated,	Roasted	4	
Beans, pod, ...	Boiled,	2	80	———, wild, ...	Roasted	4	30
Beef, fresh, lean, rare,	Roasted,	3		Eggs, fresh, . . . }	Boiled hard,	3	30
———, dry,	Roasted,	3	30				
——— steak, ...	Broiled,	3		———, . . . }	Boiled soft,	3	
———, with salt only,	Boiled,	3	36	———, ...	Fried,	3	30
———, with mustard,	Boiled,	3	10	———, ...	Roasted,	2	15
———, fresh, lean, . .	Fried,	4		———, ...	Raw,	2	
———, old, hard, salted, ... }	Boiled,	4	15	———, whip'd,	Raw,	1	30
Beets, ...	Boiled,	3	45	Flounder, fresh, . .	Fried,	3	30
Brains, ...	Boiled,	1	45	Fowl, domestic, . .	Boiled,	4	
Bread, wheat, fresh,	Baked,	3	30	———, ...	Roasted,	4	
———, corn, ...	Baked,	3	15	Gelatine, ...	Boiled,	2	30
Butter, ...	Melted,	3	30	Goose, ...	Roasted,	2	30
Cabbage head, . . .	Raw,	2	30	Heart, ...	Fried,	4	
———, with vinegar, }	Raw,	2		Lamb, fresh, ...	Broiled,	2	30
———, ...	Boiled,	4	30	Liver, beef's, fresh,	Broiled,	2	
Cake, sponge, . . .	Baked,	2	30	Meat hashed with vegetables, . . . }	Warm'd,	2	30
Carrot, orange, . . .	Boiled,	3	15	Milk, ...	Boiled,	2	
Cartilage,*	Boiled,	4	15	———, ...	Raw,	2	15
Catfish, ...	Fried,	3	30	Mutton, fresh, . . .	Roasted,	3	15
Cheese, old, strong,	Raw,	3	30	———, . . .	Broiled,	3	
Chicken, full-grown,	Fricas'd,	2	45	———, . . .	Boiled,	3	
Codfish, cured, dry,	Boiled,	2					

From Edward Jarvis's *Physiology and the Laws of Health.*

Cayley, tied to a desk on Manhattan's South Street, therefore complained of being reduced to "a useless apathetic lump with an indolent heaviness about my stomach" after dinner. His queasiness was an obvious result of the "wicked indulgence" practiced by overeaters, as Charles Paine, a recent convert to vegetarianism, pronounced. Since the stomach was a soft, fleshy bag of indeterminate size, it was capable of significant expansion "when unnaturally crowded." Such crowding was a direct outcome of the "self-gratification" commonly practiced by so many of the era's young men, T. S. Arthur attested, emblematic of "a host of imaginary wants," or of an "*artificial appetite*," as John Gunn emphasized, that transformed hunger from a natural guide to the body's sensible needs into a source of "fictitious wants." This dynamic was manifest in the partiality for well-seasoned food, which then deepened one's craving for more of the same, for dishes that "stimulate without nourishing," as was further explained in *Miss Beecher's Domestic Receipt Book*, published in 1846 as a supplement to Catharine Beecher's well-known *Treatise on Domestic Economy*. The more one ate under these circumstances, the hungrier one became.[22]

Such pathology undermined both material and moral positivism, turning need into a wholly relative experience indistinguishable from desire, a conundrum that could only be addressed by an equally artificial, self-conscious effort on the part of the eater. "Always . . . leave the table with some appetite," John Gunn consequently advised. "Don't give the stomach too much to do," the *New England Farmer* opined as well, "and it will never trouble you." Since the body's absorbents always lagged behind its secretions, skipping a meal offered the most efficacious opportunity for recalibrating a person's physiology and removing the backlog of impurities from the digestive tract, "and thereby the base of the brain." This depended on ingesting nothing more until the next scheduled meal, when no compensatory increase in the regular level of intake was permitted either. Thomas Wren Ward embraced these tenets of "scientific cuisine" upon reforming his own eating habits, restricting dinner to a single item, for instance, while expanding his consumption of nuts and raisins in accordance to the nutritional advice he read in the magazines. His "single-dish" method was just one technique from among a range of protocols and recipes designed to buttress the "interior works," remedies that were as extensive as the afflictions they were designed to forestall. The "one-meal-per-day system" was another stratagem for enhancing personal command over the stomach and overcoming the dangers posed by the age's fast eating. So was the conscious attempt to eat more slowly, arguably the most "Herculean labor" of all. "TAKE SMALL MOUTHFULS," the *American Phrenological Journal* accordingly advised . "Cut bread, sauce, pudding, every thing you eat, into SMALL PARCELS, and eat ONE AT A TIME; and eat spoon victuals with a SMALL SPOON." Full and deliberate mastication and insalivation—which also reduced the brutish habit of spitting—emerged as a corollary strategy (mobilized as well in convincing employers to grant more time for meals). Ensuring that one's food was "thoroughly imbued with saliva" prior to swallowing restrained the rate of intake while simultaneously resuscitating torpid bowels. So did increased amounts of rye mush and molasses, and more venison, which John Gunn endorsed as a worthy substitute for pork since it was easier to digest, although, as Gunn sardonically added, if victims of chronic flatulence were truly interested in achieving relief then they should go out and hunt down the animal themselves.[23]

But it was Sylvester Graham's program of dietetics, what Graham referred to as his "system of living" devised for a republic that "cannot long maintain

its existence while its members are under the dominion of an artificial, ca-
pricious appetite," which dominated the gastrointestinal discourse in industrializing America. A detailed account of the recovery from protracted ill
health by a former clerk and student was representative of the system. The
young man in question had consistently debased himself by an overfondness
for flesh meat, pies, puddings, and coffee, the *Graham Journal of Health and
Longevity* reported. "General debility" soon set in, exacerbated by an inflam-
mation of the bronchial tubes and acute soreness in the stomach and bowels, as well as a dull, persistent headache. Recovery designed around basic
"physiological principles" was his only hope. That course prescribed breakfasts consisting of six small wafer crackers baked from unbolted wheat meal
and weighing half an ounce each, to be consumed with a half pint of Indian
porridge purged of salt. Dinner, consumed precisely six hours later, included
eight ounces of Indian pudding, bereft of sauces, together with a boiled po-
tato and a sampling of fruit. A supper of boiled rice or Indian bread with
an additional half pint of unsalted Indian porridge followed after another
six hours, such strict regulation in the timing of one's meals proving to be a
key in regulating the bowels. This regime could be supplemented by small
amounts of milk, to be taken no more than twice a day. A baked apple was also
eventually introduced. Everything was to be eaten with great deliberation, of
course, thoroughly masticated in a "simple and natural" process that ultimately
restored the former overeater to good health. In fact, he was "re-engaged in
active business" within several months, his physical condition equal to that of
anyone else in the same circumstances.[24]

The Grahamite style was admittedly preachy and unrelenting, and even
bordered on the self-parodic, as contemporary references to Graham's "starvation plan for all mankind" alluded. The *North American Review* averred
that, while "books upon the subject of spare diet are succeeding one another
with marvelous speed," there were certainly better things to do with one's time
than read them. Luther Ticknor, president of the Connecticut State Medical
Society and fully cognizant of the relationship between overeating and "our
insatiable appetite for a sudden acquisition of wealth," a condition "few can
endure with safety," nonetheless derided the profusion of current attempts to
"revolutionize the diet of the whole human family, confining them to Graham
bread and water-gruel." John Gunn likewise dismissed the ultraism of true
believers who refused to eat any but fully ripened vegetables grown without manure. He also denounced vegetarianism as a violation of nature's laws,
as evidenced in the anatomical structure of the human body and the operation of the stomach's gastric fluids, which provided incontrovertible proof
that men were designed to consume meat. Benjamin Foster was another who

poked fun at such middle-class performances of scarcity. "It is hard work to make a meal from a slice of bread, and that not very good, and a glass of water," Benjamin wrote of the current fashion for making do with less. At the same time, however, he made every effort to avoid fatty meats and other oily substances that might upset his body's nutrient base and induce disease, advice originating in the pages of the *Graham Journal of Health and Longevity*. Nor were these the only changes Benjamin introduced to his diet in hopes of alleviating the "'laxness and looseness' in my interior works." William Hoffman likewise "luxuriated" on breakfasts consisting of Graham bread, which cost significantly more than a common morning roll, while Horace Greeley, who had taken up residence in a Grahamite boardinghouse upon first arriving in New York City in the late 1830s—where breakfasts of unsifted bread and filtered rainwater were served to "inmates" upon their return from a predawn bath—continued to credit the experience with having cured his chronic migraines and leaving him with "scarcely an ache of any sort."[25]

But it was John Todd who offered the most perspicacious summary of the modern relationship between eating and social order in an anecdote he included in his *Student's Manual*. Todd told of a man of affluence who had been steadily abusing his stomach for years. With his health in rapid decline, the glutton in question turned to professional help. I can cure you, sir, the physician announces after an initial examination, "'if you will follow my advice.'" The compulsive overeater promises to obey:

> "Now," says the doctor, "you must steal a horse."
> "What! Steal a horse?"
> "Yes,—you must steal a horse. You will then be arrested, convicted, and placed in a situation where your diet and regimen will be such, that in a short time your health will be perfectly restored."[26]

Todd thus made the connection between digestion and police as explicit as possible, underlining the vital relationship between stomach and government.

The most common medical diagnosis for an undisciplined appetite and its ancillary failure of will was dyspepsia. Dyspeptics suffered from a systemic imbalance in their food consumption whose effects were manifest in a wide array of symptoms that not only included a predictable sense of physical oppression after meals, sour eructations, foul breath, vomiting, constipated bowels, and a disinclination to exertion, either mental or otherwise, but enfeebled circulation, a constricted throat, impaired vision, tenderness of the scalp, and a reduced pulse that induced vertigo, headaches, and somnolence. One's vascular system was often affected if the condition was left untreated, inducing heart palpitations. A further lapse in the body's ability to discharge fluids was registered at this point, evidenced in a declining volume of urine that also exhibited a lateritious sediment and oily surface. The bowels, previously costive, gave way to chronic diarrhea, leading to an acute irritability of the alimentary tube. Such gastric dysfunction might even spread to the lungs, raising the possibility of pulmonary crisis.[27]

"As digestion is the most complex of all the organic processes, its derangements . . . are the most complicated of all morbid conditions," Russell Trall, a veteran figure in New York health circles who founded the New York Hygeio-Therapeutic College in 1854 and became a well-known retailer of Graham flour, explained in *Digestion and Dyspepsia*. And while a weak stomach was the most commonly recognized source of such morbidity, Trall observed that "they might as well say, weakness of the head, or heart, or hands, or feet; all are weak when the digestive processes fail to supply the elements of strength." Dyspepsia, as such, integrated a diverse range of derangements and disorders into a single pathognomonic narrative. The miscellaneous character of its symptoms underscored the diagnosis's development into something of a medical metacategory, an evolving rubric capable of organizing a great variety of somatic expressions into a coherent discourse concerning the whole self. Oliver Halsted, inventor of the patented chair that simulated equestrian exercise for those compelled to be sedentary, had already observed in his *Full and Accurate Account of the New Method of Curing Dyspepsia* that none of the disease's myriad etiologies were previously unknown, or had recently been discovered. What turned dyspepsia into a novel medical event, and an increasingly ubiquitous diagnosis, was science's newfound appreciation of the interdependence of all these events and their common derivation from the nervous axis connecting the brain to the stomach, which included the saturnine quality of the blood feeding the former that was directly affected by what one ate. No other pathology produces so much misery and mischief, Joel Ross concluded in his *Golden Rules of Health*. But none other also proved so curable, he further noted.[28]

"Why has dyspepsia become much more general of late years than it formerly was?" Reynell Coates asked in *Popular Medicine*. "Because our habits have been totally changed since the days of our grandfathers." Eating practices were obviously to be blamed. The menus of metropolitan boardinghouses were singled out as a particularly egregious violation of the precepts of scientific cuisine. But so was the accelerated rhythm of everyday life and the rapid reversals of personal fortune characteristic of this age of "ambition and indigestion," as Bartleby's employer so pithily identified the twin foundations of modern nervousness. "There is probably no other disease with which the human family are afflicted to so great an extent at the present day, as with

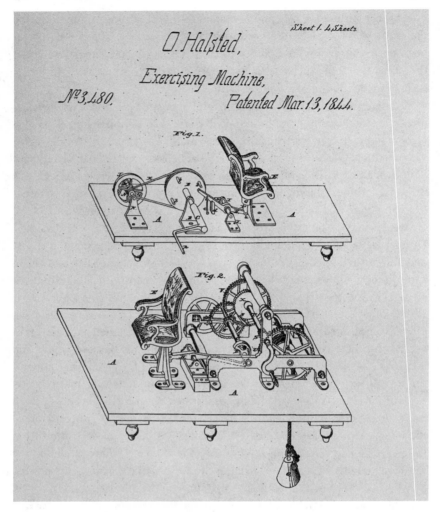

Dyspepsia," Joel Ross consequently determined. "There are very few in easy circumstances who have not occasionally suffered from some of its forms," S. W. Avery verified in *Dyspeptic's Monitor*, making note of the condition's particular excrescence among society's ease-loving classes.[29]

But a pandemic driven as much by ambition as by indigestion—by a moral dispensation no less than physical impairment—also aroused skepticism. Dr. David M. Reese, for one, documented an especially rabid outbreak in his *Humbugs of New York: Being a Remonstrance against Popular Delusion*, which was published in the wake of America's most vehement pecuniary spasm to date, the Panic of 1837. Reese depicted a metropolis succumbing to a wave of upset stomachs, "every variety of which the name dyspepsia has been stupidly and indiscriminately applied." Scarcely anyone seemed to have escaped its affects, Reese disdainfully observed of what he considered to be little more than a spate of hypochondria driven by the contagions of fashionable emulation, a figment, that is, of the popular imagination. Because such pathogens generated themselves, they lacked clinical significance, much like other phenomena being conjured out of thin air such as the fictitious book value that so exercised Joseph Hopkinson a few years earlier in his philippic addressing the "principles of commercial integrity."[30]

In a two-part study of the subject appearing in the *American Journal of the Medical Sciences* in 1840, N. Chapman sought to bridge this disparity between dyspepsia's physic and ontic expressions. Chapman, a professor of the theory and practice of medicine at the University of Pennsylvania, hoped to develop a standard epidemiology of what everyone acknowledged to be a national crisis, whether real or not. In so doing, he traced dyspepsia's mental symptoms to lesions in the spine, where the nerves controlling the digestive system's "very complex apparatus" were located. That congestive disturbance in the conduit linking mind and body effectively cast dyspepsia as a nervous breakdown whose physiology was directly expressed in one's mental impairment.[31]

No two components of anatomy more "uniformly reciprocate their affections" than the stomach and brain, Chapman reminded his readers. This made the new diagnosis an especially compelling, and coherent, instance of natural philosophy's location of mental functions on an anatomical continuum with the rest of the body's organs. Dyspepsia could thus be said to have developed in the interstices between body and soul, articulating the effect of the digestive system on muscles, lungs, heart, and brain, and the correspondent influence of the brain over all the body's organs, as well as the role of the circulating fluids in forming, supporting, and repairing those organs, "and so on," as Andrew Combe charted the ramifying interplay of anatomy so characteristic of nineteenth-century medical models. In this respect, dyspepsia integrated a seemingly random collection of disorders into a comprehensive matrix of causal interactions and common derivations. By connecting a prostrated mind to a debilitated body, moreover, contemporaries could speak of health and ethics in the same breath, and so tie the physical manifestations of conscious behavior to the conscious manifestations of physical behavior. This explained why dyspepsia was so often associated with cerebral disturbance, proof of "the intimate dependence of our moral nature on our physical constitution," as Chapman summarized his findings.[32]

According to Austin Flint, however, who published his own treatise on the subject a few months later, Chapman had not gone far enough in delineating dyspepsia's mental pathology. Flint, whom George Beard would later cite as an important influence on the latter's discovery of neurasthenia, a postbellum diagnosis that ushered in a far more psychologized understanding of mental disturbance induced by the stress of industrial life, was determined to expand dyspepsia's phenomenology. He encouraged physicians, for instance, to devote greater attention to the less tangible aspects of the disease and so win back a "class of patients" who otherwise felt that medical science had woefully little to offer them. By assigning special emphasis to dyspepsia's ambiguities, what's more—"a certain undefined sense of fear and apprehension"—Flint deliberately underscored the hysterical nature of the disease. The fact that such a broad gamut of corporeal derangements were triggered by no obvious cause save "a morbid affection of mind" even raised the possibility of what Flint called "imaginary disease," which matched common descriptions of dyspepsia as comprising a "multitude of real and imaginary woes."[33]

Flint argued that Chapman's failure to fully understand the phrenic nature of this condition issued from Chapman's improper grasp of the reciprocity between the body's digestive organs and a person's mental hygiene. True, both physicians acknowledged the close relationship that existed between "paroxysms of gastric derangement," on the one hand, and the derangement of one's powers of reason, on the other. But Flint contended that an intemperate diet and its accompanying debilitations could not possibly serve as the principal cause of mental breakdown, except among the poor, who had a different relationship with profligacy in any event. That was because there were large numbers of persons who ate with dutiful care but nonetheless suffered from "peculiarly persistent" bouts of dyspepsia. The source of the disease could not, therefore, be traced back to their diets or even, more generally, to their physical constitutions. Instead, as Flint explained, it was the sedentary nature of the dyspeptic's life—an anxious routinization and excessive cerebralness—that was to be identified as the etiology of his unhappy condition. "Moral, intellectual, and social" disquietude—what Edward Jarvis later described at the groundbreaking ceremony for Northampton's new hospital for the insane as the "perplexities, fear and anxiety" that resulted from all avenues in life being open to all persons—were not, in other words, an effect of the disease. They were its causes.[34]

Flint presented a model of psychosomatic circularity by which anomie induced gastrointestinal crisis, which exacerbated the escalating sense of gloom and dissatisfaction that had triggered the crisis to begin with. Or, as a medical student attested in his journal in 1836, "vexation disturbs the functions of the stomach inducing Dyspepsia. . . . Sorrow diminishes the energy of the nervous systems, lessens the force of the circulation, impedes the secretions and induces organic disease." In that light, David Reese's dismissal of dyspepsia as performance rather than illness rested on a false dichotomy, one that refused to acknowledge the close interrelationship between the real and the nominal, or the very possibility of imaginary disease by which individuals might themselves decide "not to be a little reasonable." Such ambiguity is common in the history of pathology, and it now proved particularly important in positioning the individual at the center of medical attention, which is why hysteria became so pronounced in the nineteenth century, abetting as it did the patient's autonomy. Only he—or, just as often, albeit for different reasons, only she—could delineate and consequently define the nature of their suffering.[35]

Dr. Valentine Mott, a prominent New York City physician, informed a young man who had come for a consultation regarding a problem with irritable bowels that his condition was the result of a localized impairment of the nerves rather than a systemic case of dyspepsia. The stricken patient knew otherwise, however, and rejected Mott's close clinical reasoning as immaterial to his experience. "The truth is that I suffer in both ways each operating to produce the other disease," he attested of the close interplay between his mental and physical ails, which he traced to an "intense suspense in all matters public and private." Andrew Combe explored that ontology in his *Physiology of Digestion*, contending that, regardless of how much attention was devoted to the particularities of diet, little relief would ensue until the dyspeptic found asylum from "the hurry and bustle [and] the anxiety and excitement of business," among other traits of modern life that overtaxed his brain. By the 1860s, the *New York Medical Journal* was thus urging physicians to recognize "how greatly the function of digestion is influenced by the mental organization of the individual." Growing appreciation of the disease's psychic context turned dyspepsia into a clinical manifestation of that peculiarly American condition by which "the brain and nervous system are kept under a very high pressure from an early age in life," as Henry Ward Beecher identified the manic effects of liberty's interaction with equality. Tocqueville described the same phenomenon in *Democracy in America*, noting in the same year Austin Flint published his findings in the *American Journal of Medical Sciences* that the minds of citizens were habitually "wearied and harassed" by the universal ambition to improve their situation. The very universality of that prospect for personal advancement then diminished the practical chances of attaining their goal. "The constant strife between the desires inspired by equality and the means it supplies to satisfy them," in other words, was the cause of a structural derangement of the national psyche, a direct effect of the market's promise of prosperity for all who were willing to make the effort. "A disappointed man of ambition is miserable," John Todd accordingly argued, "not because his loss is really so great, but because his imagination has, for years, been making it appear great to him."[36]

The great constipation that characterized the age of capital was not, as such, the simple result of "strongly-flavored foods" and "abuses of cookery." Induced by the terror that results whenever "the government of our own faculties is partially withdrawn from us," as Austin Flint wrote, dyspepsia was an expression of the existential risks inherent in a regime of sovereign selves, the nervous fallout from a world in which one was either "*self-made, or never made.*" Joel Ross, for instance, described dyspeptic headaches as a "confusion in the head" rather than the experience of any actual pain. "They feel as though they were not themselves," Ross observed of these victims, who consequently reached the forlorn conclusion that it was "useless to try to improve their condition." Such a loss of faith in improvement, and particularly in self-improvement, signaled the ultimate breakdown of personal will, of course. "Responsibility is at an end," George Moore concluded in *Man and His Motives* of the resulting degradation of the individual's "power of appealing to the mind for motives to control itself." That is why Charles Caldwell also claimed that lunatics—who had lost any semblance of self-control—commonly suffered from dyspepsia during their more lucid intervals. And that is also why Bartleby, whose employer searched in vain for signs of organic lesions that might explain his clerk's baffling behavior—perhaps all the incessant copying had damaged the scrivener's eyes, he conjectured—ended up starving himself to death.[37]

Dyspepsia's affiliation of atrophying bodies and untethered souls—the dual totems of the clerical life—epitomized the need to muster the moral discipline and physiological rigor that were required for self-government. Austin Flint pushed this discussion even further by identifying a condition of "monomania" that developed once the dyspeptic's sense of order became so distorted that his "perception of time and space" was vitiated. Concrete experience would then be replaced by "imagined or remembered impressions." Of course, such disjunctions of time and space were the sine qua non of the market, whose volatilities replaced organic certainty and absolute value with fragments of the imagination, most commonly manifest in the form of fluctuating prices. In these terms, dyspepsia proved to be a particularly ambitious attempt to incorporate the "real" and "nominal" into a single chain of personal experience during the formative decades of capitalist revolution.[38]

Bodywork

The nervous connection between the brain and the rest of the body became the subject of a distinctly new knowledge economy in the nineteenth century called physical education. "The reader will perhaps laugh at the idea of *educating* the body," Harvey Newcomb acknowledged in *How to Be a Man* in 1847, apparently having to justify the comparable status he assigned to carnal subjects as to mental and moral character. Charles Caldwell included a similar disclaimer in the preface to *Thoughts on Physical Education*. "Let no one allege that this view of education involves materialism," Caldwell announced, "or any principle unfriendly to morality or religion." And yet, had the scriptures not consistently proscribed the cultivation of the body in the Christian's regulation of himself, the *Massachusetts Teacher* remarked in a discussion of "health." And was it not true, Thomas Wentworth Higginson further observed in an essay on gymnastic exercise published in the *Atlantic Monthly* in 1858, that saints were traditionally ashamed of their bodies, their very sanctity resting on the strict opposition between a frail physique and robust spirit? "Nothing this side of ancient Greece," Higginson confessed, "will afford adequate examples of the union of saintly souls and strong bodies." Nothing until now, that is, for the identification of moral rectitude with material privation was increasingly untenable in a society that considered the accumulation of wealth to be an honest recompense for talent and tenacity, and indispensable to the progress of civilization more generally. A specifically "American saintship" had thus taken shape, according to Higginson, a Unitarian minister active in antebellum social reform, that joined strong bodies and saintly souls together into a "vigorous, manly life" against which even "dyspepsia will get the worst of it."[39]

Physical education was the means of achieving such integration, dedicated as it was to bolstering the nervous system and, as a result, stabilizing the fitful relationship between mind and matter—and nominal and real—so characteristic of the age. This required a working knowledge of one's physiology, "every thing that, by bearing in any way on the human body, might injure or benefit it in its health, vigour, and fitness for action," as Charles Caldwell explained in his *Thoughts on Physical Education*, staking out the system's expansive domain. William Hoffman became a conscientious disciple of the new catechism, health having emerged as "my chief study of late," he reported in noting a marked improvement in his physical constitution effected by a strict curriculum of Graham flour, saltwater baths, and sulfur pills ingested every evening before going to bed. Everyone needed to pay the closest attention to "the best and purest air, the best and most appropriate clothing, the best food and drink; . . . to the quantity, quality and circumstances of sleep, to cleanliness, to exercise, to ventilation, to temperature, and a thousand other things," as the *American Annals of Education* expanded on this list of prescriptions in a series of "essays on physical education." Those thousand other things were indicative of the scope of the program and its goal of "self-management," which is how Edward Jarvis referred to such a practicum in personal sovereignty. Is it any wonder that there were some who even proclaimed the new discipline to be "the basis of all rational and successful civilization?"[40]

Physical education was another effect of an industrial revolution that replaced muscle with steam. Ever since the invention of gunpowder, to cite a contemporary example, any child was capable of vanquishing Hercules. This made knowledge into "the only ground of great power," and brainwork rather than brawn into the foundation of prosperity and progress. But while "the intellect gains, the body suffers," the *Atlantic* noted of the high price of humanity's advance. Physical education would address that predicament by turning the body itself into a knowledge system, reducing flesh and blood to the level of information and so incorporating it into a telos of rational command and control. Were we not, after all, integrated mechanisms of digestive, respiratory, and neural activity operating by means of a complex circuitry of pipes and pumps? Andrew Combe, for one, marveled at the consummate skill "with which every act of every organ is turned to account," at how the chest expanded with every inhalation, pushing the bowels forward and allowing the lungs to fill themselves up—assuming that a steady supply of fresh oxygen was available—while the consequent exhalation pulled back on the ribs and contracted the bowels, which allowed the stomach to then carry out its essential tasks. Skeletons and manikins displayed at public lectures, together with sundry charts of the vital organs and diagrams of the body's musculature and circulatory system, supplemented by a vast print culture of self-diagnostics disseminated in popular vehicles of medical culture such as *Journal of Health*, *Family Library of Health*, and *Catechism of Health*, were deployed in acquainting the public with the "natural conditions on which health depends." William Alcott emphasized the importance of this technical education in his highly regarded anatomical primer for children, *The House I Live In*, which was published in 1837, the same year he cofounded the American Physiological Society. "Do we not carry about with us, throughout life, a machine . . . ingeniously constructed?" Alcott wrote of a condition that required each to attend to his or her corporeal self with the same diligence and deliberation as was commonly devoted to such other ingeniously engineered systems as steam engines and spinning jennies? The goal was to turn the individual into

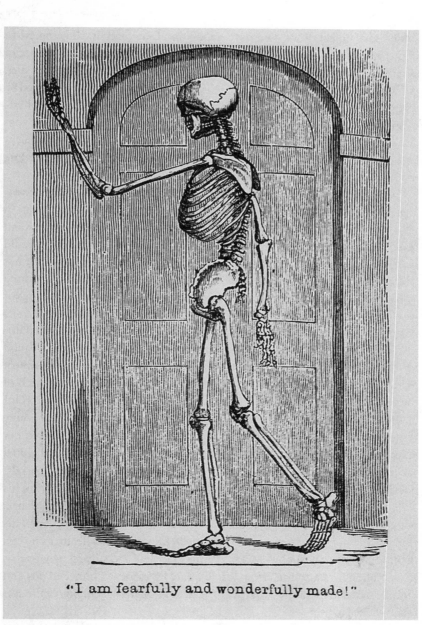

"I am fearfully and wonderfully made!"

The frontispiece of William Alcott's anatomical best seller *The House I Live In.*

a conscious object of his own observation and intervention, allowing art to improve upon nature by regulating that most important physical resource of all, namely, one's self. Attention was accordingly focused on matters of diet, evacuations, exercise, air, sleep, and passions, a roster of elements identified by science as the "non-naturals." The reference was to those aspects of our physiology that were most susceptible to conscious control, thus acquiring special significance in an age of self-making, and explaining why Eugene Becklard entitled his popular work on physiology *Know Thyself* while reminding readers in the volume's frontispiece that "knowledge is power."[41]

"Know thyself" is a noble inscription, the *Massachusetts Teacher* acknowledged. "'*Govern thyself*' would be a nobler inscription." Physical education made these goals one and the same. By training the mind to quickness and "every muscle and nerve to obedience," the autonomous individual would be transformed from a source of disorder into a pillar of stability. "Is it not strange that knowledge of such vast importance should have been so long overlooked?" Alcott asked in the preface to *The House I Live In*. In fact, it was not strange at all. The very title of Alcott's celebrated work testified to its postpatriarchal provenance. The "house" to which Alcott referred—that domicile where "I" lived—was none other than each person's own body, "good for nothing at all for any one but myself." His published tour of this most private of freeholds commenced with the thigh bone, kneepan, and arch of the foot, continued to the pores and glands, the hair and nails, and the color of the skin, of course, before concluding in those interior chambers where respiration, digestion, circulation, and excretion were organized. Such a detailed account of the assembly of one's body would accord each individual the practical means to then manage its constituent parts and so put his self-possession into practice, becoming the competent "owner and enjoyer" of his own person. "We see that the material body is not left to its own guidance, but to each one is given a mind that shall direct it," Edward Jarvis added in his *Primary Physiology for Schools*, in which he defined personal health as no less than a "mental philosophy." Much like the era's new accounting pedagogies, in fact, physical education also rejected a rote inventory of remedial dos and don'ts in favor of inculcating the public with a causal understanding of the system's internal logic.[42]

Lemuel Shattuck, who designed his *Scholar's Daily Journal* for charting one's "intellectual progress," developed an analogous program for plotting each person's physiological progress as well. This would be achieved by means of a "personal sanitary examination," Shattuck explained in a *General Plan for the Promotion of Public and Personal Health*, that promised prophylactic protection against chronic illness to anyone who maintained a log

that measured the effect of their daily activities on their physical circumstances. Those found to be particularly favorable "should be repeated," Shattuck summarized the deductive logic of physiological self-management, "and
such as are known to be unfavorable should be discontinued." That reasoning
replaced fate with risk, a definitive juncture in the history of both medicine
and the economy, while also allowing proponents of health reform to upbraid
the public for attending to their bodies only after falling ill, for failing to understand that disease was "easier to prevent than to cure," as Edward Hitchcock, the first professor of physical education in the United States, insisted
in his *Dyspepsia Forestalled and Resisted*. "Prevention is better than cure,"
the American Physiological Society also declared in promulgating an ethic
founded on the exclusive responsibility of the individual for his own health.
Only when such truths were assigned a central place in the pantheon of human enlightenment, as the *Moral Reformer*—a journal founded by William
Alcott and subtitled "Human Construction"—proclaimed in a discussion
about "educating the stomach," could the nation "expect to see the efforts of
the head, the heart and the hands united in the amelioration of the condition
of man."[43]

That amelioration found its most strenuous expression at the gym. Horace
Mann, for instance, attended a demonstration of prodigious leaps and agile
somersaults in Boston where "dyspepsia lost hold of its victim when he
mounted the flying horse" and "rheumatisms and cramps and spasms sit
coiled up and chattering in the corners" after being shaken off by the gym-
nast's supple movements. A similarly rousing display of responsible selfhood
was organized at New York's Crosby Street Gymnasium in the autumn of 1852
for an audience of more than a thousand who gathered to watch merchants,
clerks, and other professional men, wracked until recently with anxiety over
whether the dull pain in their chests was a premonition of pulmonary failure,
gliding up ropes and ladders like "young SAMPSONS." Their accomplishments
were the result of neither magic nor miracles, John Gunn explained, but of
the simple truth that a body of average size excreted a far greater amount of
fetid material by perspiring through an exercise routine than could ever be
discharged by one's "stool and urine combined." The circulation of the blood
was also enhanced, serving to build up the muscles—expanding the circum-
ference of the pectorals, for instance, by three to four inches—while removing congestions and boosting respiratory efficiency. Sedgwick's Metropolitan
Academy and Gymnasium could therefore promise to repair the splenetic
morbidity of the sedentary by transforming their "dwarfed and ungraceful
bodies," and "depressed and vacant minds," into erect, deep-chested speci-
mens of manhood. The cost of membership, furthermore, would be "but a

slight per centage on what he had heretofore paid for medicines and physicians' fees."[44]

Francis Butler, employed in the Manhattan office of his brother's paper
business whose production facilities were located across the river in Paterson,
was suitably inspired by such talk of strong, symmetrical bodies to enroll in
the Union Gymnastic Academy, where "all the best-approved gymnastic ap-
paratuses" were arranged over six thousand square feet of floor space. Francis
planned to devote an hour each morning at the gym to "the benefits of vigorous health," he announced in his diary, before then continuing to the office.
That routine would be of double benefit since Francis was not, by nature, an
early riser. The predawn start to his day would thus ward off disease while
garnering him extra hours of conscious activity, reclaiming leisure time otherwise lost to the indulgences of sleep, sloth, and indolence. Edward Tailer
exercised at the Union Gym as well, although he quit his membership a few
months before Francis Butler enrolled following an angry row with the proprietor, Mr. Rich, whom Edward accused of excessive rigidity in managing
both the gym and the gymnasts. Edward had no intention of abandoning the
program altogether, however, and, in contrast to Francis Butler, who lasted
less than a month before departing to Havana "for my health," sought a more
congenial situation for pursuing his physical education. He soon found this
at Mourquin's Gym, where, following a hurried toilet, Edward commenced
an early morning workout on the swings, parallel bars, horizontal ladders,
and dumbbells before moving on to ground exercises designed to strengthen
his back and legs, and finishing with twenty-five laps around the gym, which
"threw me into a delightful and refreshing perspiration" and stopped a late-
winter cold from developing.[45]

Edward was a fervent disciple of the modern revival of classical gymnastics that reached America in the 1820s and spawned a countless number of
similar sites of "heroic labor" over the next several decades. He effectively put
in an extra shift at the gym—unless kept late at the office the night before—
manning an assembly line of barbells, rope ladders, and pommel horses designed for the construction of his health. Physical fitness became a function
of productive prowess, in other words, applied with the same system and
conscious intent that informed the manufacture of "cloth, paper, or pins," as
William Alcott observed in his *Lectures on Life and Health*, promoting physical education into a modern work ethic as much as a branch of the health
sciences. "My progress in physical strength and development has been most
extraordinary," Edward happily reported upon renewing his membership at
Mourquin's for an additional year. "I could not dispose of my money more
advantageously to my self."[46]

From *Trall's Illustrated Family Gymnasium*, 1857.

"With a watch, a pencil, and a bill of exchange in his pocket," the *Atlantic Monthly* observed in paraphrasing Emerson's "Self-Reliance," modern Americans were steadily devolving into an enfeebled species markedly inferior to those New World primitives whose entire inventory of possessions had consisted of a club, a spear, and a mat for sleeping. The gymnasium and its exercise routines promised to alter that dismal condition and dramatically reduce the price of progress, if not fundamentally alter the balance of payments altogether. In contrast to rowing, for instance, which was thoroughly impractical in the winter, or skating, which was even less feasible in the summer—and unlike riding, too, which remained prohibitively expensive in the city—the gym was available during all seasons and all weather while at once affording "the most exercise in the shortest time," an apposite claim for the hurried conditions of the age. Gymnastics, what's more, treated "the whole body," delivering relief to one's woefully neglected shoulders and chest, abdominal muscles, and spine, and so respectively improving the function of lungs, stomach, and nerves.[47]

Exercise could also be specifically designed to channel the flow of blood to a particularly morbid limb, or to enhance the quality of intermuscular juices for overcoming constipation and improving one's general control over the body's excretions. More fundamentally, the gym made it possible to achieve a previously unknown level of conscious control over the whole self, learning to bring the muscles "into prompt and rapid action at the instant of volition" and "never make any movement whatever, except when you mean to make." A "clerk or a tailor" could thus overcome the debilitating gravity of their sedentary existence by whirling Indian clubs and riding the swings, "arms and legs flying" in a display of motion comparable to the hydraulic precision of pulleys and levers. The corporeal decline immanent to industrial civilization would, as such, be arrested by civilization's own "immense capacity for self-restoration," overturning agrarian clichés regarding the corruptions of modernity. "Life, health, size, and strength," in fact, find their highest expression "among those races where knowledge and wealth and comfort are most widely spread," John Warren, president of a Boston gymnastics society, pronounced, offering redemption to all who "had been perishing in groups for want of air and exercise." It became possible, in other words, to maximize profits without sacrificing one's health. Tired truths about aboriginal nobility and the uncorrupted nature of the savage could be assigned to the dustbin of superstition, or attributed to the obscurantist prejudices of reactionaries.[48]

It might seem paradoxical, the *Atlantic* noticed in another essay on gymnastics, that more people take exercise in the city than in the country, but "we believe it to be true." The gym, in that respect, belonged to the economy's structural shift from the household to the more flexible input of individualized labor power. At the same time, and no less significantly, the gym also moved virtue into the heart of an urban culture otherwise founded on personal aggrandizement and monetized competition. Benjamin Foster, for instance, enrolled in a Newburyport gymnasium that functioned as a virtual civic association, collecting initiation fees, electing officers, and inspiring institutional loyalty. Rutherford Hayes likewise recognized the intimate connection between fraternity and exercise when he joined a Cincinnati gym in the 1850s to socialize with other young city lawyers. The Union Gymnastic Academy in New York City even provided its members with a reading room, thus satisfying the Reverend James Alexander's vision of physical education positioning itself in a cultural alliance with public lectures and musical concerts in opposition to the evil axis of theaters, billiard rooms, and "dens of infamy." A "properly managed gym," the *New York Tribune* went on to declare, constituted "one of the most useful institutions in any city," treating a population that was occupied "with too much thinking and too little exercise" and offering the average American, "utterly exhausted in the daily effort to put ten dollars more of distance between his posterity and the poor-house," an almost utopian respite from capital's torpor and degeneracy. It certainly accorded clerks the wholesome appetite and "sound sleep . . . of the plough-man," serving as the source of a well-honed "*physical* truth as well as *moral*," William Alcott pronounced in his autobiography.[49]

"One revels in this Palace of Truth," the *Atlantic* further effused, where "absolute justice" was being rehabilitated. "That bar, that rope, that weight shall test you absolutely," doing so, what's more, in a metropolis where no one any longer swung a scythe. "Let any man test his physical condition," Thomas Wentworth Higginson remarked of such benevolent effects of exercise, "we will not say by sawing his own cord of wood, but by an hour in the gym-nasium." The gym thus emerged as an ideological landmark in the modern cityscape, a temple of health, as Catharine Beecher also proclaimed in her *Let-ters to the People on Health and Happiness*, whose high dome offered an inspi-rational analogy to the properly constructed physique, and even to Benjamin Foster's "*stocky* though not unduly *thick*" frame. But even when not boasting the monumental dimensions of New York's Seventh Regiment Gymnasium, Boston's Tremont Gym, or Chicago's Metropolitan Gymnasium, these "hu-man machine shops of busy motion" contributed a distinctly enlightened presence to an urban typography being upgraded to channel the flood of hu-manity reaching the city. In that respect, gymnasiums filled the same func-tion as hospitals, sewers, and public parks, all elements of a vast reform of social and personal hygiene in the industrial century. Ideally located on the ground floor so that all the stomping and charging would not place undue stress on the building's foundations, the gym was celebrated as a spacious and generously ventilated counteragent to decay. Exercising in vitiated air was an obvious absurdity, as Dio Lewis, a well-known publicist on matters of family life who founded the Normal Institute for Physical Education in Boston in 1861, explained in his *New Gymnastics*. The rooms also needed to be kept free of the dust raised by workouts designed to invigorate circulation in the legs and feet, a problem most conveniently addressed by washing the floor with a sticky solution of hot water and molasses that fixed the dirt into the cracks and knots rather than the lungs of gymnasts. It was no less essential to heat the space with a sufficient number of stoves, for if the temperature dipped below fifty degrees, circulation of the blood—"*the* condition of muscle-growth"—would accordingly suffer. Gymnasiums subsequently competed for membership by advertising their improved facilities and equipment, which included dressing rooms with "shower baths"—whose water temperature was fixed between thirty-five and fifty-six degrees, even in December—extended hours, reduced class sizes, and the availability of experienced coaches who ensured that personal workouts conformed to the "fundamental laws of gymnastic training."[50]

One could, of course, exercise without going to the gym. J. E. D'alfonce's *Instructions in Gymnastics*, for instance, featured routines for the head, arms, legs, and muscle development that required no apparatus whatsoever. At the same time, home versions of various exercise devices became widely available for purchase. Mann's Reactionary Lifter, constituting "a thorough gymnastic system," was one such method for drilling the whole body in private. "Ten minutes once a day" would deliver permanent relief from nervous debilities, imperfect blood circulation, and liver and bowel problems. Hinsdale's Home Gymnasium pledged the same results when put on display at the American Institute's Annual Fair in 1852, where visitors were invited to test the equipment: "Examine it thoroughly—you who are interested in the cause of Physical Education and Health—and who is not?" The *North American Review*, meanwhile, endorsed C. E. Langdon's "Home, School, and Hospital Gymnastics" since it could be utilized "at odd moments of leisure or the fragments of hours," an important consideration which also recommended Dr. Barnett's Improved Parlor Gymnasium, a version of which was adopted by New York's Board of Education for "resting the tired brain." Barnett's system, which consisted of a single elastic cable of India Rubber with handles at each end to be stretched apart by arms working in opposing fashion, was light and portable and thereby available "at any time, and in any place," including "the train or desk." Advertisements specifically targeted professional and business men "whose mental and nervous systems have been overstrained," promising that their constricted chests, weak lungs, and sluggish circulations would be emended by this simple device, which also offered a practical solution for boarders who had no place to store a set of weights, parallel bars, or suspended rings, let alone an old mattress to break their fall. A parlor rowing machine also became available from Barnett that applied the same method to the legs.[51]

Whether undertaken at home or at the gym, all this bodywork helped transplant vigorous labor from the soil and relocate it in the physical effort dedicated to one's own health, which so well suited a society of individuals no longer devoted to the making of things but to the making of themselves. In one of capitalism's more surprising inversions of common sense, productive effort became the purview of sedentary men. Office types could have their Graham bread and eat it too, and the clerk could replace the plowboy as a model citizen, ideally positioned as he was to demonstrate his skills at self-government. It was gymnasts, the *Atlantic* contended, who display those muscles that "show to such advantage in the ancient statues." Anyone who exercised, it followed by implication, became heir to the classical virtues, a para-

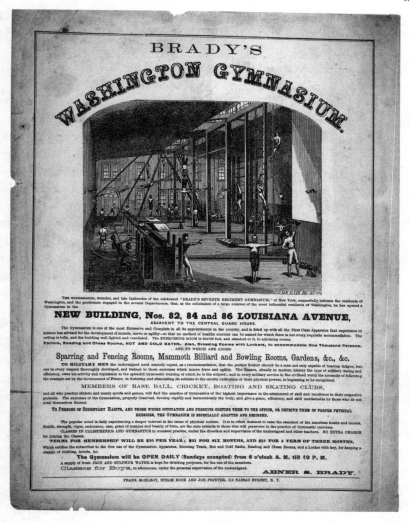

gon of constitutional integrity, self-command, and personal discipline. The bourgeoisie, which lacked—and which, in fact, had destroyed—the older, landed basis of citizenship, could thus establish a new claim to civic worth and so inherit the leadership of American society.[52]

There was another inversion at play as well, for physical education not only superseded the farm as the source of productive virtue but recast farming itself as a form of exercise. "I wish all our boys would learn to love the axe," Horace Greeley declared, for instance, in his *Recollections of a Busy*

Life, promoting the "healthiest implement that man ever handled," healthy because it threw back the shoulders, expanded the chest, and consequently opened up the lungs. That same axe allowed men to make a clearing in the forest and build a shelter for their families, becoming at once a tool of political and physiological health. Certainly, there was no better "out-of-door recreation" than farm work, Henry Ward Beecher echoed such sentiments in his treatment of "health and education," published amid reports on the mass migration of city traders back to the soil in search of the "recreation and repose" that was uniquely available in the "generous bosoms of their own farms."[53]

Clearing the land, chopping wood, burning stumps, hanging a gate, milking the cows, and digging up potatoes—digging was "peculiarly favorable to health," Edward Hitchcock determined in *Dyspepsia Forestalled and Resisted*—were transposed into techniques of medical amelioration resting on the opposition between "artificial modes of life" and "those indicated by nature," as the *Journal of Health* explained. Working on the farm therefore served as a remedial response to nervous disorder. Edward Tailer devoted an occasional hour to gardening before breakfast, for example, "and relished the sport wonderfully." William Hoffman was sent to feed the horses, clean the stable, and bring in wood to build up the morning fire on an upstate visit to the family homestead, inspiring him to proclaim that "to labor moderately is certainly very beneficial for my health." The hale countenance and strong frame that resulted from such labors, habitually juxtaposed to the pale, pimply physiognomy of deskmen entrapped in the countinghouse, constituted the "law of our physical system," the Reverend Hatfield told his audience at the Dry Goods Clerks' Mutual Benefit and Protective Association in 1850. Only physical activity could provide that "regular exercise of all the organs" which proved so critical to health. William Alcott reported on a recovering dyspeptic who was advised to move back to the farm. "Compelled . . . to practice the most rigid economy, having very little temptation to unlawful indulgence, and having an abundance of healthful exercise in the open air," this born-again agriculturalist soon embraced a "physiologically correct" life entirely free of disease.[54]

Frontiersmen splitting rails in constructing their dwellings thus proved to be worthy successors to Jefferson's "chosen people of God," models of a robust body politic cultivating personal virtue by raising its own roof and crops. Sylvester Graham, too, associated the redemptive quality of his wheat-bread recipes with the virgin soil of the nation's frontier and with those who resided in "comfortable log houses in our western country." Working the land, as such, continued to mark a counterpoint to the casualties and caprice of customers. And yet in designating the "cultivator of the soil" as the most vigorous member of society in his *Physical Education*, John Warren only seemed to be rehearsing older, agrarian truths. In fact, Warren gave expression to an entirely new perception of the land, one that defined the goal of farming to no longer be the production of goods but the production of one's own "vigorous and healthy" self. The farm was invested with a new kind of cultural capital whose value was derived from its ostensible position outside an economy now "toiling to produce more toil" and "accumulating in order to aggrandize," as the Hudson River school painter Thomas Cole denounced the corruptions of the modern industrial order. This same sense of the soil's powers of deliverance spurred the mass marketing of country cottages in these years, as well as a widespread beautification movement that strove to remake the countryside into a simulacrum of rustic refinement. The pastoral tradition was embraced, in other words, just as farming itself was being subjoined to the postagrarian logic of profit.[55]

The era's countrified platitudes were nevertheless underscored by an avalanche of statistical evidence proving that tillers of the soil lived longer, "in the ratio of 64 to 52," than either merchants or mechanics. Such data continued to mount up. A paper read by Edward Jarvis on the vital statistics of Dorchester, Massachusetts, for instance, assigned the town's farmers an average life span of forty-five years while claiming that local merchants lagged far behind, revealing a dramatic gap in personal hardiness that was attributed to the active habits of those cultivators of the earth who were, by definition, "generally free from oppressive anxieties." The same relationship between health and occupation informed the actuarial tables of life insurance companies which identified the clerk and his "artificial modes of life" as a particularly high risk. Observe, in contrast, the cultivator of the soil, John Warren exclaimed, every member of whose body was "healthful, vigorous, and well fitted for labor." Glance at the brawny arms and strong chests of sailors, John Gunn similarly urged. "Look at the strong figure of the sturdy woodman . . . and indeed at all persons who are engaged in active and laborious callings." Nature's own, sweet air was their "true gymnasium," the *Atlantic* acknowledged in yet another paean to the therapeutic effects of hard work out of doors. Henry Patterson concurred. Having "got through all my reading" on a sea voyage from New York to Richmond, he spent the rest of his time helping to haul in the rigging. "This is hard work," he satisfactorily exclaimed, "but good exercise."[56]

Henry had attended a Mercantile Library debate the year before that was devoted to determining whether "commercial pursuits [were] more favorable to the development of mind than Agricultural." At the end of the proceedings the assembled clerks declared in favor of the latter. Such pledges of allegiance to the farming life were apparently an obligatory gesture, even among those who had abandoned it. "O how happy I shall be to see the green fields again and breath the fresh air of the country," Edward Thomas enthused in anticipation of an upcoming vacation to Stamford in 1856. William Hoffman was no less insistent in embracing the pastoral ideal of health and vitality, proclaiming his preference for an "ordinary country location and residence" over the bustle and monotony of Gotham, "with all its mammon—its business— its would be luxuries—its plethoric 'markets.'" While these sentiments did not keep him from selling off the family farm and converting the land into a financial asset, William clearly recognized that such liquidity constituted a slippery ground on which to build a healthy civic life.[57]

Good Government

"Living by rule" in overcoming the omnipresent threat of disorder—"perfect obedience would be attended with perfect health," the *Massachusetts Teacher* asserted in an "address on physical education"—did not infringe on anyone's sovereign manhood. Neo-Spartan vegetarianism, cold-water baths, and predawn exercise routines were, if anything, adamant assertions of self-possession, declarations that private life preceded collective existence and that the former had become a key for guaranteeing the viability of the latter. Self-denial only appears to be an oxymoron, in other words, for it actually rests on axioms of human agency founded on the dignity, prerogative, and personal aptitude of men, and on the exclusive responsibility each assumes for his own fate. That is why the age's chronic aches and pains never provoked an identity crisis and why such desk-ridden types as William Hoffman, Edward Tailer, and Robert Graham, respectively battling constipation, miosis, and migraines, never had second thoughts about what they did for a living.[58]

James Madison's eighteenth-century rhetoric about republican government deriving its powers from the "great body of the people" thus acquired a far more tangible meaning in the nineteenth century. "The necessity of superintending the operations of life within his own body, inevitably falls upon every one, of every condition and every age," Edward Jarvis lectured audiences on the universal relevance of the "laws of physical life." "Every man is as competent as any other" in practicing those laws, the *Massachusetts Teacher* further determined, turning the question of health and disease into a means for measuring the shortcomings of those who failed to eat right or exercise properly, a natural—and neutral—source of social hierarchy in a democratic age. By establishing identifiable control over one's own constitution, that is to say, a person acquired the moral authority to judge others as being insufficiently in control. "Command yourself, and you command the world," Daniel Child wrote to himself in what was certainly the most concise aphorism for the era's new self-ruling class.[59]

But good health was much more than a means for camouflaging power. It also provided autonomous individuals with a grammar for talking to each other about themselves, turning a private habitus, ostensibly closed off from shared experience, into common sense. "A theory about how the world should be run will survive competition if it is more than a theory," the anthropologist Mary Douglas once observed.[60] Feeling sick was certainly more than a theory. Identifying one's symptoms, cataloging them on the basis of a recognizable diagnosis, and then pursuing the appropriate course of remedial action constituted a sequence of events that tied individuals together in a shared logic of cause and effect. Self-reflection could thus become the basis for mass communication.

The proliferation of desk diseases was driven, as such, by an Enlightenment ambition to make the hidden manifest and create a realm of public credibility and trust. Nervous disorders functioned as the source of that sympathy which Adam Smith considered essential for maintaining the social fabric once the market began to tear apart existing, corporate forms of community. "By the imagination we place ourselves in his situation, we conceive ourselves enduring all the same torments, we enter as it were into his body," Smith wrote. This pointed the way to a regime of personal health that offered an opportunity to simultaneously unite and separate the sovereign self from the rest of humanity. That is why physical education was never just a pedagogical initiative but a foundation of liberal political thought, physiology was not just a branch of science but a corollary of civic virtue, and medicine was not just a clinical response to disease but a redoubt against bad government.[61]

Being sick also served a market society of striving individuals because it respected neither formal privilege nor inherited status. Indeed, it pushed society in the opposite direction, placing self-government within reach of anyone who watched over his health, thus reinventing manhood for a postpatriarchal world of personal ambition, or, more to the point, reinventing patriarchy for a society in which "the boy is father of the man." The "legitimation crisis" provoked by the end of the household order, Jürgen Habermas wrote in the opening of his well-known discourse on modern politics, would be addressed by "the organism's self-healing powers," those that gave the subject "full possession of his powers." Was it not the aim of American institutions to make the whole nation into an aristocracy, the *Atlantic Monthly* asked, "to secure . . . splendid physical superiority on a grander scale?" Medicalization provided an ideal means for doing so. Did this mean that the civilizing process rested on atavistic bodies? Of course it did. Progress was the indisputable function of the ongoing interplay between biology and culture, instinct and will, and body and soul. The resulting tensions were not to be construed as contradictions, however, and certainly not as a sign of structural weakness. They were, instead, an invitation to every individual to take charge of himself by performing a well-rehearsed set of symptoms that allow each to then say to another, "I know how you're feeling."[62]

"Mankind always sets itself only such problems as it can solve," Marx once remarked. Desk diseases exemplified that practice. They encapsulated a social ethos with a highly practical agenda that envisioned a world not necessarily cured of chronic disorder, but one whose sovereign members consciously and methodically labored to bring the "constant strife" fed by their feverish ambitions under personal control, devoting their best efforts to ensuring that the object reflected in the mirror of their individuality was the "pure and beautiful" part of their character, as John Todd urged in *The Young Man*. Benjamin Franklin, as was his wont, had already identified this dynamic that became so central to market society. "Tho' I never arrived at the Perfection I had been so ambitious of obtaining, but fell far short of it," Franklin wrote in the *Autobiography*, "yet I was by the Endeavour a better and a happier Man than I otherwise should have been." The aim of physical education was not, in other words, omniscient command over one's condition, which was an unrealistic plan in such an age of fracture anyway. Instead, persons were to conscientiously pursue that sublime goal which might not be within reach, but whose very striving after was constitutive of their selves. Autonomous citizens, increasingly free of public oversight, could thus become the reliable foundation of public order, doing so, furthermore, by practicing their own autonomy. Individualism might be immune to external controls but such control was no longer necessary. Subjectivity proved to be an equally effective means of social regulation.[63]

"Civilization requires discontent," Bryan Turner has written in inverting common clichés regarding modern progress.[64] Nervous disorders, a constant in a world of flux, as well as the epitome of such flux, offered individuals a consistent selfhood that was wholly consonant with the ceaseless movement and mayhem of capitalist revolution. The sick body consequently proved vital to a healthy civic life because it negotiated the dialectics of chaos and control, fragment and whole, and particular and universal—all essential, if highly conflicted, values of modern industrial civilization. The resulting constipation, nausea, and headaches were a direct acknowledgment that the world was indeed being turned upside down, but that each individual was responsible—and able—to put it right.

5

Counting Persons, Counting Profits

In the "Vital Statistics of Boston," which was published in 1841, Lemuel Shattuck compared the previous three decades of the city's mortality rates and discovered a precipitous decline in the physical condition of its inhabitants. Extrapolating the raw numbers by race, age, sex, and residence, and applying English life insurance data as a control, he identified noxious air, poor diets, and the filthy streets of pauperized neighborhoods filling up with foreigners as the sources of an escalating medical crisis. With such big data in hand, the authorities would be equipped to undertake the broad sanitary initiatives required to ameliorate the danger, as Edward Jarvis noted in praising Shattuck's quantitative efforts on behalf of social reform. Jarvis himself was soon engaged by Congress to prepare a summary volume of the mortality figures returned by the federal census of 1850, a digest of unprecedented scope that was meant to provide a common measure of health and illness for the nation's citizenry at large.[1]

Shattuck and Jarvis were both members of the American Statistical Association, founded in Boston in 1839 to promote a view of society as the sum of its parts. This was an axiom of republican government as well, as were the allied notions of universality and transparency. Together, they positioned statistics on the barricades of political enlightenment, "developing results that can be calculated with mathematical precision," and in so doing, leading us, "step by step, to the knowledge of the laws that govern the social system," as the *Journal of the American Geographical and Statistical Society* proclaimed. The avalanche of numbers that followed, expanding enumerations of persons and property, farms and factories, marriages and migrations, and, of course, death and disease, became a critical means for reintegrating society in the fragmenting conditions of the age. Only by knowing more about one another,

the *North American Review* affirmed in an enthusiastic review of Adam Seybert's *Statistical Annals*, do "the people themselves . . . gradually shed their
local antipathies and prejudices, till mutual interest and affection spring from
acquaintance, and in time ripen into a steady and durable patriotism."[2]

Benjamin Foster, William Hoffman, Edward Tailer, Charles French, Robert Graham, Samuel Munson, Henry Patterson, Edward Thomas, and George
Cayley played no direct role in administering this new system of social accountancy. Nonetheless, the statistics were thoroughly infused with clerical production values, organized around the same tenets of paperwork that distilled the
flux of events into their constituent parts, which could then be reconfigured
into more useful patterns of causal chains and tabular sequences. By deriving
an inclusive record of collective experience from the particularities of so many
separate lives, in fact, statistics proved uniquely effective in documenting society's great transformation from stability and absoluteness into motions and
relations. Mobility, temporality, relativity, novelty, anonymity, and utility—all
those laws that "doth the man unking"—were recast into the basis of a universal
order resting in equal measure on persons and profits.

Everyone Counts

Statistics were founded on "a number of isolated facts," Francis Lieber explained in his proposed survey of the welfare of the species in 1836, "which
thus isolated have little value for human experience." Lieber, who opened a
subscription gymnasium and swimming school in Boston after arriving in
America from Germany in the late 1820s, recognized that only after all those
isolated facts were collected and classified would they become statistics, capable of leading to a knowledge of the laws that govern the social system.
In practical terms, this was accomplished by cross-referencing one fact with
another (and another, and another), either over time (by comparing, for instance, the number of unmarried men residing in New York City in 1850 to the
number residing there fifty years earlier), over space (by comparing the number of unmarried men residing in New York City in 1850 to the number residing in Charleston, South Carolina that same year), or simultaneously over
time and space (by comparing the change in the number of unmarried men
residing in both New York City and Charleston over the past fifty years). The
operative principle of all this counting was simple: the greater the number
and variety of facts that were collected, the greater the volume of comparisons
that could then be made, yielding a richer, more precise record of the human
condition. "It is only from a series of particular facts, that the mind ascends to
general truths," B. F. Foster summarized the naturalist underpinnings of his

philosophy of accounts in *Double-Entry Elucidated*. What was true of commercial science proved no less relevant to what some now began to call "political science."[3]

Census marshals had, of course, been counting the number of persons
residing in each "dwelling house" in the United States since 1790. However,
these were never more than aggregations arranged, at best, by age cohorts and
sex. Only the head of the household was personally identified, and that was
largely for bureaucratic convenience. Such meager quantifications matched
the federal constitution's original intent of establishing a decennial enumeration of the nation's population to determine its rates of taxation and representation. They also reflected the patriarchal structure of social life subsumed
under the aegis of the little commonwealth. "Little information," the *North
American Review* acknowledged of the requirements for government in the
early republic, "was sufficient to provide for the wants and exigencies of the
community . . . composed of wood-cutters and farmers."[4]

Divisions of labor had since redistributed the people "into so many classes,"
the *Review* continued, thus rendering community an elusive condition. "The
woof of time is ever being broken and the track of past generations lost," Tocqueville too observed of a democracy whose citizens were engaged in a continual
negotiation over the terms of their own happiness. Those who came before
were frequently forgotten, as a result, "and no one gives a thought to those who
will follow." Such social amnesia prompted the Boston physician and statistical
activist Jesse Chickering to write to Lemuel Shattuck in 1844 on his ongoing
frustrations in documenting the contribution of Massachusetts to the settlement of the frontier. Had a competent system of birth and domicile registration been in place over the years, Chickering complained, "we might deduce
from it a near approximation to the number of these emigrants" who have
departed their native state for other regions of the country. In the absence of
any such information, however, nothing could definitively be known about
either the numbers or the character of the great movement of population that
proved so critical to the nation's development. Americans clearly required new
sources of memory—if not collective identity—in keeping up with the fluid
circumstances of their lives.[5]

Statistics, a system of knowledge founded on the very conditions of un-
knowability prevailing in a society where ever-greater numbers of persons
found themselves living outside familiar networks of household and village,
would serve as such a source. Indeed, the proliferation of property and population so characteristic of the times was the very measure of statistical practice, as well as the practical objects of its enumerations. In generalizing from
the particular to fashion a novel relationship between the individual and the

universal, statistics proved uniquely capable of generating order out of the postpatriarchal commotion without resorting to, or restoring, any of the old hierarchies. The "age, sex, condition, occupation and numbers of a people," compared with "their moral and social state," and further cross-referenced with "their education and industry," resulted in cascading sets of regressions that turned variety and multiplicity into the foundation of regularity, and even commonality. Statistics were not, as such, intimidated by the tendency of market society to make the value of everything permanently relative. Born of comparisons, in fact, the statistical record was relative by nature, philosophically consistent with both a democratic polity and a capitalist economy, each of which promoted self-possession into an inalienable right that dispersed sovereignty over all of society. And while such relativity subverted the possibility of establishing a single, transcendent truth, statistics—not unlike the business ledger—responded by achieving a comprehensive view of social life that rested on an infinite number of autonomous fragments, or facts, as Francis Lieber called them.[6]

The archetype for this new way of knowing was Sir John Sinclair's *Statistical Account of Scotland*, an unprecedentedly inclusive record of rents, wages, climate conditions, cultivation methods, schools, roads, bridges, and inns, as well as the age, occupation, and place of birth of each member of every family, all subdivided by parish and published in twenty-one separate volumes over the course of the last decade of the eighteenth century. Sinclair's compilation of data, "a work embracing contributions from nine hundred pens," was designed to provide the raw materials for a projected "system of political economy founded on statistical researches." The initiative was lauded as the very first attempt to organize a comprehensive account of the whole fabric of social relations rather than to simply measure "the political strength of a country." This signaled a conscious advance over the mortality tables and life expectancy estimates generated a hundred years earlier under the rubric of "political arithmetic." That initial interest in attaining an overview of the kingdom derived from the lives of its subjects was, not unlike later quantifications, also driven by the disintegration of traditional structures of authority. Revolutionary unrest in seventeenth-century Britain spurred an anxious search for knowledge anchored in more certain "Terms of *Number*, *Weight*, or *Measure*," as William Petty explained at the time, an attempt to free government from the "mutable Minds, Opinions, Appetites, and Passions of particular Men." At the same time, however, political arithmetic was devoted to fortifying rather than replacing authoritarian rule. Its numbers were accordingly treated as a state secret serving a centralized apparatus of power, developed to enhance the sovereign's ability to impose order from above.[7]

Statistics inverted that relationship between knowledge and power, which is why publication of the *Statistical Account of Scotland* signaled a watershed in the history of social quantification. Its numbers were meant to reveal "the degree of happiness [society] actually enjoys" and then to circulate en masse, becoming no less than "a *new* branch of politics," as Sinclair himself declared. This marked the end of philosophical absolutism no less than political absolutism since society was to now determine its own order on the basis of the growing quantity and quality of extant knowledge available about itself, knowledge that was unavailable to personal powers of observation. "The comparative fecundity and mortality . . . as influenced by the different circumstances of location, climate, occupation, degrees of prosperity, &c.," was just one axis of human experience, for instance, that remained invisible, if not inconceivable, until the fragmentary details of thousands of separate lives were statistically organized and published. The attendant aggregations, correlations, and tabulations transcribed local particularities into a placeless universe of generalities and then returned that generalized picture back to its source, apprising citizens of the efficacy of hygienic measures in preventing disease, the influence of education on criminal behavior, the range of employments available to able-bodied adults, and the respective monetary value of goods being produced by hand or machine. Edward Jarvis even insisted that personal experience itself only became intelligible after being statistically vetted. "Such public and permanent records concerning every individual [meant] that he may be able to establish his identity, his personality, and his relation to others." Without this systematization of difference, the citizens of a large republic would find it difficult to recognize one another, let alone talk sensibly and authoritatively about such essential subjects of mutual concern as political representation, economic competition, moral emulation, and self-improvement.[8]

This growing mass of information would thus "increase the public's zest for more," J. D. B. DeBow, superintendent of the Office of the Census, declared in 1854, conjuring a population avidly embracing the recursive qualities of a measurement regime whose collations and comparisons were touted as the truest expression of an increasingly complex social reality. Statistics were clearly moving beyond their etymological roots, informed, that is, by a recognizable "concern of man in man" which mirrored the market's reinvention of society as an entity that no longer bound persons together, *a priori*, into a transcendent collective but was actively bound together by them. Community would be imposed from below, operating through a feedback loop of self-regulation that rested on "a more positive knowledge of the real state of things," as the *United States Magazine and Democratic Review* declared in explaining the need for an expansion of the federal census's catagories of inquiry. A congressional report from 1844 endorsed the establishment of a new bureau of statistics in similar terms, arguing that political oppression resulted from laws enacted on "partial and imperfect information" that invariably favored one class over another. Since government in the United States was founded on "the *mass* of the people," legislative deliberation needed to encompass "*every interest* and *every class* of the community." This is what made it incumbent on the republic to organize a thorough statistical program embracing all aspects of civic life, a tool for making government simultaneously of all and of each which accorded a new, far more plural meaning to the nation's motto, *E pluribus unum.* Archibald Russell could therefore argue in *Principles of Statistical Inquiry,* the first theoretical work on the subject written in the United States upon its publication in 1839, that "the investigation proceeds from no party feeling," and that was because "all interests, commercial and manufacturing, agricultural and professional, are alike to be represented."[9]

"Beneath this arithmetical exterior there are found the great cardinal facts of our real life," *Harper's Magazine* likewise gushed in comparing the 138 interrogatories and six separate schedules of the federal census in 1850—including a column for each person's "place of birth" that addressed Jesse Chickering's frustrations in mapping the country's migration patterns—to the lone "pamphlet" derived from the six queries comprising the nation's inaugural enumeration of 1790. The nearly limitless range of permutations that became possible when cross-referencing such a vast inventory of "isolated facts" yielded a record that "most directly concerns life, property, the promotion of happiness, and the alleviation of misery," as Joseph Kennedy, DeBow's predecessor in the Census Office, excitedly pronounced in describing the unprecedentedly expansive purview of this seventh census of the nation's social life. "The human mind dwells with satisfaction upon ascertained results, which evince a progressive knowledge respecting the real condition of the human family."[10]

And yet the "real condition of the human family" was not quite the straightforward arithmetical function that the numbers suggested. This was because the statistics were a qualitative rather than quantitative event, the outcome of a particular scheme for counting. The size of the federal census had, in fact, been dramatically expanded a decade earlier in response to the political and economic turmoil of the 1830s which revealed just how much the republic was no longer the exclusive domain of farmers and woodcutters . The population schedule was extended to seventy-four columns. Occupational categories were added. Educational institutions were enumerated. Literacy was measured. The insane were counted. And separate schedules were instituted for surveying agricultural and manufacturing enterprise—all in search of new sources of hierarchy and commonality in a market society busily dismantling the old order. Despite the ensuing volume of facts, however, the returns were widely dismissed as unusable. Even the American Statistical Association expressed its formal regret "that such documents," on whose behalf the organization had so strenuously lobbied, "have the sanction of Congress."[11]

The startlingly high rate of insanity reported among free blacks and enthusiastically embraced by pro-slavery ideologues was just the most notorious example of the skewed nature of the census numbers. The problem was, in part, administrative. Processing the thousands of manuscripts returned from the field required an intensive clerical effort for transcribing the mass of figures generated by the census's new queries onto oversized sheets subdivided into an interminable range of discrete fields. Only then could the raw data be tabulated and effectively correlated. But Congress's refusal to fund the bureaucratic apparatus necessitated by the census's far-reaching statistical program doomed the undertaking to social and scientific irrelevance. There were likewise no means for establishing a regular review procedure in the Washington office for correcting the manifold discrepancies in the completed census blanks even after the errors were discovered. The results proved "so very inaccurate, that any conclusions founded upon them are entirely unsafe" for either guiding legislation or informing public conversation.[12]

But these failures were also the result of design flaws which no amount of administrative supervision could rectify. Once we "desire to know something more than the mere numbers of the people," as Lemuel Shattuck soon explained, mere columns of figures would no longer suffice. Quantification may or may not yield statistical knowledge, that is to say: "combination and deduction are required to give them full effect." Shattuck argued that the sixth census's scheme for collecting the numbers was "too general to admit of any classification except the one originally made." This meant that the addition of so many new subjects of inquiry contributed very little additional knowledge as long as they were organized around the traditional categories of a static social order. The constitution of the household, for example, or the output of cotton mills, continued to be measured on the basis of conventional notions regarding the nature of households and cotton mills. The ensuing extrapolations could do little more than replicate those conventions, restricting the range of combinations and deductions to the patriarchal structure of family life or the long-established role of textile production in the manufacturing economy. To turn the census into a tool of statistical investigation capable of documenting "the rapid changes constantly taking place in our condition, the unyielding ambition of our people, the irregularity of enterprise, [and] the new and exciting temptations in prospects of wealth," as Nahum Capen wrote in 1849 in urging Congress to revise the taxonomy of the forthcoming enumeration of 1850, a wholly new plan for counting was required, elastic enough to allow for a mass of anonymous details to be "abstracted and combined in very many different ways." Only then, Lemuel Shattuck argued, would it become possible to generate "a much greater variety of interesting and important results."[13]

This was first achieved in 1845, in a population census of the city of Boston designed by Shattuck himself. Drawing on recent British innovations, the Boston census used a classification method that posed all queries to all persons, who were then each assigned their own separate line in the census form. This "mode of personal inquiry," as Shattuck referred to his individuated taxonomy, offered an unprecedented plan for collecting "many different classes of facts" which, due to their subsequent variety, could be combined and recombined in a rich array of relations encompassing all men, women, and children, thus revealing the extensive interplay between whole and parts in a society based on motion and relations. The "almost indefinite number of classes" of comparison that ensued had never been possible "on the plan by which the censuses have hitherto been taken" and that was because the population was hitherto counted under the collective aegis of the household, which necessarily purged the returns of all personal information, namely, the "color, sex, age, domestic condition, occupation, place of birth, wealth, education, and otherwise" of each and every member of society. The almost indefinite number of resulting comparisons, what's more, would be of "a greater or less degree of interest and importance," Shattuck further explained. Indeed, that very indeterminate quality regarding the significance of the various returns, detached as they were from any prior assumptions regarding the source of social order, was the key to this new system of enumeration and the crux of its epistemological breakthrough. The "unyielding ambition of our people," that is to say, as well as the irregularity of their enterprise and the new and exciting prospects in their wealth, would be revealed only after, rather than before, the data was collected—only after all the personalized pieces of experience were duly "abstracted and combined." This procedure inverted the older, corporate relationship between self and society by assuming that the latter was only discoverable by knowing the former. Public life thus became a function of the interaction between a horde of discrete variables entirely divorced from any peremptory notion of what they had in common, or of what even constituted commonality to begin with. Society lost its autonomous status while being reconstituted as a "combination" of ephemeral, arbitrary experiences systematically compiled from the "minute subdivisions" of individual lives. The singularity of private experience consequently became the means for discovering

| (No. 4.) | SCHEDULE of the whole number of persons within the division allotted to ... |

Completed population census blank from 1840.

"the numbers and condition of the American people in all their relations," as Joseph Kennedy announced in a lecture before the American Geographical and Statistical Society devoted to the achievements of the 1850 census returns, which had incorporated the personal mode of inquiry. "The history of each and every individual" was thus promoted into the organizing principle of the statistical project, Kennedy further declared in acknowledging that all of the nation's previous statistical surveys had constituted little more than "diversions and illusions" resting on biased schemes and narrow ideologies.[14]

These statistics were a true American system, a technology, that is, developed for transcribing the unique qualities of each citizen into an interchangeable sequence of characters that could be recombined with analogous data collected from other—indeed, from all—persons who had been duly supplied ahead of time by the newspapers with a list of interrogatories in anticipation of the census official's visit. "The heads of families; the owners, agents

SCHEDULE I.—Free Inhabitants in _Boston, Ward 11_ in the County of _Suffolk_ State of _Mass_ enumerated by me, on the _7_ day of _August_ 1850. _Geo Adams_ Ass't Marshal.

Dwelling-houses numbered in the order of visitation	Families numbered in the order of visitation	The Name of every Person whose usual place of abode on the first day of June, 1850, was in this family.	Age	Sex	Color	Profession, Occupation, or Trade of each Male Person over 15 years of age	Value of Real Estate owned	Place of Birth, Naming the State, Territory, or County	Married within the year	Attended School within the year	Persons over 20 y'rs of age who cannot read & write	Whether deaf and dumb, blind, insane, idiotic, pauper, or convict	
1	2	3	4	5	6	7	8	9	10	11	12	13	
16	16	Jane Hagan	23	f				Ireland					1
		C. Floyd	25	f									2
17	17	S. E. Guito	20	m		Counsellor	18,000	Mass					3
		Elizabeth "	25	f				"					4
		Charlotte "	2	f				"					5
		N. McGorvan	21	f				Canada					6
		Mary "	23	f				"					7
		Sarah "	40	f				"					8
18	18	S. R. Russell	27	m		Merchant		Mass					9
		Louisa "	29	f				"					10
		Ellen "	1	f				"					11
		Hannah (unknown)	50	f				"					12
19	19	G. W. Wales	34	m		Merchant		"					13
		Maria "	32	f									14
		John Mather	31	m		Saloon		Ireland					15
		Eliza Graham	42	f				Mass					16
		M. Peely	24	f				Ireland					17
20	20	G. H. Perkins	25	m		Merchant		Mass					18
		Catherine "	24	f				"					19
		G. Baylor	40	m		Saloon		England					20
		T. Hay	20	f				Mass					21
		E. Sanders	25	f				"					22
21	21	G. A. French	50	m		Merchant	7,000	"					23
		Lucy T. "	45	f				"					24
		John G. "	16	m		none		"		1			25
		Charles E. "	13	m				"		1			26
		P. Wm. "	8	m				"		1			27
		Joseph P. Williams	21	m		Clerk		R. I.					28
		Mary Morgan	20	f				Ireland			1		29
22	22	Luther Drew	40	m		Machinist	8,000	Me.					30
		Mary "	38	f				"					31
		Albert "	10	m				"					32
		Sophia Hilton	50	f				Mass					33
		Nathaniel Deanes	24	m		Carpenter		"					34
		Henry Morgan	31	m		unknown		"					35
		Mary E. "	27	f				"					36
		Augustus "	20	m		none		"					37
		William Trundy	21	m		Cand. Maker		"					38
		George "	19	m		Clerk		"					39
		Catherine Finley	20	f				Ireland			1		40
		Samuel Boice	15	m				"					41
		James Breden	10	m				"			1		42

Completed population census blank from 1850.

and occupants of farms, manufactories, stores, and workshops; the persons in charge of educational, charitable and religious institutions; the officers of the various cities, towns, and counties"—all were mobilized in generating this ledger of national experience. "Like the merchant in his books," DeBow consequently wrote in his introduction to the *Compendium* of the seventh census, "the citizen can read, at one view, all of the results of a year or of a period of years, as compared with other periods, and deduce the profit or the loss which has been made, in morals, education, wealth or power."[15]

The practical logistics of this new system of social accounting were to be observed in an otherwise innocuous genre scene painted by Francis William Edmonds in 1854 entitled *Taking the Census*. Edmonds's canvas depicted a family assembled around the open hearth of their modest cottage in welcoming a guest. Sunlight streams through the home's open windows and door in what seems, at first glance, to be little more than a rehearsal of the era's popular sentimentalizations of rural life. But Edmonds had not painted a casual visit between country neighbors. The family has assembled, rather, to welcome the census agent, who confidently assumes his place before them with quill and folio in hand, posing his questions and dutifully recording their rejoinders onto "forms made so as to be understood by any person of common sagacity," as the Census Office had directed upon mailing out the three thousand reams of paper "blanks" that comprised the raw material for the ensuing reports. That transposition of quotidian lives into standard census categories marked the very moment, in fact, when personal experience was converted into the "positive knowledge of the real state of things," turning Edmonds's country idyll into an incisive vignette of the reinvention of society.[16]

That process actually began before the census enumerator crossed anyone's threshold, for it was first necessary to engineer a system for compensating the ad hoc army of 3,276 subaltern officials recruited by the federal authorities to canvass a population dispersed over the entire continent. This was accomplished by multiplying the square root of the number of dwellings visited by each deputy marshal with the square root of the number of square miles which constituted each census district. The resulting parabola curve then became the basis of a sliding pay scale. Once all the visits were completed and the blanks filled out in triplicate, the forms were mailed back to Washington to be reviewed by Census Office clerks, who had been supplemented by extra hires in November, and returned to the field for corrections, if necessary, before then being tabulated, printed, and distributed back to a society now informed of its variable birthrates, age at marriage, and numbers of insane. At least fifty thousand bound copies of the resulting *Compendium* were printed up the same year that Edmonds made his painting, condensing "ten or fifteen millions of figures" into a single volume of ratio and comparative tables that presented a spectacular example of statistical acumen and the intrinsic efficiency of written over verbal expression. Printed on octavo rather that folio paper in order to reduce the volume's bulk and weight, thus making it easier to hold and read, and to mail, let alone arrange on the "statistical shelves" of the Mercantile Library, the *Compendium* was destined to reach almost every family in America, "where it must become, to some extent, the subject of conversation and discussion."[17]

Not everyone embraced this new system for "knowing all about everything," even if census agents were specifically instructed to behave "in such gentlemanly terms as disarms prejudice, and secures confidence and good will" when posing their queries and recording the responses. It is my business to inquire, madam, a deputy explained to a recalcitrant citizen in one anecdote that circulated throughout the country in the summer of 1850. "Well, you tell Mr. Congress, or whatever his name is, that he acts very foolish, sending you round, axing sich shaller silly questions." Prying into the domestic economy of the people was a precursor to direct taxes, the opponents of social quantification warned in mobilizing traditional fears of government conspiracy and corruption. "Old ladies were confidently told by disinterested and patriotic whig electioneerers and stump orators that the design in taking an account of their poultry, butter, eggs and homespun, was to ascertain what amount would be required from each to feed and clothe Mr. Van Buren's standing army."[18]

The census bill itself, passed only on the final day of the congressional session in 1849, incited an extended and acrimonious debate in the Senate over questions of constitutional intent and state prerogative. The most strident opposition to statistical reform came in an ultimately successful effort to strike out proposals for recording the names, birthplace, and offspring of slaves. Opponents wondered aloud as to what possible use the federal state could have for this kind of information. Doubts were even raised about the practical existence of such facts. As Senator King of Alabama explained, "the woman herself, in nine out of ten cases . . . does not know how many [children] she has actually had. [A laugh.]" In fact, the specter of census officials visiting the slave quarters in accordance with the new mode of personal inquiry was a dire portent of even graver federal interventions in the master's exclusive relationship with his chattel. At one point in the debate, William Seward sought to defuse Southern objections by assuming the matter-of-fact syntax of scientific objectivity. "The number of children that each woman has borne, the

number that are living, and the number that are dead"—all were practical details intended to no more than "ascertain . . . the question of comparative longevity," Seward explained. Certainly, no reference to or formal recognition of
Negro equality was intended. In fact, as another proponent of the census bill
reassured his colleagues, the proceeding returns were more than likely to cor-
roborate reigning racial assumptions, for by posing the same standard set of
personal queries to both slaves and free whites, direct comparisons between
the populations would become possible for the first time, no doubt providing new empirical support "for Professor Agassiz's theories" on the inherent
inferiority of the slave. But King and his colleagues were unappeased. They
recognized the threat to patriarchal authority and republican tradition that
was inherent in a statistical science which, by putting "the social and physical
condition of the masses of society" on a universal footing in order to carry
out its comparisons, replaced organic hierarchy with equivalence.[19]

Statistics did not just provoke traditional fears of "intrusive intruders" and
the "pestilence" of tyranny, let alone the abolition of slavery. A newer form
of trepidation was evident as well, driven by suspicions of an empiricism that
left "scarcely a fragment or fibre of [our] Soul, Body, and Possessions, but has
been probed, dissected, distilled, desiccated, and scientifically decomposed,"
as Thomas Carlyle complained of modern positivism. His protest found a
direct echo in the pages of the *Massachusetts Teacher*, which expressed similar concerns about an intellectual fashion that "rated, priced, and labeled according to our relative value." Statistical truth, these skeptics realized, turned
living and breathing persons into synthetic abstractions, standard deviations,
samples, estimates, probabilities, equivalencies, correlations, regressions, maximizations, likelihoods, and equations—all of which rested on a zero-sum relationship with their own humanity. That was too high a price to pay for the
civilizing process. "How many males in the family?" a census marshal asked
in another popular quip that year. "Three males a day," came the non sequitur
in response, exposing the crisis of correspondence provoked once everyone
was required to speak in the empirical grammar of universalized census categories. Another pun made the same point in even sharper terms:

> "Madam, I am out with the census, and—"
> "Well, you act out of senses, I should think, to come into my house, asking
> such questions."[20]

This resistance to the rule of "oeconomists, and calculators" was fueled by the
popular realization that statistics sought to replace one form of common sense
with another, the updated version proving far more consistent with a society
of relative value and self-making men.[21]

Taking the Census by William Edmonds.

Industrial Measures

The new common sense found its most definitive expression in the seventh census's schedule of manufactures, which was considered a crowning achievement after decades of self-professed failure in measuring the economy's inputs and outputs. Those earlier efforts dated back to a proposal by James Madison to include a query on occupation in the first federal census of 1790. It would be a most effective means for determining the relative size of each sector of the American economy, Madison contended, which was particularly important information in light of the role that factions played in government and the structural tensions that characterized the relationship between "a landed interest, a manufacturing interest, a mercantile interest, a moneyed interest, [and] many lesser interests" in the new republic. But while Congress enacted several other suggestions for expanding the nation's inaugural census beyond the simple body count mandated by the constitution—by identifying the head of each family by name, for instance, and by distinguishing not only slave from free but "whites" from "all other free persons," clear testimony to the growing importance of racial identity in American civic life—the inventory of occupations was rejected by legislators who considered it, as Madison later complained to Jefferson, to be little more than materials "for idle people to make a book." Conscious, no doubt, of the authoritarian legacy of political arithmetic—and taking a cue from English Whigs who had staunchly opposed a population census in 1753 as "utterly ruining the last freedoms of the English people"—a majority of the Senate thwarted Madison's plan to turn the federal enumeration into "an opportunity of obtaining the most useful information."[22]

Jefferson himself played a part in the next effort to expand the scope of the census, affixing his name in 1800 in his capacity as president of the American Philosophical Society to a memorial that underscored the role of the decennial census in "promot[ing] useful knowledge." The introduction of age categories was deemed especially important since these would then make it possible to construct life expectancy tables. A more elaborate version of Madison's earlier call for listing the occupation of the head of each household was taken up as well and endorsed by the Connecticut Academy of Arts and Sciences. Nine categories were identified—learned professions, merchants and traders (a definition that included bankers, insurers, brokers, and "dealers of every kind"), mariners, handicraftsmen, agricultural laborers, laborers of all other descriptions, domestic servants, paupers, and "persons of no particular calling living on their income"—of which each respondent was to be assigned just one in order to ensure that he appear "but once in this table." That rule made obvious statistical sense but posed practical difficulties in an agrarian society whose divisions of labor remained tentative and unfixed. Close to half the farmers residing in the more commercialized regions of Massachusetts, for instance, continued to toil in crafts and other pursuits, practicing a vocational versatility born of the material exigencies of a nonspecialized, preindustrial economy. Such taxonomical issues remained moot, however, since this second attempt to turn the census into a statistical digest of political economy was rejected once again by Congress.[23]

All that changed in 1810. The third federal census, which was also the first to mandate personal visits by officials to each homestead—a plan that required a division of the United States into formal enumeration districts—was also the first to feature a "Digest of Manufactures." Madison was by now, of course, president. But the critical impetus for using the census to document the nation's manufacturing activities was the trade embargo and the associated campaign on behalf of domestic industries capable of supplying substitutes for unavailable foreign goods. Tench Coxe, a former assistant secretary of the Treasury under Hamilton who played a central role in producing the landmark *Report on Manufactures* in 1791, declared in *Statement of the Arts and Manufactures of the United States of America,* which summarized the 1810 census returns, that "very useful data" had indeed been assembled, making it possible to compare the value of internal commerce (and American-made goods) to external trade, or foreign imports. Because no one was legally bound to divulge this information, however, in contrast to the formal sanctions—and monetary fines—levied against persons refusing to respond to the census's queries on population, the industrial returns were troublingly incomplete. Enumerators were also allowed personal discretion in determining what to include in their survey of manufacturing activities. The official digest of enterprise assembled by Congress was "intended merely to give a direction to inquires." As a result, the returns were judged so "imperfect" that in creating a coherent index based on the raw figures, as the *North American Review* complained a few years later, Coxe "was obliged to fill so many chasms by objecture and deduction." Historians have since discovered that more than half the totals of the value of products reported in the official *Statement* of the 1810 census were not to be found in the returns at all, but issued from Coxe's own independent estimates.[24]

Nevertheless, a precedent was established for producing a systematic body of knowledge regarding the industrializing economy and for using the administrative apparatus of the federal census in doing so. The expanded province of the census, what's more, while clearly addressing the needs of the hour, was also motivated by the general effort to develop an American statistical program which now included, in addition to Coxe's *Statement of the Arts and Manufactures,* Samuel Blodget's *Economica: A Statistical Manual for the United States of America* (1806), Timothy Dwight's *Statistical Account of the City of New-Haven* (1811), Timothy Pitkin's *Statistical View of the Commerce of the United States* (1816), and Adam Seybert's *Statistical Annals* (1818). That corpus of works was testimony to both the growing place of social quantification in public life and to its primitive condition. Adam Seybert, for instance, whose eight-hundred-page *Annals* drew on an extensive range of data assembled from a miscellany of state offices and authorities, found himself, thirty years after James Madison's initial proposal, still expostulating on the critical need for gathering information about the professions and trades, "a most useful fact" that remained unknown even though "[it] will throw more light upon the actual state of our economy, than any other." In reviewing Seybert's work on the eve of the next federal enumeration of 1820, the *North American Review* elaborated on such claims by arguing that the country's "productiveness or modes of making profit" needed to become the subject of systematic measurement. The republic required a statistics that would move beyond the world of the farmer and the mercantilist and offer "an account of all . . .

capital," a system of knowledge revealing all the avenues by which citizens exercise their "mental and physical powers" in pursuit of material happiness.[25]

This seemed to finally happen in 1820, when the fourth census of the United States incorporated Madison's original proposal for a survey of occupations—albeit with considerably less detail than proponents had hoped—while also alerting marshals to the fact that "the discrimination between persons engaged in agriculture, commerce, and manufactures, will not be without its difficulties [since] no inconsiderable portion of the population . . . will answer to all three."[26] In addition to the new "labor" data, the census also introduced far greater system into its schedule of manufactures, improving on the haphazard precedent from the previous decade by establishing a plan based on universals and equivalences, the essential conditions for generating tabular summaries. Fourteen standard queries were included in the official instructions sent from Washington to agents in the field, directing them to record the type and amounts of raw materials used in production, the number and wages of those hired to do so, further distinguished by sex, the type of machinery, if any, in use, and the quality and quantity of the finished products. Household production was excluded from the records since "it seems fairly deducible" that this type of manufacturing constituted an "incidental" effort rather than anyone's principal economic activity, and so should not be allowed to determine "the class of society to which such individual belongs." That disqualification was wholly consistent with the census's occupational taxonomy, which likewise prevented anyone from being both a farmer and an artisan for fear of helplessly skewing the statistical attempt to document society's divisions of labor. Farming might, as such, have now emerged in the historical record as a full-fledged vocation for the first time because of the census's own rules of accounting rather than the opposite.[27]

Once a fixed roster of interrogatories for manufacturing enterprises was established, it became possible to pose identical questions to all those engaged in production, which then made it possible to generate a comparable—comparisons, of course, being the crux of the statistical program—abstract of assets and expenditures encompassing all of the country's industries. The census blanks of 1820 thus came to resemble a balance sheet of earnings and expenses. In a further attempt at systematization, the Census Office issued an alphabetized manifest of those branches of manufacture that were to be surveyed. The list was extensive but not binding, for officials also acknowledged the great variety of productive activity found throughout the United States, variation that could not be exhaustively anticipated by a single set of guidelines. As such, the catalog was "intended merely to give a direction to inquires, and each will add to it every manufacture not included in it and of which he takes an account within his division." But whether this preprinted index of productive enterprise was followed to the letter, or revised at the personal discretion of the census marshals—and despite the general effort to standardize the new manufacturing schedule with a form containing fourteen common queries—the results proved no less partial and arbitrary than the numbers collected a decade earlier: the same inventory of textiles, metals, leather, glass, and shipbuilding industries that constituted the heart of the traditional mercantile economy was returned in 1820. In that respect, the formal rationalizations introduced into the design of the fourth census could still not be properly described as statistical, for they continued to count what was already known rather than uncover the realities existing beneath the "arithmetical exterior" of material life. This is what Joseph Kennedy eventually dismissed in 1859 as closed systems resting on narrow ideological habits.[28]

In fact, all surveys of American productive industry undertaken up until this point were based on the same paradigm that anchored Hamilton's *Report on Manufactures* in 1791, devoted as it was, in the words of the country's first secretary of the Treasury, to "promoting such as will tend to render the United States independent of foreign nations." These were the traditional tenets of both moral economy and political arithmetic, determining the relative importance of this or that undertaking to the commonweal and then collecting information in accordance to that same hierarchy, which subsequently came to constitute official knowledge of the economy. The explicit goal of the new schedule of industry in the census of 1810 might have been to discover "the actual condition of manufactures" in the country at large, but this referred solely to enterprises capable of replacing embargoed imports with domestically produced goods, or those industries considered essential for the settlement of new territories. Such criteria omitted "shoes, boots, saddles, bridles, harness, fur and wool hats, common smiths work, knit stockings, the making of garments in shops and families, manufactures of wool, soap, candles, potash, wares of metal (except iron) watches and clocks, and various other things actually made," and that was because such activities had never played a significant role in the import economy to begin with.[29]

The following decade witnessed a groundswell of empirical initiatives as scientific positivism converged with reformist anxieties provoked by the rise of a social order organized around the market. The American Physiology Society and American Statistical Association were, tellingly, founded just as economic Panic broke out across the country. Francis Lieber formulated his précis for surveying the welfare of the species, and Archibald Russell published his *Principles of Statistical Inquiry*, timed to coincide with congressional debate over the upcoming census bill that Russell hoped to remake into a thoroughgoing statistical instrument for measuring social relations rather than the political condition of the country, since "good order depends more upon the former than on the latter." Similar steps were undertaken outside the federal system as well, evident in the unprecedented scope of state and city censuses, many of whose innovations were incorporated in the decennial enumeration of 1840. In addition to a new interest in "vital" statistics devoted to medical subjects, the sixth federal census was also designed to amass "all such information in relation to mines, agriculture, commerce, [and] manufactures . . . as will exhibit a full view of the pursuits, industry, education, and resources of the country." This extensive registry of the country's material assets even prompted Jesse Chickering to observe that while population had constituted the principal object of national surveys in the past, the focus of investigation was shifting. "Wealth" would constitute the heart of the census project after 1840.[30]

Russell and his colleagues soon understood that the quantitative expansion of the enumeration was no guarantee of a qualitatively truer result. As the American Statistical Association explained in a memorial presented to Congress addressing the flaws of the ambitiously comprehensive sixth census, thirty-five residents of Albany, New York had been listed in the returns as engaging in commercial occupations, while in Troy, another Hudson Valley town half the size of Albany, that same column yielded a total of 796. Similar discrepancies were manifest in the account of hemp grown in Kentucky, the quality of bituminous coal mined in New Hampshire, the number of importers doing business in New Orleans, and the activity of commission houses trading in Massachusetts. These were the kind of obvious inconsistencies that Census Office clerks were hired to uncover and send back to local officials for correction, which, however, had not been done. Bureaucratic negligence was not the only problem. Some deputy marshals failed to include retail merchants in their canvas to begin with, as the Statistical Association observed, even though it was common knowledge that "every town in New England, and every county in the United States" hosted such a trade.[31]

The missing data was indicative of a problem that extended far beyond questions of administrative incompetence, for no one had equipped the enumerators with effective criteria for determining what, in fact, constituted a commercial occupation. The Census Office, an ad hoc operation established anew every ten years in carrying out the constitutionally mandated survey of the nation's population, similarly refrained from supplying marshals with a standard and binding definition of what qualified as "manufactures," which undermined the explicit aim of achieving a "full view" of the nation's industry. Instead, a putatively exhaustive list of forty-five separate branches of industry borrowed from the manufacturing schedule developed in 1820 was distributed to all agents. In thus determining ahead of time which kinds of production were worthy of being counted—a catalog resting on prior knowledge of what constituted a production economy—and then designing specific queries for each of those branches in accordance to their known practices, the census returns proved at once arbitrary and conventional. They were certainly incapable of reflecting the "rapid changes taking place in our condition" or the "irregularity of enterprise" that was so characteristic of the times and most in need of statistical ordering. As a result, the detailed roster of discrete interrogatories to be posed to the country's respective branches of industry required the addition of a forty-sixth, miscellaneous category given over to "all other manufactures," a category whose very lack of definition defied the systematic conceits of the document as a whole. And so it was that the ultimate significance of the sixth census's unprecedentedly ambitious attempt to generate a complete view of American economic development was in the operative conclusions drawn by its disappointed supporters; namely, that any attempt to measure and consequently govern life in a market society required a wholly new paradigm for counting.[32]

That happened, as we have seen, in 1850. Heartened by widespread recognition of the failures of the previous decade, the New-York Historical Society and American Statistical Association called on Congress, in appeals respectively authored by Archibald Russell and Lemuel Shattuck, to mobilize expert opinion in order to rectify past errors and create a new manner of census capable of realizing its statistical potential. Their program was not universally embraced. Congress continued to appoint political rather than professional figures to head the Census Office, for instance. It also established a new body called the "Census Board," composed of the secretary of state, the attorney general, and the postmaster general, to oversee design of the new census. The very existence of the board, however, presented statistical circles with an unprecedented opportunity to influence the structure of the upcoming survey. Joseph Kennedy was appointed secretary of the board, which meant that he became superintending clerk of the census once Congress authorized the bill in May 1850. While the Whiggish Kennedy had no professional qualifications, he was faithful enough to the new cult of useful knowledge to enlist the direct assistance of Russell and Shattuck, as well as Nahum Capen, Jesse Chickering, and Edward Jarvis, in drafting the separate schedules for surveying population (both slave and free), mortality, agricultural activity, industrial enterprise, and a miscellany of civic institutions encompassing schools, churches, prisons, and newspapers. Russell and Shattuck even traveled to Washington to track the angry Senate debate over the purview of the approaching census,

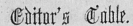

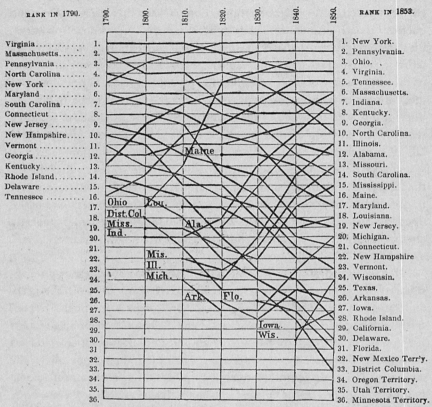

DIAGRAM SHOWING THE COMPARATIVE PROGRESS IN POPULATION OF THE SEVERAL STATES AND TERRITORIES OF THE AMERICAN UNION FOR THE LAST SIXTY YEARS.

From *Harper's Weekly Magazine*, 1854.

maintaining daily contact with Kennedy and with John Davis, the junior senator from Massachusetts and a member of the American Statistical Association who had played an instrumental role in standardizing American weights and measures and whose amendment from the previous year actually established the Census Board. Meanwhile, the divided Senate established its own special committee on the census in an attempt to counteract the activist agenda of the board.[33]

The statistical lobby itself was not of a single mind over the design of the new schedules. Those differences were particularly pronounced in regard to measuring industry. In reference to the disappointment of 1840, for instance, Jesse Chickering advised Congress that "*it is better to have a few leading facts clearly and accurately ascertained, than to attempt a great number and obtain only loose returns.*" Chickering argued that the statistical ambitions of the sixth census were doomed by the document's lack of any "clear and definite" idea of what was to be surveyed. As an example he pointed to the failed attempt to count commercial activity, asking, "What is meant by those employed in *commerce*?" "Did it include the itinerant pedlar, the small retailer, or the wholesale merchant?" The very absence of uniform definitions was the cause of the predictably meaningless results revealed in the respective returns from Troy and Albany. To avoid future fiascoes of this kind, Chickering concluded, it was necessary to standardize terms. And the best way to do that was by restricting the range of subjects to be interrogated by the census.[34]

Nahum Capen took issue with Chickering's proposal to reduce the number of subjects to be included in the census. He contended that any such quantitative sacrifice would not, in fact, result in a qualitatively more accurate return. Indeed, it would have the opposite effect. "A work is generally executed with care," Capen argued, "according to the degree of its magnitude and importance." He was most critical of the tendency "to reduce the objects of the census by making inquiries upon some subjects, and omitting others." This would entail an arbitrary selection of subjects that threatened to mar the whole statistical enterprise by compromising its inclusionary axioms. He proposed, instead, to broaden the scope of the census and so bring statistical ambitions in line with the ever-growing number of subjects of economic life in the industrial age. Capen thought that the best way to achieve such an expansion was through a system of multiple schedules, each featuring its own set of queries specifically tailored to each branch of industry. This would improve accuracy by means of more rigorous and minute interrogations without also sacrificing the principle of inclusion.[35]

At this point, J. D. B. DeBow joined the debate in a series of "letters" published in the New Orleans *Daily Picayune* and addressed to the Census Board in Washington. DeBow, who had played a leading role in Louisiana's recent state census, recognized that the old paradigm by which census categories were determined on the basis of existing hierarchies had lost any relevance once it was decided to make the census a tool of statistics. He also identified the circular nature of the old method of enumeration, that which "makes indispensable to the taking of the census the very information which the census itself can alone give!" What's more, DeBow protested, no amount of greater specification regarding the subjects of enumeration could resolve what was, in essence, an epistemological problem. But DeBow was more concerned with the political rather than philosophical implications of this question. Inspired by visions of Southern industrialization, he was troubled by Nahum Capen's proposal to institute a multiple system of specialized manufacturing schedules. Such a plan, DeBow warned, would undermine the "rule of uniformity" that was essential to the statistical ideal, and no less essential to national unity, which could no longer be taken for granted in an era of escalating sectional tensions. It followed that a universally applicable set of queries for the entire manufacturing economy was necessary to generate usable results that would be of general relevance. Designing separate schedules for separate branches of the economy would be a self-fulfilling prophecy, DeBow argued, and would further divide the nation into autonomous social and economic units. Interrogatories regarding rice, cotton, and sugarcane, for instance, would be exclusively directed toward the South, even though traces of those crops were to be found in almost all states of the union. True, they might often still be in an infant condition in the North, DeBow conceded, but so was manufacturing in Massachusetts in 1790, which everyone now regretted for not having included in the first census. Likewise, schedules devoted to surveying industrial production would be restricted to Northern states. As a consequence, the census, originally intended as "the great common measure of our representative system," would become no less than a vehicle of disunion.[36]

The plan ultimately adopted for the 1850 schedule of industry simultaneously incorporated Jesse Chickering's endorsement of a stricter definition of the subjects of inquiry, Nahum Capen's proposal to enlarge the scope of the census, and J. D. B. DeBow's argument on behalf of uniformity. The seventh census, in fact, marked another great compromise of 1850—another project for creating unity in a fragmenting reality—and a far more successful one than Henry Clay's attempt in the same year to preserve the slave republic. (The next significant changes in the method for assaying the country's manufacturing economy would only be introduced in 1880.) It offered a strikingly elegant solution to a decades-old problem, a solution "constructed on entirely different principles from any ever used previously for a like purpose," as Joseph Kennedy observed, for the census's new method of counting manufacturing enterprise was founded on the single instruction to census marshals to list every "corporation, company, or individual producing articles to the annual value of $500." This meant that all preexisting, predetermined hierarchies were unequivocally annulled. While the set of fourteen standard queries first used in 1820 was, in fact, restored, the new monetary threshold of $500 made them "applicable to the details of every branch of productive industry" for the first time. This resulted in a summary view of industry entirely divorced from any *a priori* version, or vision, of what constituted the country's production economy.[37]

In the new scheme of things, no particular form of industrial activity was more or less inherently important to the nation's material life than any other. This was to be compared to all earlier surveys in which the specific contribution or special status of certain branches of manufactures determined their position in (or exclusion from) the official record of productive practice. As a result, the 1850 census generated an unprecedentedly inclusive catalog of the industrial economy whose character would be determined only after all the returns were collated. Textile magnates in Lowell and furniture upholsterers on Manhattan's South Street, let alone slop makers in New Haven and Cincinnati, qualified for inclusion in the same material universe, which was defined solely by the value of their product. The $500 delineation of manufacturing activity consequently returned a far more extensive and variegated assemblage of "facts" than anything ever seen before. The businesses of confectioners, looking-glass makers, clothiers, tailors, and milliners, to name just a few, appeared for the first time in the nation's official record of economic life. That polyphony of voices all testifying on their own behalf—under threat of a $30 fine instituted for the first time in the case of anyone's refusal to answer the manufacturing schedule queries—underscored the authenticity of the new returns. Indeed, the massive presence in the census of so many different types of manufacturing, let alone manufacturers, provided incontrovertible proof that statistical truth was exactly what it claimed to be, namely, "a neutral ground on which all parties may cordially meet."[38]

Statistics for Profit

They all met over a bargain in a society no longer governed by any transcendent authority. In contrast to preindustrial and prestatistical visions of the commonwealth, in other words, the economy so thoroughly documented in 1850 rested on no preexisting model of the public good that was to inform public order. Commonality would be established by the opposite method: material facts would first be ascertained and only then added up into a whole. As such, this system for counting the nation's "products of industry" rested on the same axiom that underwrote the population census's novel "mode of personal inquiry." For just as the latter overturned an older classification system of the population that was incapable of discovering facts "except the one[s] originally made," the new manufacturing schedule embraced the same post-patriarchal scheme that individualized in order to universalize. The mode of personal inquiry, in other words, proved as effective in counting the growing plethora of commodities as in counting individuals.

That taxonomy not only generated an industrial panorama of unprecedented scope. It also transformed the nature of classification itself and, by so doing, the very means for producing knowledge about the economy. This was because the highly fixed sum of $500 actually constituted a most fluid boundary. Without needing to be revised every ten years, it would yield a varied picture of industrial activity in accordance to the ever-shifting conditions of doing business. The money standard proved as elastic as the market it measured. This did not mean that it lacked a stable point of reference. The $500 figure was strictly applied, not in the least because it could be. But in contrast to the notions of a general interest that informed previous enumerations and identified, those sectors of the economy essential to national life, and so worthy of investigation, the new census did not reproduce itself in the results. The opposite was the case. The 1850 returns reflected the fluctuations and relativities endemic to a volatile market, documenting the rise of new industries and the demise of old ones without requiring any prior knowledge of them. The $500 threshold became the foundation of an autonomous model of knowledge, that is to say, based on a view of change as a permanent condition. One could even conclude that the census realized the ideals of perpetual motion that became widely popular in these years, functioning as an automatic feedback mechanism of the kind that proved essential for industrial-age information systems in general. A taxonomy that abolished stable hierarchies and predictable results consequently became the basis of stability and predictability. Multiplicity and variety no longer needed to be suppressed, or subsumed, under a single sovereignty. In that respect, the seventh census provided a structural solution to capitalist disorder, bringing system and control to industrial life without sacrificing the profits that issued from the constant movement and mutability of persons and goods.

The "annual value of $500" turned money into both a common denominator and the foundation of statistical neutrality, untainted as it was by narrow political interests, traditional hierarchies, or, as improbable as it may seem, by "diversions and illusions." Not only was the manufacturing schedule a mirror of the business ledger's record of inputs and outputs but the commodity form was itself reified as statistical truth. This was indicative of how markets and statistics shared the fundamental axiom of analogy, the desideratum of making everything comparable, or exchangeable. Both systems were capable of naturalizing a man-made reality in which apples and oranges, let alone tailored suits and iron ore, became corresponding elements of a "living economy."[39]

Promoting money into the ultimate measure of value also raised a series of theoretical problems, as Henry Carey acknowledged in an essay on "the nature of commercial value." That was because money itself constituted a fluid, indeterminate variable, reflecting the relative quality of the goods being exchanged. "All we can say of value, therefore, is indefinite." The fact is, neither economists like Carey or "counting-house oracles" like B. F. Foster, nor credit agencies, Treasury officials, bankers, and manufacturers, could agree on the proper method for measuring wealth or capital. Was the $500 value of goods that qualified an enterprise for inclusion in the new census to be based on the expenses incurred in making them, for instance, or on the income earned from their sale? Was that value manifest in the business's present stock of merchandise or only in its eventual exchange? Should the sums be calculated as an undifferentiated total or categorized by article? And which dollars were being measured in the first place? There was no single answer to any of these questions, only general recognition that value in the industrial market was a relative rather than absolute event, and that both the objects and subjects of measurement were in a state of chronic flux, if not transformation. David Ricardo had already noted that there was no such thing as an invariable measure of the costs of buying and selling because "there is no commodity which is not itself exposed to the same variations as the things, the value of which is to be ascertained." His insights were echoed in *Hunt's Merchant's Magazine*, which insisted that "there is no common standard or measure of value, nor can there be any. . . . Value is in its nature relative. . . . It can never be fixed and absolute, but must vary continually with the demand and supply of all exchangeable things." Even if the value of money could be reliably stabilized, another critic wrote, it still constituted a questionable means—if not, in fact, a "statistical absurdity"—for measuring economic activity. That was because the same money, or capital, would keep getting counted over and over, "the finished products of one branch of industry being constantly the raw materials of another." Thus, for example, in the production chain leading from wool to yarn to cloth to clothing, the value of the yarn would be counted three times and that of the cloth twice.[40]

But statisticians had little interest in measuring real value. There was a more important goal in 1850 than determining return on investment. They sought, rather, to map, and consequently represent—and some might be tempted to say, invent—economic order itself. Like the account books, then, the new census numbers did not have to reflect wealth as such. They needed to provide a consistent context for making comparisons. That is what recommended the annual value of $500 to the designers of the census, who promoted this otherwise arbitrary figure to Archimedean status. Money, in that respect, was not a material substance but a function, or a referent. "I am passed and re-passed by thousands, who, with neither hold nor claim upon me, are entitled to my acquaintance," Nathaniel Willis, America's foremost magazinist, proclaimed upon assuming a first-person cash identity in an essay that appeared in the *Dollar* in 1844. It was this very promiscuity that detached money from concrete persons and things and turned it into an objective phenomenon without any inherent or transcendent qualities, only coming into being when two or more agents, however distant, were connected by it. This is exactly how statistics conceived of the relationship between discrete facts "which thus isolated have little value for human experience" until they were compared and turned into relative measurements. Money likewise replaced absolutes with what could be known only through comparison or, in market terms, through exchange. "Calculation in terms of money, and not its actual use, is thus the specific means of rational, economic provision," Max Weber also observed. The census effectively turned the relativity and fluidity of exchange into the basis of "a harmonious whole in which all interests, commercial and manufacturing, agricultural and professional, are alike to be represented," as Archibald Russell ardently proclaimed in *Principles of Statistical Inquiry*.[41]

That, at least, was the conceit. But was the census's collection of economic facts as categorically free of *a priori* impositions and qualitative judgments as the advocates of statistical truth contended? Was the new taxonomy really so much more objective, universal, and inclusive than its "crude" predecessors? Did statistics, in other words, really contain the source of their own meaning, constituting a system invulnerable to opinion and passion, a matter for "school-teachers, used to figures"? Russell himself was certainly aware of the nominalist tendencies of the new science when he compared the statistician to a compiler of dictionaries and confessed that "it is quite possible to arrange a detail of facts as to bias the reader towards one or other of the leading political creeds of the day." His point was that no fact could, or should, be collected without first explicitly determining what qualified as a fact. The census could not be executed, therefore, without a "leading idea," as was also explained in an address to the American Statistical Association in 1844, for it would otherwise become trapped in a loop between a preconception of economic life that informed the collection of facts, and a collection of facts intended to inform a conception of economic life. Russell supplied such a "leading idea" in *Principles of Statistical Inquiry* when he contended with suitable emphasis that manufacturing is "the fabrication for *wholesale trade* of any species of raw material." This meant that the transformation of nature into instruments of practical use would not be counted as an industrial activity unless those instruments circulated as commodities for sale. Money accordingly became "the incarnation and purest expression" of an economy in which goods did not acquire their value from being manufactured but from being exchanged. Statistics embraced that commercial axiom and transformed it into a science.[42]

On one level, Russell's definition was sharply anti-intuitive. He acknowledged as much in noting that manufacturing "conveys readily to the mind the general impression that it is the perfecting of raw materials." However, as he replied to his own admonition, "that is not the sense in which the [statistician] uses it." For Russell and his colleagues, aspiring as they did to invent a system of knowledge capable of epitomizing the "rapid changes . . . unyielding ambition . . . irregularity of enterprise, [and] new and exciting temptations" of the age, knitting stockings at home in the winter was of such "trifling" economic significance that it could rightly be left out of the record. So, too, the productive efforts of the village shoemaker. "What sort of return can he make, he knows not how many boots he has made, nor the value of those he has repaired but working for minute gains he does not keep accurate accounts of the progress of his business." There was simply no practical way, in other words, to translate all these local undertakings into a public accounting of the nation's industry.[43]

And yet if all productive effort whose value fell below $500 was included in the census, Gilbert Currie observed in the *Material Progress of the United States* in 1862, the result would be "of startling magnitude." Francis Walker's analysis of the 1860 census returns was more specific. "Of 43,624 coopers working at their trade"—a figure that Walker derived from the query on occupation appearing in the population schedule—"the production of only 13,750 is accounted for among the 'products of industry,'" a figure Walker took from the manufacturing schedule's list of hands employed by firms satisfying the $500 criterion. "Of 112,357 blacksmiths enumerated, only 15,720 . . . contribute to the reported production of their craft; of 242,958 carpenters, only 9,006, and of 51,695 painters, only 913." A giant gap had been created, in other words, between what was counted as "industry" in the census record and what was otherwise still recognizable as industrious labor. It was one thing to ignore household manufactures, which were surely losing their former importance in the specialized circumstances of industrial divisions of labor and cash exchange. But Walker complained that the census's classification scheme also erased the independent artisan from the formal—indeed, the official— picture of the economy.[44]

Walker thus argued that the census continued to suffer from structural flaws, the result of inquiries restricted to "the production of merchantable articles" by manufacturing corporations boasting "a corps of skilled accountants keeping its books by double entry." Joseph Kennedy responded to such criticisms by claiming that much of the labor of those who worked for "minor interests"—by which he meant enterprises producing below the monetized threshold of $500—was, in fact, contained in the reported values of the larger manufacturing concerns. "The finished products of one branch of industry are constantly the raw materials of another," he pointed out. By so reasoning, Kennedy redefined labor as a capital investment. The same was discernible in the instructions distributed to census officials in 1850 for recording employment data. "The average monthly amount paid for all the labor of all the hands," as the agents in the field were informed, was to be divided by "the number of hands employed." This would then determine the average wage paid by each enterprise, which was the figure that appeared in the blanks. The number represented an accurate summary of the firm's aggregate labor expenses, no doubt, but it did so by erasing all the fractional days and seasonal employments, not to mention the discrepancies in earnings, that constituted the experience of hired laborers themselves. The disorder of waged existence was thus transcribed into the "harmonious whole" of the ledger. Census enumerators were also told to include the cost of boarding one's hands in the same column as the amount of wages paid out. As such, once again, the price of labor reflected the capitalist's expenses, not the producer's earnings, transforming work into an interchangeable, abstract process for creating exchange value in a distinct realm of activity increasingly identified as "the economy." Six additional queries on the actual payment of wages appearing in the schedule of "social statistics," queries that often went unasked, or unanswered, did not change the picture. This disappearance of productive effort, or its subsumption under the aegis of capital, marked the loafer's ultimate victory. The sweat of the brow resulting from mixing one's labor with nature became auxiliary to the accumulation of capital by commercial enterprise.[45]

"To account for means to explain; to explain is to control; and what can be controlled will determine what is to be accounted for," as Winifred Barr Rothenberg once described the tautologies that characterized the historical transition from "market-places to a market economy." Statistics, invented to measure this transition, in fact constituted it. Industriousness—the physical act of transforming nature into objects of use—was no longer the defining act of what was now called an industrial economy. This was because such labor, unless it was waged labor, could not be integrated into an inclusive universe of common values. The census's statistics, which proved so adept at narrating the growing complexity of the economy, had no place for the producerist grammar of free-soil ideologues such as Walker, or for such homespun sentimentalists as Horace Bushnell, who waxed nostalgic in 1851 about a lost age when material standards were derived from "whatever the soil will yield" rather than what the market would bear.[46]

Counting industrial activity on the basis of the "leading idea" of producing for exchange meant, in short, that business had become synonymous with industry. New knowledge of the economy was based on an unprecedentedly expansive schedule of industrial subjects that erased old prejudices and boundaries by establishing a new boundary, namely, profit. That was because every "corporation, company, or individual producing articles to the annual value of $500" clearly did so with the intention that such values would exceed expenses. In that respect, the census's powerful common denominator, and source of objective facts, rested on no less an "ideal type" than did the moral economy of old. That updated ideal was the pursuit of gain, suitably recast by the statistics into a universal material logic. Calculating on the basis of the same assumptions that informed the account books, statistics not only documented but abetted capitalism's abandonment of labor theories of value in favor of the fraternal twins of supply and demand. Mercantile circles might complain about the new census's neglect of commercial data regarding the country's wholesale and retail trades, but the production statistics themselves turned economy into a total ecology of fungibility, making manufacturing into a function of exchange rather than vice versa.[47]

"It was necessary to establish some limit, and a proper one, it is believed, was observed," Joseph Kennedy pronounced in defense of the new system, further explaining that it was better to err on the side of accountability. Certainly, the 1850 returns were far richer and inclusive and more varied and dynamic and broadly cast than anything that had ever come before. That is why, as Francis Walker worriedly noted, they have been "quoted and indorsed, appealed to and argued from, by editors, economists, and statesmen, at home and abroad; they have been used with confidence in ascertaining the law of the national growth; economical legislation has been shaped by them; they have been made the basis of internal taxation, and have governed the distribution of banking capital among the States."[48] Who would suspect, then, that such universality rested on wholesale exclusions and hierarchies that promoted the commodity to epistemological status, resulting in an economy that worked only for profit while "bracketing" whatever social facts threatened the coherence of the data? Indeed, just as markets would not work without excluding the informal and vernacular—such as the number of boots repaired each year by the village shoemaker—neither would the census. Only that which was exchanged for a price became worthy for inclusion in the statistical record of the economy.[49]

Truck and barter thus came to underwrite both common wealth and common sense, serving as a universal grammar for making order of a reality of fast property driven by motion rather than substance. Buying and selling were no longer just a means for disposing of the products of one's hard work. They were the objects of labor in their own right in a market system that defined all value, and all values. This was the world the clerk made.

Conclusion: White Collar

In 1951, a little more than a century after William Hoffman left farm and family to install himself in business, the sociologist C. Wright Mills published an angry account of the social and psychic effects of paperwork on American life. Mills entitled his study *White Collar*, and the sense of déjà vu is inescapable. *White Collar* depicted an "American middle class" whose office routines were the engine that drove the operations of modern capitalism. This was a waged class with "no firm roots [and] no sure loyalties" whose past proved "as brief as it is unheroic." That same rootlessness was the source of a "synthetic excitement that neither eases nor releases" but only exasperates the "self-alienation" experienced each day by these "interchangeable" savants of a giant paper economy.[1]

Of course, the office had undergone considerable change since Edward Tailer seethed with frustration at having to refill the ink stands every morning at Little Alden & Co. Typewriters, vertical files, Addressographs, adding machines, and accredited university degrees in business administration were just some of the technologies that had been introduced to commercial science by the time Mills undertook his investigation. Women had also joined the ranks of clerical labor, monopolizing the office's more menial and less remunerative positions. And yet, despite the years, Mills's description of the perniciousness of mental labor presented a near-verbatim recapitulation of "the curious strange feeling, which is a compound of fear, suspense, desire, anxiety and numerous other nameless ills" ascribed by nineteenth-century critics to those "immortal sons of calico" and "dandies of the desk" manning the first generation of the office regime. The clerk's role as paragon of bourgeois discontent, in other words, was something of a tradition.[2]

"Each office . . . is a segment of the enormous file," Mills wrote of the routinization of modern life, "part of the symbol factory that produces the billion slips of paper that gear modern society into its daily shape." Rows of desks and pools of Dictaphone transcribers stacked up in the vertical serial- ity of metropolitan skyscrapers became icons of the era's "business system," "government system," "war system," and "money system" that collectively in- formed the manufacture, retrieval, and dissemination of information. Mills identified the office as a principal production site of capitalist economy, a knowledge factory operating on the basis of Fordist machine logic that orga- nized the nine-to-five work lives of its "salariat"—the book's most trenchant neologism—around those billions of slips of paper. The numbing standard- izations of this "paper routine" colonized the whole of one's waking hours, transforming the population into a "number" or "statistic" to be "filed away" by "a faceless bureaucracy."[3]

White Collar was representative of a general postwar zeitgeist that found additional expression in such other well-known treatments of American cor- porate culture as Sloan Wilson's *Man in the Gray Flannel Suit* (1955), William Whyte's *Organization Man* (1956), David Riesman's *The Lonely Crowd* (1950), and even Arthur Miller's *Death of a Salesman* (1949), the latter portraying the breakdown of patriarchal authority and the resulting crisis of manhood. Together, these texts examined the high psychic cost of the bottom line— Whyte complained of universities that neglected the humanities in favor of business education, while Riesman characterized the organization man as an "antagonistic cooperator" primed to compete with his fellow citizens over ac- cess to resources—which closely adhered to Thoreau's critique of humanity straining to fit itself into the nutshell of monetized civility. In that respect, such critiques also anticipated the popular rediscovery of *Walden* in the wake of the following decade's student rebellion against corporate hegemony. But the so- ciological trope that invoked the "small creature who is acted upon" (Mills), the individual with few opportunities to "wrench his destiny into his own hands" (Whyte), one whose existence is "habitually atomized and personalized— or pseudo-personalized" (Riesman), also gave direct expression to a Frank- furt school–inspired fear of bureaucracy's radically dehumanizing effects, so catastrophically manifested in the dark times of the twentieth century.[4]

This was, in fact, the principal distinction to be drawn between *Hunt's Merchant's Magazine*'s world of "ready men" and C. Wright Mills's enormous file of "Little Men." For while both types were the progeny of capitalist revo- lution, the twentieth-century clerk no longer personified the emancipatory effects of the commodity system. He was its unambiguous victim. The white- collared cadres of an IBM-administered economy were a defeated class, that is to say, casualties of a world they themselves administered day in and day out. Nothing personified this inversion of fortunes better than the semiotics of their very collars. An expression of personal mobility in the nineteenth century, when Benjamin Foster proudly plunged his head into a standing neckpiece on his eighteenth birthday, "as to the manner born," Mills's white collar had acquired the opposite connotation a hundred years later, serving as a symbol of profit's stranglehold over the individual soul, the definitive fashion accessory of capitalism's collectivized personality, which Mills identified as a ruinous contradiction in terms. There was no more disastrous sign, in fact, of the tragic end of an earlier golden age when "the mass of the people were the masters of the holdings which they plowed and of the tools with which they worked," as Mills quoted R. H. Tawney in his book's opening epigraph. This lost age of authentic individualism flourished before "offices replace[d] free markets" and before the entrepreneurial instincts of the "old middle classes" were trampled by the imperatives of corporate standards.[5]

Fifty years after Mills's indictment, another American sociologist, Richard Sennett, provided an update on America's ongoing clerk problem. Sennett's *Corrosion of Character*, published in 1998, similarly explored the interdynamics of economy and personality. That relationship was currently shaped, however, by post-Fordist business models that overthrew the top-down command structure that stagflated in the 1970s. Sennett described the de-bureaucratization of the office and the resulting consecration of "flex time," now deemed essential for firms having to respond to a perennially shifting market operating at ever-accelerating velocities and volatilities. This "postindustrial" capitalism was based on the axioms of "contingency" that turned "temp" employment brokered by specialized labor contractors into the fastest-growing sector of the workforce. The long-term commitment to one's "job" was systematically replaced by the specifications of the interim "project," Sennett observed, or what has since come to be known as the gig economy. "It is quite natural that flexibility should arouse anxiety," he noted of the nervous fallout from a new management plan whose "just-in-time" supply chains—an obvious incarnation of the "fast property" administered by the subaltern scribes of an earlier era—put everyone on notice.[6]

Sennett illustrated these developments with an anecdote regarding the successful son of a unionized janitor who realized his father's ambitions for the next generation, ambitions that, by definition, "rejected the way of his father." We thus follow the son's dogged pursuit of personal and professional happiness as he leverages himself into ever more gainful forms of human capital, first at business school in New York City, followed by employment with a venture capital firm on the West Coast, and then in a new job in Chicago. He leaves this last position in response to his wife's separate career path, relocating to an office park in Missouri, where he is, however, soon "downsized."

A fourth move (in the span of fourteen years) back to a New York City sub-
urb follows. "Uncertainty," Sennett concludes, "is woven into the everyday
practices of a vigorous capitalism." Flexibility's emergence as a business
value—not to mention a psychological cliché—renders personal experience
as conditional and ephemeral as the market itself. "Trust, loyalty, and mutual
commitment" give way to "fleeting forms of association" and a "detachment
and superficial cooperativeness," the new keywords for professional success.[7]

Sennett, like Mills before him, ends up in a nostalgic embrace of better
times, although in 1951 Mills yearned for the flexibility which Sennett portrays
as the bane of middle-class existence in 1998, while Mills condemned the stultifying conventions of corporate employment that Sennett celebrates as the
lost job security underwritten by Fordist strategies for avoiding rapid labor
turnover. Mills's "free markets" that guaranteed the individualism of the "old
middle classes," meanwhile, turn out to be the same "busy, bustling, disputatious" forms of sociality that alarmed nineteenth-century observers, who, in
turn, pined for those days "in which ministers, judges and governors wrought
occasionally in the field" before the shifting promise of exchange replaced the
sure results of landed labor and induced young men to sell their birthright in
serving the whims of "every painted and padded form of humanity."[8]

Market society, as such, keeps circling back on itself. The American dream
referenced by one generation turns out to have been someone else's nightmare
in a perpetually recycled declension myth. The "fast walking, fast driving, fast
eating and drinking, fast bargains, [and] fast business" of the 1850s eventually morphed into the "fast music, fast computers, and fast food" of the 1990s,
proving that the more things change, the more they stay the same. This perpetuum mobile of life under capital—of "dialectics at a standstill"— continues
to induce bouts of chronic fatigue and irritable bowels, panicked concern with
one's diet fed by a vast catechism of self-help literature, and the body-mass
ratios of exercise routines, including performances of manual labor at the local CrossFit gym. Surely, too, the standing treadmill desks of today are worthy
successors to Dr. Halsted's equestrian exercise chair of 1846. Both mediate between our humanity and the exigencies of the market, seeking to ameliorate
the fraught relationship between "Mammon and Man" that proves to be the
common denominator of capitalism's tireless reinvention of itself.[9]

Each epoch mourns the passing of an age that was already mourning
the passing of the same, turning nostalgia into the perfect expression of this
circularity. Svetlana Boym observed that the longing for a more secure past
invariably follows in the wake of social upheaval, as evidenced in eighteenth-
century France and twentieth-century Russia. Since capitalism is a system of
perennial upheaval—"Can this sweeping tide of many rushing waters now

be expected to recede, or to stand still where it is?" Ezekiel Bacon asked at the Young Men's Association of Utica in 1843 without waiting for a reply—nostalgia has assumed a particularly central place in a society where each generation keeps reexperiencing the same loss of hearth and home.[10]

"There sits Pa with his foot on the sheet iron," Horace Paine recalled of his country boyhood from the office perch of a Manhattan wholesaler. "There is Ma with her knitting work sitting by the stand." But what at first appears to be a stubborn fealty to the values of yore is, in point of fact, an ardent expression of the very relativity that replaced those values. As a creed based on irrevocable change—on a belief in a reality that, by definition, has been forever lost—nostalgia exemplifies the commodity's own inherent transmutations, which are the very condition of capital accumulation. The only permanent aspect of the yearning for permanence, in other words, is the longing itself. This leaves nostalgia as a definitive act of the imagination, constituted of memories of memories, not unlike Austin Flint's diagnosis of the "Monomania" that dissociated dyspeptics from any "real" sense of time and place. As such, it becomes yet another knowledge system for stabilizing capitalism's permanent revolution. Like the census blanks, personal diaries, contract negotiations, nervous breakdowns, and account books, nostalgia, too, helps turn "the total movement of . . . disorder" into a new source of order.[11]

This is a perilous—some might even say schizophrenic—condition, indicative of a civilization in which prosperity is inseparable from failure, industrial plenty has become coterminous with spectacles of poverty, money functions as both a common social denominator and society's ultimate divisor, and the metropolis is at once celebrated and condemned as the site of hypervisibility and a heretofore-unknown anonymity. Such inversions provoked Tocqueville's more conservative prejudices: "One feels proud to be a man, and yet at the same time one experiences I cannot say what bitter regret at the power that God has granted us over nature." Market society, he understood, was caught in a vortex of its own making, for while the tendency to render everything negotiable might be good for business—"What the French did for victory," Tocqueville also observed, Americans "do for low cost"—it was far less propitious for the social contract. One hundred seventy-five years later, even *Forbes Magazine*, that self-fashioned "capitalist tool," was forced to acknowledge "the business revolution that is destroying the American dream."[12]

The prevailing sense of loss finds consistent expression in America's political discourse as well. Every four years presidential candidates vie in conveying their concern for the condition of an embattled middle class caught in a downward spiral.[13] Barack Obama thus spoke in 2012 of "families who worked hard and believed in the American Dream but felt that the odds were

The Altwork Company's newly designed workstation.

increasingly stacked against them," while Mitt Romney promised in response that "My focus, my concern, my energy is going to be devoted to helping middle-income people . . . [who] I think have been most hurt by the Obama economy." They were both right, which meant that by the following round of presidential campaigning in 2016 the anxiety of voters increasingly subject to the "continual performance improvement algorithms" of neoliberal econometrics had only worsened, to the point where even the long-neglected "working class" was reintroduced into political discourse. The public understood only too well that the old was going down with a crash, as the *American Phrenological Journal* recognized in an earlier cycle of market-sponsored social rupture, while the new "is appearing amidst revolutions, as by magic."[14]

Such magic is manifested today in managerial fantasies of the "paperless office," which first surfaced in the late 1970s, with the advent of Reaganism. Since then, Google Docs® has made it possible to share files without printing them, Dropbox® renders the storage and dissemination of those files a wholly ethereal event, TurboScan® has digitized copying operations for convenient emailing, Doodle® coordinates office schedules through electronic synchronization, and Basecamp (whose trademark status seems to be in some dispute) instantaneously uploads commercial data to interface stations around the country, and the globe, obviating the need not only for physical documents but for one's physical presence in the office. All this information is accessed as a continual flow of real-time data streams whose inscriptions have been adapted to electronic screens by spatial anti-aliasing and subpixel rendering technologies, often utilizing such serif fonts as Georgia, whose letters feature elevated x-heights that facilitate web legibility.[15]

Paperlessness seems to be a perfect analogue to flextime, at once metaphor and technic for administering the immaterial essence of the commodity form. And yet capitalism remains saturated with paper, even if this is no longer the stuff of rags or any other form of tangible pulp. Despite all the novel methods for managing information, the economy is still organized around the same principles of storage and retrieval that made paper "the most convenient material ever discovered" in the nineteenth century. "Documents," "folders," and "files" continue to fill the function they did at Boyd & Co. Their architecture might have changed, just as the introduction of press copiers in the 1830s required a new system for "keeping one's papers," but the need to effect a seamless connection—or correspondence—between users remains unchanged. Indeed, the breakthrough effected by HTML in making all digital applications readable to each other seems to be only the latest elaboration of P. L. Spencer's original success in establishing a nationwide standard of business penmanship, that which "may be said to sway the world."[16]

The ersatz quality of the digitized files, which allow knowledge to inhabit a limitless number of surfaces all at once, replace one context for another, and travel coeval trajectories in endowing an otherwise unilinear existence with a widening array of temporalities and valences, is not then a function of machine logic but of commodity logic. Pen and paper already engendered such a virtual reality, which was the condition for capital's transmigrations from place to place, and form to form, passing between its merchant, industrial, and financial incarnations, and then back again, imbuing the human imagination with the same values of fungibility. The history of capitalism is not, then, about the economic origins of society, but about the expressions that economy assumes in society, about how capital acquired consciousness. Economists call this process "cognitive regulatory capture."[17] It was pioneered by the most unlikely of modern revolutionaries, the antebellum merchant's clerk, who made the market while making himself and so became the archetype of what we so casually call today "human capital." This is no mundane management rubric, or metaphor, however. It is the very template of contemporary life, a distressing testament to how the "disintegration, analysis, and individualizing" of the bottom line have become the measure of our very own selves.

Notes

Introduction

1. The *Tribune's* critic was Charles Dana. *New York Tribune*, July 23, 1855; Walt Whitman, *Leaves of Grass* (New York: W. W. Norton, 1965), 28. See, too, the attack on Whitman in Maximilian Schele De Vere, *Americanisms: The English of the New World* (New York: C. Scribner & Co., 1872), 141. Whitman was reportedly fired from the *Aurora* for "loaferism." Hans Bergmann, *God in the Street: New York Writing from the Penny Press to Melville* (Philadelphia: Temple University Press, 1995), 79.

2. Hawthorne, quoted in Clement Eaton, ed., *The Leaven of Democracy: The Growth of the Democratic Spirit in the Time of Jackson* (New York: George Braziller, 1963), 125; George Templeton Strong, November 5, 1838, in *The Diary of George Templeton Strong: Young Man in New York, 1835–1849*, ed. Allan Nevins (New York: Macmillan, 1952); *Southern Literary Messenger* 9, no. 4 (April 1843), 198.

"This peculiarly American word," John Russell Bartlett reported on "loafer" in 1848, "has been gradually growing into extensive use during the last twenty years." Bartlett, *Dictionary of Americanisms: A Glossary of Words and Phrases, Usually Regarded as Peculiar to the United States* (Hoboken, NJ: John Wiley & Sons, 2003), 209. Was the loafer a "peculiarly American" problem? Comparisons to the flaneur might yield an interesting cultural history. See Charles Baudelaire, *The Painter of Modern Life and Other Essays*, ed. and trans. Jonathan Mayne (New York: Da Capo, 1964).

3. *Ladies Companion*, September 1837; *New-York Daily Times*, December 10, 1852. See generally Andrew Lyndon Knighton, "Idle Threats: The Limits of Productivity in 19th-Century America" (PhD diss., University of Minnesota, 2004).

4. "Impatient of Hard Work" in Horace Bushnell, "Age of Homespun," in *Litchfield County Centennial Celebration* (Hartford, CT: Edwin Hunt, 1851), 123; Henry Ward Beecher, *Lectures to Young Men* (Boston: John P. Jewett, 1846), 15–48, and sediment on 38; Joseph G. Baldwin, *The Flush Times of Alabama and Mississippi* (New York: D. Appleton & Co., 1854), 87; draft of speech, box 4, writings and speeches, Misc. 1821–1851, n.d., Chickering Papers, Special Collections, Duke University, Durham, NC.

5. Edwin Freedley, *How to Make Money, Being a Practical Treatise on Business* (London: Routledge, Warner and Routledge, 1859), 41–2; W. Chambers and R. Chambers, *Treasury of*

Knowledge (New York: A. S. Barnes & Co., 1849), 75. As Max Weber wrote, capitalism entailed "the idea of a duty of the individual toward the increase of his capital, which is assumed as an end in itself." Weber, *The Protestant Ethic and the Spirit of Capitalism* (1904; New York: Scribner's, 1958), 51.

6. Francis Walker, "American Industry in the Census," *Atlantic Monthly* 24, no. 146 (December 1869), 691–2; Lincoln, quoted in Eric Foner, *Free Soil, Free Labor, Free Men: The Ideology of the Republican Party before the Civil War* (New York: Oxford, 1970), 30; Edwards, in *Hunt's*, vol. 1 (October 1839), 291 (hereafter in the notes, *Hunt's Merchant's Magazine* is referred to as *Hunt's*). On the merchant roots of modern industrial capitalism, see Sven Beckert, *Empire of Cotton: A Global History* (New York: Knopf, 2014), 199–242.

7. Edgar A. Poe, "The Man of the Crowd" (1840), in *The Norton Anthology of American Literature, 2nd ed.* (New York: W. W. Norton, 1985), 1:1382; Charles H. Foster, ed., *Down East Diary by Benjamin Browne Foster* (Orono: University of Maine at Orono Press, 1975), 12; Jacques Derrida, *Paper Machine* (Palo Alto, CA: Stanford University Press, 2005). "My life," as Kafka wrote of his day job at the offices of the Workmen's Accident Insurance Institution, "resembles that punishment in which each pupil must according to his office write down the same meaningless (in repetition, at least) sentence ten times, a hundred times or even oftener; except that in my case the punishment is given me with only this limitation: 'as many times as you can stand it.'" Quoted in Roy Fuller, "A Normal Enough Dog: Kafka and the Office," in *The World of Franz Kafka*, ed. J. P. Stern (London: Weidenfield and Nicolson, 1980), 193.

8. *Journal of the Geographic and Statistical Society*, July 1859, 213; B. F. Foster, *Prospectus of the Commercial Academy* (New York: 183 Broadway, New York, 1837); "oracle" in *New-York Daily Times*, May 21, 1853; Joseph Alfred Barrett, *Old Merchants of New York City* (New York: M. Doolady, 1865), 56–7; *American Phrenological Journal* (April 1853), 74; "ready to turn my hand" quoted in Brian P. Luskey, *On the Make: Clerks and the Quest for Capital in Nineteenth-Century America* (New York: New York University Press, 2010), 33; William Hoffman, Diary (1847–1850), March 31, 1848 (New-York Historical Society); Charles Edward French, Journal (1859) (Massachusetts Historical Society, Boston), 6, 15–6. On numbers of clerks, see Stuart Blumin, *The Emergence of the Middle Class: Social Experience in the American City, 1760–1900* (Cambridge: Cambridge University Press, 1989), 73–8; Luskey, *On the Make*, 5–11; Mary Ryan counted a 7,500 percent increase in the number of clerks in the commercial town of Utica, New York, between 1817 and 1850, in her *Cradle of the Middle Class: The Family in Oneida County, New York, 1790–1865* (New York: Cambridge University Press, 1981), 108, 167, 178–9. The federal census of 1850 reported that farmers and laborers were the country's most numerous occupations (among men), followed, in turn, by carpenters, cordwainers, clerks, and merchants. The "mercantile professions," in other words, had drawn even with artisanal employments by mid-century. *Hunt's*, vol. 34 (February 1856), 173.

9. Charles Frederick Briggs, *The Adventures of Harry Franco: A Tale of the Great Panic* (New York: F. Saunders, 1839), 16. Freeman Hunt: "There is gloom over society when the ship stops too long at the wharf." Hunt, *Lives of American Merchants* (New York: Hunt's Merchant's Magazine, 1856), 1:xxxviii; Ralph Waldo Emerson, "Self-Reliance" (1841), in *Norton Anthology of American Literature, 2nd ed.* (New York: W. W. Norton, 1985), 1:908. See, too, Jeffrey Sklansky, *The Soul's Economy: Market Society and Selfhood in American Thought, 1820–1920* (Chapel Hill: University of North Carolina Press, 2002), 33–72.

10. Henry Ward Beecher, *Lectures to Young Men, on Various Important Subjects*, 3rd ed. (New York: J. C. Derby, 1856), 26–9; *New York Tribune*, May 7, 1845; Virginia Penny, *The Employments*

of Women: A Cyclopaedia of Woman's Work (Boston: Walker, Wise & Co., 1863), 126; Horace Greeley, *Hints toward Reforms* (New York: Harper and Bros., 1850), 360; *Vanity Fair*, March 17, 1860. On the source of "bureaucracy" as a term of disdain and contempt, see Ralph Kingston, *Bureaucrats and Bourgeois Society: Office Politics and Individual Credit in France, 1789–1848* (London: Palgrave Macmillan, 2012).

11. Henry David Thoreau, *Walden; or, Life in the Woods* (1854; New York: Holt, Rinehart, and Winston, 1963), 275; *Hunt's*, vol. 7 (October 1842), 349; *American Whig Review*, vol. 15 (May 1852), 472; "taxes increase" in T. De Witt Talmage, *Behind the Counter: A Sermon to Clerks* (Philadelphia: George H. Hartman, 1866), 14.

12. The slaveholders' vision of America and, more specifically, that vision's relationship to capitalism, deserves additional, if marginal, discussion, if only because it has become the bon mot of so much recent scholarly attention. While there was no lack of clerks administering the Southern hubs of the global economy, it remains unclear whether the wholesale commodification of social relations that the clerk personified in antebellum America was symptomatic of slave society. Certainly, slavery would play little part in capitalism's ongoing destruction of the traditional structures of American material and cultural life over the rest of the century and into the next one. For a more detailed discussion of these questions, see Michael Zakim, "Capitalism and Slavery in the United States," in *Routledge History of Nineteenth-Century America*, ed. Jonathan Daniel Wells (New York: Routledge, 2017).

13. *United States Democratic Review*, February 1855, 119; Horatio Alger Jr., *Ragged Dick; or, Street Life in New York with Boot Black*, ed. Hildegard Hoeller (New York: Norton, 2008, 1868), 85–7; *Scribner's Monthly*, vol. 1 (February 1871), 361; Georg Simmel, *The Philosophy of Money*, ed. David Frisby, trans. Tom Bottomore and David Frisby (London: Routledge, 1990), 103; Foster, *Down East Diary*, 109 (May 13, 1848). Anyone could become a capitalist in Gary J. Kornblith, "Self-Made Men: The Development of Middling-Class Consciousness in New England," *Massachusetts Review* 26, nos. 2–3 (1985), 469.

14. Karl Polanyi, *The Great Transformation: The Political and Economic Origins of Our Time* (Boston: Beacon Press, 1944), 140.

15. For outstanding treatments of the success of the American bourgeoisie in overcoming the imbroglios of their own making, see Sklansky, *Soul's Economy*; Thomas Augst, *The Clerk's Tale: Young Men and Moral Life in Nineteenth-Century America* (Chicago: University of Chicago Press, 2003); Roy Kreitner, *Calculating Promises: The Emergence of Modern American Contract Doctrine* (Stanford, CA: Stanford University Press, 2007); Jonathan Levy, *Freaks of Fortune* (Cambridge, MA: Harvard University Press, 2012).

16. Karl Marx, "Wage Labor and Capital" (1849), in *Selected Works* (New York: International Publishers, n.d.), 1:261.

Chapter One

1. Douglass C. North, *Structure and Change in Economic History* (New York: W. W. Norton, 1981); Robert Greenhalgh Albion, *The Rise of New York Port* (New York: Charles Scribner's Sons, 1939); "Maine to Texas" in *Hunt's*, vol. 39 (October 1858), 411. "Efficiency of the markets" is a blatant anachronism, of course, and this study's sole gesture to the discipline of economic history. For more of the latter, see, for instance, Joel Mokyr, "The Industrial Revolution and the New Economic History," in *The Economics of the Industrial Revolution*, ed. Joel Mokyr (Totowa, NJ: Rowman & Allanheld, 1985), 1–51.

2. *Hunt's*, vol. 15 (October 1846), 339; F. R. R[eed], *Experience of a New York Clerk* (New York: F. R. Reed, 1877), 27–37. On older systems of exchange, see, for instance, Keith Tribe, *Land, Labour and Economic Discourse* (London: Routledge & Kegan Paul, 1978); and Margaret Schabas, *Natural Origins of Economics* (Chicago: University of Chicago Press, 2005).

3. Samuel Wells, *How to Write: A Pocket Manual of Composition and Letter-Writing* (New York: Fowler and Wells, 1857), 7; Noah J. T. George, *The Gentleman's Pocket Companion, or . . . Useful Forms of Writing* (Concord, MA: Hill and Barton, 1831); Morton ad in *St. Cloud Democrat*, December 29, 1864; Herman Melville, "Bartleby, the Scrivener: A Story of Wall-Street," *Putnam's Monthly* (November 1853), 550; *Hunt's*, vol. 1 (October 1839), 291. In the same spirit, Melville referred to civilization's transformation of "the long two-handed sword to a one-handed quill" in his story "The Paradise of Bachelors" (1855), in *Pierre; or, The Ambiguities . . . Uncollected Prose* (New York: Library of America, 1984), 1258.

4. Edward N. Tailer, Diaries, November 24 and December 17, 1849, and January 15, 1850 (New-York Historical Society); *Hunt's*, vol. 1 (October 1839), 291; "Chapters from the Experiences of a Merchant," *Hunt's*, vol. 15 (October 1846), 343–4, 347; James D. McCabe, *Lights and Shadows of New York Life* (Philadelphia: National Publishing Company, 1872), 843–7; North, *Structure and Change*, 35–7.

5. Charles H. Foster, ed., *Down East Diary by Benjamin Browne Foster* (Orono: University of Maine at Orono Press, 1975), 15, 16, 121, 219, 220–1, 229, 297, 287–8. Reports of "the demise of time and death of distance," often associated with capitalist economy, have thus proved exaggerated. If anything, capitalism marked temporality's apotheosis, not its collapse, for time acquired an unprecedented flexibility, malleability, and multidimensionality that turned the record of days and months in the account books, as well as the clock's regulation of hours on the factory floor, into a powerful means of organizing, and reorganizing, human relations. The same could be said of distance, which also played a critical role in the industrializing market. It was the distance between the exhausted soils of eastern farms, for instance, that accorded the dramatically high yields of western lands such economic significance in the global economy, thus prompting eastern cultivators to shift from grains to livestock. For a counterargument, see John J. McCusker, "The Demise of Distance: The Business Press and the Origins of the Information Revolution in the Early Modern Atlantic World," *American Historical Review* 110 (2005), 297.

6. "Rivulets" in *American Merchant* (July 1858), 141; "modern instrumentalities" in *American Merchant* (June 1858), 79; James R. Beniger, *The Control Revolution: Technological and Economic Origins of the Information Society* (Cambridge, MA: Harvard University Press, 1986), 11–2, 123–7, 130–1, 132–44, 153–68, 173–7; Thomas C. Cochran, *Frontiers of Change: Early Industrialism in America* (New York: Oxford University Press, 1981), 10, 24–5, 37–9; C. W. Moore, Diary, 218–9 (Special Collections, New York Public Library). On railroads and telegraphs, see, for instance, Richard John, "Recasting the Information Infrastructure for the Industrial Age," in *A Nation Transformed by Information: How Information Has Shaped the United States from Colonial Times to the Present*, Alfred D. Chandler Jr. and James W. Cortada, eds. (New York: Oxford University Press, 2000), 68–86.

7. *American Merchant* (May 1858), 15, and (July 1858), 131–2; B. F. Foster, *Clerk's Guide; or, Commercial Correspondence* (Boston: Perkins & Marvin, 1837), 185–201; Morton J. Horwitz, *The Transformation of American Law, 1780–1860* (Cambridge, MA: Harvard University Press, 1977), 177–9, 181–2, 193. "*No*, says the sharper, *I never told you any such thing*," which is why, according to William A. Alcott in the *Young Man's Guide*, "it is on this account that you cannot be too exact in making contracts." William A. Alcott, *Young Man's Guide* (Boston: Lilly, Wait, Colman, and Holden, 1834), 118.

8. Veteran observer in *Hunt's*, vol. 18 (May 1848), 506; "harmonize" in "A Dry-Goods Jobber in 1861," *Atlantic Monthly*, vol. 7 (February 1861), 209; "what has been done" in *Hunt's*, vol. 15 (November 1846), 484; "command of the subject" in *Hunt's*, vol. 15 (November 1846), 483.

9. *New York Star* quoted in commonplace book, box 6, Daniel F. Child Papers (Massachusetts Historical Society); Max Weber, "Bureaucracy," in *Essays in Sociology*, ed. H. H. Gerth and C. Wright Mills (New York: Oxford University Press, 1946), 197; Thomas C. Cochran, "The Business Revolution," *American Historical Review* 79, no. 5 (December 1974). See, too, JoAnne Yates, *Control through Communication: The Rise of System in American Management* (Baltimore: Johns Hopkins University Press, 1989).

10. "Arranging your papers" in *Hunt's*, vol. 15 (November 1846), 483; Weber, "Bureaucracy," 214; "competence at method" in *Hunt's*, vol. 15 (October 1846), 383, 384; Philadelphia merchant in Edward J. Balleisen, *Navigating Failure: Bankruptcy and Commercial Society in Antebellum America* (Chapel Hill: University of North Carolina Press, 2001), 51. Marshall W. Meyer, "The Growth of Public and Private Bureaucracies," in *Structures of Capital: The Social Organization of the Economy* (Cambridge: Cambridge University Press, 1990). On business plans, see Martin Giraudeau, "Seeing Like an Entrepreneur: The Dupont Family's Business Models for America (1797–1802)," *Journal of the Early Republic* (forthcoming); Wm. P. M. Ross, *The Accountant's Own Book and Business Man's Manual*, 2nd ed. (Philadelphia: Thomas, Cowperthwait & Co., 1852), 11. "The collection, digestion, and dissemination in usable form of economic information is one of the staggering problems connected with our modern large-scale social organization," as Frank H. Knight observed in *Risk, Uncertainty, and Profit* (1957; repr., Mineola, NY: Dover Publications, 2006), 261.

11. Karl Marx, *Grundrisse: Foundations of the Critique of Political Economy* (London: Penguin, 1993), 142.

12. "What is known to one is known to all," in *Hunt's*, vol. 24 (January 1850), 50; "staff of thirty" in Scott A. Sandage, *Born Losers: A History of Failure in America* (Cambridge, MA: Harvard University Press, 2005), 101; branch openings in Roy A. Foulke, *Sinews of American Commerce*, (New York: Dun & Bradstreet, 1941), 290–1. On the relationship between market and place, see Jean-Christophe Agnew, *Worlds Apart: The Market and the Theater in Anglo-American Thought, 1570–1770* (New York: Cambridge University Press, 1986).

13. Michael Boyle in Philip Hone, "Reminiscences of New York," *New-York Mirror*, February 20, 1841, 63; "shekels of silver" in *Hunt's*, vol. 1 (October 1839), 294; Michael E. Hobart and Zachary S. Schiffman, *Information Ages: Literacy, Numeracy, and the Computer Revolution* (Baltimore: Johns Hopkins University Press, 1998), 4–6, 90–1, 103; Bruno Latour, "Visualization and Cognition: Thinking with Eyes and Hands," in *Knowledge and Society: Studies in the Sociology of Culture Past and Present* 6 (1986), 22–3. See, too, Lisa Gitelman, *Paper Knowledge: Toward a Media History of Documents* (Durham, NC: Duke University Press, 2014), 3–4; Jacques Derrida, *Paper Machine* (Stanford, CA: Stanford University Press, 2005).

14. Information in this and the following two paragraphs draws on Glenn Porter and Harold C. Livesay, *Merchants and Manufacturers: Studies in the Changing Structure of Nineteenth-Century Marketing* (Baltimore: Johns Hopkins University Press, 1971), 5–6, 9, 17–18, 24–33, 74–5; Beniger, *Control Revolution*, 138–41, 151, 156; B. F. Foster, *The Merchant's Manual* (Boston: Perkins & Marvin, 1838), 36–42; *Wilson's Business Directory of New York City* (New York: John F. Trow, 1856), iv; Joseph J. Klein, "The Development of Mercantile Instruments of Credit in the United States," *Journal of Accountancy* 12, nos. 6–8 (October–December 1911), 321–45, 422–49, 526–37; Pierre Gervais, "Background Discussion: What Is the 'Industrial Revolution'?" (unpublished manuscript).

15. Freedley quoted in Harvey J. Wexler, "Business Opinion and Economic Theory, 1840–1860," *Explorations in Entrepreneurial History* 1, no. 3 (March 1949), 15; James W. Kimball, *The Dry-Goods Jobbers* (Boston: Commercial Agency, n.d.), 7.

16. "Basis of prosperity" in *Hunt's*, vol. 42, no. 4 (April 1860), 516; "capital of mind" in Granville Sharp, *Prize Essay on the Application of Recent Inventions collected at the Great Exhibition of 1851, to the Purposes of Practical Banking* (London: Waterlow & Sons, 1852), 1, and see 5–7, 15, 41–3; Lois Severini, *Architecture of Finance: Early Wall Street* (Ann Arbor, MI: UMI Research Press, 1973), 24–6, 52–9, 74–5; *Doggett's New York City Street Directory for 1851* (New York: J. Doggett Jr., 1851); *New York Journal of Commerce*, July 10, 1849; see advertisements for "offices to let" in *New-York Times*, March 15, 1854; Deborah S. Gardner, "The Architecture of Commercial Capitalism: John Kellum and the Development of New York, 1840–1875" (PhD diss., Columbia University, 1979), 101–19; *New York as It Is, in 1834* (New York: Disturnell, 1834), 18–9; William M. Thayer, *The Poor Boy and Merchant Prince; or, Elements of Success* (Boston: Gould and Lincoln, 1857), 121–3; Siegfried Giedion, *Mechanization Takes Command: A Contribution to Anonymous History* (1948; New York: W. W. Norton, 1969), 56.

17. American Desk Manufactory, *Catalogue* (New York: The Manufactory, 1873), 1–2 (Winterthur Library, Winterthur, DE); Gretchen Townsend, "Working Chairs for Working People: A History of the Nineteenth Century Office Chair" (MA thesis, University of Delaware, 1987), 16–35; Foster & Lee, Furniture Dealers (Trade Catalogues, American Antiquarian Society—hereafter AAS—Worcester, MA); Stuart Blumin, *Emergence of the Middle Class: Social Experience in the American City, 1760–1900* (New York: Cambridge University, 1989), 93–100, 340; Corlies, Macy & Co. Stationers, *Catalogue*, n.d. (Winterthur Library); Maynard & Noyes, "Black Writing Ink," ink, box 1 (Warshaw Collection of Business Paraphernalia, Smithsonian Institution, Washington, DC; hereafter Warshaw Collection); Barnes & Burr's Spring Circular to the Trade (AAS); Adel Millicent Smith, *Printing and Writing Materials: Their Evolution* (Philadelphia: Self-published, 1904), 161; Orrin N. Moore's Premium Inks, ink, box 1 (Warshaw Collection); Dolbear & Bros., penmanship, box 1 (Warshaw Collection); Michael Finlay, *Western Writing Implements in the Age of the Quill Pen* (Wetheral, UK: Plains Books, 1990), 59–62; John Murphy & Co. General Printing and Publishing Establishment (Baltimore), 1850, broadsides (AAS).

18. S. A. Potter, *Penmanship Explained; or, The Principles of Writing Reduced to an Exact Science* (Philadelphia: Cooperthwait, 1866), 21; Platt R. Spencer, *Spencerian Key to Practical Penmanship* (New York: Ivison, Phinney, Blakeman & Co., 1869), 18; *Subject-Matter Index of Patents for Inventions Issued by the United States Patent Office from 1790-1873, Inclusive* (Washington DC: Government Printing Office, 1874), 779; Joyce Irene Whalley, *Writing Implements and Accessories* (Detroit: Gayle Research Co., Book Tower, 1975), 86; Finlay, *Western Writing Implements*, 48.

19. *Hand-Book for Home Improvement, comprising How to Write. How to Talk. How to Behave. How to do Business* (New York: Samuel R. Wells, 1875), 9; Cathleen A. Baker, *From the Hand to the Machine: Nineteenth-Century American Paper and Mediums—Technologies, Materials, and Conservation* (Ann Arbor, MI: Legacy Press, 2014), 13–8, 203; Adel Millicent Smith, *Printing and Writing Materials: Their Evolution* (Philadelphia: By the author, 1904), 161; Paper and Stationery Warehouse, John Marsh, Boston, 1835–1852 (AAS); Rich & Loutrel ad in *Wilson's Copartnership Directory* (New York, 1855); "Everyday Actualities—No. XVII," in *Godey's Lady's Book* (March 1854), 199–202; forty feet in Joel Munsell, *A Chronology of Paper and Paper-Making* (Albany, NY: J. Munsell, 1857), 103, 133; "unnecessary folding" in C. R. Goodrich, ed., *Science and Mechanism* (New York: Putnam's, 1854), 176–80.

20. "Quills superseded" in *New York Tribune*, September 1, 1841; *Diary of William Dunlap* (New York: New-York Historical Society, 1930), 3:829; "extract the water" in Adam Wm. Rapp, *A Complete System of Scientific Penmanship* (Philadelphia: M. Fithian, 1832), 25; S. H. Browne, *The Manual of Commerce* (Springfield, MA: Bill, Nichols & Co., 1871), 313; B. F. Foster, *Prospectus of the Commercial Academy* (183 Broadway, New York, NY, 1837), 4–5; B. F. Foster, *Foster's System of Penmanship; or, The Art of Rapid Writing Illustrated and Explained, to Which Is Added the Angular and Anti-Angular Systems* (Boston: Perkins, Marvin & Co., 1835), 62–6; *History of the Invention and Illustrated Process of Making Foley's Diamond Pointed Gold Pens* (New York: Mayer, Merkel & Ottmann, 1875), 46. Murphy's Stationery Store in Baltimore was still advertising a selection of quills for sale in 1853. John Murphy & Co. General Printing and Publishing Establishment (Baltimore), 1850 (AAS). Even in 1875 it was still being pronounced that while "quill pens are now nearly obsolete . . . if kept well mended, none are better." *Hand-Book for Home Improvement*, 10.

21. Dolbear & Brothers, *A Chirographic Atlas* (New York: Collins, Keese, & Co., 1837); loss of pen-making skills, for instance, in Edward Everett Hale, *A New England Boyhood* (1893; repr., Boston: Little, Brown, and Co., 1964), 25; Whalley, *Writing Implements*, 43–4; Finlay, *Western Writing Implements*, 5, 10, 23. D. Hewett, *Self-Taught Penman*, 2nd ed. (Wilmington, DE: Robert Porter, 1818), 4.

22. Whalley, *Writing Implements* 44; *History of the Invention*, 7–9; Thomas Groom & Co. advertisement in James Robinson, *Merchants', Students' and Clerks' Manual* (Boston: Thomas Groom & Co., 1856); Comer's Commercial College, *Annual Register* (1866), n.p. (cover of pamphlet); *Annual Register* (1865), 4, 6, 8; Spencer's nibs in Charles H. Carpenter, *History of American Schoolbooks* (Philadelphia: University of Pennsylvania Press, 1963), 188; Mrs. L. C. Tuthill, *Any Thing for Sport* (Boston: Wm. Crosby and H. P. Nichols, 1846), 71; Frazar Kirkland, *Cyclopaedia of Commercial and Business Anecdotes* (New York: D. Appleton, 1864–5), 2:686.

23. "Economies of speed" in Alfred D. Chandler Jr., *Visible Hand: The Managerial Revolution in American Business* (Cambridge, MA: Harvard University Press, 1977); Whalley, *Writing Implements and Accessories*, 60–7; Finlay, *Western Writing Implements*, 40–3; US Patent No. 2,877 (December 12, 1842); US Patent No. 3,253 (September 9, 1843); US Patent No. 4,927 (January 13, 1847); US Patent No. 6,672 (August 23, 1849); US Patent No. 16,496 (January 27, 1857).

24. "Writing operations" in Edward N. Tailer, Diaries, May 25, 1850 (New-York Historical Society); Cayley, Diary, January 16, 1844 (New-York Historical Society); Albert Lane Norris, *Journal*, July 9, 1858 (Manuscript Collection, Winterthur Library); Graham, *Journal of Passing Events*, January 16, 1844, February 13, March 25, April 20, May 5 and 9, 1848 (New-York Historical Society); Tailer, Diaries, December 18, 19, and 20, 1849, as well as February 11, and May 25 and 28, 1850.

25. Jill Lepore, *A is for American: Letters and Other Characters in the Newly United States* (New York: Alfred A. Knopf, 2002), 66; William Alcott, *The Structure, Uses and Abuses of the Human Hand* (Boston: Massachusetts Sabbath School Society, 1856), 67; Foster, *Foster's System of Penmanship*, 10–1. See generally John Guillory, "The Memo and Modernity," *Critical Inquiry* 31 (2004), 108–32.

26. "To know just what to say" in Bryant & Stratton, *Catalogue* (1859), 30, 37; Edward N. Tailer, Diaries, February 11, 1850; Foster, *Clerk's Guide*, iv, vi–vii, 25; Boyd & Tubbs Commercial Institute, Boston, 1861 (Rare Book and Special Collections, Library of Congress).

27. Nathaniel Hawthorne, "The Custom-House" ("Introductory to 'The Scarlet Letter'"), in *Norton Anthology of American Literature*, ed. Nina Baym et al., 2nd ed. (New York: W. W. Norton,

1985), 1:1104; Foster, *Clerk's Guide*, iv, vi–vii, 25, 46–180, and "waste of words" at 25; *American Merchant* (June 1858), 84–6; Adam Smith quoted in Guillory, "Memo and Modernity," 123; Edwin T. Freedley, *How to Make Money, Being a Practical Treatise on Business* (London: Routledge, Warner and Routledge, 1859), 56–7; Roger Chartier, "Introduction: An Ordinary Kind of Writing," in *Correspondence: Models of Letter-Writing from the Middle Ages to the Nineteenth Century*, by Roger Chartier, Alain Boureau, and Cécile Dauphin (Princeton, NJ: Princeton University Press, 1997). On the end of rhetoric, also see Mary Poovey, *A History of the Modern Fact: Problems of Knowledge in the Sciences of Wealth and Society* (Chicago: University of Chicago Press, 1998).

28. "Citizen and farmer" in Munsell, *Chronology of Paper*, 43; "The Cheap Postage Question," *Young American's Magazine of Self-Improvement* (December 1847), 341, 344; David M. Henkin, *The Postal Age: The Emergence of Modern Communications in Nineteenth-Century America* (Chicago: University of Chicago Press, 2006), 21–2. Pliny Miles, "History of the Post Office," *Banker's Magazine and Statistical Register* (November 1857), 337–45; "Practical Working of Cheap Postage," in *Hunt's*, vol. 22 (January 1850), 44–6; limited use of telegraph in JoAnne Yates, "Investing in Information: Supply and Demand Forces in the Use of Information in American Firms, 1850–1920," in *Inside the Business Enterprise: Historical Perspectives on the Use of Information*, ed. Peter Temin (Chicago: University of Chicago Press, 1991), 133; and James H. Madison, "Evolution of Commercial Credit Reporting Agencies in Nineteenth-Century America," *Business History Review*, vol. 48, no. 2 (Summer 1974), 176. Allan R. Pred, *Urban Growth and the Circulation of Information: The United States System of Cities, 1790–1840* (Cambridge, MA: Harvard University Press, 1973), 81, 93.

29. Spencer, *Spencerian Key*, 24; Foster, *Foster's System*, 41; see, too, 89–104; rapid penmen in Daniel F. Child Papers, box 6, commonplace book (Massachusetts Historical Society), 1:151; B.F. Foster, *Prize Essay on the Best Method of Teaching Penmanship* (Boston: Perkins and Marvin, 1835), 50; Potter, *Penmanship Explained*, 22, 25–26, 29–30.

30. Barbara Rhodes, *Before Photocopying: The Art and History of Mechanical Copying, 1780–1938* (New Castle, DE: Oak Knoll Press, 1999), 16–24 ("easy combinations" on 24); Francis' Highly Improved Manifold Writer, 1841–1842, broadsides (AAS); Susan R. Stein, *The Worlds of Thomas Jefferson at Monticello* (New York: Harry N. Abrams, 1993), 366; Nora Wilkinson, "Copycat Copiers?" *The Conveyer: Research in Special Collections at the Bodleian Libraries* (blog), July 9, 2014, http://blogs.bodleian.ox.ac.uk/theconveyor/2014/07/09/copycat-copiers-frederick-folsch-ralph-wedgwood-and-the-improved-manifold-writer/.

31. Silvio A. Bedini, *Thomas Jefferson and His Copying Machines* (Charlottesville: University Press of Virginia, 1984), 41–54, and Peale quote on 48; "two originals" in *American Advertiser*, July 6, 1804; "one of those things" in *Philadelphia Gazette*, June 13, 1805; *New York Journal of Commerce*, January 3, 1840.

32. Bedini, *Thomas Jefferson*, 54–5, 190; Rhodes, *Before Photocopying*, 16–8.

33. "Facsimile" and portable version in "Great men attention! . . . Frank G. Johnson's portable letter copying press" (New York: John P. Prall, Printer, n.d.), printed ephemera (Library of Congress); Baker, *From the Hand*, 208–9; Granville Sharp, *Gilbert Prize Essay* (London: Groombridge and Sons, 1854), 211–27; Rhodes, *Before Photocopying*, 29–39, 63; "Copying Letters" in *Scientific American*, vol. 2 (1846), 48; William Mann advertisement; Charles Edward French, Diary, Journal No. 2, October 1 and 2, 1859 (Massachusetts Historical Society); Charles Babbage, *On the Economy of Machinery and Manufactures* (London: J. Murray, 1846), 92–3.

34. Sharp, *Prize Essay*, 212, 220–1.

35. Ibid., 222; *Hunt's*, vol. 15 (November 1846), 483–5; Rhodes, *Before Photocopying*, 4, 8–10, 12–3, 18–21, 24 (quote), 60, 63, 82–3; Cindy Sondik Aron, *Ladies and Gentlemen of the Civil Service: Middle-Class Workers in Victorian America* (New York: Oxford University Press, 1987).

36. "Sway the world" in Spencer, *Spencerian Key*, 89; "bold, free, expeditious" in Foster, *Prize Essay*, 58; "bold, free, and mercantile" was a variation on the theme. See ad for Bristow's penmanship lessons in *New York Herald*, September 30, 1839; *Potter and Hammond's System of Business Penmanship* (Philadelphia: Cowperthwaite & Co., 1865), n.p.; "plain, neat" in "Fulton & Eastman's Principles of Penmanship" in W. & R. Chambers, *Treasury of Knowledge* (New York: A. S. Barnes & Co., 1849), 24.

37. "From Turnbridge, Vermont, to London, England," *Proceedings of the Vermont Historical Society*, vol. 5, no. 3 (1937), 287; Benjamin H. Rand, *The American Penman* (Philadelphia: B. H. Rand, 1840), n.p.; Stanley Morison, *American Copybooks: An Outline of Their History from Colonial to Modern Times* (Philadelphia: Wm. F. Fell Co., 1951), 24–6; Foster, *Prize Essay*, 22, 32–3, 50–2, 57–60; Foster, *Writing and Writing Masters* (New York: Mason Brothers, 1854), n.p.; "swiftly" in Spencer, *Spencerian Key*, 93; "sacrifice everything" in *Massachusetts Teacher* (July 1855), 213–4; Boston Mercantile Academy, *Annual Catalogue* (Boston: William White, 1857), 23; Littlefield, "Before Spencerian," *Print* 3, no. 4 (1945), 33–40; Carpenter, *History of American Schoolbooks*, 184. See the polemic in *Massachusetts Teacher* (April 1855), 113–7, and in the issues of July 1855, 213–8, and November 1855, 332–7, 213–4. Tamara Plakins Thornton, *Handwriting in America: A Cultural History* (New Haven, CT: Yale University Press, 1996), 55–8.

38. "Highway" in "Penmanship," *Common School Journal*, vol. 1 (March 1839), 65; Spencer, *Spencerian Key*, 143–5; B. F. Foster, *Foster's Elementary Copy Books* (Boston: Perkins, Marvin & Co., 1833); *North American Review*, October 1825, 451–3. See generally Thornton, *Handwriting*, 47–55. "Chirythmography" also received a prominent place in the handbill announcing the opening of Folsom's Mercantile College in Cleveland in 1851. See *125 Years of Education for Business: The History of Dyke College, 1848–1973*, chap. 2 (Cleveland, OH: Dyke College, 1973).

39. Friederich A. Kittler, *Gramophone, Film, Typewriter*, trans. Geoffrey Winthrop-Young and Michael Wutz (Stanford, CA: Stanford University Press, 1999), 198–9, 230–1; Foster, *Down East Diary*, 12, 121. See, too, Darren Henry, *The Iron Whim: A Fragmented History of the Typewriter* (Ithaca, NY: Cornell University Press, 2005), 134–43.

40. Melville, "Bartleby," 548.

41. Foster, *Prize Essay*, 22; Spencer, *Spencerian Key*, 92–3.

42. Adam Wm. Rapp, *A Complete System of Scientific Penmanship* (Philadelphia: M. Fithian, 1832), 13–14; Potter, *Penmanship Explained*, 26–8, 13; Foster, *Down East Diary*, 230 (November 10, 1849); Spencer, *Spencerian Key*, 24; "Writing Desks," *American Annals of Education* (March 1837), 123–5; "Luther's Writing Desk," *American Annals of Education* (October 1838), 457–64.

43. Foster, *Foster's System*, vii; Potter, *Penmanship Explained*, 30; George W. Winchester, *Theoretical and Practical Penmanship, in Four Books*, rev. ed. (New York: Pratt, Oakley & Co., 1855); B. F. Foster, *The Origin and Progress of Book-Keeping*, 46 (London: C. H. Law, 1852); Samuel Roberts Wells, *How to Do Business: A Pocket Manual of Practical Affairs* (New York: Fowler and Wells, 1857), 31. See generally Thornton, *Handwriting in America*.

44. Cobbett in Alan Delgado, *The Enormous File: A Social History of the Office* (London: John Murray, 1979), 18; Foster, *Prize Essay*, 22, 24; Anonymous, Diary, 1834–36, June 19, 1938 (Special Collections, Bryn Mawr College); R. W. Emerson, "Doctrine of the Hands" (1837), quoted in Wai Chee Dimock, "Class, Gender, and a History of Metonymy," in *Rethinking Class: Literary Studies and Social Formations*, ed. Wai Chee Dimock and Michael T. Gilmore (New York:

Columbia University Press, 1994), 58. Generally see Jonathan Goldberg, *Writing Matter: From the Hands of the English Renaissance* (Stanford, CA: Stanford University Press, 1990).

45. "Strong arm" in Mrs. Francis S. Osgood, "Labor," in *American Phrenological Journal*, vol. 12 (September 1850), 293–4. Also, "Is there in the wide world a factory containing a tenth part as much curious and complicated machinery as the hand?" Alcott, *Structure, Uses and Abuses*, 116. See, too, Francis Barker, *The Tremulous Private Body: Essays on Subjection* (Ann Arbor: University of Michigan Press, 1995), 70–80.

46. Frederick Beck, *The Young Accountant's Guide; or, An Easy Introduction to the Knowledge of Mercantile Book-Keeping* (Boston: Stimpson and Clapp, 1831), 5; N. S. B. Gras, *Business and Capitalism: An Introduction to Business History* (1939; repr., New York: Augustus M. Kelley, 1971), 116–9; Sidney Pollard, *The Genesis of Modern Management: A Study of the Industrial Revolution in Great Britain* (1965; repr., Hampshire, United Kingdom: Gregg Revivals, 1993), 209–19, 221–2; Frederick Michael E. Hobart and Zachary S. Schiffman, *Information Ages: Literacy, Numeracy, and the Computer Revolution* (Baltimore: Johns Hopkins University Press, 1998), 148–50; G. A. Lee, "The Concept of Profit in British Accounting, 1760–1900," *Business History Review* 49, no. 1 (Spring 1975), 10–17, 29–32.

47. James Barnard Blake, Diary, March 5 and April 4, 1851 (Manuscripts, American Antiquarian Society); Foster, *Origin and Progress*, 15; Eve Chiapello, "Accounting and the Birth of the Notion of Capitalism," *Critical Perspectives on Accounting* 18 (2007), 263–96; B. S. Yamey, "Scientific Bookkeeping and the Rise of Capitalism," *Economic History Review*, 2nd ser., 1, nos. 2–3 (1949), 99–113.

48. "Display" in C. C. Marsh, *The Science of Double-Entry Book-Keeping* (New York: John C. Riker, 1857), 5; repeated in *Duties of Employers and Employed, Considered with Reference to Principals and Their Clerks or Apprentices* (New York: J. S. Redfield, 1849), 23; "equilibrium of results" quoted in John J. Williams, "A New Perspective on the Development of Double-Entry Bookkeeping," in *The Development of Double-Entry: Selected Essays*, ed. Christopher Nobes (London: Routledge, 1984), 144.

49. "Musical notes" in "What Constitutes a Merchant," *Hunt's*, vol. 1 (October 1839), 286; Lee, "Concept of Profit," 9–10; W. T. Baxter, "Accounting in Colonial America," in *Studies in the History of Accounting, by* A. C. Littleton and B. S. Yamey (London: Sweet & Maxwell, 1956), 274–5; Pollard, *Genesis of Modern Management*, 211–23.

50. Terry K. Sheldahl, "Foreword to C. C. Marsh's 1835 'Lecture on the Study of Book-Keeping,' with a Balance Sheet,'" *Accounting Historians Journal* 15, no. 2 (Fall 1988), 201; Baxter, "Accounting in Colonial America," 278–81; Pollard, *Genesis of Modern Management*, 209–19, 221–2; Jonathan Levy, "Accounting for Profit and the History of Capitalism" (unpublished manuscript).

51. Sheldahl, "Foreword," 5; C. C. Marsh, *The Science of Double-Entry Book-Keeping, Simplified* (New York: John C. Riker, 1857), 7, 8; Henry A. Patterson, Diary, September 1, 8, and 16, 1836 (New-York Historical Society); S. W. Crittenden, *An Elementary Treatise on Book-Keeping* (Philadelphia: E. C. & J. Biddle & Co., 1860), 5–8; Irvine Hitchcock, *A New Method of Teaching Book-Keeping* (Boston: Nichols & Hall), iii, 9.

52. Foster, *Origin and Progress*, 6; Crittenden, *Elementary Treatise*, 6; James Bennet, *The American System of Practical Book-Keeping (New York: B. & S. Collins, 1839)*, 12.

53. Horace Mann, "Means and Objects of Common School Education," in *Lectures on Education* (Boston: Ide and Dutton, 1855), 41; *Massachusetts Teacher* (June 1852), 168, 170–1; Foster, *Concise Treatise on Commercial Book-keeping* (Boston: Perkins and Marvin, 1837), 11; "drilling the learner into a calculating machine" in "Foster's Mercantile Agency Establishement," B. F.

Foster, *Counting-House Assistant* (London: Charles H. Law, 1847), 8; "to reason upon and comprehend what he is doing" in *New-York Daily Times*, March 28, 1853; "plain and philosophical principles" in Boyd & Tubbs Commercial Institute, Boston, 1861 (Rare Book and Special Collections, Library of Congress). On school reform, see Rush Welter, *The Mind of America: 1820–1860* (New York: Columbia University Press, 1975), 276–97. Bookkeeping "is necessary for every person engaged in the ordinary pursuits of life," Samuel Wells observed in quoting Ira Mayhew, yet another prolific promoter and author of accounting systems. Wells, *How to Do Business*, 125.

54. Marsh, *Science of Double-Entry*, 7; "a person" in Sheldahl, "Foreword," 191; Foster in *New York Daily Times*, March 28, 1853; Mann, "Means and Objects," 41; and see, too, 25–6; *Massachusetts Teacher* (June 1852), 168, 170–1; Foster, *Concise Treatise*, 11; Marsh, *Science of Double-Entry*, 7. And see Edward J. Burke, "Objectivity and Accounting," *Accounting Review* 39, no. 4 (October 1964), 837–49.

55. "Hieroglyphics" in Kirkland, *Cyclopedia*, 2:672, 677; Alden in Balleisen, *Navigating Failure*, 52, 70; Foster in *New York Daily Times*, December 2, 1852; Crane in Judith A. McGaw, "Accounting for Innovation: Technological Change and Business Practice in the Berkshire County Paper Industry," *Technology and Culture* 26, no. 4 (October 1985), 714.

56. Thomas Jones in *Hunt's*, vol. 1 (September 1839), 257; Edwin J. Perkins and Sherry Levinson, "Partnership Accounting in a Nineteenth Century Merchant Banking House," *Accounting Historians Journal* 7, no. 1 (Spring 1980), 59–68. See, too, "Problems in Accountantship," *Hunt's*, vol. 7 (December 1842), 567–9.

57. Spencer in *Hunt's*, vol. 37 (December 1857), 702.

58. Joseph Hopkinson, *Lecture upon the Principles of Commercial Integrity* (Philadelphia: Carey and Lea, 1832), 13, and republished in *Hunt's*, vol. 1 (November 1839), 377–89. For biographical details concerning Hopkinson, see *Hunt's*, vol. 7 (November 1842), 397–416.

59. *Hunt's*, vol. 11 (December 1844), 573–4, including "constant and ever-varying"; "a world of goods" in Asa Greene, *Perils of Pearl Street, including a Taste of the Dangers of Wall Street* (New York: Betts and Anstice, 1834), 6; *American Phrenological Journal*, vol. 10 (1848), 253; Karl Marx and Friedrich Engels, "Manifesto of the Communist Party" (1848), in *The Marx-Engels Reader*, 2nd ed., ed. Robert C. Tucker (New York: W. W. Norton, 1978), 476.

60. Thomas Carlyle, *The French Revolution: A History* (1837; London: Chapman and Hall, 1898), 1:29; Horace Bushnell, "Age of Homespun," in *Litchfield County Centennial Celebration* (Hartford, CT: Edwin Hunt, 1851), 115; Émile Durkheim, "Sociology of Knowledge," in *Selected Writings*, ed. Anthony Giddens (Cambridge: Cambridge University Press, 1972), 251; Georg Simmel, *The Philosophy of Money*, ed. David Frisby, trans. Tom Bottomore and David Frisby (London: Routledge, 1990), 107–8. See, most famously, Friedrich Nietzsche, "On Truth and Lies in a Nonmoral Sense" (1873), in which he compares the invention of truth to a game of craps "using every die in the designated manner, counting its spots accurately, fashioning the right categories, and never violating the order of caste and class rank." See, too, Maurice Dobb, *Theories of Value and Distribution since Adam Smith: Ideology and Economic Theory* (Cambridge: Cambridge University Press, 1973), 74–9, 82.

61. *Hunt's*, vol. 20 (February 1849), 223–5.

62. Ibid.

63. Foster, *Foster's System*, v.

64. Carey in "Political Economists," *American Whig Review* 12 (October 1850), 382; Lorraine Daston and Peter Galison, "The Image of Objectivity," *Representations* 40 (Fall 1992), 84–9; Theodore M. Porter, "Quantification and the Accounting Ideal in Science," *Social Studies of Science*

22 (1992), 633, 640–1; Donald MacKenzie, *Engine, Not a Camera: How Financial Models Shape Markets* (Cambridge, MA: MIT Press, 2006), 143–77.

65. "Self-evident truths" in Thomas Jones, *Hunt's* (December 1842), 30, reprinted in "Analysis of Bookkeeping as a Branch of General Education," *Accounting Historians Journal* 4, no. 2 (Fall 1977), 45; Simmel, *Philosophy of Money*, 224, 210–4. Also see Peter Miller, "Accounting as Social and Institutional Practice: An Introduction," in Anthony Hopwood and Peter Miller, *Accounting as Social and Institutional Practice* (New York: Cambridge University Press, 1994); and Porter, "Quantification."

Chapter Two

1. Spencer in *Hunt's*, vol. 37 (December 1857), 702; T. S. Arthur, *Advice to Young Men* (Philadelphia: G. G. Evans, 1860), 69, 79, "whole theory of accounts" on 72, and "fair business hand" on 71; T. S. Arthur, "The Use of Learning," *Youth's Companion*, March 23, 1841, 181; the story was republished in *Youth's Companion* (without the last paragraph) on December 27, 1849. On the market's hermeneutics, see, too, T. S. Arthur, "Don't Be Discouraged," *Godey's Lady's Book* (September 1843), 121–4. "If there ever was a place where thinkers for thinking's sake were few and unimportant as compared with thinkers for the sake of action, it is here." Henry W. Bellows, *The Leger and the Lexicon* (Cambridge, MA: John Bartlett, 1853), 6.

2. Samuel Roberts Wells, *How to Do Business: A Pocket Manual of Practical Affairs* (New York: Fowler and Wells, 1857), 41; Charles H. Foster, ed., *Down East Diary by Benjamin Browne Foster* (Orono: University of Maine at Orono Press, 1975), 210–1 (July 25, 1849); "goaheadativeness" in *Scientific American* (June 4, 1853), 301. See more generally Stephen Carl Arch, *After Franklin: The Emergence of Autobiography in Post-Revolutionary America, 1780–1830* (Hanover, NH: University Press of New England, 2001), 20–53.

3. "Anxious" quoted in John G. Cawelti, *Apostles of the Self-Made Man* (Chicago: University of Chicago Press, 1988), 48; Petty in Eric Roll, *A History of Economic Thought* (London: Faber and Faber, 1973), 104–6; James L. Huston, *Securing the Fruits of Labor: The American Concept of Wealth Distribution* (Baton Rouge: Louisiana State University Press, 1998), 3–10, 14–5, 31, 42–5, 52, 130, 162–4, and "hard earned" on 41. And see generally Gregory S. Alexander, *Commodity and Propriety: Competing Visions of Property in American Legal Thought, 1776–1970* (Chicago: University of Chicago Press, 1997), 26–42.

4. J. Hector St. John de Crevecoeur, *Letters from an American Farmer* (New York: Penguin Books, 1981), 54; "toing and froing" quoted in Harvey J. Graff, *Conflicting Paths: Growing Up in America* (Cambridge, MA: Harvard University Press, 1995), 76; Carole Shammas, *A History of Household Government in America* (Charlottesville: University of Virginia Press, 2002), 58–63.

The nature of household patriarchy in America has generated an enormous literature of the highest standards. Most helpful to this study is Winifred Barr Rothenberg, *From Market-Places to a Market Economy: The Transformation of Rural Massachusetts, 1750–1850* (Chicago: University of Chicago Press, 1992); Toby Ditz, "Ownership and Obligation: Inheritance and Patriarchal Households in Connecticut, 1750–1820," *William and Mary Quarterly* 47, no. 2 (April 1990), 235–65; Nancy R. Folbre, "The Wealth of Patriarchs: Deerfield, Massachusetts, 1760–1840," *Journal of Interdisciplinary History* 16, no. 2 (Autumn 1985), 199–220; Carole Shammas, Marylynn Salmon, and Michel Dahlin, *Inheritance in America: From Colonial Times to the Present* (New Brunswick, NJ: Rutgers University Press, 1987); Martin Bruegel, *Farm, Shop, Landing: The Rise of a Market Society in the Hudson Valley, 1780–1860* (Durham, NC: Duke University

Press, 2002); James Henretta, "Families and Farms: Mentalite in Pre-Industrial America," *William and Mary Quarterly 35*, no. 1 (January 1978), 3–32; Richard Lyman Bushman, "Markets and Composite Farms in Early America," *William and Mary Quarterly 55*, no. 3 (July 1998), 351–74; William James Booth, *Households: On the Moral Architecture of the Economy* (Ithaca, NY: Cornell University Press, 1993); Christopher Clark, *The Roots of Rural Capitalism: Western Massachusetts, 1780–1860* (Ithaca, NY: Cornell University Press, 1990).

5. Robert W. Gordon, "Paradoxical Property," in *Early Modern Conceptions of Property,* John Brewer and Susan Staves, eds. (London: Routledge, 1995), 96–8.

6. Eli Cook, "The Pricing of Progress" (PhD diss., Harvard University, 2012), 65.

7. Bruegel, *Farm, Shop, Landing,* 67; L. Ray Gunn, *The Decline of Authority* (Ithaca, NY: Cornell University Press, 1988), 105–41. On the "dynamic" nature of industrial property, see James Willard Hurst, "The Release of Energy," in *Law and the Conditions of Freedom* (Madison: University of Wisconsin Press, 1956), 1–32.

8. Karl Marx, *Grundrisse* (London: Penguin, 1973), 276–7; Capt. Marryat, *Diary in America* (Philadelphia: Carey and Hart, 1839); Harding in Joyce Appleby, ed., *Recollections of the Early Republic: Selected Autobiographies* (Boston: Northeastern University Press, 1997), 136; "Where there is a will there will be a way" also in James W. Alexander, "The Merchant's Clerk Cheered and Counselled," in *The Man of Business, Considered in His Various Relations* (New York: Anson D. F. Randolph, 1857), 39; "he can do anything" in Joseph F. Kett, *Rites of Passage: Adolescence in America, 1790–Present* (New York: Basic Books, 1977), 96–7.

9. *American Phrenological Journal* (January 1853), 2. See also issues from March, April, and May 1853. As the most widely read magazine in the country, see Jayme M. Sokolow, *Eros and Modernization: Sylvester Graham, Health Reform, and the Origins of Victorian Sexuality in America* (Rutherford, NJ: Fairleigh Dickinson University Press, 1983), 156–8; Guild in Chris Clark, "The Agrarian Context of American Capitalist Development," in *Capitalism Takes Command: The Social Transformation of Nineteenth-Century America,* Michael Zakim and Gary J. Kornblith, eds. (Chicago: University of Chicago Press, 2011), 25; William Hoffman, Diary, March 30 and 31, 1848 (New-York Historical Society).

10. Hoffman, Diary, April 17, 1847, as well as March 1, 30, and 31, 1848, and April 3, 1848.

11. Hoffman, Diary, March 31 and April 3, 6, 10, 1848.

12. Alexander, "Merchant's Clerk," 8; Jackson biography in Michael Paul Rogin, *Fathers and Children: Andrew Jackson and the Subjugation of the American Indian* (Piscataway, NJ: Transaction Publishers, 1991), 39–40; Frazar Kirkland, *Cyclopaedia of Commercial and Business Anecdotes* (New York: D. Appleton 1864), 1:16–7; John Angell James, *The Young Man from Home* (New York: D. Appleton, 1840), 19; Foster, *Down East Diary,* 229 (November 7, 1849). Both advice literature and children's fiction, which emerged as a distinct literary genre after 1820, often featured a dead or missing father. Shawn Johansen, *Family Men: Middle-Class Fatherhood in Early Industrializing America* (New York: Routledge, 2001), 1.

13. "Every son" and "*Let everyone who is below*" in "Young Men's Department," *Cultivator* (April–May 1835), 47; Edward Everett in Nian-Sheng Huang, *Benjamin Franklin in American Thought and Culture, 1790–1990* (Philadelphia: American Philosophical Society, 1994), 54; and see Mercantile Library Association of the City of New-York, *The Thirty-Eighth Annual Report* (1859), 23; S. G. Goodrich, *Recollections of a Lifetime; or, Men and Things I Have Seen* (New York: Miller, Orton and Mulligan, 1856), 415; Mellon in introduction to *The Autobiography of Benjamin Franklin,* by Benjamin Franklin, ed. Leonard W. Labaree, Ralph L. Ketchum, Helen C. Boatfield, and Helene H. Fineman (New Haven, CT: Yale University Press, 1964), 10.

14. "All the promise" in Kett, *Rites of Passage*, 94; Lincoln in Daniel Walker Howe, *Making the American Self: Jonathan Edwards to Abraham Lincoln* (Cambridge, MA: Harvard University Press, 1997), 138-9; Adam Smith, *The Wealth of Nations*, ed. Edwin Cannan (Chicago: University of Chicago Press, 1976), 111; "visible horizon" in *American Phrenological Journal* (August 1848), 252; Edward Jarvis, *Address, Delivered at the Laying of the Corner Stone of the Insane Hospital at Northampton, Massachusetts* (Northampton, MA: J. & L. Metcalf, 1856), 8; Alexis de Tocqueville, *Democracy in America*, ed. J. P. Mayer (New York: Doubleday & Co., 1969), 537; Tocqueville on insanity quoted in Joseph F. Kett, *The Pursuit of Knowledge under Difficulties: From Self-Improvement to Adult Education in America, 1750-1990* (Stanford, CA: Stanford University Press, 1994), 52.

15. Cooper in Steven Stoll, *Larding the Lean Earth: Soil and Society in Nineteenth-Century America* (New York: Hill and Wang, 2002), 166; "stops payment" in *American Phrenological Journal*, vol. 17 (March 1853), 49; "loafers" in *Cultivator* (April 1845), 108; Edwin T. Freedley, *Practical Treatise on Business* (Chicago: D. B. Cooke, 1853), xii-xiii; capital intensive responses in Thomas S. Wermuth, *Rip Van Winkle's Neighbors: The Transformation of Rural Society in the Hudson River Valley* (Albany: State University of New York Press, 2001), 103-9, 115-27; Bruegel, *Farm, Shop, Landing*, 65-79, 85-6, 110-4; Hoffman, Diary, March 9, 1847; "astonishing" in William Hunter, "Annual Address before the Rhode-Island Society for the Encouragement of Domestic Industry" (Providence: By the Society, 1826), 6-7; Carey in Paul Keith Conkin, *Prophets of Prosperity: America's First Political Economists* (Bloomington: Indiana University Press, 1980), 264-6, 269, 272; "remunerating" in Bruegel, *Farm, Shop, Landing*, 97. See, too, "American Agriculture," *Journal of American Geographical and Statistical Society* (March 1859), 76-86.

16. "Henry Homespun Jr." in Stoll, *Larding the Lean Earth*, 29; *Catskill Messenger* in Bruegel, *Farm, Shop, Landing*, 68; increasing debt in Fred Bateman and Jeremy Atack, *To Their Own Soil: Agriculture in the Antebellum North* (Ames: Iowa State University Press, 1987), 11; Robert A. Gross, "Culture and Cultivation: Agriculture and Society in Thoreau's Concord," *Journal of American History* 69, no. 1 (June 1982), 42-4, 48, 50; Clark, *Roots of Rural Capitalism*, 124-6; William J. Gilmore, *Reading Becomes a Necessity of Life: Material Cultural Life in Rural New England, 1780-1835* (Knoxville: University of Tennessee Press, 1992), 344-74.

17. *Country Gentleman* in Clarence H. Danhof, *Change in Agriculture: The Northern United States, 1820-1870* (Cambridge, MA: Harvard University Press, 1969), 54-5, 96-100, quote on 96; Rothenberg, *From Market-Places to a Market Economy*, 62-3; Bennett in Bruegel, *Farm, Shop, Landing*, 66; *Cultivator* (February 1837), 165; full-time farming in Eric Nellis, "The Working Lives of the Rural Middle Class in Provincial Massachusetts," *Labor History* 36, no. 4 (Fall 1996), 514-7; four sons in Howard S. Russell, *A Long, Deep Furrow: Three Centuries of Farming in New England* (Hanover, NH: University Press of New England, 1976), 343. See, too, Jesse Chickering, *A Statistical View of the Population of Massachusetts, from 1765 to 1840* (Boston: Charles C. Little and James Brown, 1846).

18. Hoffman, Diary, January 15 and March 4, 1849, 199, as well as January 26, July 21, August 22 and 24, 1850.

19. *Hints to Young Tradesmen, and Maxims for Merchants* (Boston: Perkins & Marvin, 1838), 53; Hubbard Winslow, *The Young Man's Aid to Knowledge, Virtue, and Happiness* (Boston: Crocker and Brewster, 1839), 354; B. F. Foster, *Clerk's Guide; or, Commercial Correspondence* (Boston: Perkins & Marvin, 1837), 224; James Nixon, *The Rudiments of Book-Keeping, Designed for Schools and Self-Instruction* (New York: F. J. Huntington, and Mason Brothers, 1854), 1-2; Marryat in Burton J. Bledstein, *The Culture of Professionalism: The Middle Class and the Development of Higher Education in America* (New York: W. W. Norton, 1978), 214.

20. Edward Jarvis, *Traditions and Reminiscences of Concord, Massachusetts, 1779–1878* (Amherst: University of Massachusetts, 1993), 109; *Hunt's*, vol. 7 (October 1842), 349; Charles Edward French, Diaries, 1851–1904, July 19 and 30, September 30, October 1, 1851 (Massachusetts Historical Society); Henry A. Patterson, Diaries, 1832–1849, February 28, 1837 (New-York Historical Society); Hoffman, Diary, 1847–1850, March 7, 1849; Edward Isaiah Thomas, Diary, June 6 and 15, 1853, Thomas Family Papers, 1815–1887 (American Antiquarian Society, Worcester, MA); Morgan in William O. Stoddard, *Men of Business* (New York: Charles Scribner's Sons, 1897), 112–6. See, too, Henry Pierce, Diaries, 1845–1895, letter dated March 3, 1850 (Massachusetts Historical Society). On the end of American patriarchy, see Hendrik Hartog, *Man and Wife in America: A History* (Cambridge, MA: Harvard University Press, 2000); and Holly Brewer, *By Birth or Consent: Children, Law, and the Anglo-American Revolution in Authority* (Chapel Hill: University of North Carolina, 2005).

21. Father's "empire" in John Locke, *Second Treatise of Government* (1690; Indianapolis, IN: Bobbs-Merrill Co., 1952), 37, and see generally chap. 6 ("Of Paternal Power"); "this day" in Thomas Augst, *The Clerk's Tale: Young Men and Moral Life in Nineteenth-Century America* (Chicago: University of Chicago Press, 2003), 20; Mary Ryan, *Cradle of the Middle Class: The Family in Oneida County, New York, 1790–1865* (New York: Cambridge University Press, 1981), 108, 167, 178–9.

22. George S. Hillard, "The Dangers and Duties of the Mercantile Profession," in *An Address Delivered before the Mercantile Library Association at Its Thirtieth Anniversary, November 13, 1850* (Boston: Ticknor and Fields, 1854), 38; *American Phrenological Journal*, vol. 10 (1848), 252.

23. *Hunt's*, vol. 5 (December 1841), 536; William A. Alcott, *The Physiology of Marriage* (Boston: J. P. Jewett, 1856) 209–13; *United States Economist*, June 18, 1853; Stephen Elias, *Alexander T. Stewart: The Forgotten Merchant Prince* (Westport, CT: Praeger Publishers, 1992); Tappan in Walter Barrett, *The Old Merchants of New York City* (New York: Carleton, 1864), 230–1.

24. Frazar Kirkland, *Cyclopaedia of Commercial and Business Anecdotes* (New York: D. Appleton, 1864–5), 2:672.

25. "Abuses" in Benjamin Penhallow Shillaber, Journal, January 6, 1849 (Special Collections, Columbia University); Daniel N. Haskell, *An Address Delivered before the Boston Mercantile Library Association* (Boston: Dutton and Wentworth, 1848), 19. See, too, Ayn Rand, *The Virtue of Selfishness: A New Conception of Egoism* (New York: New American Library, 1964).

26. Robert Hone, Diary, April 25, 1840, 3; "Mercantile Agency," in *Hunt's*, vol. 24 (January 1851), 46–53; Edward J. Balleisen, *Navigating Failure: Bankruptcy and Commercial Society in Antebellum America* (Chapel Hill: University of North Carolina Press, 2001), 103, 130–1. In general, see James Willard Hurst, *Law and the Conditions of Freedom in the Nineteenth-Century United States* (Madison: University of Wisconsin Press, 1956); Morton J. Horwitz, *The Transformation of American Law, 1780–1860* (Cambridge, MA: Harvard University Press, 1977).

27. Wells, *How to Do Business*, 114–5.

28. Georg Simmel, *Simmel on Culture: Selected Writings*, ed. David Frisby and Mike Featherstone (London: Sage Publications, 1997), 235; Marx, *Grundisse*, 225–6. A credit agency circular announced in 1858 that there were 157,394 stores around the country that each owed an average of $14,500 to metropolitan jobbers, a total indebtedness that amounted to $2.25 billion. Rowena Olegario, *A Culture of Credit: Embedding Trust and Transparency in American Business* (Cambridge, MA: Harvard University Press, 2006), 26.

29. T. S. Arthur, *The Mother's Rule; or, The Right Way and the Wrong Way* (Philadelphia: H. C. Peck & Theo. Bliss, 1856), 286–7; Hoffman, Diary, April 8, 1848.

30. Henry W. Bellows, *The Leger and the Lexicon* (Cambridge, MA: John Bartlett, 1853), 26–7; Horwitz, *Transformation of American Law*, 178–9; Christopher Tomlins, *Freedom Bound: Law, Labor, and Civic Identity in Colonizing English America, 1580–1865* (New York: Cambridge University Press, 2010), 337–9, 366–71; Roy Kreitner, *Calculating Promises: The Emergence of Modern American Contract Doctrine* (Stanford, CA: Stanford University Press, 2007), 22–3, 31–3, 42–5, 84–6. Georg Simmel: "What we regard as freedom is often in fact only a change of obligations." Simmel, *The Philosophy of Money*, ed. David Frisby, trans. Tom Bottomore and David Frisby (London: Routledge, 1990), 283.

31. "Memorial from Francis Lieber," April 18, 1836, 24th Cong., 1st Sess., Senate, Doc. 314, 10 (1836); Archibald Russell, *Principles of Statistical Inquiry; as Illustrated in Proposals for Uniting an Examination into the Resources of the United States with the Census to Be Taken in 1840* (New York: D. Appleton, 1839), 201–16. See, too, John E. Crowley, "The Sensibility of Comfort," *American Historical Review* (June 1999), 749–82, or, more fundamentally, David Ricardo, *Principles of Political Economy and Taxation* (London: John Murray, 1817).

32. *New York Tribune*, May 27, 1851; *Hunt's*, vol. 34 (April 1856), 403–15. Henry C. Carey, "Wealth and Land," in Carey, *Past, Present, and Future* (Philadelphia: Carey and Hart, 1848), 142–3. The debate over capitalism's empirical effect on the standard of living has been ferociously rehearsed by historians. The result of such a quantitative focus on purchasing power, however, is to bring the population into the commodity fold rather than examine how the commodity enfolded them. See, for instance, E. J. Hobsbawm, "The Standard of Living during the Industrial Revolution: A Discussion," *Economic History Review*, n.s., 16, no. 1 (1963), 119–34; T. S. Ashton, "The Standard of Life of the Workers in England, 1790–1830," supplement, *Journal of Economic History* 9 (1949), 19–38; Donald R. Adams Jr., "The Standard of Living during American Industrialization: Evidence from the Brandywine Region, 1800–1860," *Journal of Economic History 42*, no. 4 (1982), 903–17; Hacker in F. A. Hayek, ed., *Capitalism and the Historians* (Chicago: University of Chicago Press, 1954); T. S. Ashton, "The Treatment of Capitalism by Historians," in Hayek, *Capitalism and the Historians*, 33–63. See Hobsbawm generally in *Age of Empire: 1875–1914* (New York: Pantheon, 1987).

33. Edwin T. Freedley, *How to Make Money* (London: Routledge, 1859), 62 (the same discussion in Freedley, *A Practical Treatise on Business*, 121). "Profitably spent" "investment," "accounting for himself," "fame, glory, and principle," and "greatest profit" in *Hunt's*, vol. 1 (November 1839), 411; "honary motive" in *Hunt's*, vol. 36 (January 1857), 49. William Alcott expanded on the importance of a personal budget in the following conversation between two clerks, as reported in his *Advice to Young Men:* "Boarding costs three and a half dollars a week, or a little over $180 a year. Add the washing and that comes to $200. Clothing is $125 and boots and shoes and sundry additions another $75. " 'Where are the three hundred and fifty remaining?' 'Dear knows, for I don't . . .' 'What does your account book say?' 'Account book! I don't keep an account book. . . .' 'That is strange! Why, I keep my own cash account as carefully as I do my employer's.' 'Keeping an account of your money doesn't make it go any further.' 'O, yes, it does. Keep an account of every item spent for a month, and read it over carefully on the first of the succeeding one . . . it will cause you to be more careful of your money.' " Arthur, *Advice to Young Men*, 28–9.

34. New York Association for the Improvement of the Condition of the Poor, *Annual Report* (New York: The Association, 1845); *Godey's Lady's Book* (March 1851), 206; William A. Alcott, *Young Man's Guide* (Boston: T. R. Marvin, 1849), 108–9; Benjamin Franklin Foster, *Foster's School Book-Keeping: The Theory and Practice of Book-Keeping* (Boston: Perkins and Marvin, 1840), 5; Hoffman, Diary, "An Account of Expenses," 1847, 340.

35. Lawrence in William M. Thayer, *The Poor Boy and Merchant Prince; or, Elements of Success* (Boston: Gould and Lincoln, 1857), 116–7; *Duties of Employers and Employed, Considered with Reference to Principals and Their Clerks or Apprentices* (New York: J. S. Redfield, 1849), 30; Edwin L. Theiss, "The Beginnings of Business Budgeting," *Accounting Review* 12, no. 1 (March 1937), 43–4, box 1 (Lemuel Shattuck Papers, Massachusetts Historical Society). Without learning to keep accounts of their own expenditures, one would never learn "the proper use of money" or "the real value of property," as Theodore Dwight pronounced in *The Father's Book* (Springfield, MA: G. and C. Merriam, 1834), 176.

36. *New-York Times*, November 8, 1853; Marx, *Grundisse*, 792–4. See, too, Moishe Postone, *Time, Labor and Social Domination: A Reinterpretation of Marx's Critical Theory* (New York: Cambridge University Press, 1993). And: "As it is the nominal or money price of goods, therefore, which finally determines the prudence or imprudence of all purchases and sales, and thereby regulates almost the whole business of common life in which price is concerned, we cannot wonder that it should have been so much more attended to than the real price [of labor]." Adam Smith, *Wealth of Nations* ed. Edwin Cannan (Chicago: University of Chicago Press, 1976), 43 (bk. 1, chap. 5).

37. *North American Review* 97 (October 1863), 307; Elizur quoted in Jonathan Ira Levy, "Ways of Providence: Capitalism, Risk, and Freedom in America, 1841–1935" (PhD diss., University of Chicago, 2008), 141.

38. "Income" quoted in Sharon Murphy, *Investing in Life: Insurance in Antebellum America* (Baltimore: Johns Hopkins University Press, 2012), 131; "prudence" in J. H. Phillips, *Life Assurance Agent's Manual* (London: William Tweedy, 1857). On clerks as a principal market for life insurance policies, see Sharon Ann Murphy, "Security in an Uncertain World: Life Insurance and the Emergence of Modern America" (PhD diss., University of Virginia, 2005), 284–8, 316–7; Viviana A. Rotman Zelizer, *Morals and Markets: The Development of Life Insurance in the United States* (New Brunswick, NJ: Transaction Publishers, 1983), 92; "Contributions to Vital Statistics," *North American Review* (October 1863), 302–3. See generally John Fabian Witt, *The Accidental Republic: Crippled Workingmen, Destitute Widows, and the Remaking of American Law* (Cambridge, MA: Harvard University Press, 2004), 43–70.

39. *New England Family* quoted in Jonathan Levy, *Freaks of Fortune: The Emerging World of Capitalism and Risk in America* (Cambridge, MA: Harvard University Press, 2012), 88; *North American Review* 97 (October 1863), 309, 307; Wright in Levy, *Freaks of Fortune*, 86 and generally 60–103. See, too, Angel Kwolek-Folland, *Engendering Business: Men and Women in the Corporate Office, 1870–1930* (Baltimore: Johns Hopkins University Press, 1998), 18–20; and, more generally, Frank H. Knight, *Risk, Uncertainty and Profit* (1921; Mineola, NY: Dover Publications, 2006); Francois Ewald, "Insurance and Risk," in *The Foucault Effect: Studies in Governmentality*, Graham Burchell, Colin Gordon, and Peter Miller, eds. (Chicago: University of Chicago Press, 1991), 197–210.

40. Tocqueville, *Democracy in America*, 508.

41. "Providence" and " 'tis God alone" in Levy, *Freaks of Fortune*, 72, and "best of all banks" on 67. On the general role of insurance in the nineteenth century's construction of the acquisitive individual, see Kreitner, *Calculating Promises*, 97–104.

42. *Hunt's*, vol. 8 (February 1843), 124; Murphy, *Investing in Life*, 156–61.

43. Foster, *Foster's School Book-keeping*, 5; Foster, *Down East Diary*, 229 (November 7, 1849); "artificer" in Mercantile Library Association of the City of New-York, *Seventeenth Annual Report* (New York: The Association, 1838), 7; *American Annals of Education* (June 1837), 285.

44. B. F. Foster, *Prospectus of the Commercial Academy* (183 Broadway, New York, NY, 1837), 3, 8; *125 Years of Education for Business: The History of Dyke College, 1848–1973*, chap. 2 (Cleveland, OH: Dyke College, 1973); Hugh P. Hughes, "Some Contributions of and Some Controversies Surrounding Thomas Jones and Benjamin Franklin Foster," *Accounting Historians Journal*, vol. 9, no. 2 (Fall 1982), 47–8.

45. *New-York Daily Times*, May 5, 1853; May 8, 1856; September 20, 1858; January 10, 1853; May 18, 1855; and December 7, 1854. Also Terry K. Sheldahl, "Foreword to C. C. Marsh's 1835 'Lecture on the Study of Book-Keeping,' with a Balance Sheet,'" *Accounting Historians Journal* 15, no. 2 (Fall 1988), 191; Winterton in *New York Tribune*, April 22, 1845; Goldsmith in *Tribune*, September 19, 1845.

46. Charles E. Rogers, *Diary*, 1864–1865 (Manuscripts and Archives, New York Public Library), July 11 and 27, 1864; September 6 and 8, 1864; and December 2, 1864. See also Samuel Lyman Munson, Diary, 1861–1862 (New-York Historical Society), May 8, 1862; August 26, 1862; September 9, 1862; and May 1858, 42–5. Hours in *Circular and Catalogue of Bryant and Stratton's Mercantile Colleges* (New York: Office of the American Merchant, 1859), 17, 24–5.

47. Spencer in *Circular and Catalogue* (New York: American Merchant, 1859), 14; Warren P. Spencer, *Origin and History of the Art of Writing* (New York: Ivison, Phinney, Blakeman & Co., 1869), 27; "emporiums" and "continuous chain" at *Circular and Catalogue*, 15; "can be learned" in *Circular and Catalogue*, 11; James Bennett, *American System of Practical Bookkeeping* (New York: Collins, Keese, 1839), 12, 3; Chicago opening in *American Merchant* (June 1858), 88; metamorphosis in *American Merchant* (September 1858), 288–9; Konstantin Dierks, *In My Power: Letter-Writing and Communications in Early America* (Philadelphia: University of Pennsylvania Press, 2011), 62–81.

48. James Barnard Blake, Diary, February 1 and 5, March 5 and 7, 1851 (American Antiquarian Society); Comer's Commercial College, *Annual Register* (1865), 6; *Boyd & Stubbs Commercial Institute* (Library of Congress); Comer's Commercial College, *Annual Register* (1866), cover; *New York Herald*, March 4, 1836.

49. John Rule, "The Property of Skill in the Period of Manufacture," in *The Historical Meanings of Work, ed.* Patrick Joyce (Cambridge: Cambridge University Press, 1987), 104–11; Rockefeller in Gary John Previts and Barbara Dubis Merino, *A History of Accounting in America: An Historical Interpretation of the Cultural Significance of Accounting* (New York: Ronald Press, John Wiley & Sons, 1979), 25; Lewis Tappan, *The Life of Arthur Tappan* (New York: Hurd and Houghton, 1870), 40–1. See, too, Paul E. Johnson, *Sam Patch, the Famous Jumper* (New York: Hill and Wang, 2003), 53–61.

50. "Copying machine" in *Hunt's*, vol. 24 (May 1851), 533; Charles H. Foster, ed., *Down East Diary by Benjamin Browne Foster* (University of Maine at Orono Press, 1975), July 22, 1850, 297; Hoffman, Diary, March 6 and March 9, 1849, as well as March 4, June 21, July 3 and 7, August 31, November 1, September 19 and 24, 1850.

51. "Ten to one" in Arthur Cohen, "Arthur Mervyn and His Elders: Ambivalence of Youth in the Early Republic," *William and Mary Quarterly* 43, no. 3 (July 1986), 369; Henry David Thoreau, *Walden; or, Life in the Woods* (1854; New York: Holt, Rinehart and Winston, 1963), 25; "foolish ambition" in *Herbert Tracy; or, The Trials of Mercantile Life, and the Morality of Trade* (New York: John C. Riker, 1851), 5–6; "undue eagerness" and "loud accost" in Alexander, "Merchant's Clerk," 29; "anxious to come up" in Hoffman, Diary, 217, June 21, 1850; Tailer quoted in Augst, *Clerk's Tale*, 60; Mercantile Library Association of the City of New-York, *The Seventeenth Annual Report* (1838), 7; Hoffman, Diary, August 31, 1850; "possessor and

proprietor" in *American Merchant* (June 1858), 104; "two hands" and "handmaid" in *American Merchant* (June 1858), 104; "I look about me" in Anonymous, Diary, 1834–1838, August 29, 1836 (Special Collections, Bryn Mawr College); Foster, *Down East Diary*, 220 (October 6, 1849).

52. Hoffman, Diary, August 31, 1848; September 4, 1848; and August 31, 1850. See also *Hunt's*, vol. 17, 4 (October 1847), 441; Wells, *How to Do Business*, 58–9; Thomas Tyson, "Nature and Environment of Cost Management Among Early Nineteenth Century U.S. Textile Manufacturers," *Accounting Historians Journal*, vol. 19, no. 2, 5–6; on costing and budgeting, see Peter Miller and Ted O'Leary, "Accounting and the Construction of the Governable Person," *Accounting, Organizations and Society* 12 (1987): 235–65; C. W. Moore, Diaries, 1842–1871 (Manuscripts and Archives, New York Public Library), 92–3.

53. Augst, *Clerk's Tale*, 60; French, *Diary*, Journal 2, October 3, 1851, as well as March 3 and 4, and June 24, 1856.

54. Edward N. Tailer, Diaries, 1848–1917, December 12, 15, 1849 (New-York Historical Society); Alexander, "Merchant's Clerk," 20–2. On no compensation paid in the first year, see, for instance, *New York Journal of Commerce*, August 7, 1849. "We are not 'prentices, we are clerks." Mrs. L. C. Tuthill, *Get Money* (New York: Charles Scribner, 1858), 34–6.

55. Tailer, Diary, March 22, June 3, December 5 and 17, January 19 and 21, February 11 and 28, April 30, March 27, May 3 and 25, 1850.

56. George Francis Train, *Young America in Wall-Street* (1857; repr., New York: Greenwood Press, 1968), iii–iv; Tailer, Diary, January 15, 1852, and February 2, 1850; John Todd, *The Student's Manual* (Northampton, MA: Hopkins, Bridgman & Co., 1859), 217; Hoffman, Diary, May 5, 1848.

57. Tailer, Diary, February 2, 1850.

58. *Hunt's* (September 1852), 392; Rogers, Diary, March 2 and 3, 1864; Walter Barrett, *Old Merchants of New York City* (New York: Carleton, 1864), 111.

59. Haskell in *Hunt's*, vol. 18 (June 1848), 622; French, Journal No. 4, February 29 as well as March 1 and 4, 1856.

60. French, Journal No. 4, March 2, 1856.

61. French, Journal, December 31, 1856, and January 4, 9, 1857.

62. French, Journal, January 17, 1857.

63. French, Journal, January 28 and March 14, 1857.

64. *Hunt's*, vol. 15 (November 1846), 483; *Hunt's*, vol. 29 (1853); Michael Warner, "The Mass Public and the Mass Subject," in *Habermas and the Public Sphere*, ed. Craig Calhoun (Cambridge, MA: MIT Press, 1992), 159–69; Eran Shalev, *Rome Reborn on Western Shores: Historical Imagination and the Creation of the American Republic* (Charlottesville: University of Virginia Press, 2009), 151–87.

65. "Admiration of wealth" in Adam Ferguson, *An Essay on the History of Civil Society* (1767; Edinburgh: Edinburgh University Press, 1966), 186: "if you wish" in *Hunt's*, vol. 29, 2 (August 1853), 264; Adam Smith, *An Inquiry into the Nature and Causes of the Wealth of Nations* (1776; repr., Chicago: University of Chicago Press, 1976), chap. 2; See, too, C. B. MacPherson, "The Economic Penetration of Political Theory: Some Hypotheses," in *The Rise and Fall of Economic Justice and Other Papers* (Oxford: Oxford University Press, 1985), 101–17.

66. Ralph Waldo Emerson, "Nominalist and Realist" (1844) in *Essays and Lectures* (New York: Library of America, 1983), 575–87; Washington Irving, *Rip Van Winkle* (Philadelphia: David McKay Co., 1921), 58; "searching always" in Alexis de Tocqueville, *Democracy in America*, ed.

J. P. Mayer (Garden City, NY: Doubleday, 1969), 453. "You have an apparatus of total and circulating mistrust, because there is no absolute point. The perfected form of surveillance consists in a summation of malveillance." Michel Foucault, "The Eye of Power," in *Power/Knowledge: Selected Writings and Interviews, 1972-1977,* ed. Colin Gordon (New York: Pantheon, 1980), 158. See, too, Georg Simmel, "The Stranger," in *On Individuality and Social Forms* (Chicago: University of Chicago Press, 1971), 143-9.

Chapter Three

1. Joseph Schumpeter would call this syllogism the first postulate of classical economic theory. *A History of Economic Analysis* (1954; New York: Routledge, 1996), 576-7.

2. Theodore Parker, "Thoughts on Labor," in "Critical and Miscellaneous Writings of Theodore Parker," *The Dial: A Magazine for Literature, Philosophy, and Religion* (April 1841). A generation later even the liberal journal *Putnam's Monthly* was using the same rhetoric: "Seven hundred and twenty six thousand human beings lie down to sleep on this little island, and rise up to eat. And yet not one of them even produced a grain of wheat of an ounce of food." *Putnam's Monthly* 11, no. 1 (January 1868), 91.

3. *American Phrenological Journal,* "What Shall I Do for a Living," vol. 17 (April 1853), 67; Weems in Scott E. Casper, *Constructing American Lives: Biography and Culture in Nineteenth-Century America* (Chapel Hill: University of North Carolina Press, 1999), 71-3; William Ellery Channing, *Self-Culture* (Boston: James Munroe & Co., 1839), 11; "Who has not read with deep interest the incident in the life of Washington, who, when he had injured a favorite tree of his father's, frankly confessed his offense?" "Integrity the Foundation of Mercantile Character," *Hunt's,* vol. 24 (May 1851), 649.

4. William Thayer, *The Printer Boy; or, How Ben Franklin Made His Mark,* n.p. (preface); repeated by Hatfield in his appearance before the New York Association of Dry Goods Clerks, in Rev. E. F. Hatfield, *The Night No Time for Labor: A Sermon on the Early Closing of Stores* (New York: D. A. Woodworth, 1850), 138. On "individualism," see Tocqueville, *Democracy in America,* 506-13, 525-8; Wordsworth's original text: "The Child is father of the Man," in "My Heart Leaps Up When I Behold" (1802) in *William Wordsworth: The Poems,* vol. 1, ed. John O. Hayden (New Haven, CT: Yale University Press, 1977), 522; "Means of Self-Acquaintance," *Young American's Magazine of Self-Improvement* (May 1847), 137-43. Sixty-seven new entries—ranging from "self-abhorring" to "self-worshipping"—and all commencing with the prefix "self-," appeared in the second edition of Webster's *American Dictionary* in 1841. Noah Webster, *An American Dictionary of the English Language . . . Revised Edition with an Appendix, Containing All the Additional Words in the Last Edition of the Larger Work* (New York: Harper Brothers, 1846). See, too, James Livingston, "Modern Subjectivity and Consumer Culture," in *Getting and Spending: European and American Consumer Societies in the Twentieth Century,* Susan Strasser, Charles McGovern, and Matthias Judt, eds. (New York: Cambridge University Press, 1998), 413-30.

5. "However dismal" in *United States Democratic Review,* February 1855, 120; Thomas Jefferson, *Notes on the State of Virginia,* ed. William Peden (New York: Norton, 1954), 165; *American Whig Review* (May 1852), 472; "catfish" in Walter Barret (pseud.), *The Old Merchants of New York* (New York: Carlton, 1863), 25; "starched cravat" in *Hunt's,* vol. 10 (February 1844), 143; Charles H. Foster, ed., *Down East Diary by Benjamin Browne Foster* (Orono: University of Maine at Orono Press, 1975), 233; Parker, "Thoughts on Labor," 511-12; Joel Ross, *What I Saw in New York* (Auburn, NY: Derby and Miller, 1851), 142.

6. Ezekiel Bacon, *Recollections of Fifty Years Since: A Lecture Delivered before the Young Men's Association of the City of Utica, February 2, 1843* (Utica: R. W. Roberts, 1843), 24; "Demand of the Age on Young Men," *American Phrenological Journal, vol. 10 (August 1848)*, 252; Horace Greeley, *Hints toward Reforms* (New York: Harper and Bros., 1850) 360; "hearth-stone" in *Young American's Magazine of Self-Improvement* (March 1847), 86; *Cultivator* (June 1854), 175.

7. Channing, *Self-Culture*, 41; Ralph Waldo Emerson, "Ode, Inscribed to W. H. Channing," in *Norton Anthology of American Literature*, 2nd ed. (1846; New York: W. W. Norton, 1985), 1:984; Emerson, "The Transcendentalist" (1843) in *Essays and Lectures* (New York: Library of America, 1983), 194. Thoreau: "We do not ride on the railroad, it rides upon us," quoted in Leo Stoller, "Thoreau's Doctrine of Simplicity," *New England Quarterly* (December 1956), 446. See, too, Karl Polanyi, "Our Obsolete Market Mentality," in *Primitive, Archaic, and Modern Economies*, ed. George Dalton (Boston: Beacon Press, 1968), 59–77; Gregory S. Alexander, *Commodity and Propriety: The Competing Visions of Property in American Legal Thought* (Chicago: University of Chicago Press, 1997).

8. "Amidst so many tears" in John Angell James, *Young Man's Friend and Guide through Life to Eternity* (New York: R. Carter and Bros., 1857), 38; James W. Alexander, "The Merchant's Clerk Cheered and Counselled," in *The Man of Business, Considered in His Various Relations* (New York: Anson D. F. Randolph, 1857), 8–9; H. A. Boardman, *The Bible in the Counting House* (Philadelphia: Lippincott, Grambo and Co., 1853), 395; George W. Whitehouse, Diary, 1844 (Manuscripts and Archives, New York Public Library), 8; Charles Frederick Briggs, *The Adventures of Harry Franco: A Tale of the Great Panic* (New York: F. Saunders, 1839), 12–4, 37.

9. On Greeley's association with this phrase, see Coy F. Cross II, *Go West Young Man! Horace Greeley's Vision for America* (Albuquerque: University of New Mexico Press, 1995); also see *New York Tribune*, July 13, 1865; Clarence H. Danhof, *Change in Agriculture: The Northern United States, 1820–1870* (Cambridge, MA: Harvard University Press, 1969), 7; Frederick Jackson Turner, *The Frontier in American History* (New York: Henry Holt, 1921), 30. Migration rates in Patricia Kelly Hall and Steven Ruggles, "'Restless in the Midst of Their Prosperity': New Evidence on the Internal Migration of Americans, 1850–2000," *Journal of American History* 91, no. 3 (December 2004), 829–31; "Steam-boat" in John Todd, *The Young Man: Hints Addressed to the Young Men of the United States* (Northampton, MA: Hopkins, Bridgman & Co., 1854), 120; New York State Census, Manhattan Co., manuscript returns, 1855 (New York Public Library); president and secretary in *New York Tribune*, January 12, 1850; Newburyport in Stephen Thernstrom, *Progress and Poverty: Social Mobility in a Nineteenth Century City* (Cambridge, MA: Harvard University Press, 1964), 15, and on population movement in Newburyport, see 85, 87. Charles H. Foster, ed., *Down East Diary by Benjamin Browne Foster* (Orono: University of Maine at Orono Press, 1975), 219; "locomotive" in Lemuel Shattuck, "Contributions to the Vital Statistics of the State of New-York," 1850 (pamphlet collection, New York Public Library), 9–10. A statistical sample of all New York City wards from the 1855 state census, the first to document place of birth, showed that almost three-quarters of the city's clerks were born elsewhere. Brian P. Luskey, *On the Make: Clerks and the Quest for Capital in Nineteenth-Century America* (New York: New York University Press, 2010), 10.

10. "Brilliant and attractive" in *Hunt's*, vol. 17, no. 3 (September 1847), 324; parlor stoves in Duncan Faherty, *Remodeling the Nation: The Architecture of American Identity, 1776–1858* (Hanover, NH: University Press of New England, 2007), 179–80; "ruddily" quoted in Martin Bruegel, *Farm, Shop, Landing: The Rise of a Market Society in the Hudson Valley, 1780–1860* (Durham, NC: Duke University Press, 2002), 183; Albert Prescott Paine, *History of Samuel Paine, Jr.* (n.p., 1923),

88; Horace Bushnell, "Age of Homespun," in *Litchfield County Centennial Celebration* (Hartford, CT: Edwin Hunt, 1851), 119; Andrew Jackson Downing, *Architecture of Country Houses* (New York: D. Appleton, 1851), vi, 137–44; S. G. Goodrich, *Fireside Education* (New York: F. J. Huntington, 1838), 64. Vincent J. Bertolini, "Fireside Chastity: The Erotics of Sentimental Bachelorhood in the 1850s," *American Literature* 68, no. 4 (December 1996), 707–8. See, too, Herman Melville, "I and My Chimney (1856) in *The Writings of Herman Melville*, vol. 9 (*The Piazza Tales and Other Prose Pieces*) (Evanston, IL: Northwestern University Press, 1987), 352–77.

11. *Hunt's*, vol. 29 (November 1853), 647.

12. H. A. Boardman, *Suggestions to Young Men Engaged in Mercantile Business* (Philadelphia: Lippincott, Grambo and Co., 1851), 8; James D. McCabe, *Lights and Shadows of New York Life* (Philadelphia: National Publishing Co., 1872), 502; *Trow's City Directory* (1855); Hoffman, Diary (New-York Historical Society), March 9, June 25, and July 20, 1849; Whitman in Elizabeth Hardwick, "Bartleby in Manhattan," in *Bartleby in Manhattan and Other Essays* (New York: Random House, 1983), 223; Robinson in Timothy J. Gilfoyle, *City of Eros: New York City, Prostitution, and the Commercialization of Sex, 1790–1920* (New York: Norton, 1992), 97; Patricia Cline Cohen, *The Murder of Helen Jewett* (New York: Knopf, 1999).

13. "Sleepless" in Horace Mann, *A Few Thoughts for a Young Man: A Lecture Delivered before the Boston Mercantile Library Association* (Boston: Ticknor, Reed, and Fields, 1850), 7; Wendy Gamber, *The Boardinghouse in Nineteenth-Century America* (Baltimore: Johns Hopkins University Press, 2007), 8, 30–2, 72–3, 102–5, 112–3.

14. Henry Ward Beecher, "The Lecture System," in *Eyes and Ears* (Boston: Ticknor and Fields, 1862), 106–7; "damp underground" in *Atlantic* (January 1869), 60–1; Edward Jarvis, *Lecture on the Necessity of the Study of Physiology* (Boston: W. D. Ticknor & Co., 1845), 24–32; Andrew Combe, *The Principles of Physiology* (New York: Harper & Brothers, 1834), 177, 179, 185; James Wynne, *Report of the Vital Statistics of the US, Made to the Mutual Life Insurance Company of NY* (New York: H. Baillière, 1857), 207–10; "Health Insurance," *Chronotype*, May 2, 1846; "Ventilation of School Rooms," *Common School Advocate* (September 1841), 352; Importance of Fresh Air," *American Magazine of Useful and Entertaining Knowledge*, June 1, 1836, 439; See, too, "Contributions to Vital Statistics," *North American Review* (October 1863), 324.

15. *Hunt's*, vol. 22, no. 3 (March 1850), 361–2; E[dward] J[arvis], [Untitled review of works on vital statistics], *American Journal of the Medical Sciences* (July 1852), 133, 135–40; Granville Sharp, *Prize Essay on the Application of Recent Inventions Collected at the Great Exhibition of 1851, to the Purposes of Practical Banking* (London: Waterlow & Sons, 1852), 5–12; C. W. Moore, Diary, 1842–1871, March 16, 1847 (New York Public Library). See, too, Morrill Wyman, *A Practical Treatise on Ventilation* (Boston: James Munroe, 1846).

16. Combe, *Principles of Physiology*, 183; Wolfgang Schivelbusch, *Disenchanted Night: The Industrialization of Light in the Nineteenth Century* (Berkeley: University of California Press, 1995), 50–1; "The Character of Franklin," *North American Review*, vol. 83 (October 1856), 411; "whole street" in John Donaldson, *Jack Datchett, the Clerk: An Old Man's Tale* (Baltimore: H. Colburn, 1846), 5; Rev. E. F. Hatfield, *The Night No Time for Labor: A Sermon on the Early Closing of Stores* (New York: D. A. Woodworth, 1850), 126, 135–6, 139. And see Louis Bader, "Gas Illumination in New York City, 1823–1863" (PhD diss., New York University, 1970), 228–54, 331–8.

17. Cayley in Luskey, *On the Make*, 12; Diary, 1834–1838, September 2, 1836 (Canaday Special Collections Manuscript Collection, Bryn Mawr College); Edward N. Tailer, Diary, December 5,

1849 (New-York Historical Society); Edward Isaiah Thomas, Diary, 1852–1858, June 18 and 19, 1853 (American Antiquarian Society).

18. *Atlantic Monthly*, March 1861, 296; *Massachusetts Teacher* (August 1850), 246; "his arm, his hand" in Platt R. Spencer, *Spencerian Key to Practical Penmanship* (New York: Ivison, Phinney, Blakeman & Co., 1869), 24; Foster, *Down East Diary*, 148; *New England Farmer*, May 15, 1833; "mouthful" in "Merchant's Clerk," *Hunt's*, vol. 29 (November 1853), 646, and repeated in Frazar Kirkland, *Cyclopaedia of Commercial and Business Anecdotes* (New York: D. Appleton, 1864–5), 2:686–7. See generally Andrew Lyndon Knighton, "Idle Threats: The Limits of Productivity in 19th-Century America" (PhD diss., University of Minnesota, 2004). On the dangers of mental labor, see Joan Burbick, *Healing the Republic: The Language of Health and the Culture of Nationalism in Nineteenth-Century America* (New York: Cambridge University Press, 1994), 156–67. "It was pleasanter for him to sit on the log and sing, and see Jonas mend the wheelbarrow, than to go to work himself; and he mistook that feeling for being tired," as one particularly popular children's story explained: *Rollo at Work; or, The Way for a Boy to Learn to be Industrious*, 5th ed. (1837; Philadelphia: Hogan & Thompson, 1841), 14.

19. "Brows" in Melville, "The Paradise of Bachelors," 1257; *Vanity Fair*, March 17, 1860, 183; Asa Greene, *Perils of Pearl Street; Including a Taste of the Dangers of Wall Street* (New York: Betts and Anstice, 1834), 25–6; on rings, see *Democratic Review*, February 1855, 121; "painted and padded" from an editorial titled "Stick to the Farm," *Cultivator*, June 1854, 175; Henry David Thoreau, "Life without Principle," *Atlantic Monthly*, October 1863, 488; Walter Harding, "A Checklist of Thoreau's Lectures," *Bulletin of the New York Public Library* 52 (1948), 84.

20. Henry David Thoreau, *Walden; or, Life in the Woods* (1854; New York: Holt, Rinehart and Winston, 1963), 4, 47–8. "Instead of enjoying the abundance of the earth, as you have been accustomed to do, you begin to associate the idea of dollars and cents, with the food on your table; you are compelled to vex yourself with economizing in the details of living, instead of by system, and to feel your soul gradually narrowing in, to a conformity with narrow circumstances." "Stick to the Farm," *Cultivator* (June 1854), 176. See, too, Michael Warner, "Walden's Erotic Economy," in *Comparative American Identities: Race, Sex, and Nationality in the Modern Text*, Hortense J. Spillers, ed. (New York: Routledge, 1991).

21. *A Collection of the Political Writings of William Leggett* (New York: Taylor & Dodd, 1840), 2:164; *Cultivator*, June 1854; T. R. Malthus, *An Essay on the Principle of Population* (1797; New York: Cambridge University Press, 1992); Thoreau, *Walden*, 8. See generally Jeffrey Sklansky, *The Soul's Economy: Market Society and Selfhood in American Thought, 1820–1920* (Chapel Hill: University of North Carolina Press, 2002).

22. Channing, *Self-Culture*, 22; "Manual Labor: Its Influence upon the Mind," *Phrenological Journal* 15 (March 1852), 54–5; Johnson in Jean-Christophe Agnew, "Banking on Language: The Currency of Alexander Bryan Johnson," in *The Culture of the Market: Historical Essays*, ed. Thomas L. Haskell and Richard F. Teichgraeber III (New York: Cambridge University Press, 1996), 256; Tyler in Marilyn S. Blackwell, "Growing Up Male in the 1830s: Thomas Pickman Tyler (1815–1892) and the Tyler Family of Brattleboro," *Vermont History* 58, no. 1 (Winter 1990), 12. Anyone with ambition must recognize that he must draw on his own resources, like "the patient skill and energy of the smith to bring it from its crude condition to one of glaring brilliancy, elasticity, and keenness." "Self-Culture," in *American Phrenological Journal*, vol. 14 (1851), 60.

23. "Held by a precarious tenure at best" in *Cultivator* (March 1835), 32; Thoreau, *Walden*, 1; Blackstone quoted in Robert W. Gordon, "Paradoxical Property," in *Early Modern Conceptions*

of Property, John Brewer and Susan Staves, eds. (New York: Routledge, 1996), 95; Channing, *Self-Culture,* 11.

24. *Family Lyceum,* September 1, September 29, and October 13, 1832; Charles C. B. Seymour, *Self-Made Men* (New York: Harper & Bros., 1858), 15–6, 31–3.

25. Leo Stoller, "Thoreau's Doctrine of Simplicity," 458; Foster, *Down East Diary,* 232; *Young American's Magazine of Self-Improvement,* March 1847, 85; *Phrenological Journal* 15 (1852), 54. "Mr. Thoreau is spoken of as an oddity, as the Yankee Diogenes, as though the really ridiculous oddity were not in us of the 'starched shirt-collar' rather than in this devotee of Nature and Thought," quoted in Walter Harding, ed., *Thoreau: A Century of Criticism* (Dallas, TX: Southern Methodist University Press, 1954), 10.

26. James, *Young Man's Friend,* 31; Channing, *Self-Culture,* 13; *Harper's* (November 1854), 862.

27. Charles Edward French, Journal No. 4, February 7, 1857, as well as Journal No. 3, Fall 1852, and Journal No. 2, October 29, 1851 (Massachusetts Historical Society); Mercantile Library Association of the City of New-York, *Seventeenth Annual Report* (1838), 7; Eliza Cope Harrison, *Philadelphia Merchant: The Diary of Thomas P. Cope* (South Bend, IN: Gateway Editions, 1978), 423; *Hunt's,* vol. 3 (July 1840), 9. On the Mercantile Library generally, see Thomas Augst, *The Clerk's Tale: Young Men and Moral Life in Nineteenth-Century America* (Chicago: University of Chicago Press, 2003), 158–206. On "useful knowledge," see generally Alan Rauch, *Useful Knowledge: The Victorians, Morality, and the March of Intellect* (Durham, NC: Duke University Press, 2001).

28. "Especial benefit" in Thirty-fifth Annual Report of the Mercantile Library Association of Boston (Boston: Dutton and Wentworth, 1855), 4; "centripetal force" in Alexander, "Merchant's Clerk," 8; "schoolhouse" in Daniel N. Haskell, *An Address Delivered before the Boston Mercantile Library Association* (Boston: Dutton and Wentworth, 1848), 17; "social invention" in *Hunt's,* vol. 29 (July 1853), 43; Jürgen Habermas, *Structural Transformation of the Public Sphere: An Inquiry into a Category of Bourgeois Society* (Cambridge, MA: MIT Press, 1991), 5; Donald M. Scott, "The Popular Lecture and the Creation of a Public in Mid-Nineteenth Century America," *Journal of American History* 66, no. 4 (March 1980), 800–1.

29. Hoffman, Diary, March 31, 1848, and September 8, 1848; Foster, *Down East Diary,* 256–7 (February 8, 1850), and Mann on 227 (November 2, 1849), Greeley on 241 (December 21, 1849); Tailer, Diaries, January 14 and 15, 1850; Charles E. Rogers, Diary, 1864–1865, February 5, January 4 and 5, and October 5, 1864 (Special Collections, New York Public Library); Samuel Lyman Munson, Diary, 1861–1862, February 7, 1861 (New-York Historical Society); A Journal of Albert Lane Norris, 1857–1862 (Manuscript Collection, Winterthur Library), February 18, 1859; Henry A. Patterson, Diaries, 1832–1849, October 2, 1841 (New-York Historical Society); Robert Graham, Journal, 1848–1849, February 11, 1848 (New-York Historical Society).

30. William M. Thayer, *The Poor Boy and Merchant Prince; or, Elements of Success* (Boston: Gould and Lincoln, 1857), 235; James Carlile, *Wrongs of the Counter* (London: B. Green, 1848), iv; Diary, 1834–1838, August 25 and October 19, 1836; Hoffman, Diary, January 7 and 20, 1849, and May 13, 1848; Rev. E. F. Hatfield, *The Night No Time for Labor: A Sermon on the Early Closing of Stores* (New York: D. A. Woodworth, 1850), 135; *New York Tribune,* September 1, 1841; Charles E. Rogers, Diary, April 4, 1864.

31. "Chained" in Channing, *Self-Culture,* 52; "emancipation of the clerks" in *New York Tribune,* August 31 and September 1, 1841; on degradation, see *Tribune,* January 12, 1850. For appeals to women shoppers, see, for instance, *Tribune,* September 1 and 6, 1841; January 12, and February 28,

1850 (quotes at January 12, 1850). See also *The Young Americans' Magazine of Self-Improvement* 1 (1847), 122–3; David Scobey, "Anatomy of the Promenade: The Politics of Bourgeois Sociability in Nineteenth-Century New York," *Social History* 17, no. 2 (1992), 203–27.

32. *New York Tribune*, August 20, 21, and 31; September 1 and 3, 1841; December 14 and 24, 1846; January 12 and 23; February 28; March 1; May 15 and 20; and July 12, 1850; *New York Herald*, August 23, 1841; Hoffman, Diary, January 7, 20, 1849; Charles French, Diary, Journal No. 5, June 13, 1857 (Massachusetts Historical Society). Association quoted in *Tribune*, January 23, 1850; *Tribune*, February 28, 1850; "clinched desks" and "nailed to benches" in Herman Melville, *Moby Dick* (1851; New York: W. W. Norton & Company, 1967), 12–13; "inasmuch as it is not money but time they want" in *Tribune*, May 15, 1850; Marten Estey, "Early Closing: Employer-Organized Origin of the Retail Labor Movement," *Labor History* 13, no. 4 (1972), 560–70.

33. "Leisure—Its Uses and Abuses" *Hunt's*, vol. 1 (November 1839), 404.

34. "Mercantile Library Associations," *Hunt's*, vol. 29 (October 1853), 439; "mere sordid" in *Tribune*, February 28, 1850; Thayer, *Printer Boy*, 79–81; *Duties of Employers*, 29, 38; John Gourlie, *An Address Delivered before the Mercantile Library Association* (New York: James Van Norden, 1839), 16–17; Guy Aiken, "Educating Tocqueville: Jared Sparks, the Boston Whigs, and *Democracy in America*," *Tocqueville Review* 34, no. 1 (2013), 180. Compare, most famously, to Thorstein Veblen, *Theory of the Leisure Class: An Economic Study of Institutions (1899; New York: Modern Library, 1934)*, esp. chap. 3.

35. John Locke, *Two Treatises of Government, ed.* Peter Laslett (1698; Cambridge: Cambridge University Press, 1988), 172 (First Treatise); "The Money or Commercial Value of the Man," *Hunt's*, vol. 35 (July 1856), 37; Franklin quoted in box 6, commonplace book, vol. 3, 155, Daniel F. Child Papers (Massachusetts Historical Society); E. J. Hundert, "The Making of *Homo faber*: John Locke between Ideology and History," *Journal of the History of Ideas* 33, no. 1 (1972), 268 and passim. "An increase of free time," as Marx noted, can be used for "the production of fixed capital, this fixed capital being man himself." *Grundisse* (London: Penguin, 1973), 711–2. On working-class leisure, see Steve J. Ross, *Workers on the Edge: Work, Leisure, and Politics in Industrializing Cincinnati, 1788–1890* (New York: Columbia University Press, 1985).

36. Thomas Jefferson, *Notes on the State of Virginia (1787; New York: W. W. Norton & Co., 1954)*, 165; O. S. Fowler, *Self-Culture and Perfection of Character, Including the Management of Youth* (New York: Fowlers and Wells, 1847); Channing, *Self-Culture*, 115, 118.

37. Max Weber, *The Protestant Ethic and the Spirit of Capitalism* (1904; New York: Scribner's, 1958), 51–2; George S. Hillard, "The Dangers and Duties of the Mercantile Profession," *An Address Delivered before the Mercantile Library Association at Its Thirtieth Anniversary, November 13, 1850* (Boston: Ticknor and Fields, 1854), 38; "occidental rationalism" quoted in Franco Ferrarotti, "Weber, Marx, and the Spirit of Capitalism," in *A Weber-Marx Dialogue*, ed. Robert J. Antonio and Ronald M. Glassman (Lawrence: University Press of Kansas, 1985), 267; Michael Chevalier, *Society, Manners, and Politics in the United States* (Boston: Weeks, Jordan and Co., 1839), 334; William A. Alcott, *The Physiology of Marriage* (1866; New York: Arno Press, 1972), 96; John Todd, *The Young Man: Hints Addressed to the Young Men of the United States* (Northampton, MA: Hopkins, Bridgman & Co., 1854), 16–7. See, too, Paul du Gay, "Max Weber and the Moral Economy of Office," *Journal of Cultural Economy* 1, no. 2 (2008), 129–44; Margaret C. Jacob and Matthew Kadane, "Missing, Now Found in the Eighteenth Century: Weber's Protestant Capitalist," *American Historical Review* 108, no. 1 (2003), 20–49.

38. "Turning the mind" in Channing, *Self-Culture*, 13; Mary Cayton, *Emerson's Emergence*, 105–6; J. S. Holliday, *The World Rushed In: the California Gold Rush Experience* (Norman:

University of Oklahoma Press, 1981), 361; John Todd, *The Student's Manual* (Northampton, MA: Hopkins, Bridgman & Co., 1859), 120–1.

39. Hoffman, Diary, 101, April 10, 1848; Foster, *Down East Diary*, 59 (October 3, 1847); *North American Review*, vol. 64 (January 1847), 269.

40. Michael Zuckerman, "The Fabrication of Identity in Early America," *William & Mary Quarterly* 34, no. 2 (April 1977), 183–91; Hugh J. Dawson, "Fathers and Sons: Franklin's 'Memoirs' as Myth and Metaphor," *Early American Literature* 14 (1979–80), 277–81, Mather on 277; "haughty" in Gregory Nobles, "The Politics of Patriarchy in Shay's Rebellion: The Case of Henry McCulloch," *Dublin Seminar for New England Folklife Annual Proceedings* (Boston: Boston University, 1985); John Angell James, *The Young Man from Home* (New York: American Tract Society, 1845), 19.

41. "Mr. Greeley's Comments," in *Love, Marriage, and Divorce and the Sovereignty of the Individual: A Discussion by Henry James, Horace Greeley, and Stephen Pearl Andrews* (New York: Stringer & Townsend, 1853), 34; box 7, commonplace book, vol. 5, Daniel F. Child Papers (Massachusetts Historical Society), 200; Benjamin Franklin, *The Autobiography of Benjamin Franklin*, ed. Leonard W. Labaree, Ralph L. Ketchum, Helen C. Boatfield, and Helene H. Fineman (New Haven, CT: Yale University Press, 1964), 160; Thomas Hobbes, *Leviathan* (1651; New York: Barnes & Noble, 2004), 33. See, too, R. Jackson Wilson, *Figures of Speech: American Writers and the Literary Marketplace, from Benjamin Franklin to Emily Dickinson* (Baltimore: Johns Hopkins University Press, 1989), 29–40.

42. Alexis de Tocqueville, *Democracy in America*, ed. J. P. Mayer (New York: Doubleday, 1945), 508. "Curious strange feeling" quoted in Scott A. Sandage, *Born Losers: A History of Failure in America* (Cambridge, MA: Harvard University Press, 2005), 24–5; Herman Melville, "Bartleby, the Scriviner," *Putnam's Monthly* 2 (November–December 1853), nos. 11–12; Andrew Lyndon Knighton, "Idle Threats: The Limits of Productivity in 19th-Century America" (PhD diss., University of Minnesota, 2004), 49–52. Also see Elizabeth Hardwick, "Bartleby in Manhattan," in *Bartleby in Manhattan and Other Essays* (New York: Random House, 1983); Liane Norman, "Bartleby and the Reader," *New England Quarterly* 44, no. 1 (1971), 22–39. Richard Henry Dana wrote to Edward Evert about Melville's story: "The secret power of such an inefficient and harmless creature over his employer who all the while has a misgiving of it, shows no common insight." In Hershel Parker, *Herman Melville: A Biography* (Baltimore: Johns Hopkins University Press, 2005), 2:179.

43. Tocqueville's translator in F. O. Matthiesen, *American Renaissance: Art and Expression in the Age of Emerson and Whitman* (New York: Oxford University Press, 1941), 6; Sylvester Graham, *A Defence of the Graham System of Living; or, Remarks on Diet and Regimen* (New York: W. Applegate, 1835), 88; "Arrest of the Confidence Man," *New York Herald*, quoted in Herman Melville, *The Confidence-Man: His Masquerade*, ed. Hershel Parker (New York: W. W. Norton, 1971), 228 (emphasis in original); Charles Baudelaire, *Intimate Journals*, trans. Christopher Isherwood (1947; Mineola, NY: Dover Publications, 2006), 8–9. See, too, Susan Buck-Morss, "The Flaneur, the Sandwichman and the Whore: The Politics of Loitering," *New German Critique*, no. 39 (Autumn 1986), 99–140. Herman Melville, "Billy Budd," in *Billy Budd and Other Tales* (New York: New American Library, 1961). Benjamin Franklin: "The Plague, and the Hero, are both of a trade!" quoted in Steven Forde, "Benjamin Franklin's 'Machiavellian' Civic Virtue," in *Machiavelli's Liberal Republican Legacy*, ed. Paul Rahe (Cambridge: Cambridge University Press, 2006), 157. Joseph Schumpeter: "Industrial and commercial activity is essentially unheroic in the knight's sense ... and the ideology that glorifies the idea of fighting for fighting's sake and of

victory for victory's sake understandably withers in the office among all the columns of figures." *Capitalism, Socialism, and Democracy* (London: George Allen & Unwin, 1947), 128.

44. "Own reward" quoted in Margaret R. Hunt, *The Middling Sort: Commerce, Gender, and the Family in England, 1680–1780 (Berkeley: University of California Press, 1996)*, 71; "Industry," *Cultivator* (March 1835), 18; Todd, *Student's Manual*, 30–1, 367, 370–1; "to create" quoted in George Gusdorf, "Conditions and Limits of Autobiography," in *Autobiography: Essays Theoretical and Critical*, ed. James Olney (Princeton, NJ: Princeton University Press, 1980), 44. See Louis A. Sass, *Madness and Modernism: Insanity in the Light of Modern Art, Literature, and Thought* (New York: Basic Books, 1992), 1–39.

45. Haskell, *Address Delivered*, 31; New York Mercantile Library, *Seventeenth Annual Report*, 7; Spencer in *Hunt's*, vol. 37, no. 6 (December 1857), 701.

46. Nian-Sheng Huang, *Benjamin Franklin in American Thought and Culture, 1790–1990* (Philadelphia: American Philosophical Society, 1994), 42–3; "Benjamin Franklin," *Cultivator* (August 1834), 83; Seymour, *Self-Made Men*, 429. For instance, Harper & Brothers issued a two-part "splendidly illustrated edition" of *Life of Franklin*, a "universal favorite." *New York Journal of Commerce*, January 13, 1850.

47. *North American Review*, no. 21 (September 1818), 289–323. See, too, Charles Francis Adams on Franklin: "That nice sense which revolts at wrong for its own sake, and that generosity of spirit which shrinks at participating in the advantages of indirection, however naturally obtained, were not his." Quoted in Nian-Sheng Huang, *Benjamin Franklin*, 53. See generally Thomas N. Baker, *Sentiment and Celebrity: Nathaniel Parker Willis and the Trials of Literary Fame* (New York: Oxford University Press, 1999).

48. On a conservative, antidemocratic model of the self (ultimately not adopted by Americans) that does not rise in the world, see Stephen Carl Arch, *After Franklin: The Emergence of Autobiography in Post-Revolutionary America, 1780–1830* (Hanover, NH: University Press of New England, 2001), 58–9.

49. *North American Review*, vol. 83, no. 173 (October 1856). Characteristic, too, was the portrait of Franklin that adorned the frontispiece of volume 1 of *Young American's Magazine of Self-Improvement* (1847).

50. Sesquicentennial in Luskey, *On the Make*, 23; Franklin, *Autobiography*, 71 ("near 300 miles"), 105. On Franklin as an archetype of the loyal clerk, also see Seymour, *Self-Made Men*, 434–7. On Franklin's strained relationship with his own son, see, for instance, Gordon S. Wood, *The Americanization of Benjamin Franklin* (New York: Penguin Press, 2004), 139, 160–3.

51. Cayley in Luskey, *On the Make*, 33; Ralph Waldo Emerson, "History" (1841) in *Essays and Lectures* (New York: Library of America, 1983), 240; James Brewster, *An Address . . . to the Young Men of New Haven, CT* (New York: Isaac J. Oliver, 1857), 26; Arthur quoted in John G. Cawelti, *Apostles of the Self-Made Man* (Chicago: University of Chicago Press, 1988), 41.

52. Augst, *Clerk's Tale*, 32–4, 53, 60; James, *Young Man's Friend*; Foster, *Down East Diary*, 77 (November 27, 1847). Larzer Ziff, "Autobiography and the Corruption of History," in *Benjamin Franklin, an American Genius*, ed. Luigi Sampietro and Gianfranca Balestra *(Rome: Bulzoni, 1993)*; Michael Mascuch, *Origins of the Individualist Self: Autobiography and Self-Identity in England, 1591–1791* (Cambridge, UK: Polity, 1997), 51; Georges Gusdorf, "Conditions and Limits," 32–3. On the antebellum invention of celebrity, a closely related subject, see Baker, *Sentiment and Celebrity*.

53. *Franklin, Autobiography*, 155; Greeley, "Self-Made Men," in *Life and Times of Benjamin Franklin*, by James Parton (New York: Mason Brothers, 1864), 677–9.

54. Franklin, *Autobiography*, 151; Frederick Beck, *The Young Accountant's Guide; or, An Easy Introduction to the Knowledge of Mercantile Book-Keeping* (Boston: Stimpson and Clapp, 1831), 5; Weber, *Protestant Ethic and the Spirit of Capitalism*, 47–57; Charles Baudelaire, "Further Notes on Edgar Poe," in *The Painter of Modern Life and Other Essays*, trans. Jonathan Mayne (London: Phaidon Press, 1964), 101. Another political theorist of the age, the rabidly pro-slavery George Fitzhugh, likewise identified Franklin as the archetype of American capitalism.

55. Charles Hudson, "Memoir of Lemuel Shattuck," *Proceedings of the Massachusetts Historical Society* 18 (1880), 155; "District of Massachusetts Clerk's Office," November 26, 1842, box 1 (Lemuel Shattuck Papers, Massachusetts Historical Society); A Parent, *The Scholar's Daily Journal* (Boston: Lemuel Shattuck, 1843), in box 2 (Lemuel Shattuck Papers, Massachusetts Historical Society).

56. William A. Alcott, *The Young Man's Guide* (Boston: T. R. Marvin, 1849), 226. "I always carried my little Book with me." Benjamin Penhallow Shillaber, Journal (Special Collections, Columbia University), January 1, 1849; "maxims" in *Harper's*, May 1851, 840; "strict regard" in Thayer, *Poor Boy*, 116–7; Hoffman, Diary, n.d. (opening page). Charles Taylor, *Sources of the Self: The Making of the Modern Identity* (Cambridge, MA: Harvard University Press, 1989), 175–6.

57. "Book of memorandums" in Walter Taylor Marvin, Diary (Special Collections, Rutgers University), opening entry; *Hunt's*, vol. 15 (October 1846), 383–4; T. S. Arthur, *Advice to Young Men* (Philadelphia: G. G. Evans, 1860), 40.

58. Munson, Diary, January 1 and February 2, 1861; Thomas, Diary, July 1, 1853.

59. Marilyn S. Blackwell, "Growing Up Male in the 1830s: Thomas Pickman Tyler (1815–1892) and the Tyler Family of Brattleboro," *Vermont History* 58, no. 1 (Winter 1990), 12; Charles Richard Williams, ed., *Diary and Letters of Rutherford Bichard Hayes* (Columbus: Ohio State Archaeological and Historical Society, 1922), 1:358; Foster, *Down East Diary*, 77 (November 27, 1847).

60. Channing, *Self-Culture*, 23; Bradley Newcomb Cumings, Journal, 1828–47 (Massachusetts Historical Society); Shillaber, Journal, January 1, 1849; Thoreau in Richard F. Teichgraeber III, "'A Yankee Diogenes,'" in *The Culture of the Market: Historical Essays*, ed. Thomas L. Haskell and Richard F. Teichgraeber III (New York: Cambridge University Press, 1996), 294; James Barnard Blake, Diary, 1851 (American Antiquarian Society). John Todd's *Index Rerum; or, Index of Subjects, Intended as a Manual to Aid the Student and the Professional Man, in Preparing Himself for Usefulness* (1837), which was long popular, designed to improve on the traditional commonplace book by creating an easily accessible taxonomy for recording and then accessing information one had read in books, magazines, or newspapers. Parker, *Herman Melville*, 1:108–9. See generally Augst, *Clerk's Tale*, 19–61.

61. Hoffman, Diary, April 16, 1848; Marx, *Grundisse*, 244. "The effect that one element produces upon another then becomes a cause that reflects back as an effect upon the former, which in turn repeats the process by becoming a cause of retroaction." Georg Simmel, *The Philosophy of Money*, ed. David Frisby, trans. Tom Bottomore and David Frisby (London: Routledge, 1990), 119.

62. Carl Menger, *Principles of Economics* (Auburn, AL: Ludwig von Mises Institute, 1976), 133–41; Daniel Defoe, *The Life and Adventures of Robinson Crusoe* (London: Penguin, 1965), 101–6: "This our friend Robinson soon learns by experience, and having rescued a watch, ledger, and pen and ink from the wreck, commences, like a true-born Briton, to keep a set of books." Karl Marx, *Capital* (Moscow: Progress Publishers, 1954), 1:81 ("The Fetishism of Commodities and the Secret Thereof").

63. Foster, *Down East Diary*, 210–1 (July 25, 1849). On "plastic," see John Demos and Virginia Demos, "Adolescence in Historical Perspective," *Journal of Marriage and the Family* 31, no. 4 (1969), 634; Maurizio Lazaratto, *The Making of the Indebted Man: An Essay on the Neoliberal Condition* (Cambridge, MA: MIT Press, 2012), 49.

Chapter Four

1. S. G. Goodrich, *Recollections of a Lifetime; or, Men and Things I Have Seen* (New York: Miller, Orton and Mulligan, 1856), 64; Edward Jarvis, *Lecture on the Necessity of the Study of Physiology* (Boston: W. D. Ticknor & Co., 1845), 34–5. Another list of modern panaceas: "animal magnetism, Owenism, Matthiasism, Mormonism, Maria Monkism, Fanny Wrightism, etc., etc.," *Boston Medical and Surgical Journal*, November 21, 1838, 253. Or, as another contemporary observed, "one sort of ism generally begets another": quoted in Jayme M. Sokolow, *Eros and Modernization: Sylvester Graham, Health Reform, and the Origins of Victorian Sexuality in America* (Rutherford, NJ: Fairleigh Dickinson University Press, 1983), 146. On finance capital's purportedly "unrepresentable symptoms," see Fredric Jameson, "Culture and Finance Capital," *Critical Inquiry* 24 (Autumn 1997), 252.

2. Peter Melville Logan, *Nerves and Narratives: A Cultural History of Hysteria in Nineteenth-Century British Prose* (Berkeley: University of California Press, 1997), 2; "ears polite" is a quote from Walter Channing, William Ellery's younger brother, in Lamar Riley Murphy, *Enter the Physician: The Transformation of Domestic Medicine, 1760–1860* (Tuscaloosa: University of Alabama Press, 1991), 113; W. M. Wallace, *A Treatise on Desk Diseases* (London: T. Griffiths, 1826). See, too, Michel Foucault, "Technologies of the Self," in *Ethics: Subjectivity and Truth*, ed. Paul Rabinow (New York: New Press), 248–9.

3. "Unknown to our forefathers" in Robert Tomes, "Why We Get Sick" (1856) in Gert H. Brieger, *Medical America in the Nineteenth Century* (Baltimore: Johns Hopkins University Press, 1972); Edward Jarvis, *Primary Physiology for Schools* (Philadelphia: Thomas Cowperthwait, 1850), 156; John C. Gunn, *Gunn's Domestic Medicine* (Knoxville: University of Tennessee Press, 1986), 10, 270–1, 275–6, 211. Joan Burbick, *Healing the Republic: The Language of Health and the Culture of Nationalism in Nineteenth-Century America* (New York: Cambridge University Press, 1994), 16–8.

4. Hoffman, Diary (New-York Historical Society), 184–5, 198, n.d.; Edward N. Tailer, Diaries, May 30, 1850 (New-York Historical Society); Robert Graham, Journal of Passing Events (New-York Historical Society), March 25, 1848; Allen Richmond, *The First Twenty Years of My Life* (Philadelphia: American Sunday-School Union, 1859), 129; Charles Edward French, Diary, Journal No. 6 (1859), 83 (Massachusetts Historical Society).

5. "Fast walking" quoted in James H. Cassedy, *Demography in Early America: Beginnings of the Statistical Mind, 1600–1800* (Cambridge, MA: Harvard University Press, 1969), 158; Beecher quoted in Harvey Green, *Fit for America: Health, Fitness, Sport and American Society* (Baltimore: Johns Hopkins University Press, 1986), 31; Hoffman, Diary, January 26, 1850.

6. *Atlantic Monthly*, vol. 3 (May 1859), 540; *New-York Daily Times*, October 15, 1852; *Boston Medical and Surgical Journal*, July 24, 1856, 505–6; Wallace, *Desk Diseases*, 5–6, 41–2.

7. "Contaminated" in Wallace, *Desk Diseases*, 5–6, 41–2; "vegetate behind the salesman's counter" in *Medical and Surgical Journal*, July 24, 1856, 506; Hoffman, Diary, March 8, 1847; "thousand excuses" in *Massachusetts Teacher* (July 1849), 217; Andrew Combe, *The Principles of Physiology* (New York: Harper & Brothers, 1834), 125; "Why We Get Sick," *Harper's*, October

1856, 646; Gretchen Townsend, "Working Chairs for Working People: A History of the Nine-teenth Century Office Chair" (MA thesis, University of Delaware, 1987), 16–25. "Not only have we overlooked the purity of the air, but we have actually rendered it, by our contrivances, more and more impure": "Importance of Fresh Air," *American Magazine of Useful and Entertaining Knowledge*, June 1, 1836, 439.

8. *Massachusetts Teacher* (April 1851), 107, 10; Combe, *Principles of Physiology*, 22; Charles E. Rosenberg, "Disease and Social Order in America," in *Explaining Epidemics and Other Studies in the History of Medicine* (Cambridge: Cambridge University Press, 1992), 266–7; *Annals of American Education*, June, 1833, 243. Also see Simon Schaffer, "States of Mind: Enlightenment and Natural Philosophy," in *The Languages of Psyche: Mind and Body in Enlightenment Thought*, ed. G. S. Rousseau (Berkeley: University of California Press, 1990); Guenter B. Risse, "Medicine in the Age of Enlightenment," in *Medicine in Society: Historical Essays, ed. Andrew* Wear (Cambridge: Cambridge University Press, 1992); H. Tristam Engelhardt Jr., "The Concepts of Health and Disease" in *Evaluation and Explanation in the Biomedical Sciences, ed. H. Tristam* Engelhardt Jr. and Stuart F. Spicker (Dordrecht, The Netherlands: D. Reidel, 1974), 125–41; John Harley Warner, *The Therapeutic Perspective: Medical Practice, Knowledge, and Identity in America, 1820–1885* (Princeton, NJ: Princeton University Press, 1997); Bruce Haley, *The Healthy Body and Victorian Culture* (Cambridge, MA: Harvard University Press, 1978); Nancy Tomes, *The Gospel of Germs: Men, Women, and the Microbe in American Life* (Cambridge, MA: Harvard University Press, 1998).

9. Hoffman, Diary, 191 (July 16, 1849); Graham in Stephen Nissenbaum, *Sex, Diet, and Debility in Jacksonian America: Sylvester Graham and Health Reform* (Chicago: Dorsey Press, 1980), 93–7, quote on 97; Beecher in Clifford E. Clark Jr., "The Changing Nature of Protestantism in Mid-Nineteenth Century America: Henry Ward Beecher's Seven Lectures to Young Men," *Journal of American History* 57, no. 4 (March 1971), 836. Compare cholera and desk diseases in J. D. B. DeBow, *Mortality Statistics of the Seventh Census of the United States, 1850* (Washington, DC: Nicholson, 1855). See, too, Charles E. Rosenberg, *The Cholera Years: The United States in 1832, 1849 and 1866* (Chicago: University of Chicago Press, 1962); Claudine Herzlich and Janine Pierret, *Illness and Self in Society* (Baltimore: Johns Hopkins University Press, 1987), 3–23.

10. *Harper's*, February 1857, 409; "Dietetics—Dr. Alcott's Work—No. II," *Boston Medical and Surgical Journal* (October 24, 1838), 222–3.

"Mr. Lewis Tappan said when he came into that place a few minutes ago, he met a Physician at the door,—he did not say it to his disadvantage, for he believed he was favorable to their cause—who had told him as he went out that he had sat and heard as much against his interests as he could bear. (Laughter.)" *A Report of the Proceedings of the Second American Health Convention* (Boston and New York, 1839), 11. Alcott had a close relationship with *Boston Medical and Surgical Journal* and published there extensively. The attack was part of a widespread debate within medicine, largely along generational lines, over the physician's healing powers (versus those of nature). Warner, *Therapeutic Perspective*, 23–38; Murphy, *Enter the Physician*, 116–20; Hebbel E. Hoff and John F. Fulton, "The Centenary of the First American Physiological Society founded at Boston by William A. Alcott and Sylvester Graham," *Bulletin of the Institute of the History of Medicine* 5, no. 8 (October 1937), 687–734. See generally Nikolas Rose, "Medicine, History and the Present," in Roy Porter and Colin Jones, *Reassessing Foucault: Power, Medicine, and the Body (New York: Routledge, 1994)*, 48–70; and Paul Starr, *The Social Transformation of American Medicine* (New York: Basic Books, 1982).

11. "Constantly in danger" in Wallace, *Desk Diseases*, 13; Jarvis, *Lecture*, 33; *Young American's Magazine of Self-Improvement* (May 1847), 139; Thomas Wren Ward Papers, Diary, 1827–1853,

May 8, 1853 (Massachusetts Historical Society); *Massachusetts Teacher* (August 1850), 245; Waterhouse in Charles E. Rosenberg, "Catechisms of Health: The Body in the Prebellum Classroom," *Bulletin of the History of Medicine* 69, no. 2 (Summer 1995), 193; Walt Whitman, *The Gathering of the Forces,* ed. Cleveland Rodgers and John Black (New York: G. P. Putnam's Sons, 1920), 2:131-3.

12. On the subaltern body, see, for instance, Peter Stallybrass and Allon White, *The Politics and Poetics of Transgression* (Ithaca, NY: Cornell University Press, 1986); Charles Bernheimer, *Figures of Ill Repute: Representing Prostitution in Nineteenth-Century France* (Cambridge, MA: Harvard University Press, 1989); Logan, *Nerves and Narratives*; Steven Bruhm, *Gothic Bodies: The Politics of Pain in Romantic Fiction* (Philadelphia: University of Pennsylvania Press, 1994); Griselda Pollack, "Feminism/Foucault—Surveillance/Sexuality," in *Visual Culture: Images and Interpretations,* ed. Norman Bryson, Michael Ann Holly, and Keith Moxey (Hanover, NH: Wesleyan University Press, 1994); Karen Halttunen, *Confidence Men and Painted Women: A Study of Middle-Class Culture in America, 1830-1870* (New Haven, CT: Yale University Press, 1982); Carroll Smith-Rosenberg, *Disorderly Conduct: Visions of Gender in Victorian America* (New York: Oxford University Press, 1985).

13. "Midnight horrors" in William A. Alcott, *Forty Years in the Wilderness of Pills and Powders* (Boston: John P. Jewett, 1859), 275. On the immaculate body, see, for instance, Michael Warner, "The Mass Public and the Mass Subject," in *Habermas and the Public Sphere, ed.* Craig Calhoun (Cambridge, MA: MIT Press, 1992); Karen Sanchez-Eppler, *Touching Liberty: Abolition, Feminism, and the Politics of the Body* (Berkeley: University of California Press, 1993); Carole Pateman, *The Disorder of Women: Democracy, Feminism, and Political Theory* (Stanford, CA: Stanford University Press, 1989); Francis Barker, *The Tremulous Private Body: Essays on Subjection* (Ann Arbor: University of Michigan Press, 1995); Susan L. Roberson, "'Degenerate Effeminacy' and the Making of a Masculine Spirituality in the Sermons of Ralph Waldo Emerson," in *Muscular Christianity: Embodying the Victorian Age,* Donald E. Hall (Cambridge: Cambridge University Press, 1994). Victor J. Seidler, "Reason, Desire, and Male Sexuality," in *The Cultural Construction of Sexuality,* ed. Pat Caplan (London: Tavistock Publications, 1987).

14. Hoff and Fulton, "Centenary," 724; box 7, commonplace book, vol. 4, 252, Daniel F. Child Papers; Barker, *Tremulous Private Body,* 86-95; Dror Wahrman, *The Making of the Modern Self: Identity and Culture in Eighteenth-Century England* (New Haven, CT: Yale University Press, 2004), 296-7.

15. Roy Porter, "Consumption: Disease of the Consumer Society?" in *Consumption and the World of Goods, ed.* John Brewer and Roy Porter (London: Routledge, 1993), 59-61.

16. *Wallace, Desk Diseases,* 41; Whitman, *Gathering of the Forces,* 199, 202-3; "Labor a Necessity and Duty," *American Phrenological Journal,* vol. 11 (October 1849), 308; "frequent lavations" in Green, *Fit for America,* 57; Hoffman, Diary, June 26 and July 1, 14, and 15, 1849; Catharine Maria Sedgwick, *Means and Ends, or Self-Training* (Boston: Marsh, Capen, Lyon & Webb, 1839), 43-5; "chest of medicine" in *Massachusetts Teacher* (August 1850), 248; coarse towel in Alcott, *Forty Years,* 17; Gunn, *Domestic Medicine,* 118-9; New York Mercantile Library, *Thirty-First Annual Report (New York: Printed for the Association, 1852),* 25; *Thirty-Fourth Annual Report (New York: Printed for the Association, 1855),* 30. Alex Berman, "The Heroic Approach in 19th Century Therapeutics," in *Sickness and Health in America,* Judith Walzer Leavitt and Ronald L. Numbers, eds. (Madison: University of Wisconsin Press, 1978), 77-86. It was also important "not to bathe soon after taking food." See *American Phrenological Journal,* vol. 8 (May 1846), 138.

17. "Due management" in "Proper Feeding of the Body," *American Phrenological Journal,* vol. 11 (April 1849), 131; George Moore, *The Use of the Body in Relation to the Mind* (London,

Longman, 1846), 283; "more immediately" in Oliver Halsted, *A Full and Accurate Account of the New Method of Curing Dyspepsia* (New York: O. Halsted, 1830), 14.

18. *Report of the Proceedings of the Second American Health Convention* (Boston and New York, 1839), 16; "cheap bread" in *Niles (MD) Weekly Register,* October 1840, 314; Lemuel Shattuck, *Report of a General Plan for the Promotion of Public and Personal Health* (Boston: Dutton & Wentworth, 1850), 241; Sylvester Graham, *A Defence of the Graham System of Living; or, Remarks on Diet and Regimen* (New York: W. Applegate, 1835); Gunn, *Domestic Medicine,* 12; Henry David Thoreau, *Walden; or, Life in the Woods* (1854; New York: Holt, Rinehart and Winston, 1963), 26. Men frequently starve, "not for want of necessities, but for want of luxuries," as Thoreau wrote in *Walden* (50). James Vernon, *Hunger: A Modern History* (Cambridge, MA: Harvard University Press, 2007), 1–20. See, too, J. A. Etzler, *The Paradise within the Reach of All Men, without Labour, by Powers of Nature and Machinery: An Address to All Intelligent Men* (London: J. Brooks, 1836).

19. Charles Caldwell, *Thoughts on Physical Education* (Edinburgh: Maclachlan, Stewart, & Co., 1844), 52; *Atlantic,* vol. 1 (March 1858), 593; pastry in Joel H. Ross, *Golden Rules of Health and Hints to Dyspeptics* (New York: A. Fraetas, 1849), 24; "steam engine rapidity" in Sarah Josepha Hale, *The Good Housekeeper; or, The Way to Live Well and to Be Well While We Live* (Boston: Weeks, Jordan & Co, 1839); Alexis de Tocqueville, *Letters from America,* ed. Frederick Brown (New Haven, CT: Yale University Press, 2010), 24; hotcakes in *New England Farmer,* May 11, 1836, 347; *Massachusetts Teacher* (August 1850), 244. On the modern abundance of food, see Cindy R. Lobel, *Urban Appetites: Food and Culture in Nineteenth-Century New York* (Chicago: University of Chicago Press, 2014), 39–72. "In short, America is the Land of Labor and by no means what the English call Lubberland and the French Pays de Cocagne where the Streets are said to be pav'd with half-peck Loaves, the Houses tiled with Pancakes, and where the Fowls fly about ready roasted, crying, Come eat me": Benjamin Franklin, *Information for Those Who Would Remove to America* (1752) in Franklin, *The Autobiography and Selections from His Other Writings* (Indianapolis, IN: Bobbs-Merrill, 1952), 196.

20. "Ease-loving" in Ross, *Golden Rules,* 56; turtle soup and lobster salads in Horace Mann, *A Few Thoughts for a Young Man: A Lecture Delivered before the Boston Mercantile Library Association* (Boston: Ticknor, Reed, and Fields, 1850), 17; Mann in Michael B. Katz, *The Irony of Early School Reform: Educational Innovation in Mid-Nineteenth Century Massachusetts* (Cambridge, MA: Harvard University Press, 1968), 41; "bread-nexus" in E. P. Thompson, "Moral Economy of the English Crowd," in Thompson, *Customs in Common* (New York: New Press, 1993), 189–200. On how little has changed, see Susan Bordo, "Hunger as Ideology," in *Unbearable Weight: Feminism, Western Culture, and the Body* (Berkeley: University of California Press, 1993), 99–138.

21. "Simple life" and "no small part" in Horace Bushnell, "The Age of Homespun," in *Litchfield County Centennial Celebration* (Hartford, CT: Edwin Hunt, 1851), 124; hickory nuts at 116; "abuses" in Gunn, *Domestic Medicine,* 125; from the constitution of the American Physiological Society (1837), in Hebbel E. Hoff and John F. Fulton, "Centenary of the First American Physiological Society," *Bulletin of the Institute of the History of Medicine,* vol. 5 (October 1937), 725; *Miss Beecher's Domestic Receipt Book,* 3rd ed. (New York: Harper & Brothers, 1856), 3; Jarvis, *Lecture,* 22; "wholesome food" in W. Chambers & R. Chambers, *Treasury of Knowledge* (New York: A. S. Barnes & Co., 1849), 148; "natural diet" in *Medical and Surgical Journal,* December 19, 1838, 319; Karl Marx, *Economic and Philosophical Manuscripts of 1844,* ed. Dirk J. Struik (New York: International Publishers, 1964), 150; Emerson in Roberson, " 'Degenerate Effeminacy,' " 160.

22. *Putnam's*, vol. 11, no. 1 (January 1868), 91; *Boston Medical and Surgical Journal*, July 24, 1856, 506–7; Cayley in Brian P. Luskey, *On the Make: Clerks and the Quest for Capital in Nineteenth-Century America* (New York: New York University Press, 2010), 11–2; Albert Prescott Paine, *History of Samuel Paine, Jr.* (1923), 140; Jarvis, *Lecture*, 14–17; Arthur, *Advice to Young Men*, 27; Gunn, *Domestic Medicine*, 12–13; *Miss Beecher's Domestic Receipt Book*, 11, 23. There are obvious parallels to masturbation, another of the age's medical pandemics, which "instead of giving relief to its excitement, always increases it," according to Samuel Woodward, who studied the prevalence of the disease among inmates under his charge at the Worcester Insane Asylum. Woodward, *Hints for the Young*, 8.

23. Gunn, *Domestic Medicine*, 12–13; *New England Farmer*, May 11, 1836; "base of the brain" in Hoff and Fulton, "Centenary," 710, 715; Thomas Wren Ward Papers, Diary, December 3, 1852, and March 22, 1853; Edward Hitchcock, *Dyspepsia Forestalled and Resisted* (Amherst, MA: J. S. & C. Adams, 1831), 23, "single dish" at 64; "Herculean" in "Patent Right for Eating Slowly," *American Phrenological Journal*, vol. 11 (February 1849), 71; "one-meal-per-day system" in *American Phrenological Journal*, vol. 11 (April 1849), 132; "SMALL MOUTHFULS" in *American Phrenological Journal*, vol. 11, 71; John C. Warren, *Physical Education and the Preservation of Health* (Boston, William D. Ticknor, 1846), 42; salivation in Ross, *Golden Rules*, 20; Dr. Philip Mason, *A Legacy to My Children* (Cincinnati, OH: Moore, Wilstach & Baldwin, 1868), 421; Gunn, *Domestic Medicine*, 147. On need and desire, see Bryan S. Turner, "The Mode of Desire," in *The Body and Society: Explorations in Social Theory* (Los Angeles: Sage Publications, 2008), 17–32.

24. Sylvester Graham, *A Defence of the Graham System of Living; or, Remarks on Diet and Regimen* (New York: W. Applegate, 1835), 12; "Recovery from Protracted Ill Health," *Graham Journal of Health and Longevity*, September 29, 1838, 305–8; Hubbard Winslow, *Young Man's Aid to Knowledge, Virtue, and Happiness* (Boston: D. K. Hitchcock, 1837), 328.

25. "Starvation plan for all mankind" in *Boston Medical and Surgical Journal*, November 21, 1838, 255; *North American Review*, October 1838, 381; Luther Ticknor, *New York Journal of Medicine and Collateral Sciences*, September 1846, 188; Gunn, *Domestic Medicine*, 144; Charles H. Foster, ed., *Down East Diary by Benjamin Browne Foster* (Orono: University of Maine at Orono Press, 1975), 75 (November 21, 1847; July 24, 1847), 38; Hoff and Fulton, "Centenary," 710, 715; Hoffman, Diary, August 25, 1850. See also William Colgate, January 1843: bread .06, Graham crackers (.25) on February 4, 1843, Colgate-Colby Family Household Accounts (New-York Historical Society); Horace Greeley, *Autobiography; or, Recollections of a Busy Life* (New York: E. B. Treat, 1872), 105. It proved very difficult to sell a loaf made with coarse whole-wheat flour, so a dough was prepared from fine white flour to give it the necessary adhesive quality and then cracked wheat and coarse flour were added, as was molasses, for coloring, although the heavy dough still did not rise well. Hoff and Fulton, "Centenary," 710.

26. John Todd, *The Student's Manual* (Northampton: Hopkins, Bridgman & Co., 1859), 281.

27. Wallace, *Desk Diseases*, 7–9; Oliver Halsted, *A Full and Accurate Account of the New Method of Curing Dyspepsia* (New York: O. Halsted, 1830), 34–50.

28. R. T. Trall, *Digestion and Dyspepsia* (New York: S. R. Wells, 1875), 82–3; Trall in Jayme M. Sokolow, *Eros and Modernization: Sylvester Graham, Health Reform, and the Origins of Victorian Sexuality in America* (Rutherford, NJ: Fairleigh Dickinson University Press, 1983), 146, 161; Trall also in Green, *Fit for America*, 63–5; Halsted, *Full and Accurate Account*; Ross, *Golden Rule*, 155.

29. Coates in Stephen P. Rice, *Minding the Machine: Languages of Class in Early Industrial America* (Berkeley: University of California Press, 2004), 105; "ambition and indigestion" in

Melville, "Bartleby," *Putnam's Monthly*, vol. 2 (November 1853), 548; Ross, *Golden Rule*, 141; S. W. Avery, *Dyspeptic's Monitor* (New York: E. Bliss, 1830), iii.

30. Reese quoted in Gert H. Brieger, "Dyspepsia: The American Disease? Needs and Opportunities for Research," in *Healing and History: Essays for George Rosen*, Charles E. Rosenberg, ed. (New York: Dawson Science History Publications, 1979), 186; Joseph Hopkinson, *Lecture upon the Principles of Commercial Integrity* (Philadelphia: Carey and lea, 1832), 13. See attack on Halsted in *Boston Medical and Surgical Journal*, December 28, 1830. See generally Roy Porter, "The Body and the Mind, the Doctor and the Patient," in *Hysteria beyond Freud*, Sander Gilman, Helen King, Roy Porter, G. S. Rousseau, and Elaine Showalter, eds. (Berkeley: University of California Press, 1993), 225–66.

31. N. Chapman, "On Dyspepsia, or Indigestion," *American Journal of the Medical Sciences* 50 (February 1840), 323. See, too, "A Full and Accurate Method for Curing Dyspepsia," *American Quarterly Review*, vol. 19 (March 1831), 233–46.

32. Chapman, "On Dyspepsia," 330, vol. 51 (May 1840), 108; Combe, *Principles of Physiology*, 25; Chester R. Burns, "Diseases versus Healths: Some Legacies in the Philosophies of Modern Medical Science," in *Evaluation and Explanation in the Biomedical Sciences*, ed. H. Tristam Engelhardt Jr. and Stuart F. Spicker (Dordrecht, The Netherlands: D. Reidel, 1974), 39–41; Simon Schaffer, "States of Mind: Enlightenment and Natural Philosophy," in *The Languages of Psyche: Mind and Body in Enlightenment Thought*, G. S. Rousseau, ed. (Berkeley: University of California Press, 1990); George Rousseau, "Cultural History in a New Key: Towards a Semiotics of the Nerve," in *Interpretation and Cultural History*, Joan H. Pittock and Andrew Wear, eds. (London: Macmillan, 1991).

33. Austin Flint, "Remarks upon Dyspepsia as connected with the Mind," *American Journal of the Medical Sciences* (January 1841), "class of patients" at 74, "fear and apprehension" at 66, "imaginary disease" at 66, 66–74; "real and imaginary" in Halsted, *Full and Accurate Account*, 236. George Miller Beard, *Practical Treatise on Nervous Exhaustion* (New York: William Wood, 1880), xi. "A disease that seldom, if ever, obtains its due share of sympathy, because it is neither seen nor can be fully conceived by those who have never actually felt it but is too often treated with unfeeling contempt, or aggravated by ridicule." Avery, *Dyspeptic's Monitor*, vi.

34. Chapman, "On Dyspepsia," 108, vol. 51 (May 1840); Flint, "Remarks upon Dyspepsia," 66, 64; Edward Jarvis, *Address, Delivered at the Laying of the Corner Stone of the Insane Hospital at Northampton, Massachusetts* (Northampton: J. & L. Metcalf, 1856), 15–6.

35. Medical student in Charles Rosenberg, "Body and Mind in Nineteenth-Century Medicine," in *Explaining Epidemics and Other Studies in the History of Medicine* (New York: Cambridge University Press, 1992), 80; Engelhardt, "Concepts of Health and Disease," 127, 132; Porter, "Body and the Mind," 234; Logan, *Nerves and Narratives*, 38–41; Bartleby: "At present I would prefer not to be a little reasonable," in *Putnam's* (December 1853), 613. On women's specific use of hysteria in the gender wars being waged in the newly domesticated home, see T. Walter Herbert, *Dearest Beloved: The Hawthornes and the Making of the Middle-Class Family* (Berkeley: University of California Press, 1993).

36. Dr. Mott in Rosenberg, "Body and Mind," 83, *Medical Journal* at 84; Combe quoted in Ralph James Savarese, "Nervous Wrecks and Ginger-Nuts: Bartleby at a Standstill," *Leviathan: A Journal of Melville Studies* 5, no. 2 (October 2003), 28–9; Henry Ward Beecher, *Eyes and Ears* (Boston: Ticknor and Fields, 1862), 203; Alexis de Tocqueville, *Democracy in America*, ed. J. P. Mayer (New York, 1945), 537; Todd, *Student's Manual*, 373.

37. Flint, "Remarks upon Dyspepsia," 65; "self-made or never-made" in O. S. Fowler, *Self-Culture, and Perfection of Character; Including the Management of Youth* (New York: Samuel R.

Wells, 1847); Ross, *Golden Rules*, 142; George Moore, *Man and His Motives* (New York: Harper & Brothers, 1848), 121, and generally 121–3; Caldwell, *Physical Education*, 25–9. As was remarked of Bartleby, "his body did not pain him; it was his soul that suffered." *Putnam's*, November 1853, 554.

38. Flint, "Remarks upon Dyspepsia," 65.

39. Harvey Newcomb, *How to Be a Man: A Book for Boys* (Boston: Gould, Kendall, and Lincoln, 1847), 100–1; Caldwell, *Physical Education*, iv; *Massachusetts Teacher* (August 1850), 244; *Atlantic Monthly*, vol. 1 (March 1858), 582–6. The religious press objected to Beecher's lecture "Laws of Nature" by arguing that "admiration of physical strength belonged to the barbarous ages of the world," to which Higginson's bemused modernism responded, "So it certainly did, and so much the better for those ages." See *Atlantic Monthly*, March 1858, 585.

40. Caldwell, *Physical Education*, 8; Hoffman, Diary, 157, October 30, 1848; *American Annals of Education 8, no. 7* (July 1838), 315; Jarvis quoted in Rosenberg, "Catechisms," 192; see, too, "Progress of Physical Education," *American Journal of Education* (January 1826), 19–23; and Michael Sappol, *A Traffic of Dead Bodies: Anatomy and Embodied Identity in Nineteenth-Century America* (Princeton, NJ: Princeton University Press, 2002), 175–84.

41. Gunpowder in J. E. D'alfonce, *Instructions in Gymnastics* (New York: George F. Nesbitt & Co., 1851), i; Caldwell, *Physical Education*, 27; *Atlantic*, vol. 7 (March 1861), 285; Combe, *Principles of Physiology*, 125; Murphy, *Enter the Physician*, 140–1, 146; William A. Alcott, *The House I Live In; or, The Human Body* (Boston: Light & Stearns, 1837), v–vi, 28; Eugene Becklard, *"Know Thyself": The Physiologist; or Sexual Physiology Revealed*, trans. M. Sherman Wharton, from the 4th Paris ed. (Boston: Bela Marsh, 1859; rpt., New York: Arno Press, 1974).

42. "Know thyself" in *Massachusetts Teacher* (September 1853), 258; "every muscle and nerve" in *Duties of Employers and Employed, Considered with Reference to Principals and Their Clerks or Apprentices* (New York: J. S. Redfield, 1849), 23; Alcott, *House I Live In*, v–vi, 28; "owner and enjoyer" in *Massachusetts Teacher* (November 1850), 344; Jarvis in Rosenberg, "Catechisms," 192.

43. Lemuel Shattuck, *Report of a General Plan for the Promotion of Public and Personal Health* (Boston: Dutton & Wentworth, 1850), 240–1; Hitchcock, *Dyspepsia*, 14–15; American Physiological Society quoted in James C. Whorton, *Crusaders for Fitness: The History of American Health Reform* (Princeton, NJ: Princeton University Press, 2014), 110; *Moral Reformer* quoted in Rice, *Minding the Machine*, 99–100. See generally Starr, *Social Transformation*, 17–21, 30–59.

44. Mann quoted in *North American Review*, July 1855, 62; *New-York Daily Times*, October 15, 1852; *Atlantic Monthly* (March 1861), 283–4, 286; Gunn, *Domestic Medicine*, 109; Charles Fayette Taylor, *Theory and Practice of the Movement Cure* (Philadelphia: Lindsay and Blakiston, 1861), 3–6; Sedgwick's in *New-York Daily Times*, February 27, 1854.

45. Diary, Francis Eugene Butler, Papers 1830–1900 (Special Collections, Rutgers University), January 7, 8, and 9; February 5, 1850. Tailer, Diary, October 20, November 21, December 14 and 25, 1849; January 18, 24, and 31, 1850; March 2, April 9, May 24 and 28, 1850.

46. Bruce Bennett and Deobold B. Van Dalen et al., *A World History of Physical Education* (Englewood Cliffs, NJ: Prentice-Hall, 1953), 362–419; "heroic labor" in *Atlantic*, March 1861, 299; Alcott in Murphy, *Enter the Physician*, 176; Tailer, Diary, January 17, March 6, and April 12, 1850.

47. "With a watch" in *Atlantic* (March 1861), 283–4; "most exercise" and "whole body" in *Atlantic*, vol. 7 (March 1861), 287. See, too, Taylor, *Theory and Practice*.

48. "Volition" in *The Gymnastic Free Exercises of P. H. Ling*, ed. and trans. M. Roth (Boston: Ticknor, Reed and Fields, 1853), x; repeated in *Duties of Employers and Employed*, 23–4; "clerk or tailor" and "arms and legs" in *Atlantic* (March 1861), 284; Frederic L. Holmes and Kathryn M. Olesko,

"The Images of Precision: Helmholtz and the Graphical Method in Physiology," in M. Norton Wise, *The Values of Precision* (Princeton, NJ: Princeton University Press, 1997), 198–9; "self-restoration" in *Atlantic*, vol. 7 (January 1861), 56; Warren in Murphy, *Enter the Physician*, 183. See, too, Ezra Champion Seaman, *Essays on the Progress of Nations* (New York: Charles Scribner, 1852), 35–46.

49. *Atlantic*, vol. 3 (May 1859), 540; Foster, *Down East Diary*, May 14, 1850, 287; Charles Richard Williams, ed., *Diary and Letters of Rutherford Bichard Hayes* (Columbus: Ohio State Archaeological and Historical Society, 1922), 1:284–5; James W. Alexander, "The Merchant's Clerk Cheered and Counselled," in *The Man of Business, Considered in His Various Relations* (New York: Anson D. F. Randolph, 1857), 35; *New York Tribune*, December 24, 1846; "sound sleep" in *Atlantic*, vol. 7 (March 1861), 296; Alcott, *Forty Years*, 17.

50. *Atlantic*, March 1861, 298; Higginson in *Atlantic* (March 1858), 587; Beecher in Michael Newbury, "Healthful Employment: Hawthorne, Thoreau, and Middle-Class Fitness," *American Quarterly* 47, no. 4 (December 1995), 690; Foster, *Down East Diary*, 76 (November 23, 1847). At Dr. Trall's gym there is a portrait of a model body on the wall. *Atlantic*, March 1858, 592; "human machine shops" in *Atlantic* (March 1861), 284; Dio Lewis, *The New Gymnastics for Men, Women and Children, 25th ed.* (New York: Fowler & Wells Company, 1891), 15–6; *New York Tribune*, December 24, 1846. see advertisements for Ottignon and Metropolitan gymnasiums in *New-York Daily Times*, December 9, 1852. On heating the gym, see Foster, *Down East Diary* (December 13, 1849).

Also: "When I reached Canal St I extended my walk to Othingham's Gymnasium, where I found several engaged in exercising, with no other instructor then their own common sense and judgement, which is at any time liable to err, and to lead them into grievous difficulties at variance with the fundamental laws of Gymnastic training. Some were lifting heavy weights, in a manner burdensome, as well as dangerous to themselves, and all the exercises were performed with no regard to grace, or to the suitable and appropriate maintenance of the body whilst exercising. The entire establishment wore a dirty aspect, and the dressing rooms can only compare in the most unfavorable manner with those of Mr. Mourquin's." Tailer, Diaries, November 22, 1849.

51. D'alfonce, *Instructions in Gymnastics*, 5–7; Van Dalen, *World History*, 371, 376–7; *Atlantic*, March 1861, 287–8; May 1859, 542–3; Halsted, *Full and Accurate Account*; Townsend, "Working Chairs," 26–7; Green, *Fit for America*, 183–4, Mann's on 199; "examine it thoroughly" in *New York Daily-Times*, November 6, 1852; *North American Review*, July 1855, 64; Dr. Barnett's Improved Parlor Gymnasium, "Gymnasium," box 1 (Warshaw Collection).

52. *Atlantic* (March 1861), 287.

53. Horace Greeley, *Recollections of a Busy Life* (New York: J. B. Ford & Co., 1869), 303. For a variation on this theme of the axe, see Thoreau, *Walden*, 32; Beecher, "Health and Education," in *Eyes and Ears* (Boston: Ticknor and Fields, 1862). 204; "recreation and repose" in "What Shall I Do for a Living, No. II," *American Phrenological Journal*, vol. 17 (March 1853), 49.

54. Hitchcock, *Dyspepsia*, 221; *Journal of Health* in Green, *Fit for America*, 88; Tailer, Diaries, May 1, 1850; Hoffman, Diary, January 26, 1850; Rev. E. F. Hatfield, *The Night No Time for Labor: A Sermon on the Early Closing of Stores* (New York: D. A. Woodworth, 1850), 126; Combe, *Principles of Physiology*, 121–3; Alcott, *Forty Years*, 278.

55. Sylvester Graham, *A Treatise on Bread, and Bread-Making* (Boston: Light and Stearns, 1837), 34; John C. Warren, *Physical Education and the Preservation of Health* (Boston: William B. Ticknor, 1846), 68; Cole in Andrew Lyndon Knighton, "Idle Threats: The Limits of Productivity

in 19th-Century America" (PhD diss., University of Minnesota, 2004), 139; Adam W. Sweeting, *Reading Houses and Building Books: Andrew Jackson Downing and the Architecture of Popular Antebellum Literature, 1835–1855* (Hanover, NH: University Press of New England, 1996), 11, 18–9, 23–4; Richard L. Bushman, *Refinement of America: Persons, Houses, Cities* (New York: Knopf, 1992), 242–50. Anne C. Rose, *Voices of the Marketplace: American Thought and Culture, 1830–1860* (Lanham, MD: Rowman & Littlefield, 2004), 65–7. See, too, Roderick Nash, *Wilderness and the American Mind* (New Haven, CT: Yale University Press, 1967), 67–83.

56. Edward Jarvis and Thos. Laycock, "Notice of Some Vital Statistics of the United States, in a Letter to the Hon. Horace Mann," *Journal of the Statistical Society of London*, vol. 9 (October 1846), 278–9; *North American Review*, vol. 97 (October 1863), 324; Warren, *Physical Education*, 11; Gunn, *Domestic Medicine*, 152; *Atlantic* (May 1859), 542; Patterson in Thomas Augst, *The Clerk's Tale: Young Men and Moral Life in Nineteenth-Century America* (Chicago: University of Chicago Press, 2003), 62. "Contributions to Vital Statistics," *North American Review* (October 1863), 324; James Wynne, MD, *Report on the Vital Statistics of the United States, Made. to the Mutual Life Insurance* (New York: H. Baillière, 1857), 207–10. Also, Jay, "American Agriculture," *Journal of the American Geographical and Statistical Society* (March 1859), 84. E[dward] J[arvis], [Untitled review of works on vital statistics], *American Journal of the Medical Sciences* (July 1852), 162–4.

57. Henry A. Patterson, Diary, January 1841, vol. 3, 47 (New-York Historical Society); Edward Isaiah Thomas, Diary, 1852–1858, June 11, 1856 (American Antiquarian Society); Hoffman, Diary, 101, April 10, 1848.

58. "Extracts from an Address on Physical Education," *Massachusetts Teacher*, vol. 6 (August 1853), 232. See generally Louis Dumont, "A Modified View of Our Origins: The Christian Beginnings of Modern Individualism," in *The Category of the Person*, by Michael Carrithers, Stephen Collins, and Steven Lukes (New York: Cambridge University Press, 1988), 93–122.

59. James Madison, "Federalist No. 39" (1787; New York: Modern Library, n.d.), 243; Jarvis, *Lecture*, 8; *Massachusetts Teacher*, vol. 3 (November 1850), 347; Daniel Child Papers, box 6, commonplace book, vol. 1, 171. This was a subject who was irreducibly defined by his corporeality, which is why David Hume, in *An Enquiry Concerning the Principles of Morals* (1751), had already precociously addressed the subject of physical exercise dedicated to maintaining health and warding off painful illness as the essence of self-possession. Michel Foucault, *The Birth of Biopolitics: Lectures at the Collége de France, 1978–79* (New York: Palgrave, 2008), 272. On the new centrality of the life process in politics resulting from Jefferson's substitution of the "pursuit of happiness" for "public happiness" in the republic's founding creed, see Hannah Arendt, *On Revolution* (New York: Viking Press, 1963), 115–40.

60. Mary Douglas, *How Institutions Think* (Syracuse, NY: Syracuse University Press, 1986), 73.

61. Adam Smith, *Theory of Moral Sentiments* (1759; New York: Augustus M. Kelley, 1966), 4.

62. Jürgen Habermas, *Legitimation Crisis*, trans. Thomas McCarthy (Boston: Beacon Press, 1973), 1; *Atlantic Monthly*, vol. 7 (January 1861), 60.

63. Marx in Toby Miller, *The Well-Tempered Self: Citizenship, Culture, and the Postmodern Subject* (Baltimore: Johns Hopkins University Press, 1993), 5; John Todd, *The Young Man: Hints Addressed to the Young Men of the United States* (Northampton, MA: Hopkins, Bridgman & Co., 1854), 139–40; Benjamin Franklin, *The Autobiography of Benjamin Franklin*, ed. Leonard W. Labaree (New Haven, CT: Yale University Press, 1964), 156.

64. Bryan S. Turner, *The Body and Society: Explorations in Social Theory* (Oxford, UK: Basil Blackwell, 1984), 62.

Chapter Five

1. Lemuel Shattuck, "On the Vital Statistics of Boston," *American Journal of the Medical Sciences* (April 1841), 373–84; Walter F. Willcox, "Lemuel Shattuck, Statist, Founder of the American Statistical Association," *Journal of the American Statistical Association* 35, no. 209, pt. 2 (March 1940), 469–70. See, too, James H. Cassedy, *Demography in Early America: Beginnings of the Statistical Mind, 1600–1800* (Cambridge, MA: Harvard University Press, 1969), 244–50, 294–303.

2. *Journal of the American Geographical and Statistical Society* (February 1859), 56; *North American Review*, vol. 9 (September 1819), 219. See, too, Michael E. Hobart and Zachary S. Schiffman, *Information Ages: Literacy, Numeracy, and the Computer Revolution* (Baltimore: Johns Hopkins University Press, 1998), 146–72.

3. "Memorial from Francis Lieber" (24th Cong., 1st Sess., Senate, Doc. 314), 3. Lieber's influence is evidenced in "The Approaching Census," *United States Magazine and Democratic Review* 5 (January 1839), 77–85. Lieber also lectured in these years at the Boston Society for the Diffusion of Useful Knowledge: *First Annual Report* (Boston: Daily Advertiser, 1830), 5. Foster in J. G. C. Jackson, "The History of Methods of Exposition of Double-Entry Book-Keeping in England," in *Studies in the History of Accounting, by* A. C. Littleton and B. S. Yamey (London: Sweet & Maxwell, 1956), 302. "Political science" found in "Approaching Census," 79.

4. For a convenient anthology of federal census schedules and queries, see Carroll D. Wright, *The History and Growth of the United States Census* (Washington, DC: Government Printing Office, 1900); *North American Review*, vol. 3 (September 1816), 364, 367.

5. *North American Review*, vol. 3 (September 1816), 364; Alexis de Tocqueville, *Democracy in America*, ed. J. P. Mayer (New York, 1945), 507; letter from Chickering, February 5, 1844, box 1 (Lemuel Shattuck Papers, Massachusetts Historical Society). Shattuck had devised his "Complete System of Family Registration" a few years before (1841, box 1).

6. "Age, sex, condition"; "moral and social state"; "education and industry" in J. D. B. DeBow, *Statistical View of the United States . . . Being a Compendium of the Seventh Census* (Washington, DC: Beverely Tucker, 1854), 9. See generally Peter Stallybrass, "Marx and Heterogeneity: Thinking the Lumpenproletariat," *Representations* 31 (Summer 1990), 69–95; James C. Scott, *Seeing Like a State: How Certain Schemes to Improve the Human Condition Have Failed* (New Haven, CT: Yale University Press, 1998).

7. Sir John Sinclair, *Statistical Account of Scotland* (Edinburgh: William Creech, 1791), vii–x; "nine hundred pens" in Joseph Kennedy, "The Origin and Progress of Statistics," *Journal of the American Geographical and Statistical Society* (1860): 100; Petty quoted in *The Economic Writings of Sir William Petty*, ed. Charles Henry Hull (New York: Augustus M. Kelley, 1963), 1:244 (*Political Arithmetick*, 1690); Walter Francis Willcox, *Studies in American Demography* (Ithaca, NY: Cornell University Press, 1940), 81–2; Eric Roll, *A History of Economic Thought* (London: Faber and Faber, 1973), 100; Theodore M. Porter, *The Rise of Statistical Thinking 1820–1900* (Princeton, NJ: Princeton University Press, 1986), 23; Peter Buck, "Seventeenth-Century Political Arithmetic: Civil Strife and Vital Statistics," *Isis, no. 241* (1977), 73–4, 77–80; also see Peter Buck, "People Who Counted: Political Arithmetic in the Eighteenth Century," *Isis* 73, no. 1 (March 1982), 28–45; Keith Tribe, "The Structure of Political Oeconomy," in *Land, Labour and Economic Discourse (London: Routledge & K. Paul, 1978),* 90–1.

8. Sinclair quoted in David Eastwood, "'Amplifying the Province of the Legislature': The Flow of Information and the English State in the Early Nineteenth Century," *Historical Research* 62, no. 149 (October 1989): 288–9; "comparative fecundity" in *Democratic Review*, March 1845,

292; E[dward] J[arvis], [Untitled review of works on vital statistics], *American Journal of the Medical Sciences* (July 1852).

9. J. D. B. DeBow, *Statistical View of the United States . . . being a Compendium of the Seventh Census* (Washington: A. O. P. Nicholson, 1854), 10; "concern of man in man" in James Garfield, *Report* (41st Congress, 2d Session, House of Representatives, Report No. 3), 8; "The Approaching Census," *United States Magazine and Democratic Review*, vol. 5 (January 1839), 80; "Report on Bureau of Statistics and Commerce" (28th Congress, 1st Session, Report No. 301), March 8, 1844, 3; Archibald Russell, *Principles of Statistical Inquiry; as Illustrated in Proposals for Uniting an Examination into the Resources of the United States with the Census to Be Taken in 1840* (New York: D. Appleton, 1839), 11. For more on the Bureau of Statistics, see *United States Magazine and Democratic Review*, vol. 16 (March 1845), 291–303. The need "of understanding as clearly and fully as possible the composition of the social forces which, so far, Governments have been assumed to control, but which now, most men agree, really control Governments." Or: "Men are gradually finding out that all attempts at making or administering laws which do not rest upon an accurate view of the social circumstances of the case, are neither more nor less than the imposture in one of its most gigantic and perilous forms." "Some Observations on the Present Position of Statistical Inquiry," *Journal of the Statistical Society of London* 23 (September 1860), 363. And, generally, Oz Frankel, *States of Inquiry: Social Investigations and Print Culture in Nineteenth-Century Britain and the United States* (Baltimore: Johns Hopkins University Press, 2006). On the end of early republican (or pre-Jacksonian) notions of the public in America, see Mary Kupiec Cayton, *Emerson's Emergence: Self and Society in the Transformation of New England, 1800-1845* (Chapel Hill: University of North Carolina Press, 1989); and Thomas N. Baker, *Sentiment & Celebrity: Nathaniel Parker Willis and the Trials of Literary Fame* (New York: Oxford University Press, 1999).

10. "Heads of families" in *Milwaukee Daily Sentinel and Gazette*, June 7, 1850; "Curiosities of the Census," *Harper's New Monthly Magazine*, vol. 8, no. 44 (January 1854), 264–9; Kennedy, "The Origin and Progress of Statistics," 92–4.

11. Wright, *History and Growth of the United States Census*, 32–9; "Memorial of Errors Sent to Congress by the American Statistical Association," in *Hunt's*, vol. 12 (February 1845), 125–39. For more on errors in the sixth census, see House Reports, 28th Congress, 1st Session (1844), Report No. 579; Senate Documents, 28th Congress, 2nd Session, Doc. 4; 28th Congress, 2d Session, Doc. No. 116 (1845). On the problems of 1840, also see Shattuck, *Report on the Subject of the State Census of 1850*, House Report No. 127, Commonwealth of Massachusetts, April 1849, 6–10. "An inaccurate census is not only useless, but it may be positively injurious, by being made the false basis of theories in law" (9).

The quantitative expansion of the sixth census in 1840 has led historians to overemphasize its role in a developing culture of calculation. See, for example, Margo J. Anderson, *The American Census: A Social History* (New Haven, CT: Yale University Press, 1988); Patricia Cline Cohen, *A Calculating People: The Spread of Numeracy in Early America* (Chicago: University of Chicago Press, 1982).

12. On the specific controversy over black insanity, see Edward Jarvis, "Insanity among the Coloured Population of the Free States," *American Journal of the Medical Sciences*, vol. 7 (January 1844), 71–84; "Reflections on the Census of 1840," *Southern Literary Messenger*, vol. 9 (June 1843), 340–52; on tabulating occupational returns, see Willcox, *Studies in American Demography*, 87–8; Nahum Capen and Jesse Chickering, *Letters Addressed to the Hon. John Davis Concerning the Census of 1849*, 30th Congress, 2nd Session, Senate Miscellaneous No. 64 (Washington, DC:

Tippin & Streeper, 1849), 20; Lemuel Shattuck, *Report to the Committee of the City Council . . . Census of Boston for the Year 1845* (Boston: John H. Eastburn, 1846), 7–16, 6–8; *American Almanac and Repository of Useful Information* (1845), 154.

13. Lemuel Shattuck, *Report of the Sanitary Commission of Massachusetts, 1850* (Boston: Dutton and Wentworth, 1850), "desire" on 127, "combination and deduction" on 283; "much greater variety" on 130; "too general" in Lemuel Shattuck, *Report to the Committee of the City Council . . . Census of Boston for the Year 1845* (Boston: John H. Eastburn, 1846), 18, and "would truly exhibit" at 1; "abstracted and combined" in Shattuck, *Report of the Sanitary Commission*, 130; Capen in *Letters Addressed to the Hon. John Davis*, 4. The concept of numeracy, sometimes applied by scholars, proves a problematic category of historical analysis since numbers do not always mean the same thing, despite appearances.

14. "Many different classes" and "greater or less," in Shattuck, *Report to the Committee of the City Council*, 18; "abstracted and combined" in Lemuel Shattuck, *Report of a General Plan for the Promotion of Public and Personal Health* (Boston: Dutton & Wentworth, 1850), 130; "indefinite number of classes" and "minute subdivisions" in Shattuck, *Report of a General Plan*, 20; British precedent in D. V. Glass, *Numbering the People: The Eighteenth-Century Population Controversy and the Development of Census and Vital Statistics in Britain*, (Farnborough: D. C. Heath, 1973), 9–10, 90–5; Kennedy, "Origin and Progress," 109. The 1850 census was the first "which really amounted to an attempt at scientific work," according to Carroll D. Wright, "Address," *American Statistical Association*, n.s., no. 81 (March 1908), 7. See, too, McCulloch, in *A Descriptive and Statistical Account of the British Empire* in 1847, who also dismissed the value of earlier enumerations when "statistical science could hardly be said to exist." Quoted in Glass, *Numbering the People*, 11.

15. "Heads of families" in *Cleveland Herald*, June 25, 1850; DeBow, *Compendium*, 10.

16. Edmunds's painting is in the collection of the Metropolitan Museum of Art, New York; "common sagacity" in *Congressional Globe*, 31 Congress, 1 Session (Washington, DC: John C. Rives, 1850), 283; three thousand reams in DeBow, *Compendium*, 29; "positive knowledge" in "Approaching Census," 80.

17. On compensation, see *Congressional Globe*, 31st Cong., 1st. Sess., 568–9; Franklin B. Hough, "On the Principles of Statistics as Applied to the Census," *Proceedings of the American Association for the Advancement of Science* (Cambridge, MA: Joseph Lovering, 1869), 154–7; 3,276 and 148 in *Harper's*, vol. 4 (March 1852), 561; fifty thousand bound volumes in J. D. B. DeBow, *Statistical View of the United States . . . Compendium of the Seventh Census* (Washington, DC: Nicholson, 1854), 11, in addition to 320,000 other volumes, "to say nothing of countless abstracts"; on being returned to the field for corrections, see National Archives, Records Group 29, Letter Book, 1851–2; "ten or fifteen millions" in J. D. B. DeBow, *The Seventh Census of the United States: 1850, an Appendix* (Washington, DC: Robert Armstrong, 1853), v; Oz Frankel, *States of Inquiry*, 46–8, 58–9; statistical shelves in *Hunt's*, vol. 29 (October 1853), 442.

18. "Gentlemanly terms" in Lemuel Shattuck, *Report on the Subject of the State Census of 1850* (Commonwealth of Massachusetts, House, Doc. No. 127), April 1849, 18; "Mr. Congress" in *Fayetteville Observer*, May 28, 1850; "old ladies" in *Daily Ohio Statesman*, May 6, 1850—rhetoric that was clearly recycled from 1840. See Johnson Hooper, "Taking the Census" in *A Quarter Race in Kentucky and Other Sketches*, ed. William T. Porter (Philadelphia: Carey and Hart, 1847), 80–1. This fear has not disappeared, as is manifest in the fact that no one still wants to be "reduced to a statistic." Kathleen Woodward, "Statistical Panic," *A Journal of Feminist Cultural Studies* 11, no. 2 (1999), 181.

19. "The Seventh Census," *Congressional Globe*, 31 Congress, 1 Session, 672–7; Kennedy, "Origin and Progress," 107; "social and physical condition" in *Congressional Globe*. The *Democratic Review* observed that the statisticization of the census was opposed by "the strictest class of the strictest school of the States-Rights doctrine": "The Approaching Census," 80. On the problem of the census's revelation of the growing population differentials between North and South, see Anderson, *American Census*, 23–5. On the constitutionality of government investigations of subjects not explicitly placed under its authority, see Russell, *Principles of Statistical Inquiry*, 21–3.

20. "Intrusive intruders" in *Fayetteville Observer*, September 10; "pestilence" in Franklin Hough, "On the Manner of Taking a Census," *Journal of American Geographical and Statistical Society* (April 1859), 120; Carlyle, *Sartor Resartus* (1831), quoted in George Levine, "Defining Knowledge: An Introduction," in *Victorian Science in Context*, Bernard Lightman, ed. (Chicago: University of Chicago Press, 1997), 17; for Carlyle's influence on American thinking, see Kenneth Marc Harris, *Carlyle and Emerson* (Cambridge, MA: Harvard University Press, 1978); *Massachusetts Teacher* (April 1852), 122; "How many males" in *Daily Ohio Statesman*, September 16, 1850; "senses" in *Fayetteville Observer*, May 28, 1850; *Natchez Courier*, June 4, 1850; *Chattanooga Gazette*, June 14, 1850; *Cleveland Herald*, June 17, 1850; *Bangor Daily White & Courier*, July 6, 1850. See, too, William T. Porter, "Taking the Census," in *A Quarter Race in Kentucky* (Philadelphia: Carey and Hart, 1847), 80–1. Perhaps the most famous satirical critique of the new statistical sensibility is found in Dickens's character Thomas Gradgrind: "Stick to Facts, sir!" *Hard Times* (1854; New York: W. W. Norton, 1990).

21. "Oeconomists" is from Burke, quoted in Emma Rothschild, *Economic Sentiments: Adam Smith, Condorcet, and the Enlightenment* (Cambridge, MA: Harvard University Press, 2001), 17. Brinkley Messick, *The Calligraphic State: Textual Domination and History in a Muslim Society* (Berkeley: University of California Press, 1992).

22. Madison in *Annals of Congress* (1st Cong., 2nd Sess., 1790), 1115, 1145–7; Federalist No. 10 in *The Federalist* (1787; New York: Modern Library, n.d.), 56; Robert C. Davis, "The Beginnings of American Social Research," in *Nineteenth-Century American Science: A Reappraisal, ed.* George H. Daniels (Evanston, IL: Northwestern University Press, 1972), 154–6; *American State Papers*, Miscellaneous, vol. 1 (6th Congress, 1st Session), 202–3; 1753 in Alain Desrosières, *The Politics of Large Numbers: A History of Statistical Reasoning* (Cambridge, MA: Harvard University Press, 1998), 24. James H. Cassedy, *Demography in Early America: Beginnings of the Statistical Mind, 1600–1800* (Cambridge, MA: Harvard University Press, 1969), 215–20; Cline, *Calculating People*, 161–4.

23. Census, Communicated to the Senate, January 23, 1800, in *American State Papers: Miscellaneous*, vol. 1 (Washington, DC: Gales and Seaton, 1834), 202–3 (1800); Willcox, *Studies in American Demography*, 81–2; Garfield, *Report*, 35–7; Winifred Barr Rothenberg, *From Market-Places to a Market Economy: The Transformation of Rural Massachusetts, 1750–1850* (Chicago: University of Chicago Press, 1992), 118.

24. Anderson, *American Census*, 18–19; Jacob E. Cooke, *Tench Coxe and the Early Republic* (Chapel Hill: University of North Carolina Press, 1978), 497–502; *A Statement of the Arts and Manufactures of the United States of America, for the Year 1810: Digested and Prepared by Tench Coxe* (Philadelphia: A. Cornman, 1814), xxvii. The digest was anticipated by Coxe's *Essay on the Manufacturing Interest of the United States* (1804); "Manufactures," in *The Federal Census: Critical Essays* (New York: Macmillan, 1899), 259; *North American Review*, September 1819, 221. See, too, Judy L. Klein, "Reflections from the Age of Economic Measurement," in *The Age of*

Economic Measurement, Judy L. Klein and Mary S. Morgan, eds. (Durham, NC: Duke University Press, 2001).

25. *North American Review,* September 1819, 217–21; Timothy Dwight, *A Statistical Account of the City of New-Haven* (New Haven, CT: Walter and Steele, 1811); D. B. Warden, *A Statistical, Political, and Historical Account of the United States of North America* (Edinburgh: Archibald Constable, 1819); Timothy Pitkin, *A Statistical View of the Commerce of the United States* (Hartford, CT: Charles Hosmer, 1816).

26. Adam Seybert, *Statistical Annals* (Philadelphia: Thomas Dobson & Son 1818), 217–21; *North American Review,* September 1819, 217–21; "the discrimination between persons" in "Instructions to Marshalls" (1820), in Wright, *History and Growth,* 135. William C. Hunt, "The Federal Census of Occupations," American Statistical Association, new series, no. 86 (June 1909), 468–9.

27. Wright, *History and Growth,* 309; "It seems fairly deducible," in Wright, *History and Growth,* 135. "In every improved society the farmer is generally nothing but a farmer," as Adam Smith noted in the first chapter of *Wealth of Nations,* 9. See generally Steven Stoll, *Larding the Lean Earth: Soil and Society in Nineteenth-Century America* (New York: Hill and Wang, 2002).

28. "Intended merely" in Wright, *History and Growth,* 135; Secretary of State, *Digest of Accounts of Manufacturing Establishments* (Washington, DC: Gales & Seaton, 1823); "arithmetical exterior" in "Glances at Our Moral and Social Statistics," *Harper's New Monthly Magazine,* vol. 10, no. 57 (February 1855), 334.

29. Alexander Hamilton, "Reports on Manufactures," *Annals of Congress,* 971 and 1018–34; Shattuck, *Report to the Committee of the City Council,* 18; *Statement of the Arts,* xxvii, and "shoes, boots, saddles" on vi. See, too, Russell, *Principles of Statistical Inquiry,* 52–8.

30. Cline, *Calculating People,* 175–204; Franklin B. Hough, *History of the Census in New York* (Albany, NY: J. Munsell, 1866); "Memorial from Francis Lieber," 24th Congress, 1st Session, Sen. Doc. No. 314; Wright, *History and Growth,* 36, 143; Chickering in Chickering and Capen, *Letters Addressed to the Hon. John Davis,* 21. J. H. Middleton, "Growth of the New York State Census," vol. 9 (September 1905), 292–306.

Niles (MD) Weekly Register already contended in 1818 that statistics had been neglected and that the government should establish a permanent office to collect such information, in Davis, "Beginnings of American Social Research," 160. For a well-known example of the use of the returns, see George Tucker, *Progress of the United States in Population and Wealth in Fifty Years . . . with An Appendix* (New York: Press of Hunt's Merchant's Magazine, 1855; reprinted by Augustus M. Kelley, 1964).

31. On tabulating occupational returns, see Willcox, "Development of the American Census," 87–8; 28th Cong., 2nd Sess., House, Doc. No. 116; Chickering and Capen, *Letters Addressed to the Hon. John Davis,* 20; 28th Cong., 2nd Sess., Senate, "Memorial," December 10, 1844; *American Almanac,* 1845, 156; Shattuck, *Report to the Committee of the City Council,* 7–16; 6–8; Memorial of Errors Sent to Congress by the American Statistical Association in *Hunt's,* vol. 12 (February 1845), 125–39.

32. Wright, *History and Growth,* 36, 144; John Cummings, "Statistical Work of the Federal Government of the United States," in John Koren, *The History of Statistics: Their Development and Progress in Many Countries* (New York: Macmillan, 1918), 672–4; Shattuck, "Report on the Subject of the State Census," 6–10.

33. J. D. B. DeBow, *Statistical View of the United States* (Washington, DC: A. O. P. Nicholson, 1854), 13; DeBow, *Seventh Census,* iv; Paul J. FitzPatrick, "Statistical Societies in the United States

in the Nineteenth Century," *American Statistician* 11, no. 5 (December 1957), 14; *DeBow's Review* (March 1848), 243; *Hunt's*, vol. 12 (June 1845), 549–51; Russell to Shattuck, January 2, 9, 16, and 24, and March 20, 1850 (Lemuel Shattuck Papers, Massachusetts Historical Society); Edward Jarvis, *The Autobiography of Edward Jarvis*, ed. Rosalba Davico (London: Wellcome Institute for the History of Medicine, 1992), 98–101.

The creation of the Census Board was part of a more general bureaucratic reform: the Department of Interior was established on the same day, and it assumed responsibility—instead of the Department of State—for administering the federal census and publishing its results. Wright, *History and Growth*, 39–41; Cummings, "Statistical Work," 674; Davis, "Beginnings of American Social Research," 163–6. For details on the work of the Census Bureau, see W. Stull Holt, *The Bureau of the Census* (Washington, DC: Brookings Institution, 1929), 16. For an alternative taxonomy, see the plan for the census, which included ten schedules, as proposed by the Senate committee in De Bow, *Compendium*, 13–4. See, too, *DeBow's Review*, vol. 8 (May 1850), 422–44.

34. Chickering and Capen, *Letters to the Hon. John Davis*, 19–30. See Russell, *Principles of Statistical Inquiry*, 62–98.

35. Chickering and Capen, *Letters to the Hon. John Davis*, 1–19. Capen's letter was later privately printed by Thomas Ritchie and issued in pamphlet form.

36. *Daily Picayune*, September 27; October 6, 7, 10, and 13; November 10, 1849. See, too, *DeBow's Review*, July 1850.

37. Kennedy, "Origin and Progress," 115–6.

38. "Meet" in "Approaching Census," 77.

39. "Living economy" in Gilbert E. Currie, *The Material Progress of the United States during the Past Ten Years* (New York: Gilbert E. Currie, 1862), 6. See, too, Jack Amariglio and Antonio Callari, "Marxian Value Theory and the Problem of the Subject: The Role of Commodity Fetishism," in *Fetishism as Cultural Discourse*, ed. Emily Apter and William Pietz (Ithaca, NY: Cornell University Press, 1993), 201–2.

40. "All we can say of value" in *Hunt's*, vol. 40 (March 1859), 310; "no common standard" in *Hunt's*, vol. 40 (March 1859), 309; *Hunt's*, vol. 38 (January 1858), 57–8; *Hunt's*, vol. 19 (September 1848), 523–7; Ricardo quoted in Maurice Dobb, *Theories of Value and Distribution since Adam Smith: Ideology and Economic Theory* (Cambridge: Cambridge University Press, 1973), 82; *Federal Census*, 265, 275–8, 284; Joseph A. Schumpeter, *History of Economic Analysis* (New York: Routledge), 589, 625–6.

41. Willis in Andrew Lyndon Knighton, "Idle Threats: The Limits of Productivity in 19th-Century America" (PhD diss., University of Minnesota, 2004), 249; Max Weber, *Economy and Society: An Outline of Interpretive Sociology*, ed. Guenther Roth and Claus Wittich (Berkeley: University of California Press, 1978), 86; "harmonious whole" in Russell, *Principles of Statistical Inquiry*, 10–1. See, too, Simmel, *Philosophy of Money*, 103, 240, 376. Marx had similar things to say; see *Grundisse* (London: Penguin, 1973), 141–2, 190–3, 215, 790–1, 793, 796, 808–9. "The task of constructing a classification of intangibles is not primarily a scientific one. There is no logic of discovery or construction, just of validation." Jan-Erik Grojer, "Intangibles and Accounting Classifications: In Search of a Classification Strategy," *Accounting, Organizations and Society* 26 (2001), 698, also see 710; *Hunt's*, vol. 1 (October 1839), 294.

42. Russell, *Principles of Statistical Inquiry*, 11–2, 55–6; *Constitution and By-Laws of the American Statistical Association . . . and an Address* (Boston: T. R. Marvin, 1844), 16; and see DeBow in *Daily Picayune*, October 13, 1849. "*Making* and *manufacturing*" no longer meant the same thing, Charles Babbage noted in 1834. The manufacturer "must attend to other principles besides those

mechanical ones on which the successful execution of his work depends; and he must carefully arrange the whole system of his factory in such a manner, that the article he sells to the public may be produced at as small a cost as possible." Babbage, *On the Economy of Machinery and Manufactures* (1835; New York: Augustus Kelley, 1963), 121. See, too, Julian Hoppit, "Reforming Britain's Weights and Measures, 1660–1824," *English Historical Review* 108 (January 1993), 91.

43. Russell, *Principles of Statistical Inquiry*, 50–1, 121–2.

44. Francis Walker, "American Industry in the Census," *Atlantic Monthly* 24, no. 146 (December 1869), 689, 691–2; see, too, Walker, "Defects of the Census of 1870," *Discussions in Economics and Statistics* (1899; New York: Augustus M. Kelley, 1971), 1:51–3; see, too, "Memorial of the American Statistical Association, Praying the Adoption for the Correction of Errors in the Returns of the Sixth Census," December 10, 1844, 28th Congress, 2nd Session, no. 5 (Senate), 4–8. See generally Francis A. Walker, *Discussions in Economics and Statistics* (1899; New York: Augustus M. Kelley, 1971), 1:6–18.

45. "Restricting" in Walker, *Discussions*, 690, and "corps of accounts" at 692. See also Kennedy, "Origin and Progress," 118. The social statistics' queries included the following questions: "average monthly wage to a farm hand with board; average to a day laborer with board; average to a day laborer without board; average day wages to a carpenter without board; weekly wages to a female domestic with board; price of board to laboring men per week." Wright, *History and Growth*, 647.

46. Rothenberg, *Market-Places to a Market Economy*, 62; Georg Simmel, *Simmel on Culture: Selected Writings*, ed. David Frisby and Mike Featherstone (London: Sage Publications, 1997), 235; Bushnell, "*Age of Homespun*," *Litchfield County Centennial Celebration* (Hartford, CT: Edwin Hunt, 1851), 114–5. On the tautologies endemic to economic science, see Melvin W. Reder, *Economics: The Culture of a Controversial Science* (Chicago: University of Chicago Press, 1999), 15–39.

47. Memorial of the Chamber of Commerce of New York, 36th Congress, 1st Session, Senate Misc. Doc. No. 14 (February 14, 1860), 1–3.

48. Kennedy, "Origin and Progress," 117–8; Walker, *Discussions*, 689; *Hunt's* created a whole national division of labor based on the manufacturing schedule returns: see vol. 45 (August 1861), 139–44.

49. Kreitner, *Calculating Promises*, 12, 22–3, 34, 87; on complaints about the absence of commerce as the subject of a separate schedule in the census see "Memorial of the Chamber of Commerce of New York," 36th Cong., 1st Sess., Senate, Misc. Doc. No. 14, February 14, 1860. Also see Timothy Mitchell, "The Properties of Markets," in *Do Economists Make Markets? On the Performativity of Economics*, ed. Donald MacKenzie, Fabian Musiesa, and Lucia Siu (Princeton, NJ: Princeton University Press); and Eli Cook, "Pricing of Progress" (PhD diss., Harvard University, 2012). On bracketing, see Paul Hirsch, Stuart Michaels and Ray Friedman, "Clean Models vs. Dirty Hands: Why Economics Is Different from Sociology," in *Structures of Capital: The Social Organization of the Economy*, ed. Sharon Zukin and Paul DiMaggio (Cambridge, MA: Cambridge University Press, 1990), 39–56; Desrosières, *Politics of Large Numbers*, 239–60.

Conclusion

1. C. Wright Mills, *White Collar: The American Middle Classes* (New York: Oxford University Press, 1956), xvi–xvii.

2. "Curious strange feeling" in Scott Sandage, *Born Losers: A History of Failure in America* (Cambridge, MA: Harvard University Press, 2005), 24–5; "calico" and "desk" in *United States Democratic Review* (February 1855), 120.

3. Mills, *White Collar*, 189, 289.

4. "What sphinx of cement and aluminum bashed open their skulls and ate up their brains and imagination?" Allen Ginsberg, *Howl* (1955; San Francisco: City Lights, 1996). Mills, *White Collar*, xii; William Whyte, *The Organization Man* (New York: Simon and Schuster, 1956), 14; David Riesman, in collaboration with Nathan Glazer and Reuel Denny, *The Lonely Crowd: A Study of the Changing American Character* (New Haven, CT: Yale University Press, 1950), 21. The Frankfurt school was particularly focused on the lumpen-bourgeois roots of fascism. See Siegfried Kracauer, *The Salaried Masses: Duty and Distraction in Weimar Germany* (1930; London: Verso, 1998), which, when first published, was a pioneer in depicting the white-collar class as both agent and victim of modern capitalism. For a general contextualization, see Richard Gillam, "White Collar from Start to Finish: C. Wright Mills in Transition," in *Theory and Society* 10, no. 1 (1981), 1–30.

5. Mills, *White Collar*, xvi, 3, 15; Foster, *Down East Diary*, 232–3 (November 16 and 23, 1849). For William Hoffman, as well, the collar was part of a confident mercantile persona to be presented to country buyers. William Hoffman, Diary, 1847–1850 (New-York Historical Society), July 3, 1850.

6. Richard Sennett, *The Corrosion of Character: The Personal Consequences of Work in the New Capitalism* (New York: W. W. Norton, 1998), 9, 11. See generally Michael E. Hobart and Zachary S. Schiffman, *Information Ages: Literacy, Numeracy, and the Computer Revolution* (Baltimore: Johns Hopkins University Press, 1998) and Dan Lyons, "Congratulations! You've Been Fired," *New York Times*, April 10, 2016.

7. Sennett, *Corrosion of Character*, 18–31; Charles H. Foster, ed., *Down East Diary by Benjamin Browne Foster* (Orono: University of Maine at Orono Press, 1975). See generally David Harvey, "Money, Time, Space and the City," in *The Urban Experience* (Baltimore: Johns Hopkins University Press, 1989), 165–99.

8. Washington Irving, *Rip Van Winkle* (Philadelphia: David McKay Co., 1921); S. G. Goodrich, *Recollections of a Lifetime; or, Men and Things I Have Seen* (New York: Miller, Orton and Mulligan, 1856), 64; "painted and padded" in *Cultivator*, June 1854, 175. Log cabin imagery is also relevant. See Joyce Appleby, ed., *Recollections of the Early Republic: Selected Autobiographies* (Boston: Northeastern University Press, 1997), 6, 42.

9. "Fast walking" from *Boston Medical and Surgical Journal*, quoted in James H. Cassedy, *Demography in Early America: Beginnings of the Statistical Mind, 1600–1800* (Cambridge, MA: Harvard University Press, 1969), 158; "fast music" in Benjamin Barber, *Jihad vs. McWorld: Terrorism's Challenge to Democracy* (New York: Ballantine Books, 1995), 4; "dialectics at a standstill" quoted by Rolf Tiedemann in Walter Benjamin, *The Arcades Project*, trans. Howard Eiland and Kevin McLaughlin (Cambridge, MA: Harvard University Press, 1999), 943. See Pamela Paul, "Why Can't We Sit Still Anymore?" *New York Times*, October 9, 2015.

10. Svetlana Boym, *The Future of Nostalgia* (New York: Basic Books, 2001), xvi; Ezekiel Bacon, *Recollections of Fifty Years Since: A Lecture Delivered before the Young Men's Association of the City of Utica, February 2, 1843* (Utica: R. W. Roberts, 1843), 24.

11. Albert Prescott Paine, *History of Samuel Paine, Jr.* (1923); Austin Flint, "Remarks upon Dyspepsia as Connected with the Mind," *American Journal of the Medical Sciences* (January 1841), 65; Karl Marx, "Wage Labor and Capital" (1849), in *Selected Works* (New York: International Publishers, n.d.), 1:261. See Georg Lukacs on "transcendental homelessness" in Lukacs, *Theory of the Novel: A Historico-Philosophical Essay on the Forms of Great Epic Literature* (1920; London: Merlin Press, 1988), 40.

12. "One feels proud" quoted in Albert Boime, *The Magisterial Gaze: Manifest Destiny and American Landscape Painting c. 1830–1865* (Washington, DC: Smithsonian Institution Press, 1991), 6; Alexis de Tocqueville, *Democracy in America*, ed. Harvey C. Mansfield and Delba Winthrop (Chicago: University of Chicago Press, 2000), 386; Edward Hess, "The Business Revolution That Is Destroying the American Dream," *Forbes*, February 24, 2011. See Louis A. Sass, *Madness and Modernism: Insanity in the Light of Modern Art, Literature, and Thought* (New York: Basic Books, 1992).

13. The rhetoric, and reality, of this crisis is not confined to the United States; it is common to the whole of the deindustrializing West.

14. *American Phrenological Journal*, vol. 10 (1848), 253. See, too, Luc Bultanski and Eve Chiapello, *The New Spirit of Capitalism* (London: Verso, 2005).

15. "Will paper be as important in the information systems of the year 2000 as it is today? Almost certainly not." F. W. Lancaster, *Toward Paperless Information Systems* (New York: Academic Press, 1978), 1; Kate Harrison, "5 Steps to a (Nearly) Paperless Office," *Forbes*, April 19, 2013. See, too, the federal Paperwork Reduction Act of 1980, which was amended in 1995, and, for that matter, the Plain Writing Act of 2010 (H.R. 946, Pub. L. No. 111-274).

16. Abigail J. Sellen and Richard H. R. Harper, *The Myth of the Paperless Office* (Cambridge, MA: MIT Press, 2002), 6.

17. T. J. Clark, "Should Benjamin Have Read Marx?" *Boundary 2* (2003), 43, 44. See, too, Maurizio Lazaratto, "Immaterial Labor," in *Radical Thought in Italy: A Potential Politics*, Paolo Virno and Michael Hardt, eds. (Minneapolis: University of Minnesota Press, 2006).

Index